Drafting for Corporate Finance

Concepts, Deals, and Documents

Second Edition

PLI'S COMPLETE LIBRARY OF TREATISE TITLES

ART LAW

Art Law: The Guide for Collectors, Investors, Dealers & Artists

BANKING & COMMERCIAL LAW

Asset-Based Lending: A Practical Guide to Secured Financing
Consumer Financial Services Answer Book
Documenting Secured Transactions: Effective Drafting and Litigation
Equipment Leasing–Leveraged Leasing
Hillman on Commercial Loan Documentation
Maritime Law Answer Book
Structured Finance: A Guide to the Principles of Asset Securitization

BANKRUPTCY LAW

Bankruptcy Deskbook
Personal Bankruptcy Answer Book

BUSINESS, CORPORATE & SECURITIES LAW

Accountants' Liability
Anti-Money Laundering: A Practical Guide to Law and Compliance
Antitrust Law Answer Book
Broker-Dealer Regulation
Business Liability Insurance Answer Book
Conducting Due Diligence in a Securities Offering
Consumer Financial Services Answer Book
Consumer Product Safety Regulation: Impacts of the 2008 Amendments
Corporate Compliance Answer Book
Corporate Legal Departments: Practicing Law in a Corporation
Corporate Political Activities Deskbook
Corporate Whistleblowing in the Sarbanes-Oxley/Dodd-Frank Era
Covered Bonds Handbook
Derivatives Deskbook
Deskbook on Internal Investigations, Corporate Compliance and White Collar Issues
Directors' and Officers' Liability
Doing Business Under the Foreign Corrupt Practices Act
EPA Compliance and Enforcement Answer Book
Exempt and Hybrid Securities Offerings
Fashion Law and Business
Financial Institutions Answer Book
Financial Product Fundamentals: Law, Business, Compliance
Financial Services Regulation Deskbook
Financially Distressed Companies Answer Book
Hedge Fund Regulation
Initial Public Offerings: A Practical Guide to Going Public
Insider Trading Law and Compliance Answer Book
International Corporate Practice: A Practitioner's Guide to Global Success
Investment Adviser Regulation: A Step-by-Step Guide to Compliance and the Law
Legal Opinions in Business Transactions
Mergers, Acquisitions and Tender Offers: Law and Strategies
Mortgage Finance Regulation Answer Book
Mutual Funds and Exchange Traded Funds Regulation
Outsourcing: A Practical Guide to Law and Business
Private Equity Funds: Formation and Operation
Proskauer on Privacy: A Guide to Privacy and Data Security Law in the Information
    Age

Public Company Deskbook: Sarbanes-Oxley and Federal Governance Requirements
Securities Investigations: Internal, Civil and Criminal
Securities Law and Practice Handbook
The Securities Law of Public Finance
Securities Litigation: A Practitioner's Guide
Social Media and the Law
Soderquist on Corporate Law and Practice
Sovereign Wealth Funds: A Legal, Tax and Economic Perspective
Telecommunications Law Answer Book
Variable Annuities and Variable Life Insurance Regulation

COMMUNICATIONS LAW

Advertising and Commercial Speech: A First Amendment Guide
Sack on Defamation: Libel, Slander, and Related Problems
Telecommunications Law Answer Book

EMPLOYMENT LAW

Corporate Whistleblowing in the Sarbanes-Oxley/Dodd-Frank Era
Employment Law Yearbook
ERISA Benefits Litigation Answer Book
Labor Management Law Answer Book

ESTATE PLANNING AND ELDER LAW

Blattmachr on Income Taxation of Estates and Trusts
Estate Planning & Chapter 14: Understanding the Special Valuation Rules
International Tax & Estate Planning: A Practical Guide for Multinational Investors
Manning on Estate Planning
New York Elder Law
Stocker and Rikoon on Drawing Wills and Trusts

HEALTH LAW

Health Care Mergers and Acquisitions Answer Book
Medical Devices Law and Regulation Answer Book

IMMIGRATION LAW

Immigration Fundamentals: A Guide to Law and Practice

INSURANCE LAW

Insurance Regulation Answer Book
Reinsurance Law

INTELLECTUAL PROPERTY LAW

Copyright Law: A Practitioner's Guide
Faber on Mechanics of Patent Claim Drafting
Federal Circuit Yearbook: Patent Law Developments in the Federal Circuit
How to Write a Patent Application
Intellectual Property Law Answer Book
Kane on Trademark Law: A Practitioner's Guide
Likelihood of Confusion in Trademark Law
Patent Claim Construction and Markman Hearings
Patent Law: A Practitioner's Guide
Patent Licensing and Selling: Strategy, Negotiation, Forms
Patent Litigation
Pharmaceutical and Biotech Patent Law
Post-Grant Proceedings Before the Patent Trial and Appeal Board
Substantial Similarity in Copyright Law
Trade Secrets: A Practitioner's Guide

LITIGATION

American Arbitration: Principles and Practice
Electronic Discovery Deskbook
Expert Witness Answer Book
Evidence in Negligence Cases
Federal Bail and Detention Handbook
How to Handle an Appeal
Medical Malpractice: Discovery and Trial
Product Liability Litigation: Current Law, Strategies and Best Practices
Sinclair on Federal Civil Practice
Trial Handbook

REAL ESTATE LAW

Commercial Ground Leases
Friedman on Contracts and Conveyances of Real Property
Friedman on Leases
Holtzschue on Real Estate Contracts and Closings:
 A Step-by-Step Guide to Buying and Selling Real Estate

TAX LAW

The Circular 230 Deskbook: Related Penalties, Reportable Transactions, Working
 Forms
Internal Revenue Service Practice and Procedure Deskbook
International Tax Controversies: A Practical Guide
Langer on Practical International Tax Planning
Transfer Pricing Answer Book

GENERAL PRACTICE PAPERBACKS

Anatomy of a Mediation
Attorney-Client Privilege Answer Book
Drafting for Corporate Finance: Concepts, Deals, and Documents
Legal Opinions in Business Transactions
Pro Bono Service by In-House Counsel: Strategies and Perspectives
Thinking Like a Writer: A Lawyer's Guide to Effective Writing & Editing
Working with Contracts: What Law School Doesn't Teach You

Drafting for Corporate Finance

Concepts, Deals, and Documents

Second Edition

Carolyn E.C. Paris

Practising Law Institute
New York City

#60412

This work is designed to provide practical and useful information on the subject matter covered. However, it is sold with the understanding that neither the publisher nor the author is engaged in rendering legal, accounting or other professional services. If legal advice or other expert assistance is required, the services of a competent professional should be sought.

QUESTIONS ABOUT THIS BOOK?

If you have questions about billing or shipments, or would like information on our other products, please contact our **customer service department** at (800) 260-4PLI.

For library-related queries, **law librarians** may call toll-free (877) 900-5291 or email: libraryrelations@pli.edu.

For any other questions or suggestions about this book, contact PLI's **editorial department** at: editorial@pli.edu.

For general information about Practising Law Institute, please visit **www.pli.edu**.

Legal Editor: Jacob Metric

Copyright © 2007, 2014 by Practising Law Institute.

First edition 2007, originally published as *Drafting for Corporate Finance: What Law School Doesn't Teach You*, Carolyn E.C. Paris.

Library of Congress Control Number: 2007931826

ISBN: 978-1-4024-2313-0

To Clifford and Marjorie Carter

About the Author

CARRIE PARIS (BA University of Illinois at Urbana-Champaign 1973; MA University of Texas at Austin 1975; JD Stanford Law School 1978; MBA Columbia Business School 2001; Columbia University Second Majors Program (Computer Science) 2002) was at Davis Polk & Wardwell in New York City from 1978 to 1980 and from 1983 through 1999, where she was a partner from 1989 through 1998, and Director of Practice Information and Professional Development in 1999. Her practice at Davis Polk encompassed a broad range of debt finance, including acquisition and leveraged finance, on behalf of both financial institutions and corporate clients. From 1980–1983, she was with Coudert Brothers in Singapore, involved principally with Indonesian lending and project-related work.

During 2001–2002, Ms. Paris was a Fellow at the Deming Center for Quality, Productivity and Competitiveness at the Columbia Business School (New York City). From 2003–2007, she worked in risk management and systems development for Mayer Brown in London. Ms. Paris earned an MSc (2008) and PhD (2013) in Information Systems and Innovation Group, Department of Management, at the London School of Economics; her thesis "Information Technology, Contract and Knowledge in the Networked Economy: A Biography of Packaged Software for Contract Management" is available online at LSE Theses Online (etheses.lse.ac.uk).

Ms. Paris is the author of *How to Draft for Corporate Finance* (Practising Law Institute 2001 & Supps. 2002–06). She is also author of "Selecting a Bankruptcy Remote Entity," in *New York and Delaware Business Entities* (eds. Arthur Norman Field and Morton Moskin, West 1997), and co-author of "Operational Due Diligence," in *Due Diligence for Global Deal Making* (ed. Arthur Rosenbloom, Bloomberg Press 2002). She is based in London but visits New York City on a regular basis.

Table of Chapters

Table of Contents

Foreword to the Second Edition—Reflections on the Financial Crisis

Dear Reader,

It is something of an understatement to say that much has happened in the world of finance since I prepared the first edition of this book. Even as that first edition went to press, in the summer of 2007, there were indications in the markets that something was amiss, as LIBOR rates shot up, and other signs of liquidity distress appeared. Since then, we have experienced the worst financial crisis since the Great Depression. Given the magnitude of the crisis, the effects of which are still playing out, it was with some trepidation, as they say, that I took up a review of the book to prepare a second edition. And it was with some relief, as I note below, that I concluded that the basic principles of sound finance practice remain unchanged, being perhaps more important than ever.

It is not my intention to discuss the "Great Recession" in any detail in this introduction, or to embellish the core text with the many interesting observations that might be made throughout relating to the financial crisis. Many people, including government bodies and key participants, have already written about the crisis, important legal cases have only recently been brought and settled, and we can expect to see additional academic and policy research for some time to come. Economic historians would say not only that it is far too early for anyone to prepare a definitive account of the crisis, but that no such thing will ever exist.

Instead in this brief introduction I will offer a few reflections on the financial crisis and subsequent events, in terms of what they suggest about the purpose and meaning of finance in the 21st century, and then draw out several implications for finance professionals and this book. Some of these reflections and implications relate to the impact of information technology on finance as historically developed and understood.

Let me begin by suggesting that finance professionals should be familiar with the key events of the financial crisis. A good place to start is *The Financial Crisis Inquiry Report* produced by the Financial Crisis Inquiry Commission (Public Affairs 2011), an independent panel of ten persons charged by Congress to report on the causes of the financial crisis. While the report was criticized by the dissenting members of the panel for being too US-centric and perhaps for laying too much of the blame on deregulation, it provides an excellent chronology (and is a remarkably good read as well).

At a very high level, one might say that the financial crisis involved a global excess of savings, or money available for investment, being directed to real estate—too much money chasing too few investments in a low interest rate environment. This resulted in a bubble in the real estate asset class—notably in the U.S. residential market but in some European residential and commercial real estate markets as well. When the bubble burst, there was a collapse in real estate valuations and an overall tightening of liquidity. Money stopped moving around the system based on trust. This started occurring in 2007, and the Federal Reserve Bank provided additional liquidity support in the U.S. and to foreign institutions as well.

Historically, a collapse of asset values would affect not only the owners of the assets but the banks that had lent directly against the assets, and then of course the investors in the banks (including, potentially, bank depositors)—triggering the classic "run on the bank." The collapse in asset values might potentially implicate bank solvency but in any case since banks typically fund themselves short and lend long, widespread questions about bank asset valuations can quickly turn into a generalized liquidity crisis because banks not only make loans but constitute the payment system as well as effective agents or fiduciaries with respect to money as a store of value. Thus banking crises have the potential of doing widespread damage to the general economy, and governments have an interest in intervening in bank crises to limit this damage. When time is short and information inadequate, the government as ultimate guarantor of money and the payments system has to step in. As the full consequences play out, a kind of rolling crisis can ripple across the economy, affecting businesses, government budgets, governmental and other workers, and taxpayers.

In the case of the recent financial crisis, the dynamic was amplified by a number of recent developments. To put it in few words, interests in questionable real estate loans were widely dispersed and had proliferated not only throughout the traditional banking sector in the U.S. and abroad but among non-traditional market participants—the so-called "shadow banking" sector—and were very difficult to trace. It was not possible to "contain" the problem—for example by facilitating the writedown and restructuring of bad loans by banks holding mortgages directly. Instead these loans had been securitized, in some cases through multiple steps and vehicles, so that indirect interests in a single loan might be held (and borrowed against) by a number of different institutions in the form of CDOs (collateralized debt obligations). In addition, credit default swaps had been used to move the credit risk associated with various CDOs around the financial system. In a synthetic CDO, the technologies were combined as investors in the synthetic CDO effectively underwrote the creditworthiness of identified CDOs that were not actually held in the investment vehicle. Thus the risk associated with questionable real estate loans was not only widely dispersed but was subject to a multiplier or leverage effect generated by both the potentially many layers of borrowing and the amplification through credit default swaps and synthetic CDOs. Many types of organizations—including not only banks but also hedge funds, insurance holding companies, and pension funds— found themselves holding securities or being obligated under financial contracts that were difficult to value or representing significant losses. The questionable valuation of two hedge funds at Bear Stearns in February 2008 precipitated the collapse of that institution and it was absorbed by JPMorgan.

In August 2008, the U.S. government took over the giant mortgage lending agencies Fannie Mae and Freddie Mac. These agencies, though owned by private stockholders, had long enjoyed favorable borrowing rates in world markets based on an implicit guarantee by the U.S. government. When real estate valuations collapsed, the government had in effect to make good on that guarantee.

It was in September 2008 that the world of finance turned upside down. By the end of the month, Lehman Brothers had entered bankruptcy, with unforeseen repercussions worldwide. Merrill Lynch had agreed to be acquired by Bank of America. The Federal Reserve Bank of New York had bailed out AIG, paying hundreds of millions of dollars to its bank counterparties under credit default swaps. The U.S. government guaranteed money market funds as if they were bank deposits, and Morgan Stanley and Goldman Sachs had become bank holding companies in order to get the benefit of government guarantees and funding from the Federal Reserve. Congress approved $700 million of funding for the Troubled Asset Relief Program. In the following months the Federal Reserve and Treasury took many other steps to support financial institutions and create additional liquidity in the financial system. Years later, interest rates remained at historic lows. Fortunately, Federal Reserve Chairman Ben Bernanke, who was a student of the Great Depression, applied his learning, and the Great Recession did not develop into something worse. Still, the rolling economic damage was immense, and widespread. In Europe, Iceland's enormously outsized banking sector collapsed, Ireland effectively nationalized the banking system at huge cost to taxpayers, and the financial crisis became conflated with weaknesses in the design of the Euro to create ongoing severe economic stress in several other countries' economies (Greece, Spain, Portugal and, to a lesser extent, Italy), damaging their status as sovereign borrowers and the banks that held their bonds. The institutions, the understandings and the trust that had for decades been taken for granted were fundamentally undermined.

In light of the financial crisis, what might be some reflections on the purpose and meaning of finance in the twenty-first century? Some observers, focusing on globalization and the development of information technology, envision a new, more efficient and less costly system that "seamlessly" moves funding around the world from willing investors to worthy (and transparent) enterprises, and that constitutes (again) a "seamless" payments system as well as a reliable store of value. In this vision, money is abstracted as information, and finance is an information system.

There has been a fair amount of experimentation along these lines, some of it quite successful, for example micro-finance and the use of mobile phones for payments in developing countries. Crowd-funding over the Internet, peer-to-peer lending, Internet-based foreign exchange and payment providers, and virtual currencies such as Bitcoin all represent attempts to bypass traditional financial institutions and practices. There is an underlying theme that information technology will generate and support more perfect, transparent markets in goods, services, and intangibles, including money. In this vision, price more perfectly reflects all information, financial resources are efficiently allocated, and risk is optimally dispersed to those best able to bear it.

Though it is hard to gainsay that finance (like other industry sectors) is more and more an information systems-based and information systems-dependent industry, what are the lessons of the financial crisis for the future of technology-driven finance?

First, in the twenty-first century as in preceding centuries, the supply of money can be a major driver in finance. That is, the market may be from time to time shaped more by the need of investors to find investment opportunities—the search for yield—than by the ability of borrowers to put the money to good use. The financial crisis has thus opened many interesting debates about the nature of global capitalism and provoked challenges to received wisdom concerning markets and economics.

What is new is the hyper-development of what we might call metafinance: finance about finance, sometimes discussed under the heading of "financial innovation." In the metafinance business model, financial institutions create financial products and the associated markets and indices that may relate to (be derivative of) prices or to underlying "real world" financial obligations (for example, bonds of XCorp.), credit default swaps being an example. The trading of these financial products in their associated markets can be a source of profits to the traders. There is no outside limit to the creation or proliferation of such products and markets,[1] which are generally designed with the use of, or centered around, information technology capabilities. In these metafinance markets, actions of traders can result in values of these derived products both detaching from the real values, and in some cases affecting prices, of the underlying. That is, there is a dynamic two-way relationship between values in the derivative market

---

1. "Under what conditions do the theories of finance produce impossible scenarios that are bound to backfire and fail? They are not 'bound' to do this for causal or dialectical reasons, but because they seek to derive endless possibilities from limited resources." Judith Butler, *Performative Agency*, 3 J. of Cultural Econ. 147, 153 (2010).

and the market in the underlying. For example, this is institutionalized when changes in CDS prices result in gain or loss for the obligor on the underlying loan, back-propagating the imputed risk of default as reflected in the CDS market, to the market value of debt, to the debtor's balance sheet, even though the debtor remains obligated for 100% repayment.

One could argue that the existence of and prices in the derivative market can actually drive the market in the underlying. At this point I make my second reading recommendation—the 2007 and 2008 annual reports of AIG.

AIG Financial Products (AIGFP), a unit of AIG, wrote credit default swaps to earn revenue on credit exposure in an unfunded form, focusing on a "super senior" layer of exposure in CDOs and other securitized debt, above other AAA-rated layers. Terms were "negotiated by AIGFP for each transaction to provide that the likelihood of any payment obligation by AIGFP under each transaction is remote, even in severe recessionary market scenarios. The underwriting process for these derivatives included assumptions of severely stressed recessionary market scenarios to minimize the likelihood of realized losses under these obligations."[2]

Put in terms of price arbitrage, the premium AIGFP earned, even if it was very low, was more than its funding cost, which was zero. AIGFP was run as a trading desk, not as a credit underwriting business, and they relied on statistical risk models, not analysis of the underlying credits. An AIG executive is reported to have said: "The models suggested that the risk was so remote that the fees were almost free money."[3]

Of the $527 billion in notional exposure of the super senior credit default swap portfolio (SSCDSP) at the end of 2007, approximately $379 billion consisted of a "regulatory capital relief" portfolio written specifically for purposes of lowering capital charges for (mostly Euro-

---

2.   AIG 2007 Annual Report (2008) [hereinafter AIG 2007 Annual Report], at 122–33, *available at* http://www.aig.com/Chartis/internet/US/en/ 2007annualreport_tcm3171-440907.pdf.

3.   Brady Dennis & Robert O'Harrow Jr., *A Crack in the System*, WASH. POST, Dec. 30, 2008. *Available at* www.washingtonpost.com/wp-dyn/content/ article/2008/12/29/AR2008122902670.html.

pean) banks under Basel I capital adequacy rules, "rather than risk mitigation". That is, this portion of the portfolio supported classification arbitrage.

Just over half of the remainder of the SSCDSP related to "multi-sector CDOs," most of it involving some exposure to U.S. subprime mortgages. As of year-end 2007, AIG booked $11.25 billion of unrealized market valuation loss on the multi-sector CDO portion of the SSCDSP, but "continue[d] to believe that the unrealized market valuation losses recorded on the AIGFP super senior credit default swap portfolio are not indicative of the losses AIGFP may realize over time."[4]

However, AIG's accountants identified a material weakness in internal controls over financial reporting and oversight relating to the valuation of the SSCDSP. For 2008, AIG booked an additional $28.6 billion of unrealized market valuation loss on the SSCDSP, most of which related to the multi-sector CDO swaps. Due to degradation of the underlying CDOs and AIG ratings downgrades, there were collateral calls on the SSCDSP portfolio that (together with collateral demands in AIG's securities lending program) precipitated a liquidity crisis by mid-September 2008. The U.S. government determined that a collapse of AIG threatened unacceptable systemic risk and rescued AIG with emergency financial assistance. By the end of 2008, a majority of the multi-sector CDO swaps (face amount $62 billion) had been liquidated in a transaction funded by the U.S. government. The underlying CDOs were purchased and the associated CDSs were terminated for a total purchase price of $59.3 billion, or nearly face value. (To put this figure in perspective, shareholders' equity at year-end 2007 was $95.8 billion, net loss for 2008 was $99.3 billion, and shareholders' equity at year-end 2008 was $52.7 billion (giving effect to significant equity infusions by the U.S. government).)

Through credit default swaps, major financial institutions had been exposed to AIG in an amount at least equal to the payments they received in 2008 from settling out those CDS obligations. This effective risk-shifting was in addition to the capital support (for regulatory purposes) that AIG was providing to banks under its regulatory capi-

---

4.   AIG 2007 Annual Report, at 33.

tal relief book. The exposures appear to be in some respects reciprocal. At year-end 2008, AIG identified as a risk factor its continuing concentrated credit risk exposure to financial institutions, particularly money-center/global banks (160% of shareholders' equity; 65.6% attributable to the top five). From a systems perspective, AIG was a critical point of failure in a small and tightly interdependent network, operating in an information environment characterized by hedging, netting and other accounting conventions that mask gross exposures.

Participants in the network assessed their positions principally by reference to market-based valuation techniques. AIG's 2008 annual report includes extensive discussion of its valuation methodologies, including detailed explication of their modified version of the BET (binomial expansion technique) model used to value the SSCDSP. BET was originally developed by a rating agency in 1996 to generate expected loss estimates for CDO tranches. The modified BET model implied default probabilities and cash flows from price estimates on the individual securities comprising the portfolio of a CDO. AIG obtained prices from CDO collateral managers where these prices were available, but for 2008 CDO collateral managers provided these prices for only 61.2% of the underlying securities. For the rest, AIG derived the price based on a "matrix pricing" technique by comparison to similar securities.

In its 2008 annual report, AIG acknowledges a number of issues around valuation: counterparty disputes; problems with reliance on historical data; unanticipated high correlations; concentration of risk; and the possibility that loss of market access could prevent the execution of hedging strategies. It opens a discussion on risk factors by noting: "Many of these risks are interrelated and occur under similar business and economic conditions, and the occurrence of certain of them may in turn cause the emergence, or exacerbate the effect, of others."[5] A principal advisor on AIG's risk models commented on the effective tainting throughout the financial system caused by the "dis-

---

5.   AIG 2008 Annual Report (2009), at 21, *available at* http://www.aig.com/Chartis/internet/US/en/2008annualreport_tcm3171-440902.pdf.

person" of risk: "You have this very, very complicated chain of the movement of the risk, which made it very opaque about where the risk finally resided. And it ended up residing in many places. So the whole infrastructure of the financial market became kind of infected, because no one knew exactly where the risk was."[6]

One might argue, or at least consider the possibility, that the willingness of traders at AIG Financial Products to underwrite the risk of certain CDOs facilitated the creation of those CDOs and, indirectly, the funding of the underlying real estate loans. In any case, there can be a profit incentive to participate in metafinance markets that has relatively little to do with the traditional purpose of finance—efficient allocation of capital—and more to do with matching counterparties who take different views on a particular risk. In some cases, trading in these markets, and thus risk, can be highly concentrated among a small group of participants. As I have noted, there is no limit to the number of derivative risk-view trades that can be made with reference to a single underlying "real economy" (or other metafinance) price or other event, for example if there are multiple levels of securitization or if there is no requirement to hold any interest in the underlying. Thus finance can come to take an outsized role in relation to the "real economy"—wealth-producing trade in goods and non-financial services.

This leads to the question: what is the proper role of financial institutions vis-à-vis the "real economy," on the one hand, versus the financial industry per se, on the other? And then: what are the implications for the appropriate scope of government intervention in the event of market dysfunction? As various commentators unpicked the financial crisis, they noted the concentration of market activity, and there were allegations that in some cases financial institutions had conflicts of interest, did not put their customers first, or favored customers on one side of a risk trade as against the interests of customers on the other side of the risk trade. In addition, "shadow banking" participants (such as hedge funds)—frequent counterparties in lucrative transactions—might be implicated or disadvantaged, but in any case were important participants in the trading markets. Though

---

6. Gary Gorton, Yale University School of Management, transcript reported in THE WALL STREET JOURNAL, October 31, 2008.

outside the purview of regulators, they were part of the bigger picture, and the effects of their participation in the market had to be considered.

The case of AIG dramatically illustrates the systemic dynamics of leverage, whether in the form of borrowing, or in the case of AIG's CDS book, in the form of "unfunded credit exposure," especially where leverage involves collateral arrangements. An important predecessor case involved the hedge fund Long Term Capital Management (LTCM). In 1998, LTCM experienced a liquidity crisis judged by U.S. federal regulators to entail excessive systemic risk, and they orchestrated a bailout. The crisis demonstrated that the hedge fund industry, positioned to exploit arbitrage opportunities using borrowed money (leverage), no longer stood outside the markets but was capable of moving them. MacKenzie[7] has analyzed the events leading up to this crisis as the "creation of a superportfolio," where a relatively small group of hedge fund arbitrageurs, using similar risk models, ended up with similar positions on macro-economic events. As the macro-portfolio played out, adverse events in Russia and Asia propagated and amplified across the holdings of many financial institutions, affecting asset prices and liquidity in apparently unrelated (and supposedly uncorrelated) markets. In particular, margin calls on losing positions forced the liquidation of "good" assets at distressed prices. The dynamics of leverage thus quickly transmitted distress across firms and markets in a "cascade" of non-linear cumulative and interactive effects, or "contagion," not easily anticipated through simple aggregation but which look more like features of high-risk technologies as described by Perrow.[8]

Just as in the case of Long Term Capital Management in 1998, it was collateral requirements that generated the liquidity crisis for AIG: as valuations of various CDOs collapsed, AIG's counterparties demanded collateral to support the credit default swaps on those CDOs.

---

7. Donald Mackenzie, *How a Superportfolio Emerges: Long Term Capital Management and the Sociology of Arbitrage*, in THE SOCIOLOGY OF FINANCIAL MARKETS (Karin Knorr Cetina and Alex Preda eds., Oxford University Press 2005).

8. Charles Perrow, *Normal Accidents: Living with High-Risk Technologies* (Basic Books 1984).

Collateral requirements (margin calls) can transmit and amplify price weakness. As borrowers sell high quality assets to meet the demands of counterparties, the market prices of those high quality asset classes fall. In this way, the existence of highly levered participants in the market (such as some hedge funds) puts other market participants at risk as, under mark-to-market accounting, they may have to write down the value of their holdings in the event the levered participants confront liquidity problems.

In addition, the case of AIG demonstrates the very serious problem of valuation of financial assets and obligations. There is a significant reliance on informational shortcuts—on "market" values and indices, on models and on rating agencies—in lieu of traditional underwriting. Much has been written about the faulty models, based on inapt historical data, that were used in securitizing U.S. residential real estate loans. Such heuristics may be essential elements of some financial technologies—Donald MacKenzie of the University of Edinburgh has argued that full calculation of values and thus prices of CDOs using individual loan data represents a problem of computational intractability—but they need to be understood as imperfect, and their construction and sponsorship questioned.

Thus the case of AIG, and the unfolding of the financial crisis more generally, revealed the extent of opacity not only across the financial markets generally but within financial institutions. Knowledge across the production chain—from mortgage borrowers to investors in synthetic CDOs—was partial and fragmented, and the use of informational shortcuts was extensive. The reliance on informational shortcuts extended to the preparation of financial statements and disclosure. Though the accounting profession has been given a relative "pass" in the wake of the financial crisis, it would be hard to argue that the disclosure provided or, according to generally accepted accounting principles and mark-to-market accounting, could have provided an accurate picture of financial assets and obligations and thus the financial condition of various entities. Furthermore, entity-by-entity accounting (where for example, XBank transfers the risk associated with a portfolio on the basis that it holds AAA-rated credit default swap protection from YCorp covering the portfolio, while YCorp values its CDS obligation at zero) effectively hides risk at the systemic level. In sum, certain corners of finance had been transformed into a largely self-reflexive information and trading business that concealed latent systemic risk.

The Great Recession has caused many to question the scope of the obligation of the government to underwrite banking, sometimes under the headings of "moral hazard" and "too big to fail." In the case of AIG the US government determined that it needed to support a private company's obligations to major banking institutions because the failure to do so would have triggered a catastrophic cascade of financial failure—the financial system would have seized up. The government also stepped in with many other critical fixes to support asset values, financial institutions and liquidity. In so doing, one might argue, the government rewrote on an ad hoc basis the rules of contract and perhaps bankruptcy. Reliance on the "market" was set aside. Yet I would say that overall we have been well-served by these government interventions, and that, indeed, there is an unstated but perhaps essential expectation in the "market" that the government will intervene in a catastrophic market failure for the sake of the larger economy. You can reach your own conclusion about this important policy question. In any event, the financial crisis has prompted a debate about the proper scope of the implicit government guarantee in relation to money, the payments system, and ordinary course "Main Street" commercial banking on the one hand, and in relation to non-traditional and metafinance activities that banks had taken up, on the other.

Since the onset of the financial crisis there has been a flurry of regulatory activity, much of it focusing on increased capital requirements, more supervision of bank liquidity, the reduction of perceived risky activity in the regulated (de facto government-underwritten) financial sector, increased transparency in some markets such as derivatives, expanded scope of financial regulatory authority and attempts to understand systemic risk, including on a global scale. While some in the financial industry find the new requirements onerous, others ask whether enough has been done. The shadow banking sector is still active and thriving and, given the new regulatory environment, perhaps more attractive than ever. Finance continues to be characterized by opacity and fragmentation. This can lead financial institutions to demand more in terms of protective tripwires and collateral arrangements in the ordinary course of business. While this can make the individual institution more safe and sound, it makes the network of finance more vulnerable to a dynamic of "cascade" or "contagion." In other words, it can increase (largely latent and often invisible) systemic risk.

A rather demoralizing series of developments has continued to erode trust in banks and in the integrity, indeed even operational robustness, of the "market." As lawsuits against major banks arising from the financial crisis have made their way through the courts, the LIBOR and other price- and index-fixing scandals have revealed bankers manipulating key market indicators, around which billions of dollars of financial transactions have been structured. "Rogue traders" have caused huge losses at major banks. It has been alleged that holders of credit default swaps have confounded the management of troubled debt situations, from which they are set to profit, and that the CDS market has had an outsized effect on bond prices, to the advantage of traders in the underlying. Metafinance still thrives, and new forms are emerging: "dark pools" and high frequency trading are representative of a fragmentation of markets, where privileged participants trade on restricted platforms or using technology that operates on a time scale where ordinary investors cannot compete. Automated trading was implicated in the "Flash Crash" of 2010, and there are indications that sponsors or owners of markets (markets-as-products) may run them to their own advantage. At the same time, traditional market-making and specialist activities intended to provide liquidity in market disruptions have fallen away. There have always been public companies effectively controlled by founding families or other voting blocs, but tiered equity has become more common for companies coming to market, effectively disenfranchising public investors in favor of continuing control by company insiders. In the meantime, in the ultra-low interest rate environment, the search for yield continues, with the recent return of PIK (pay-in-kind) and covenant-lite debt. In many respects in the world of finance, business is back to business as usual.

What are some implications of the financial crisis and subsequent events for finance professionals and for this book? There are no doubt many, but let me suggest four issues to think about.

First, while lawyers have emerged relatively unscathed from the financial crisis in terms of assigning blame, this may not be the case in the future. I would like to emphasize the message in this book that it is important to understand the purpose and the context of the transaction or other project you are working on, and to raise questions when anything about the situation makes you uncomfortable. Given the fragmentation of knowledge across the production chain in metafinance, as described above, it can be difficult to get the big picture and to think through how things might be viewed in hindsight. In particular, consider whether anyone might allege a conflict of interest.

Second, the financial crisis revealed that many supposedly sophisticated investors and other parties did not really understand what they were buying or committing to, but relied on the representations of intermediaries, informational shortcuts like models and ratings, or simply the "brand name" of the sponsor. They did not conduct due diligence on the obligor or other counterparty, and did not think through the consequences of various scenarios. Who is the obligor and what is the obligation? What is each party committing to? What due diligence has been done and is it sufficient? These fundamentals of corporate finance practice remain critically important, and apply equally in the relatively disembodied and abstract realm of metafinance.

Third, although they have not received much attention, I believe that the financial crisis revealed many weaknesses in accounting and disclosure practices. Questions have been raised about accounting for derivatives and about the effects of mark-to-market accounting, and I have already noted the problem of valuation. But there are other issues. Just as in the Enron case, the contingencies associated with many contractual arrangements—such as liquidity backstops which could bring off-balance sheet obligations or assets onto the balance sheet or collateral arrangements that could generate liquidity crises—were not clearly or consistently understood or disclosed, even within the relevant institution. This resulted in an informational void when the system came under stress. Finance professionals should absorb this point in thinking through where current accounting and disclosure practices fall short and then perhaps in time work toward better practices that promote more effective disclosure and "transparency."

Lastly, the financial crisis should provoke lawyers and other finance professionals to consider their roles with respect to financialization and financial technology. Clearly financial technologies permit ever faster, global, and more abstract and disembodied transactions, and the drive toward speed and automation is not going to slow. For example, the interbank payments processing organization

SWIFT is promoting the use of "bank payment obligations" to reduce manual processing of letters of credit in international trade. But the financial crisis should prompt increased scrutiny and reflection. A technological determinist would say that the existence of new financial technologies in fact does not just facilitate but actually generates transactions (including profits and losses) that would otherwise not exist. The financial crisis and subsequent events show that it is not enough just to be able to execute a trade—financial institutions and other market participants need to understand what they are doing. The multiple layers of informational shortcuts that support financial innovation and speed of execution can result in fragmentation and opacity; they are not a substitute for careful underwriting. Data on screens is just that, and it is essential to look beyond.

What are the professional (including ethical) obligations of lawyers and other finance professionals with respect to the design and use of these systems? Do they have the necessary skills? Where are the checks and balances? What are the unintended consequences? What should continue to be "manual"?

In raising these issues, I am not intending to sound overly pessimistic. Instead I want to argue for the continuing importance, indeed criticality, of finance for enterprise, investment and trade, and for the integrity of the payments system and of money as a store of value. These are the underpinnings of the wealth-creating real economy. Even technologies such as credit cards and Internet-based payment systems ultimately depend on robust and trustworthy banking infrastructure, and banking infrastructure for the foreseeable future depends on some form of government oversight and backstop. I would like to argue for the continuing importance of "situated knowledge"—due diligence and real underwriting—in finance. With finance operating at hyperspeed, it has never been more important. In sum, I argue for the worth of finance—not as an end in itself, but in its legitimate, indeed critical, support relationship vis-á-vis the real economy—and for the practices and work of finance professionals. It is in this spirit that I offer the second edition of this book.

In the preface, I mention reading the *Wall Street Journal*. Let me recommend now that you also regularly read the *New York Times Dealbook*, the *Economist*, and the *Financial Times*.

I would like to thank James Florack and Tiffany Boydell of Davis Polk & Wardwell for their invaluable help in preparing this second edition and to express my appreciation to Dr. Susan Scott of the London School of Economics for her collaboration in developing some of the themes discussed in this Foreword to the Second Edition. The opinions expressed in this book are my own, and of course I am responsible for any errors.

CARRIE PARIS
London, October 2014

Preface

Hello young lawyers (or lawyers, young or not, new to corporate finance)!

A few parts of this book have their antecedents in some writing that I did over twenty years ago, when I was a young lawyer. I had spent a few years working on Wall Street and was living in Singapore. Much to my surprise, I found I had really enjoyed the first few years of law practice in New York, and I missed the pace and the challenge.

While still in law school I had subscribed to the *Wall Street Journal*, taking advantage of a student discount, and I read it regularly. At the beginning, it meant next to nothing to me, being a typical liberal arts student. Over the three years of law school, things became a bit less foggy, but it was still a report from a foreign country—until I got to New York, when everything started to click into place.

Of my work, in particular I enjoyed drafting. I was lucky to learn from partners who—if not always patient—were still painstaking and willing to invest the time (in me and my peers) to explain what worked and what did not. But I still missed having that overarching view of the whole, and at times found it frustrating to feel like a climber ascending a peak one slow step at a time.

I thought that drafting was a skill that, given sufficient time and resources, could be taught and learned in a systematic fashion. I still believe that, though it would take a semester or two to do it right. *How to Draft for Corporate Finance* (referred to in Appendix A, Notes and Resources) is a set of materials that can be used to teach (or to teach yourself) drafting skills.

This book is not a comprehensive training manual, nor is it an authoritative reference, but is intended to give you that overview perspective. I hope you find it useful and that you enjoy your labors (and the fruits of your labors) in the credit and capital markets.

CARRIE PARIS
London, July 2007

Chapter 1

Introduction

§ 1:1   What Is Corporate Finance, and Why This Book

Most business transactions involve money changing hands, but corporate finance is *all* about money. A company needs money to run or grow its business, including by buying other businesses. Banks and investors have money to lend or invest. Corporate finance is the business of getting money from those who have it to lend or invest to companies that can put the money to work.

At least, that is, the front-end, high-profile part of corporate finance. Corporate finance is also about how the company will live with its financial agreements, and when and how the banks and investors will get their money back. This part matters just as much in the long run.

The role of the corporate finance lawyer is to represent companies, banks and investors, and various and sundry other parties—intermediaries, sponsors, trustees—in corporate finance matters. A lot of what corporate finance lawyers do is to help their clients get deals done—that is, to closing. But they are also expected to assist and advise their clients after closing.

After closing, lawyers get questions about how to interpret financial agreements and additional queries concerning clients' rights and obligations. Often, these questions arise due to something important—a big transaction is in the offing, there's a dispute about wording, or the company is in some kind of difficulty, including of a

1

financial nature. Sadly, a client rarely calls a lawyer to say everything is going well and isn't it wonderful that the finance agreement anticipated all eventualities.

The problem you face working on a deal as a new lawyer is that you're down at ground level. Some of the work you do may be more about logistics and deal management than anything else—moving the deal from Point A to Point B. Most of those logistics and deal management skills are not particular to corporate finance, and this book, for the most part, is not about those things.

Sooner or later, though, you will be asked to work on corporate finance documents—a loan agreement or an indenture. You will be given a form or some precedents to start with, and a term sheet. If you look at the form or precedent, and if you have worked with any other contracts, the general structure and the "boilerplate" terms at the end will look familiar. Conditions precedent and representations and warranties are basic elements of a contract you probably learned about in law school. But much of the contract is pretty specific to the world of corporate finance. That is what this book is about. Understanding those terms and getting them right is very important to the client, and the consequences of getting them *not* quite right can be significant—for the client and sometimes for the lawyer.

It is important to understand where the terms of the contract come from—which ones are essentially fixed or given and will be demanded by the market, and which ones are negotiable. Clients are generally in a hurry, and there is no point in using up time and goodwill haggling over items that are truly standard or unimportant. That is the mark of inexperience.

In addition, it is especially important to know which terms are most likely to have operational effect in the future, and thus will matter the most in hindsight.

There is no way, looking at a contract as a "flat" or linear document and reading it straight through like a novel, to tell what is important. The critical terms don't leap off the page, and they won't be bolded or highlighted. It is not a question of pure thinking and analysis, but a question of knowing where to look and what to look for. Knowing more about the company, finance, and the universe of comparable agreements will let you spend your time wisely, produce better work more quickly, and impress your clients, senior lawyers, and opposing counsel. Knowing more about what you are doing makes it less likely that you will make a mistake. Knowing why you are doing what you are doing and being better at doing it makes it more interesting and less stressful.

§ 1:2   What This Book Covers

This book introduces you to the players, the markets, and the instruments that make up corporate finance, and sets forth some of the fundamental accounting and bankruptcy concepts key to corporate finance lawyering.

You will learn how to analyze the nature and rank of the corporate finance instrument. You will also work through major issues relating to corporate structure within the obligor group, look at external credit support, and be introduced to concepts of commitment, conditions, risk, and liquidity.

We will go through the deal life cycle from inception through closing and post-closing, describing the role of the lawyer at each step.

Then we will examine corporate finance contracts element by element and look at how the pieces fit together. There is a detailed analysis of debt and lien covenants, business covenants that may impact corporate transactions, and financial covenants. Amendment, control, and refinancing provisions are given special attention as these may be particularly important "in hindsight."

To help you spend your time wisely and avoid errors, the book offers guidance on how to review contracts with a risk-weighting in mind, as well as suggested best practices.

Indicative terms for bank credit agreements and public debt, balance sheets for the various stages of corporate evolution, and a "diary of a liquidity crisis" are included as illustrations.

§ 1:3   What This Book Doesn't Cover

This book is not an encyclopedia of corporate finance, but only an introduction to the basic concepts. The focus is principally on debt, not equity; and convertible debt is only touched on, as are structured finance and derivatives. Structured finance and derivatives are significant legal specialties in their own right and constitute huge and diverse markets. Though not the subject of this book, they have become increasingly important, and were substantially implicated in the financial crisis commencing in 2007–2008.

Though this book talks about the effect of security on rank, the details of how to attain a perfected security interest are not addressed at all, and indeed are technical and quite specific to the type of collateral and the jurisdiction.

The book is mostly about the financial contract provisions that directly affect the company and does not address the securities laws, or other legal or operational aspects of placement or underwriting, or the activities of broker-dealers. There are other regulatory schemes relevant to money-raising, such as the Investment Company Act and the Investment Advisers Act, that are not touched upon here; each of these represents an area of special legal expertise. Likewise, the Trust Indenture Act is only mentioned in passing.

The book is not an introduction to corporate finance from a quantitative perspective, and neither is it about the markets where debt, equity, and other financial instruments are traded.

Issues and documentation relevant to private equity or to mutual funds or other pooled investment structures and vehicles are not within the scope of this book, and neither are specialty areas of finance such as leasing, project finance, sovereign lending, municipal finance, oil and gas, and real estate.

Hopefully this long list of what is not covered will encourage you to look forward to many years of learning about new practice areas!

Though much more is left out of this book than could be contained in it, what is presented here will give you some basic tools of understanding applicable to any area of finance. Perhaps more importantly, you will learn to orient yourself so that, when you are working in a new area of finance, you will apply what you know and ask the right questions—What is the purpose of the deal? What are the relevant markets and precedents? Who is the obligor? What are the conditions? What are the outs? and so forth—and position yourself to provide good and effective client service. In a novel or challenging situation, an experienced lawyer can quickly orient herself in this way and take charge, without overreaching the boundaries of expertise. Over time, you too will learn to do this.

§ 1:4   Caveat

This book is a general introduction to legal and financial topics. It cannot be relied upon as providing definitive or up-to-date guidance. In all cases the reader should carry out appropriate legal research and analysis and consult with senior and expert supervising lawyers for guidance.

Chapter 2

The Players

---

§ 2:1   The Company Perspective

From time to time most companies will have a need for cash that cannot be met with internally generated cash flow. For example, a company may need cash to balance out its regular inward and outward cash flows. Or it may need cash to finance growth, including through acquisitions. A company may decide to seek financing to optimize or rationalize its capital structure and to increase returns to its shareholders.

The company will also have options for capital raising based on its maturity, its existing capitalization and creditworthiness, the stability of its cash earnings, and the value of its assets. Market conditions provide the backdrop for decision-making, defining what is available, the cost, and the terms and conditions.

Sound financial management consists of making the optimal decisions in designing the company's capital structure, matching its needs (or the goals of its shareholders) against the demands of lenders and investors, as reflected in the credit and capital markets.

§ 2:1.1   Debt Versus Equity

In any capital-raising exercise the most fundamental choice is between debt and equity. There are two relevant perspectives—that of the business and that of the equity owners in the business.

Equity owners in a growing business or in a low interest environment are generally happy to see relatively high levels of debt, as that ensures that returns beyond what is necessary to service debt will accrue to the more concentrated equity position. The most extreme version of this scenario is the leveraged recapitalization, where debt is incurred to finance direct payouts to shareholders, shrinking their position in the remaining capital structure even to the point of negative net worth on a book value basis. A levered capital structure is also thought sometimes helpful in warding off unwanted approaches from potential acquirers.

On the other hand, management may see a high level of debt as draining on the business and a straitjacket on their decision making, and certainly for every business there is a level of debt that is not sustainable. A high level of debt may be difficult or impossible to manage for a business with volatile cash flows, and reduces the margin of error and flexibility for a company that runs into unexpected difficulties. At some stages in a company's life—for example, before it is in a positive cash earnings position—debt can be a problematic form of financing.

Some generalizations are useful: Given the relative ranking and associated risk, holders of equity demand higher rates of return, and over time and in general get these. (Some people may ask: Why ever invest in bonds when stocks provide a better return? The answer is that risk of loss and volatility are both higher for stocks. If you are looking for assurance of maintenance of value or may need to pull the money out in the near term or on short notice, bonds are the safer bet.) Interest is deductible for tax purposes; dividends are not. So interest is paid with before-tax dollars, and dividends and other returns of capital (stock buy-backs) are not. For these reasons, debt is "cheaper" than equity. As a corollary, equity issuance is dilutive to existing equity holders, whereas the incurrence of debt is not. Instead, debt levers equity.

§ 2:1.2　*Short-Term or Long-Term Debt*

In the normal interest rate environment, short-term interest rates are lower than longer-term interest rates; this is the normal "yield curve." An "inverted yield curve" refers to the situation where short-term rates have risen above the longer-term rates—for example, because there is expected near-term inflationary pressure but the long-term inflation picture is more benign.

9

So why don't companies always, or at least in the normal interest rate environment, finance with short-term debt rather than long-term debt? If they did, they would have to constantly go to their lenders or the credit markets for new funds. In addition to and more important than the transaction overhead, this would entail too much risk: A negative event affecting either the company or the markets could deprive the company of its cash overnight, precipitating a liquidity crisis.

§ 2:1.3   *Illiquidity Versus Insolvency*

The classic "run on the bank" is exactly this situation. Suppose the local bank takes in demand deposits from the local citizens (creating short-term liabilities) and lends the money out to the same citizens in the form of thirty-year mortgages (long-term assets). The cash in the bank's vault is enough to meet regular withdrawals but is just a fraction of the deposits it holds. (If it took in interest-bearing deposits and kept all the cash in a vault, it would do nothing but lose money.) In the ordinary course this works fine and all is well. However, if a financial panic occurs and all the depositors show up on the same day to withdraw all their savings, the bank will not be able to meet the depositors' demands.

Every liquidity crisis is a version of the "run on the bank" scenario. Being short of cash to meet immediate needs—illiquidity—is different from insolvency, which means that aggregate liabilities exceed aggregate assets. Insolvency cannot be fixed by short-term financing, whereas a liquidity crisis, if properly identified and promptly addressed, often can be fixed. Of course, a company could be insolvent but still liquid (until its insolvency becomes apparent, or results in breaches of financial tests, so that its lenders withdraw financial support), or both insolvent and illiquid.

§ 2:1.4   *Matching Liabilities to Assets; Managing Maturities*

To avoid liquidity problems, it is generally considered prudent to match debt maturities to corresponding assets or cash flows from which the debt will be repaid. You can see what this means on a personal level by comparing an uncommitted demand overdraft facility, to student loans, to a mortgage. The bank overdraft facility is not a good source of funds to buy a house because you probably wouldn't be able to repay the loan on short notice (on demand), and you wouldn't want to risk losing your house. Student loans are generally repayable over time out of expected earnings, and a mortgage is secured against the house and is repayable over the term of occupancy or at sale.

In the corporate context, matching liabilities to assets means that the typical company will have a revolving credit facility providing short-term working capital or cash management financing, as well as longer-term debt either matching capital assets or otherwise representing more long-term ballast in the capital structure, taking into account anticipated refinancings.

Bankers and financial analysts use the ratio of short-term liabilities to short-term assets as a measure of liquidity. A ratio of more than 1:1 indicates that the company is going to have to come up with cash in the near term but does not have an obvious source for the cash. As a corollary, when there is an unwaived default permitting acceleration of long-term debt, the long-term debt turns into short-term debt for financial accounting purposes. This can be a very negative event for a company, turning a stable financial situation into a looming liquidity crisis. One of the reasons that companies try to stay in compliance with covenants in their debt agreements is to avoid their short-term debt ballooning up due to unwaived defaults, particularly at quarter end. You may find that quarter end is a busy time for waiver requests.

In addition to matching assets to liabilities, financial officers generally try to manage maturities so that a company does not have large long-term debt repayments all coming due at once—creating the so-called exploding balance sheet.

Whether it is through default on long-term debt or mismanagement of debt maturities, it is not a pretty picture when a large chunk of the company's capital structure is coming due in the immediate future. At a minimum this exposes the company to the risks and costs of a forced refinancing of its capital structure, in possibly unfavorable market conditions.

§ 2:1.5   *Market Conditions*

Company CFOs do keep an eye on general market conditions. For equity this means the appetite for equity issues and the price-earnings ratios at which equity is trading. Companies are not eager to sell pieces of the equity pie for too cheap, and will be looking for high price-earnings ratios on comparables.

For debt the key market indicators are interest rate and the general availability of credit. Low interest rates and an abundance of funds can mean that it is a good time to go to the credit markets. Easy credit can propel M&A activity and can mask credit problems (artificially depressing default rates), because debt that would otherwise be in default can be easily refinanced. During a "credit crunch," when interest rates may be higher and funding and conditions for loans tighter, companies at the margin may be unable to find financing and highly levered companies with floating-rate debt may find it hard to service their debt.

§ 2:1.6   *Fixed-Rate Financing and Call Protection*

Debt can be fixed rate or floating rate. Floating-rate debt is "cost-plus" financing, where lenders price loans at a spread or margin over a defined cost of short-term funds that is subject to periodic resetting. Most syndicated bank financing is on a floating-rate basis. Fixed-rate notes or bonds bear interest at a stated rate of interest.

CFOs are generally looking to take advantage of low interest rate environments by "locking in" long-term fixed-rate financing. On the other hand, a company does not want to be "locked in" to paying interest on debt financing it does not need, and it would like to be able to refinance high-cost debt with lower-cost debt when general interest rates fall or the company's credit rating improves.

Fixed-rate lenders and investors have the opposite set of concerns. They are looking to buy or invest in a stream of income priced appropriately at the time of investment for the full term of the investment. They are choosing among alternative investments and will be looking at potential lost opportunities (in the form of reduced "spread" over their own costs of funds) if the debt is repaid early. If they aren't offered appropriate call protection (protection for repayment prior to scheduled maturity), they will invest in an alternative asset that does have this feature or they will demand a higher interest rate reflecting the higher risk of early repayment.

The conflicting interests of the company and its lenders and investors on this score are dealt with in the "call" or optional redemption provisions relating to fixed-rate debt. In descriptions of bonds, you will see the references to call versus non-call, the earliest call dates, and call protection, which can be in the form of prohibitions on repayment or in the form of "make-whole" provisions. "Make-whole" provisions look at alternative investment streams available at the time of early repayment and provide to the lender or investor a lump sum that "makes them whole" for what they have lost, calculating the net present value of the difference between what they would have gotten had the debt remained outstanding and what they can earn on an alternative investment (usually U.S. treasuries or some other conservative benchmark investment) for the remainder of the original term.

§ 2:1.7   *Short-Term Pricing with Medium-Term Assurance of Access to Funds Through a Backstop*

Companies with strong credit ratings can have their cake and eat it too—at least in a competitive lending environment. They do this by issuing very-short-term notes—commercial paper—with maturities to match their actual cash management needs, and in anticipation of being able to continue to do so. By staying very short, they can match their actual cash needs closely and not incur any more interest cost than is absolutely necessary, borrowing overnight or for a week or a month.

They also pay a small commitment fee to banks to stand by and fund them if, for some reason, they cannot or choose not to "roll" commercial paper at its maturity but still need the funds, that is, if they cannot or choose not to issue new commercial paper notes to pay off maturing notes. The combination of low interest on the commercial paper notes and commitment fee can provide the lowest all-in cost of medium-term financing.

As you would guess, the key term of the standby commitment or so-called backstop, which will be in the form of a revolving credit agreement, is its conditionality. It does not provide much comfort if the same events that make the commercial paper market inaccessible would excuse the banks from lending.

Commercial paper is rated, with the highest rating of A-1 by Standard & Poor's, and P-1 by Moody's. Many investors are limited to A-1/P-1 commercial paper. Except for the most creditworthy and liquid companies, the rating agencies will require a backstop to be in place and will need to be comfortable that the conditions to lending are not too strict before rating the commercial paper A-1/P-1.

§ 2:1.8   *Nature of the Business*

The nature of the company's business is directly related to its needs for cash. In this respect the financial needs of two companies in the same line of business will tend to be similar, and for this reason bankers have industry-specific finance groups.

For example, the retail apparel business is all about getting the right product to the customer at the right price at the right time, and then dealing as economically as possible with what isn't sold. The business typically runs on design and manufacturing cycles somewhere from six months to eighteen months in length. A wholesaler or retailer in the business may have to pay for goods shipped from abroad months before they can be sold in stores. So there can be a lot of money tied up in inventory. For many retail companies the inventory cycle is seasonal, and it may even be that a majority of the company's business is done at Christmas. During certain periods of the year, the company may be a net user of cash, and at other times its business generates cash. A wholesaler or retailer that sells through franchisees may give its customers or franchisees thirty to forty-five days to pay, and there may be adjustments or returns.

This business model depends heavily on working capital to fund receivables and inventory, and the company may be going to its banks on an ongoing basis to arrange financing for short periods of time, including in the form of letters of credit for overseas payments to suppliers. Key production assets may consist of talent, intellectual property, and information and logistical systems, and the company may have no fixed assets other than its headquarters and perhaps some distribution centers. To sum up: A financial program for a business like this may include inventory finance, possibly trade finance involving letters of credit, factoring or other arrangements to monetize receivables from customers or franchisees, and the long-term financing of distribution centers and logistical systems.

Businesses that are dependent on capital assets such as buildings, factories, physical networks like pipelines or laid cable, or transportation equipment, including rolling stock (train cars), containers, ships and airplanes, need and use cash in a different way and across a different time frame. They have to finance the purchase of these expensive physical assets up front, whereas the earning capacity of the asset is spread over years into the future. They usually have to spend money along the way on maintenance to keep the asset in good operating condition, but even so should also be paying back the purchase money debt and saving for the renewal of the asset. A business like this is heavily dependent on capital expenditures and capital expenditure financing, which should correspond in tenor to the life of the asset. If you have a chance to cast your eye over an old-style first mortgage indenture for a railroad or a utility, you will see lots of detailed provisions about the capital expenditure cycle and capital expenditures increasing borrowing capacity under the indenture, for example, through so-called additions and betterments. Leasing is another way to finance capital assets.

Other business models are not tied to the production or use of physical assets. Banks, very roughly speaking, make money in two ways: by borrowing money and then investing it at a higher rate of return, and by acting as a middleman and taking a fee for services. Insurance companies take in funds (premiums), invest the funds, and stand by to make claims payouts to policyholders. Both businesses depend on the ability of the managers to find the right mix of investments and risk underwriting. In both cases, extremely high leverage against equity can produce outsized returns but also pose outsized risks. Regulators impose minimum capital levels to guard against liquidity and insolvency problems.

Reserves (against, for example, warranty claims, litigation risks, bad assets, or expected policyholder claims) are big items on the liability side of the balance sheets of some companies, particularly financial institutions. Actuaries, who are statisticians specialized in calculating the likelihood of particular events, can play a key expert role in making reserve calculations, for example, in the insurance industry. Actual losses realized (for example, due to warranty claims, litigation, bad debts, or claims experience) can be charged against the corresponding accrued reserves (reducing the reserve) and feed into the analysis for setting the appropriate level of reserves going forward.

Whatever the business, you should have a sense of how it is that it makes money, how it might potentially lose money, and how its business model relates to financial statement items such as revenues, assets, and liabilities, including reserves. In many cases, the relationship of the company's money-making model to the financial statements is entirely straightforward. In other cases, it takes some digging around to see what is going on, and it might be there are some obvious areas of "softness," where management judgment and accounting treatment can have inordinate effect. More on this later.

§ 2:1.9   *Maturity of the Business*

It is also worth understanding where the company stands in terms of the "maturity" of its business model.

A start-up needs money to finance asset acquisition or maybe even just research and development (R&D), to develop some ideas or to turn ideas into marketable goods and services. Cash earning capability may be off in the future, or just ephemeral, in any case highly speculative. A business in this formative stage should not be borrowing money, but instead looking for equity investments from venture capital investors ("angel" investors), who are running a book of such investments expecting that some of them will win big while others will go nowhere. (The "dot-com" initial public offering (IPO) boom can be seen as a case of public investors lining up to be "angels," with the predictable outcome that many fell to earth.)

Borrowing—incurring debt that the lender expects will be timely repaid, with interest—should be against an asset (as a mortgage is a loan against real property) or, once a business is up and running, against a cash flow. During growth, both equity and debt can be sound financial strategies from the company perspective, but from the equity perspective more debt, provided cash flow is reasonably certain, may be better—as debt levers returns to equity holders. Simply put, equity holders do not have to "share" the upside beyond what it takes to service the debt.

Finally, as a company runs to the end of the cycle it may be throwing off steady cash but not growing; it may even be shrinking. Fresh injections of capital at this stage, unless targeted at new growth initiatives, do not make sense, though the company may be a solid and stable credit risk as it runs down over the medium term.

Some businesses are cyclical, meaning that the industry as a whole will go through ups and downs depending on factors to a significant degree out of management's control, such as the prices of underlying commodities or macro-economic conditions. Other businesses are very stable and steady cash earners. For many years utilities threw off predictable cash earned in a heavily regulated but monopolistic environment. Though this is still characteristic of some utilities, the industry as a whole is not the safe and predictable investment environment it once was. Deregulation can turn stable and steady producers of predictable cash flows into cyclical or even speculative businesses.

§ 2:1.10   *Where Does the Company's Cash Come From?*

You should try to understand not only how the company generates its reported income, but where it gets its cash. The two are not the same.

For example, a company may book revenues (income) based on when contracts are signed or when goods are shipped, on the basis that there is likely to be little further performance required of the company, but payment may be spread over a period of time, and the company may need to finance its costs in advance of receiving payment (accounts receivable financing). Revenues may be booked but subject to returns, chargebacks, or other adjustments. So there may be a time lag or even uncertainty in turning revenue into cash. In too many cases in the recent past, purported revenues based on "swaps" or trades of goods or services turned out to be illusory in terms of ultimate cash realization, or inflated through "roundtripping" of the same goods or services with cooperating counterparties, or both. "Channel-stuffing," which is the practice of pushing goods out to customers, in advance of orders or with an expectation of high returns in order to make quarterly sales targets, is another improper activity that can inflate income figures.

A company in its early stages of development may not be earning any cash at all from its business but instead living off cash proceeds from capital-raising activities. Sales of assets outside the ordinary course of business can be another source of cash, but of course these cash receipts are not part of ordinary operating income and are likely to be one-shot (non-recurring).

Income statements report income on a Generally Accepted Accounting Principles (GAAP) basis and are intended to convey a sense of the company's earnings performance for a period, almost always on an accrual basis, not a cash basis. Ebbs and flows in working capital, period-to-period adjustments and capital transactions such as the issuance of equity for cash, borrowings and repayments are reflected on the statement of cash flows for the company. Both views of a company are relevant, but keep in mind that it is cash that repays debt, not book income.

§ 2:1.11   *Implications for Lawyers*

When you are working on a deal, take a little time to learn about the company's business, by reading recent SEC filings, analysts' reports, or the information package for the deal. Your review should include a look at the company's financial statements including the footnotes. Make sure that you understand how your deal fits in with the company's overall capital structure, how it is positioned in the market (so that you can identify the correct precedents), and what the use of proceeds will be. You should understand the company's overall financial strategy. If the company is borrowing money, how do the company and the bankers expect the company to pay it back? If the plan is that debt will be repaid with equity infusions, asset sales, or refinancings, then the financing agreements should permit this to happen.

In particular, if refinancings are anticipated and need to be secured with collateral, or be senior to subordinated debt, or otherwise inherit the benefits of the debt to be refinanced, the documents must be precisely worded to make sure this will be the unqualified result and that lawyers will be able to give opinions to this effect. This is an area where the company's lenders, both the lenders that expect to be refinanced and those that may provide the refinancing, have an especially keen interest in the provisions of debt agreements other than their own. It is, to say the least, unpleasant to have to explain and deal with drafting oversights that end up making an anticipated refinancing (or other anticipated transaction) difficult or impossible to do.

§ 2:2   Investors and Intermediaries

§ 2:2.1   *Individual and Institutional Investors in the Public or Quasi-Public Markets; Underwriters and Placement Agents*

Equity or debt can be raised through offerings to retail and institutional investors of SEC-registered securities in the public markets, or of similar but unregistered securities to sophisticated and overseas investors, including institutional investors (in a Rule 144A/Reg. S offering). In this public or quasi-public market, banks act as underwriters to bring the issue to market. Since many retail investors invest through mutual funds, in fact the public or quasi-public market is dominated by institutional investors. These sorts of deals, whether or not SEC-registered, are viewed as "capital markets" deals, and the documentation and practices, including due diligence and the preparation of a selling document, are driven by the public offering model.

The typical documentation in this market consists of:

- an engagement letter between the company and an investment bank providing a mandate for the financing to the bank for a period;

- a disclosure or selling document (the prospectus or offering memorandum);

- an underwriting or purchase agreement signed at pricing and just before issuance and containing the conditions precedent to purchase and the representations; and

- shares and any required related corporate documents (for equity) or notes and an indenture (for debt).

Until pricing and the signing of the underwriting or purchase agreement there is no commitment on the part of the underwriters.

Under an indenture, there is a trustee who acts as a paid agent for the company in administering the indenture but is also charged with acting in trust for and on behalf of the note- or bondholders after funding. The trustee is not a principal, but an agent and fiduciary. For public debt, the indenture must be a qualified indenture under the Trust Indenture Act, which contains provisions governing the role, rights, and obligations of the trustee.

Transfer provisions and arrangements designed to ensure compliance with the securities and tax laws and to promote trading and liquidity may be complex, but are relatively standard. Bearer securities (relatively rare today for U.S. issuers) are securities that are held and transferable in physical form, with interest and principal paid on presentment to a paying agent. Holders of registered securities are listed on a register of holders, transfer is by change of the registered owner, and there is typically no need for physical securities; instead there is reliance on the book entries kept by the registrar. However, many holders of registered securities are not listed on the books of the issuer or its registrar because they hold through accounts at broker-dealers (in so-called street name). Global notes are physical notes that are held by a depositary, which maintains a register of the holders of interests in the global note. Provisions relating to the form of security and transfer of interests in the security need to be right, in terms of the desired tax and securities laws results, but aren't controversial.

Compensation to the banks in this "public" market is in the form of a spread between what the company gets and what the purchasers of the securities pay at initial issuance. For an equity IPO, the spread might be 5–7%; in the high-yield debt market it might be 2.25–3%; and for investment grade bonds it would be less than 1%. Getting to closing is critical to the bankers; if there is no closing, they get nothing. For this reason, the engagement letter will provide that if the company does a comparable deal with other bankers during the exclusivity period covered by the engagement letter, it will owe a fee equal to the spread to its original bankers.

Commercial paper is offered under an exemption from registration requirements, usually in a program managed by a bank acting as dealer (and taking a spread). Documentation consists of a form of a simple promissory note and, if a dealer is used to market the notes, a dealer agreement, though there is no firm commitment on the part of the dealer to actually purchase or place the commercial paper. There may also be an agreement with a bank to act as agent to handle the mechanics of issuing and paying the notes.

The capital markets practice in a law firm is typically resourced with lawyers who are versed in securities laws requirements and underwriters' practices. The business of underwriting is outside the scope of this book, but lawyers who work in this area need to be sensitive to the underwriting perspective, to how underwriters and individual bankers are compensated, and to the relationships among the underwriters in a deal where there is more than one underwriter. Financial institutions are very much oriented to claiming credit for deals in so-called league tables, and a lot of the dynamics you will observe drive off this orientation. League tables are the various industry tabulations of deals and the bankers and other professionals involved, and are taken to be rough guides to competitive ranking, market share, and relevant experience. (Lawyers care about league tables too.)

§ 2:2.2 *Banks and Other Lenders in the Bank Loan and Private Placement Markets*

In contrast to the capital markets, the private credit market has developed out of the historical practice of commercial (deposit-taking) banks lending their own funds directly to companies. The banks typically act in a syndicate with an agent bank. The agent bank drives the deals and negotiates with the company on behalf of the banks, but does not take on any underwriting or risk assessment for the banks, each of which is expected to make its own credit assessment. In big deals there can be a number of agents with different titles such as syndication agent, documentation agent, and so forth. Again, the league table orientation can be at work here.

The typical documentation in this sort of deal consists of a commitment letter with term sheet and providing for fees; possibly a bank book for syndication for a large deal, for an acquisition or leveraged deal, or for a non-public company; and a credit agreement with attached notes, forms of opinions, and, as relevant, other forms of documents such as security agreements and guarantees.

The banks that put the deal together will get closing fees (paid at initial funding or at closing). Banks that commit will get commitment fees (based on the amount of unused or unfunded commitment) from the time they commit (which can be starting from or after the commitment letter date depending on when initial commitments made by the lead banks are sold down in the course of syndication), with commitment and/or facility fees (which accrue based on the total amount of the facility whether used or unused) running from closing on definitive documentation through the life of the commitment. And, of course, banks earn interest on loans made. There may be separate compensation for banks issuing or participating in letters of credit and providers of "swingline" loans (short-term loans made by a small and manageable subset of the bank group), if the credit agreement includes these facilities. An important development in the past decade is the non-investment grade "Term Loan B" market, targeted at CLOs, hedge funds and other non-traditional institutional investors. Many of them are also participants in the high-yield bond market.

Insurance companies lend money directly to companies under note purchase agreements. When several insurance companies agree to make loans at the same time on the same terms, this is done under multiple parallel note purchase agreements. All insurance companies will have an independent say on the terms, but one typically acts as an unofficial lead in negotiations. There is no agent or trustee, but there may be voting and collective action that runs across the parallel agreements.

§ 2:2.3   Competition and Consolidation in the Banking Industry

In 1933, the Glass-Steagall Act required the separation of commercial banking (the business of taking deposits and lending money) from investment banking (the sale of securities). As a result, and as an example, the "House of Morgan" was split in two, and the successor firms, Morgan Stanley and JPMorgan Chase, are still around. The investment banks and broker-dealers stayed in the securities business, and the commercial banks were restricted to the private lending business.

Over time, and particularly after the deregulation of interest rates, commercial banks came to the view that being shut out of the securities business was detrimental to their business activities and, particularly, to profitability. In 1999, Glass-Steagall was repealed and former commercial banks have since built up formidable securities and other investment banking units, competing with the traditional investment banks across most lines of business. The business of loan syndication does, however, still remain largely in the hands of the traditional commercial banks.

A second significant trend in the banking industry as a whole has been massive consolidation. Many storied names of the not-too-distant past, such as Drexel, Chemical Bank, First Boston and Bankers Trust, which played a dominant role in the leveraged buyout business in the late 1980s, have disappeared, often as the result of mergers. In the financial crisis, Bear Stearns was acquired by JPMorgan Chase and Merrill Lynch by Bank of America. Globalization, competitive pressures, and a revolution in systems and information requirements all drive toward scale and global scope as key elements of success and survival. Massively increased market transparency, where formerly closely held market information is now widely disseminated in close to real time, is also a factor. While some niche players still manage to thrive, in general all the big global banks compete against each other across nearly all lines of financial services and are facing commoditization of many types of financial services. Unsurprisingly given the shifting and shrinking landscape, there is a large amount of employee mobility among bankers, and moving from bank to bank over the course of a career is now the accepted norm.

§ 2:2.4 *Implications for Lawyers*

Bankers are working in a pressurized and highly competitive environment, and the lawyers they select are part of the service package they offer to the client companies. Sensible and efficient lawyering is appreciated; tendentious, ill-informed, inexpert, or time-wasting lawyering is not.

Whether paid for by the company (in the case of a bank loan) or the underwriters (in the case of securities offering), legal costs are pure overhead on the deal. No one likes to see higher-than-expected legal bills.

Some areas of finance practice are subject to significant fee pressures and so-called commoditization, where either the clients or the lawyers work off standard forms and on a volume basis. Some areas of legal work have been taken in-house and organized for low-cost execution by paralegals. And some very large sectors of the financial markets (for example, certain kinds of derivatives) are relatively light users of outside legal talent on a transactional basis.

Decisions about hiring lawyers have been institutionalized and may be politicized within financial institutions. Many global banks have a preferred provider or panel designation, and law firms not on the approved list cannot be hired without special dispensation. Big deals or preferred provider or panel relationships are put out for competition among law firms, so that lawyers must prepare responses to RFPs (requests for proposals) and attend beauty contests, explaining their relevant expertise, in order to be hired. Internal counsel is often charged with keeping a close eye on legal costs and expected to manage relationships with law firms to show cost-effectiveness. On the other hand, some lawyer-hiring decisions are still within the business units, and as bankers move from one institution to another they may bring along their favorite lawyers.

There is little institutional loyalty running from a financial institution to a law firm, at least compared to what there was thirty years ago. Lawyers are under more pressure to demonstrate, on a deal-by-deal basis, market-specific expertise and execution efficiency. On the other hand, where a relationship can be built up over time based on a shared history of deals and documents, and continuity in staffing, it can be highly rewarding, both financially and professionally.

§ 2:3　Exchanges, Regulators and Industry Associations

§ 2:3.1　*Another Kind of Liquidity; Trading and Exchanges*

Liquidity refers to both having cash and being able to turn non-cash assets into cash. Investors and lenders are interested not only in the liquidity of the issuer or borrower, but in their own liquidity, and, in particular, in having the ability to sell their own financial assets as freely as possible. So (although this is not a focus of this book) a lot of corporate finance is about the markets where debt and equity are traded.

Shares of publicly traded companies are traded on stock exchanges or stock trading systems, such as the New York Stock Exchange and NASDAQ. Exchanges are not only trading platforms but have rules and apply sanctions relevant to promoting market fairness and efficiency. When a company is first selling shares to the public, it is called an initial public offering (IPO). Subsequent offerings may be made by the company, or by its existing shareholders of large amounts of previously unregistered shares (secondary offerings). The first would be dilutive to existing equity, while the second would not be. Note that bringing a company public, in terms of selling shares to the public, does not guarantee that control of the company is in public hands.

There are many companies where insiders, for example, a founding family or other founders of the business, retain effective control either through majority stock ownership or by holding a class of stock with special voting rights.

Stock exchanges are also businesses in their own right. They have areas of specialization and compete with one another. An NYSE listing has traditionally been a sign that a company has "arrived," in the sense that it is a large creditable business appropriate as an investment for public stockholders, including so-called widows and orphans. Foreign company shares can be available for trading in the United States in the form of American Depositary Receipts (ADRs). However, foreign or global companies often consider listing on non-U.S. exchanges such as the London Stock Exchange or the Hong Kong Stock Exchange. Online trading systems present another competitive pressure on the historic exchanges. In general, the same pressures toward scale, global scope and borderless execution, standardization, and transparency that affect the banking industry apply to the exchanges.

Some corporate and other bonds are exchange-traded and listed. However, many bonds are traded over-the-counter (meaning off an exchange and directly between financial institutions and other counterparties). High-yield bonds, though often publicly registered, tend to trade rather narrowly among market participants that specialize in this sector (including mutual funds, hedge funds and securitization vehicles such as CDOs (collateralized debt obligations) or CBOs (collateralized bond obligations)). The fixed-income market has generally been more opaque than the public equity markets, but now terms and prices of many corporate bonds are available through online information services. The market in U.S. Treasury bills, notes, and bonds has opened up considerably with the availability of direct online investment, whereas the market used to be dependent on so-called primary dealers. And various online information services provide trading information about corporate and municipal bonds, and other fixed-income investments.

Private equity interests, bank loans, and private placement notes are, of course, not exchange traded, though in the case of bank loans there is considerably more information than there used to be through the services of various industry groups, the rating agencies, and information service providers.

§ 2:3.2   *Primary Regulators and Self-Regulatory Organizations*

The Securities and Exchange Commission (SEC) is the primary regulator of the securities markets in the United States, acting under the Securities Act of 1933 and the Securities Exchange Act of 1934. Oversight of the mutual fund industry is through the Investment Management Division of the SEC, operating under the Investment Company Act of 1940 and Investment Advisers Act of 1940. The National Association of Securities Dealers (NASD) was a self-regulatory organization regulating the activities of underwriters and broker-dealers. In 2007, it merged with New York Stock Exchange member regulation, enforcement, and arbitration operations to form the Financial Industry Regulatory Authority (FINRA).

Commercial banks (banks taking deposits) are established and regulated as either state banks or as national banks (by the Comptroller of the Currency). With very few, if any, exceptions they are also subject to regulation by the Federal Reserve Board (FRB) (the Federal Reserve System being the central bank and lender of last resort) and the Federal Deposit Insurance Corporation (FDIC) (which provides insurance on deposits). Insurance companies are chartered for operation in the fifty states and the District of Columbia, but the National Association of Insurance Commissioners (NAIC) runs national-level programs including the setting of standards for prudential investment (NAIC ratings).

§ 2:3.3   *Industry Associations*

Industry associations are extremely important in the financial services business. The Loan Syndications and Trading Association (LSTA) and the Loan Market Association (LMA) promulgate forms and standards for the trading of bank loans. The International Swaps and Derivatives Association (ISDA) promulgates forms and standards to deal with practices and issues in the over-the-counter derivatives market, and, more or less, defines the market.

§ 2:3.4   *Implications for Lawyers*

Apart from the obvious point that lawyers must understand the laws and regulations and exchange and trading rules applicable to the market in which they work, lawyers should also consider the growing impact of trade association involvement in monitoring and addressing legal needs and issues for their constituencies. In particular, industry associations can be expected to promote market efficiency and transparency, making previously closely held specialized market information available to a broader audience, supporting or developing trading and transactions platforms, and promulgating standards including standard documentation. Lawyers are expected to be familiar with the standard forms and use them correctly, and to be knowledgeable about issues (such as issues of document interpretation) mooted and resolved by the industry groups. Advice to financial institutions that is not informed by this knowledge is likely to be off-market and incorrect.

Lawyers should also be aware that key goals of industry groups are to reduce uncertainty in transaction outcomes and to reduce transactions costs, including unnecessary legal expenses. This means that they will push, and appropriately so, for more standardization and automation in transaction execution, including standard documentation and execution platforms and practices that reduce the role of lawyers.

§ 2:4   Ancillary Players

§ 2:4.1   *Providers of Trustee and Administrative Services*

Ancillary businesses provide a host of critical administrative services in connection with corporate finance: corporate trustees under trust indentures, paying agents, registrars, transfer agents and solicitation agents; custodians, depositaries and clearing agencies; and collateral agents and servicers. These companies take care of all the mechanics of corporate finance, which can be significant. The services are provided for a fee, and may combine ministerial and processing tasks with some prudential or fiduciary obligations.

Advising corporate trustees or custodians or clearing agents are legal specialties separate and apart from representing companies raising money and the bankers assisting them. Carefully defining processes and standards of care, as well as limitations of liability and indemnification provisions, are the most important documentation issues in the agreements that define these parties' roles. The documentation for these services is relatively standard, the services themselves strictly limited in scope, and the customary providers quite expert, so it is rare that defining the role of an administrative provider will be especially problematic in the course of getting to closing. However, it is critical to coordinate with these participants and to take their comments on documentation, and to make sure they are ready to do what is necessary at closing and thereafter.

Take time to make yourself familiar with the outlines of the Trust Indenture Act of 1939. One relevant provision requires a conflicted trustee to resign in certain circumstances. As many banks have shed their corporate trust services and the industry has become more specialized, this provision is less of a concern but is still worth knowing about.

§ 2:4.2   Rating Agencies

The rating agencies—Standard & Poor's, Moody's and Fitch—are the gatekeepers to the debt and securitization markets. You will become familiar with their rating systems and how they view the world. In particular, the distinction between investment grade (BBB-/Baa3 or higher) and non-investment grade (also called high-yield or junk) debt drives much of the debt markets. For many deals, it will be necessary to liaise with the rating agencies and with their attorneys to make sure you address their concerns and obtain the desired rating.

The rating agencies not only rate an issue at closing but continue to monitor the issuer after closing to keep the rating up to date. They may raise a rating, downgrade the debt securities of a company, or put the company on credit watch with negative or with positive implications. A change in rating has a direct effect on the price at which the debt trades. It can also change the universe of investors because, for example, some investors cannot hold non-investment grade debt. Further, a change in rating can affect the pricing of other debt of the company through the operation of pricing grids applicable to bank loans. An improved credit rating up to investment grade may cause some leveraged-style covenants to become inoperative. A downgrade may give lenders or counterparties the right to require collateral or even accelerate the obligations owed to them.

Rating agencies rate securities, not companies. If you want to use a rating to refer to a company's creditworthiness, you would refer to the rating of the company's unsecured unsubordinated long-term debt.

§ 2:4.3   Accountants

Accountants audit companies for the purpose of preparing audited financial statements and help public companies comply with the SEC's accounting rules. Company management cannot prepare a public disclosure document meeting SEC requirements without accountants at their side, providing not only the financial statements but a lot of other financial analysis and content.

There is a tendency among lawyers to tune out during discussion of accounting issues, but you will quickly note that the best and most senior securities lawyers are paying close attention. Accounting issues can have a ripple effect on disclosure drafting, and accounting issues that are not properly identified and addressed can delay registration statements becoming effective consistent with the underwriters' timetable for bringing the issue to market. Accounting problems from prior periods can require the restatement of prior period financial statements, a time-consuming exercise that can delay timely filing of quarterly or annual reports. Sometimes accounting issues relate to legal documents or issues, or accounting problems give rise to legal issues—as in the case of stock options backdating reported during 2006 and 2007.

Lawyers and accountants interact in other contexts. Lawyers are called upon to provide audit comfort letters under a long-standing protocol promulgated by the American Bar Association (ABA) and agreed to by the accounting profession. These letters are used by accountants in analyzing litigation and other contingent obligations in the course of preparing financial statements. Responding to requests for these letters is not a casual exercise, but requires expertise and judgment on the part of the responding lawyers.

In the securitization context, accountants may directly or indirectly rely on so-called true sale opinions. These opinions reach a qualified conclusion that the terms of a sale of assets from the originator to the securitization special purpose vehicle will pass muster under governing bankruptcy law precedents as a "true sale" transferring the assets from seller to purchaser. Accountants may also rely on legal opinions in other areas, such as tax.

Accountants take on potentially significant liabilities in providing audit services and assisting client companies, and are justifiably concerned about limiting their liability as much as possible. Lawyers, for their part, are also wary of taking on too much liability, especially where their advice might affect financial statements of public companies. Worries about liability and reliance are an important backdrop to the interactions between lawyers and accountants.

§ 2:4.4   *Financial Printers*

Information technology has revolutionized the financial printing industry. It used to be that corporate finance lawyers, or at least those in the securities practice, could look forward to spending many days, nights, and weekends at the printers, laboriously preparing registration statements, prospectuses, and other printed documents for filing and large distributions. A lot of actual work—drafting and negotiation—went on in the printers' conference rooms. But there were dead times too. While waiting for documents to be turned around, the lawyers and the rest of the party—company employees, bankers, and accountants—might amuse themselves by watching television and gorging on lobster and steak. If there was a morning filing deadline in Washington, some junior lawyer might be sent off at 4:00 A.M. to catch a plane that would be (inevitably, or so it seemed) delayed in taking off. And so on. Older corporate finance lawyers all have some sort of tale to tell about their nights at the printers.

These days the fun and games at the printers are pretty much over. Most filings are done electronically, and final documents can be prepared without the aid of professional printers. Financial printers, who for much of the twentieth century had a lock on a very lucrative and specialized niche, have diversified into all sorts of other mostly computer-based printing and distribution businesses. We note them here partly as a sentimental nod to the past, but also to point out that legacy financial printers do stay on top of the latest technologies for document production and electronic filing and, of course, are still necessary for bulk printing and distribution.

§ 2:4.5   Lawyers

Yes, for sake of completeness we round out the roster of ancillary players with a mention of the lawyers. Though lawyers and the legal press may forget this, lawyers are not principals in their deals, but service providers, or even (from a corporate procurement perspective) vendors. Nevertheless, it is important for the individual lawyer, for the firm, and for the profession that lawyers not forsake professional standards, or moral or intellectual integrity, in the course of serving their clients.

§ 2:5   The Evolving Market; Hedge Funds and Private Equity; Derivatives

§ 2:5.1   The Status Quo Ante

To review: Investors and lenders have traditionally broken down into several classes: individual investors (some of whom might qualify as high net worth individuals or sophisticated investors, while others are retail investors); institutional investors, such as pension funds and mutual funds; and banks, divided from 1933 to 1999 between investment banks, like Goldman Sachs and Morgan Stanley, and commercial banks, like Citibank and JPMorgan Chase.

Publicly issued stocks and (investment grade) bonds, including Treasury securities and municipal bonds, might be held by individual investors; institutional investors (including mutual funds) would invest across the range of public debt and equity; investment banks would typically likewise run proprietary positions and trade across these markets; insurance companies would lend money privately in so-called private placements; and banks would make bank loans.

Registered debt and equity securities trade in the public markets. The "price" of access to the public markets is SEC registration and compliance with disclosure and corporate governance requirements applicable to public companies, which are, in theory, answerable to their shareholders. The trading of securities is on the basis of public information, which is supposed to be made available to all investors on an equal basis.

Historically, private placement notes and bank loans were intended, or at least designed, to be held to maturity, with some limited liquidity. If a company got into trouble, its agent bank and other private lenders would get together and do what they could to help. These private lenders often worked closely with management as, in effect, financial advisers and were given access on a regular basis to non-public information, which was expected to be closely held within the lending community and, in particular, not shared across to any traders or brokers in the bank.

§ 2:5.2   Change Happens

This relatively static picture prevailed for decades, and in many respects is still descriptive of a "norm." However many aspects of the picture have shifted.

As we noted above, the barrier between investment banking and commercial banking came down when Glass-Steagall was repealed. Consolidation has continued across the financial services industry as scale (for systems) and scope (around the world) became key.

Changes in the securities laws permitted the wider distribution of public-like securities without SEC registration. The penetration of the financial markets by ubiquitous computing and open information platforms has dispersed and accelerated the activity. Many financial services and products are widely available and increasingly commoditized. At the same time, technologically-driven fragmentation and tiering of markets (such as "dark pools" and high-frequency trading) have created new types and sources of opacity.

Capital requirements imposed on banks that affect their profitability made them less interested in a "hold to maturity" model of lending or in traditional market-making (standing by to buy in order to support a market). Instead, loans are originated by banks but then sold into an expanded group of bank loan investors, including securitization vehicles such as CLOs (collateralized loan obligations), mutual funds, hedge funds, and other sophisticated investors.

Though there had always been distress buyers of bankrupt company debt, this has become more institutionalized. So-called vulture funds were formed to be strategic purchasers of debt in troubled credit situations, anticipating, for example, the conversion of subordinated debt into equity of the company that would emerge from bankruptcy. Non-traditional investors such as private equity funds and hedge funds may make strategic acquisitions of multiple layers of a company's capital structure to maximize overall gain. These investors have become very important players in the world of corporate finance.

§ 2:5.3   *Private Equity and Leveraged Buyouts*

The private equity industry, which began as a handful of so-called leveraged buyout (LBO) shops, has grown to become a major factor in M&A (mergers and acquisitions), attracting institutional investors, building multi-billion dollar war chests, and tapping enormous capacity to borrow in the leveraged finance markets. With closing fees, management fees (standard 2% of assets under management), and carry (share of gain on profits at 20%), private equity has been extremely profitable, taking equity ownership of even very large public companies back to private. Many companies now end up as reporting companies because they are issuers of high-yield debt, not because they have public equity. Going full circle, private equity houses are taking their management companies public (though without giving up management control).

Investors in private equity funds include the same institutional investors, such as pension funds, that invest the savings of individuals in the stock markets. One way of looking at private equity is that it is a different way for managed capital to make its way to businesses. Rather than rely on stockholder voting rights to elect or boot out boards of directors, the managers of the institutional investors put their faith in the management skills and, in particular, the corporate finance acumen of the private equity houses. The exclusive focus of the private equity business is on the return to equity and on the exit at a profit, which distinguishes it from the views that other types of investors and constituencies may have.

§ 2:5.4   *Hedge Funds*

Separately, pools of lightly regulated capital became concentrated in so-called hedge funds, which are often offshoots of the banks' proprietary trading desks and headed up by former traders who got tired of racking up trading gains for someone else's account. Hedge funds typically take strategic trading positions in financial asset classes or particular risks, borrowing money to magnify the effect of their bets. Some early hedge funds specialized in a macro-economic view and trading strategy, and there was one spectacular early flameout: Long-Term Capital Management, which had to be rescued in a government-monitored bailout when macro events went the wrong way. Other hedge funds are interested in shareholder activist positions or in finding and exploiting unexpected leverage in subordinated debt against the company or against senior debtholders.

Hedge funds are also important customers on Wall Street. They borrow heavily against a constantly changing portfolio. The prime brokerage business is all about serving these heavy traders and borrowers.

Much has been made of the fact that hedge funds, together with their brokers and lenders, are in a position to know about the funds' potentially market-moving activities. And when hedge funds buy bank loans, they may become privy to inside information. The market has developed principles for communication and use of confidential information by loan market participants, which contain guidance on how public-side and private-side loan market participants should analyze and handle information they receive about borrowers, including suggested information control policies and procedures.

§ 2:5.5   *Derivatives, and Credit Derivatives in Particular*

Derivatives—which enable investors to hedge their positions and reduce risks on balance sheets, as well as speculate in financial or other assets or particular risks—applicable to nearly all classes of financial assets have become a huge business. These instruments can, on the one hand, cushion and spread risk, and, on the other hand, magnify and concentrate risk. Some participants in these markets are there for hedging purposes, but there has always been a gray line between hedging and speculating. In addition, once you start looking at a derivatives contract as representing a value in its own right, the "trading" part begins, and long chains of transactions can develop. Leverage, using borrowed funds to support hedge obligations, will magnify both the upside and the downside.

By their very nature, derivative transactions are generally leveraged transactions. To make serious money in the business, parties take on potential risk beyond the level of funds they have actually put into the transaction. Players in the market run risk quantification models over their book of business in order to determine, at any given time, that their risk levels are tolerable. But there are several inherent limitations on risk modeling. First of all, risk models are designed by people, and subject to the limitations on the abilities of people, even with computer modeling tools to assist them, in considering all possible outcomes. Second, if negative events or confluent downside scenarios that the risk assessment team, even correctly, deemed remote do in fact come to pass, then the fact that these events were deemed remote will not make them less real nor less costly. Lastly, when increasing numbers of market participants use similar modeling techniques and decision models, and take actions based on the resulting analyses, they are, as a group, probably undoing some of the assumptions that they have used.

Because derivative transactions are more abstract than other financial contracts, it has not always been the case that parties have understood what they were agreeing to. Procter & Gamble's lawsuit against Bankers Trust (in the mid-1990s), alleging that it sold P&G inappropriate derivatives, was a severe reputational blow. Enron, before its collapse, was running essentially a large derivative position with respect to its own stock price, but it is unclear whether the people at the top of the organization understood or quantified the level of risk undertaken with respect to a falling stock price. Certainly, it was not disclosed.

Credit derivatives are of particular interest. The concept of a credit derivative is that a bank or other investor holding a loan or debt can contractually lay off to others the risk that the obligor will default. The volume of credit derivatives is now tremendous. It has been suggested that since credit derivatives are traded, this is another market that might potentially reflect non-public information, as banks and other private lenders take positions on certain obligor names based on the information they have about potential deals or other factors affecting credit risk.

§ 2:5.6   *Playing a Game of Catch-Up*

In sum, the relatively static world of public versus private finance, debt versus equity with very little else on the menu, senior debt trumping subordinated debt, a clear distinction between inside information and public disclosure, and close and stable relationships between a company and long-term investors and financial advisers has become one where the lines and the rules are less clear. In particular, in the leveraged finance area, the loan and bond markets continue down a long path of convergence, including on covenants and other terms, due to the growth of non-bank crossover investors driven more by yield than covenant protections, as well as the complex tiering of the issuer's capital structure. So-called covenant-lite deals reflect the recognition that tight covenants for a borrower and non-traditional opportunistic investors rather than relationship bankers can be problematic. The old assumptions about what is intended and what "everybody knows" are being put to the test. As the markets continue to evolve, the coming years will bring a review of legal and documentary standards. In the meantime, there is a lag and many of the forms and conventions hark back to the earlier era.

§ 2:6   The M&A Connection

§ 2:6.1   *Financial Engineering and Financial Buyers*

A company might look for strategic acquisitions or be sought by a strategic purchaser, meaning that the company is a "good fit" with another company based on what it is that they do.

A "financial buyer," on the other hand, looks for businesses—or perhaps more accurately, cash flows—that have not been optimized from an equity-holder's perspective. The optimization or "fine-tuning" might include improvements in operations (combining and reducing redundant activities, or identifying new markets to increase revenues), but to a large degree may consist of increasing leverage—that is, by borrowing the maximum amount against the cash flows and accruing all of the earning potential over and above debt service to a smaller and, thus, richer group of equity investors.

This is what the private equity business and leveraged finance is all about. An acquisition where borrowed funds make up a majority of the purchase price and the acquired company assumes the acquisition debt is called a leveraged buyout or LBO.

The private equity house looks for opportunities to buy equity in businesses, including public companies, that appear undervalued in view of what the private equity house believes it can do with the underlying assets and cash flow. After a period of operational improvement and with a new capital structure, the company is ready to be sold for more, hopefully much more, than what it cost to buy. There is always an exit strategy.

§ 2:6.2   *Assessment of the Target Company Debt*

Due diligence for an M&A deal requires close scrutiny of the existing debt instruments of the target and thorough understanding of the proposed deal. Can the existing debt remain in place or will it have to be refinanced? This is the threshold question. The answer may determine timing and feasibility of the deal, and of course will have a big impact on holders of the target company debt. Of particular interest:

- Is the proposed deal permitted under the merger covenant and any change of control provisions?

- Will the deal trip any other covenants (for example, debt or lien covenants) or create any other defaults under the existing debt agreements?

- If the deal is not permitted under the existing debt agreements, can they be amended and, if so, how? Or can the debt be paid off?

Floating-rate bank loans generally can be repaid at any time, and any outstanding letters of credit, which cannot be simply revoked, can be dealt with under new arrangements. If the target company has outstanding bonds, it is more likely that they cannot be prepaid, and it may be that change of control provisions permit holders to put their bonds but do not permit the issuer to unilaterally call the bonds. Where the proposed deal would violate the terms of target company bonds, the answer may be a consent solicitation or tender offer with consent solicitation. Bondholders are offered consideration to amend the bond terms or, in the second alternative, offered an opportunity to put their bonds at a premium simultaneously executing an "exit consent." Through one or the other method, the goal is to end up with amended agreements (in the latter case, perhaps for just a small remaining outstanding amount of bonds) permitting the deal to go forward. It is the essentially covenant-free investment grade public debt of the target that is most likely to remain outstanding post-acquisition. When the yield on the new debt goes up to reflect the target company's new junk status, the price on those bonds can drop precipitously.

§ 2:6.3   The Acquisition Debt

Again, a thorough understanding of the proposed deal is absolutely key. Finance lawyers should be familiar with the M&A documentation and keep fully informed regarding the state of disclosure and timing. Key items to consider and manage include:

- How is the acquisition being financed, precisely? How do the pieces of debt and equity work together and which companies will be the issuers and obligors?

- What are the plans for target company debt? Does the proposed acquisition financing contain terms that will be breached by target company debt still outstanding after the deal, or by the terms of such debt? As an example, the acquisition debt may prohibit any limitation on the ability of subsidiaries to upstream money to the parent company, but the target (or subsidiary) debt may contain such limitations, such as a minimum net worth covenant.

- What terms in the acquisition documents and any disclosure documents specifically interrelate with or refer to the financing documents? In particular, what terms of the financing appear in disclosure documents (and must be kept up to date if the financing terms change)?

- If (as is usually the case) the target company is taking on the acquisition debt, then what is the fraudulent conveyance analysis? Obligations that a company incurs for inadequate consideration may be set aside as invalid unless, after giving effect to them, the company is still solvent, meaning that the fair market value of assets exceeds liabilities. Clearly the target company does not receive consideration when it assumes debt, the proceeds of which have been paid to its shareholders, so the typical LBO scenario presents fraudulent conveyance risk as a structural matter. This is addressed by establishing the solvency of the company.

- What are the mechanics of funding, including the payoff of any debt? What are the logistics of getting security in place by closing?

- Is the acquisition financing staged, with bridge loans at closing and an anticipated takeout?

In a deal of any size, there are many moving parts. To ensure that the moment of closing is in good order requires advance planning and preparation.

§ 2:6.4   *Bridge Loans, PIK, Staple or Stapled Financing . . . Innovation Is the Rule*

To make the deal happen, M&A finance is always pushing at the boundaries of what is feasible on the financial side. If it is going to take some time to get the permanent financing in place, more time than is in the deal schedule to closing, then funding at closing will be provided in the form of a bridge. This is pretty typical when a high-yield debt placement is planned, and there might also be a bridge receivables facility. Full-scale fees compensate the bridge lenders, and if the bridge isn't timely taken out there is a further fee at extension. There have also been "equity bridges," where banks fund over to expected equity that might not be in place at closing. After closing of the acquisition, there is a big push to put the permanent financing in place—no one wants to be stuck with a "hung bridge," or "bridge to nowhere"!

A different type of "bridge" might be the financing of a tender offer, as part of a two-step tender offer to merger, where the only condition to funding is that sufficient shares have been tendered to guarantee approval of the merger in a shareholder vote. A facility like this has to be very carefully structured to eliminate any risks and to ensure that the merger takes place. Failure to get to the merger would result in another type of "bridge to nowhere." Advising on a loan like this requires careful analysis of the margin rules to assure compliance, probably by making sure that the loan is unsecured (including that there be no negative pledge applicable to the tendered shares) and that there is no chance whatsoever that the merger will not be consummated (so that the tendered shares' days as publicly traded securities are essentially over). This points to another requirement for M&A finance lawyers: If the target is a public company, expertise in the margin rules is essential. These are rules promulgated by the Federal Reserve Board that limit loans secured by tradable securities.

Leveraged finance is also the home of pay-in-kind (PIK) debt, where interest on notes is paid through the issuance of additional notes. This structure can enable the company to get through some projected low-cash-flow years with reduced risk of debt service default. "Toggle" notes let a company choose the PIK option as an alternative to cash pay. "Covenant-lite" deals give the company more maneuvering room than deals with traditional covenant structures— and less leverage to the (now broadly based) lenders and investors.

Staple or stapled financing refers to a package offered by a bank acting as adviser to a seller that includes the buyout financing, so that the seller's bank is standing by to finance the purchase of the target. This arrangement puts the bank on both sides of the deal, so the bankers and their lawyers need to manage potential conflicts of interest or allegations of such.

To address the needs of non-traditional investors in bank loans, "B term" loans have some bond-like attributes (longer term, minimal amortization, some call protection, perhaps less covenant protection and higher yield). Second lien finance is (often unsubordinated) debt that is not in the topmost secured position, but that often has real (if not clearly understood) rights as a holder of a second lien position on collateral. Bonds might be priced to yield higher than the market of comparables to guarantee full subscription, in some cases giving the initial purchasers an immediate upside just after issuance, which is more of an equity placement dynamic than something normally seen for debt. Mezzanine finance refers to subordinated debt that often has associated equity options or warrants, so there is a blend of debt and equity features. In all these cases, there is a blend of debt and equity type features or a "slicing and dicing" of the capital structure that would not be warranted except at the aggressive margins of corporate finance where the limits of the achievable are constantly being tested. Innovation is the rule.

§ 2:6.5   *Implications for Lawyers*

Leveraged buyouts depend on the availability of credit. When cheap money abounds and other conditions are right (this is cyclical!), M&A deal flow not only keeps the M&A lawyers busy, but provides interesting and challenging work for finance lawyers.

Tight time frames and high stakes up the ante considerably over garden variety bank loans and investment grade debt offerings. Speed, responsiveness, and understanding the context are all critical elements of client service. You will need to work closely with the M&A lawyers, have a clear grasp of their timing and their documents, and make sure you understand both the short-term financing plans and the overall exit strategy.

You need to know what information needs to remain in the strictest confidence. At the early stages of the deal, even its existence may be confidential and, certainly, leaking to the other side or a competitive bidder could be (from a client's perspective) disastrous. If the target is public, everyone has to worry about the inadvertent disclosure of material inside information and potential insider trading. This concern is particularly acute before announcement of a deal, but does not go away at that time because developments may continue to move the markets. You also need to understand the banks' possible multiple roles, any attendant conflicts of interests, and how these are being managed, including through internal information barriers. Lawyers should be careful to make sure that they are not the source of information leaks from one side of a bank's information wall to the other. Likewise, lawyers who are representing clients in multiple roles need to analyze and manage their own possible conflicts of interest. These issues are not terribly obvious to new lawyers, but when the team makes a mistake in handling confidential information it tends to attract the attention of clients and, in the worst cases, the media or regulatory authorities. Supervising lawyers may also forget to explain the ground rules, so it is safest to assume, unless instructed otherwise, that information should stay within the team and the designated client contacts for the team.

The practice of corporate finance is very much market driven, so it is of significant advantage to be up to date with comparables, trends, and the newest tricks. There is a special premium on the ability to analyze and design debt agreements, and to understand the intricacies of covenants, including financial covenants.

In sum, M&A or private equity is a high profile and challenging area where talented finance lawyers with market knowledge and strong technical skills can really make a difference.

Chapter 3

The Instruments

---

§ 3:1   Review of the Basic Terms

§ 3:1.1   Scheduled Maturity; Mandatory Repayment; Optional Repayment; and Call Versus Non-Call

Equity, except for mandatorily redeemable preferred stock, is in perpetuity and has no maturity date. The essence of debt, on the other hand, is that it has a maturity date at which it must be paid off and that it bears a yield. Debt is usually defined by its maturity date and its coupon—for example, 3.5% bonds due August 15, 2030.

The simplest form of debt payment is a repayment of the full amount of principal at a final maturity date and periodic (monthly, semiannual, or annual) payment of interest from the date of issue to maturity. But there are alternatives. Some debt is issued at a discount to its face value, and the yield is obtained by the holder when the face value is paid at maturity. In other cases, there are scheduled installments or mandatory prepayments or redemptions due in advance of final maturity. These are sometimes called sinking fund payments.

So-called mortgage-style repayment schedules reflect flat payment amounts across the life of the loan, with each repayment reflecting a portion of principal (small at first and larger as you go along) and interest (large at first then diminishing). These are unusual in the world of corporate finance.

Unscheduled or early repayments of principal can occur at the election of the company, if this is permitted; on a mandatory basis because of an event or out of certain funds (this may apply ratably or to all of the debt issue on an automatic basis, or apply to all of the debt issue based on collective debtholder action, or be optional with each of the holders on an individual basis); or upon acceleration after default.

Being able to pay off ("call") debt on an optional basis and without a premium is obviously an advantage for the company since it would permit the company to refinance at a lower cost when interest rates drop, or pay down its debt and reduce interests costs when it no longer needs the borrowed funds. Fixed-rate debt usually includes limitations on the ability to call the debt, ranging from absolute prohibitions, to make-whole requirements, to limitations on amount or on source of funds for the payment, to premiums. Callable debt will trade lower than comparable debt that is non-call or that has some call protections or disincentives (soft-call).

§ 3:1.2   *Yield and Coupon; Yield and Price; Accrual; Fixed Rate Versus Floating Rate; Margin and Spread*

Common stock, of course, does not have a fixed yield. It may pay dividends declared periodically by the board of directors, and for some companies and industries (generally in mature or regulated industries) regular dividends are the norm. For other companies, particularly those in a growth mode, investors don't want or expect dividends; they want to see earnings plowed back into the business. Companies flush with cash will buy back shares to reduce the base of equity and increase the stock price. But for a common equity holder the return is, albeit indirectly, through earnings, accreting to an eventual higher stock price, and in a trading market. Stock price and the price-earnings ratio are key indicators.

On the other hand, yield together with maturity defines debt, which doesn't enjoy any share of earnings or benefit from upside potential vis-à-vis the company. Preferred stock can also have a yield in the form of a stated dividend, which normally accumulates, so that if it is not declared in one period it will carry forward until the board of directors determines that it should be paid. Yield or interest is measured as a percentage per annum, with 100 basis points equal to 1%.

Yield is not the same as stated interest rate or coupon. Yield is calculated based on the purchase price of the instrument at the time of purchase, taking into account all payments scheduled to be made. By adjusting price, a $1,000 bond paying interest at 5% per annum can be made to yield 3% per annum or 10% per annum. For a stated coupon, the higher the price, the lower the yield, and vice versa. If a bond is currently trading at a price to yield 9%, that means that the company would have to issue bonds bearing 9% if it were to issue debt at par (100 cents on the dollar) for the same maturity today. However, regardless of the yield and price of debt in a trading market, the obligation of the company is as per the contract. In the case of the 5% bond, the company is obligated to pay $50 a year of interest and $1,000 at maturity. Some instruments, such as Treasury bills and commercial paper, are issued at a discount to par, and thus have yield but no coupon.

The interest accrual method is another feature of the debt instrument, with the variables being the number of days of the year (360 or 365/366), whether the daily rate accrues for actual days elapsed or a year of twelve thirty-day months, and how frequently the interest compounds. Interest accrual is nearly always a function of market convention for the particular type of interest rate, with the Prime rate calculated on the basis of 365/366 days (360 days for lesser credits) and actual days elapsed, and LIBOR-based interest calculated for actual days elapsed but on a 360-day basis, while bonds typically bear interest on the basis of 360 days and twelve months of thirty days each. Interest usually accrues from the date of issue, but it is possible to issue a note or bond with interest accruing from an earlier date; in that case the purchase price will reflect the interest amount already accrued at issuance.

Interest is generally of two types—fixed rate, with a set interest rate, and floating rate. Treasury bills, notes and bonds, commercial paper, private placement term notes, and public or Rule 144A corporate debt are nearly all fixed rate, which is set at issuance based on prevailing market conditions for debt of that credit quality and tenor.

The syndicated bank loan market is predominantly a floating-rate market. This is based on its traditional premise of the bank as a cost-plus or "match-funding" lender that does not take interest rate risk per se. Floating-rate debt bears an interest rate that is comprised of two elements: a base or reference rate, and a margin. Standard reference rates include the London interbank offered rate (LIBOR) or Eurodollar rate; and a "base rate" (typically the greater of the Prime rate and the Federal Funds overnight rate plus 1/2 of 1%). As a result of the recent LIBOR-rate scandal, there have been changes made to the process of setting LIBOR rates and thus to the definitions in credit agreements.

Each bank has its own standard definitions for these reference rates and standard related provisions for interest periods and interest accrual. There is also a set of standard yield protection provisions covering the inability to obtain the reference rate; the illegality of using a particular reference rate; capital adequacy costs (permitting banks to charge borrowers for costs due to capital requirements attributable to the loan); increased costs due to change in law after commitment; and the fact that interest is to be received free of withholding. Generally, lawyers should not fool with these standard definitions and provisions, but just make sure they are correct and reflect the bank's current standard form. Occasionally a borrower with some leverage may extract some concessions in the yield protection provisions, but these must always be cleared within the bank. These may relate to mandating a change in the bank's booking office if that would reduce costs payable by the borrower, or restricting the transfer of loans where that might cause the borrower to incur increased costs.

In a bank loan, the company can usually choose the floating rate to apply to a particular interest period, with short-term or stub rates (shorter than a month) typically restricted to the Prime or other over-night rate. Loans can be paid off at the end of interest periods without any extra cost; if they are paid off mid-period, then the borrower owes a break-funding cost calculated on the theoretical basis that the bank incurred a matched cost of funds.

The margin is set according to market conditions and the credit-worthiness of the borrower. It is not uncommon in bank loan agreements to find complex tables showing what margin will apply, based on credit ratings or financial ratios.

Spread usually refers not to the margin over a base or reference rate but the difference between two interest rates or yields that are being compared. The typical benchmark for spread is the yield on debt of comparable tenor issued by the U.S. Treasury.

§ 3:1.3   Rating

At any point in time some industries are in better shape than others, and within an industry some companies are thriving while others are not. Luck, skill, and prudence all play their part, but one of the measures of business success or failure is the company's creditworthiness. Just like people, some companies are good bets and others are more likely to turn out to be deadbeats. The rating agencies—Standard & Poor's, Moody's and Fitch—are in the business of assessing and monitoring the creditworthiness of debt issues and issuing ratings accordingly in the form of grades. Securities issued by companies, countries, municipalities, and securitization vehicles can all have debt ratings. Commercial paper is also rated, with paper rated lower than A-1/P-1 being much harder to place.

Rating agencies rate the creditworthiness of particular debt instruments. Long-term debt ratings down to level BBB-/Baa3 are considered "investment grade," and lower ratings are considered "non-investment grade." The credit rating of a particular issue, and particularly the distinction between investment grade and non-investment grade, is highly determinative of the market in which the issue can be placed and the terms it will contain. What this means is that for some deals, obtaining a particular credit rating may be key, and bankers may be asked to adjust various terms, and lawyers asked to issue various opinions, in order to satisfy the rating agencies so that the desired rating will be issued.

A downgrade can be a significant event in the life of a company. It can close off its short-term funding or make loans more expensive. Likewise being put on "credit watch with negative implications"—meaning that the rating agency is studying the situation but believes a downgrade to be likely—can be a serious matter.

§ 3:2   Plain Vanilla Finance

So what are the key terms relevant to particular financial instruments?

§ 3:2.1   *Common Stock*

Common stock is of course mostly defined by the issuer and attributes of the stock as and where it trades—most particularly its price. The rights of holders of common stock are found in the corporate law of the state of incorporation and the company's charter documents. The board of directors can declare dividends (ordinary or extraordinary) or initiate stock buy-back programs, but these are entirely within the discretion of the board. They might also define rights programs to give existing shareholders preemptive rights to subscribe to new issuances so that they will not be diluted, or as a "poison pill" to discourage takeovers. Stock can be combined (if the price becomes too low for convenient trading) or split (if the price becomes too high). (Common stock has a par value but as it is usually set quite low, the theoretical right of the company to require shareholders to make good on unpaid par value is effectively irrelevant in nearly all cases.)

§ 3:2.2   *Preferred Stock*

Preferred stock has a liquidation preference and a stated dividend that accrues on the liquidation preference. In liquidation or dissolution the holders of preferred stock are entitled to recover the amount of the liquidation preference plus accrued and unpaid dividends ahead of any distribution to common stockholders. Some preferred stock is mandatorily redeemable, but the failure to redeem generally does not create a breach of contract nor the right to enforce against the assets of the corporation. Likewise, the preferred dividend is not a contract right of the holders of the preferred stock unless and until the board of directors declares the dividend. Instead, if the stock is not timely redeemed or the dividend is not declared, there may be other rights and remedies, such as the right to appoint directors, and common stock dividends are blocked. The rights of holders of preferred stock are found in the corporate law of the state of incorporation and the company's charter documents. You should be aware that there may be important issues relating to the characterization of (especially redeemable) preferred stock as such or, instead, as debt for various purposes.

§ 3:2.3   *Convertible Debt*

Convertible debt is fixed-rate debt that contains an embedded option to convert the debt into common equity. Because of this potential equity upside, the coupon on the debt will be significantly lower than what would apply to debt issued without the convert feature. Convertible debt is issued with a conversion price that is set so that the option is "out of the money," with the conversion price higher than the market price so that converting at issuance would not make economic sense. Instead the holders of convertible debt are making a bet that the stock price will go up.

As you would guess, the conversion price has to be adjusted to take account of all the technical events—not relating to underlying performance of the company—that might occur to change the market price of the stock. For example, if there were a two for one stock split, the option price should be reduced by half in order to keep the parties in the same relationship and keep the benefit of the bargain. But this is a very simple example, and there could be much more complex transformations of the company's equity, including mergers and recapitalizations. The anti-dilution provisions in a convertible debt indenture are highly technical and must cover a lot of unknowns. This is an area where a drafting error might cost a client big money.

§ 3:2.4   *Commercial Paper*

Commercial paper refers to short-term promissory notes issued by corporations or by financial vehicles such as securitization special purpose vehicles (SPVs). These notes have essentially no events of default or covenants, but they do have a fixed maturity. Their coupon (or discount) is based on the credit quality of the issuer and the maturity, and is usually priced in a very straightforward way based on current market conditions. An issuer can issue commercial paper to meet its short-term cash needs by managing issuance and maturities—more or less treating the commercial paper market as its short-term lender.

The problem with relying solely on the commercial paper market for short-term liquidity is that when the maturity date comes around the company must, on that date, come up with the money to pay in full. It would be the unusual issuer that would have a sudden inflow of cash on that particular day, and to sit with money in the bank to pay off on the maturity date is not an economically rational decision—the company would normally be paying more interest on the commercial paper than it could earn in similarly rated but even shorter term deposits ("negative arbitrage"). The usual assumption is that whatever amount of maturing commercial paper the company wants to remain outstanding will be rolled over in the commercial paper market, that is, paid off with the proceeds of new commercial paper issued on the day that the old commercial paper matures.

A commercial paper rating of A-1 or P-1 is usually required to issue commercial paper. This takes into account the rating agencies' assessment that the commercial paper will in fact be paid at maturity. But what if something happens between the date of issuance and the maturity date that affects either the company's general liquidity position or its ability to maintain an A-1/P-1 rating, meaning that it will not be able to roll over its commercial paper? In other words, the issuer cannot say (unless it is extremely creditworthy and holding reserves of ready cash, in which case one must wonder why it is issuing debt at all) that its only plan for paying commercial paper at maturity is to issue more commercial paper. Instead, both the company and the rating agencies will want to know that it will be able to get funds from a bank group under a committed revolving credit facility—for this purpose called a commercial paper backstop.

Conditions to lending under the backstop can be meaningful, but usually must not include vague conditions that are unlikely to be met in the very circumstances where the company is blocked from the commercial paper markets—or the backstop isn't worth very much!

50

Instead, the conditions must be set so that in nearly all cases (but not, for example, including the bankruptcy of the company) the commercial paper holders will be made whole, and the banks must take over the credit. The rating agencies can thus take comfort that in most troubled credit situations the banks will be taking out the commercial paper holders as their notes come due.

§ 3:2.5   Bank Debt—Revolving Credits

Under revolving credit facilities, banks agree to provide extensions of credit to meet short-term or unexpected cash needs. For example, a company may have cash flow that predictably brings in cash at certain times during the week, month, or year, but these positive cash flows do not correspond to needs for cash, for example, to pay taxes or meet payroll. A different type of cash need addressed by revolving credit is one that occurs when a company unexpectedly finds itself cut off from a financing source or when another type of unexpected liquidity need arises. A revolving credit that is provided principally for the latter situation is often called a backstop, and one of the most common arrangements in investment grade financing is, as noted above, a revolving credit facility backstopping commercial paper.

For a multinational, the revolving credit facility may include foreign currency subfacilities and arrangements for non-U.S. subsidiaries to be borrowers with a parent company guarantee.

In a big facility with lots of banks, there is usually a swing-line facility. This permits the borrower to borrow very fast (usually on the same day) from a small group of lead banks. If the swing-line loans are out for more than a few days, they will be converted into a regular loan from the entire revolving credit syndicate.

Some facilities incorporate an "auction"-type feature permitting banks to bid to make short-term loans on a non-ratable basis.

Banks are compensated for a revolving commitment with a commitment fee (based on unused commitments) or, if there are multiple facilities, and particularly if there are non-ratable facilities, a facility fee (based on the total amount of the facility whether used or unused).

The remedy for default on a revolving credit facility includes not only acceleration of loans but also termination of the commitments so that no more loans will be made, and in the case of bankruptcy, the termination of commitments is automatic.

§ 3:2.6   *Bank Debt—Letters of Credit*

Letters of credit are issued by banks on behalf of an account party (the bank's customer) to a beneficiary (a party to whom the bank's customer owes or may owe money). The letter of credit is a way of bridging the gap of time, risk, or trust between the account party and the beneficiary. In each case the account party may owe money to the beneficiary and needs to provide assurance of payment, but there is a condition that must be met before the beneficiary is paid. The conditions, which must be documentary in nature and not require the bank to make any "real world" judgments or exercise discretion, are set out in the letter of credit. Once the beneficiary has the letter of credit in hand, it knows that if it delivers documents meeting the conditions, then the letter of credit issuing bank will pay. Making demand on the letter of credit issuing bank to pay is called drawing on the letter of credit. If there is a draw on the letter of credit, the letter of credit bank looks to be reimbursed by its account party. The letter of credit represents a contractual undertaking by the bank, and if conforming documents are presented for a draw on the letter of credit, the bank must pay, absent fraud or the like.

Letters of credit can be issued under an umbrella revolving credit facility or under separate letter of credit arrangements.

In the case of a direct pay letter of credit, the letter of credit is a straightforward payment mechanism. For example, if a company needs to order goods being manufactured in China, then it will ask its bank to issue a letter of credit to the manufacturer stating that upon presentment of documents evidencing delivery of the described goods to the company's importer, the purchase price will be paid. If the company's bank does not have an office or branch in China, then it will ask a local Chinese bank to pay on the letter of credit, and that Chinese bank becomes a confirming bank. Without the letter of credit, the company and the manufacturer could never come to agreement on how to move their arrangement forward—the manufacturer doesn't want to make goods against a mere promise to pay, and the company isn't going to pay in advance.

A standby letter of credit is intended to cover a performance short-fall by the account party—for example, a failure to meet a contract deadline or a failure to pay. The reimbursement obligation in this case is more contingent than in the case of a direct pay letter of credit.

If the account party goes into default under its agreement with the letter of credit issuing bank, there is no effect on already outstanding letters of credit, on which the beneficiaries are relying and that cannot be withdrawn. There is also no loan outstanding that can be accelerated, and the reimbursement obligation may never be more than a contingent obligation if, for example, the conditions to draw are not met before the letter of credit expires. Instead, to "prepay" a letter of credit reimbursement obligation requires the company to put up cash collateral that the issuing bank will either apply to pay the reimbursement obligation immediately upon draw, or release back to the borrower in the event the letter of credit expires undrawn. "Prepaying" a letter of credit reimbursement obligation on an already outstanding letter of credit in this manner would be subject to preference risk.[1] Given the higher level of commitment and risk, particularly for longer term letters of credit, letter of credit fees are typically significantly higher than revolving credit commitment fees—equal to the margin over LIBOR in the leveraged market.

In a case where a company can provide cash collateral to a letter of credit issuer, why doesn't it pay the beneficiary of the letter of credit directly, and remove the letter of credit issuer as intermediary? If the letter of credit backstops a contingent, rather than a fixed, payment obligation, then the company would obviously not want to give over the cash to the beneficiary directly. A second reason may be that the backstopped obligation may not permit early payment or redemption, and there may be no mechanics for providing funds (for example, to a trustee) in advance of the maturity date. A third reason is alluded to above: such a payment directly by the company may be subject to preference attack, whereas payments made by the letter of credit issuer to the beneficiary will not be subject to preference attack so long as the letter of credit was put into place simultaneously with the original financing or has been in place longer than the preference period.

---

1. *See* chapter 5.

How can a company and its bank manage long-running letter of credit requirements? Where letters of credit are used to backstop financial obligations such as notes or bonds, why are letters of credit used instead of, for example, put agreements? These are legitimate questions. There are many arrangements for "evergreen" letters of credit, which renew, for example, on an annual basis unless the issuing bank declines to renew. In some cases where a letter of credit is needed to support a long-term debt obligation, the letter of credit may have a shorter expiry date than the maturity of the notes or bonds, but the expiry (or non-renewal) of the letter of credit may be a default or mandatory redemption event so that holders of the notes or bonds are always entitled to letter of credit-quality protection. A simple put would generally not suffice because the banks providing the letter of credit typically want more covenant and other protection than is contained in the original agreement running to the benefit of the note- or bondholders.

Revolving credit commitments and outstanding letters of credit behave differently in a troubled credit or bankruptcy scenario. Whether lenders have to lend under their revolving credit commitments as a company's financial situation deteriorates is a matter of the lending conditions; and in all cases the lenders will not have to fund after the company is in bankruptcy. The issuer of the letter of credit, however, is in a different situation—the letter of credit is unaffected by the status of the account party; in fact, the point of the letter of credit is to substitute the credit of the issuer for that of the account party. (It is not unheard of, though, for letter of credit issuers to become more particular about documentary requirements for draw when the account party is in financial difficulty.)

It is not usually the case that the bankruptcy of the account party will be a drawing condition under the letter of credit, so the issuer is left hanging with an obligation to honor the letter of credit sometime out in the future. In some cases, it is crystal clear the draw will occur—for example, if the letter of credit backstops a fixed payment obligation that has not occurred before bankruptcy. In other cases, the obligation of the letter of credit issuer is contingent, based, for example, upon whether the company performs a certain obligation out in the future. In these cases, the contingent claim of the letter of credit issuer will have to be valued and provided for in the bankruptcy of the account party.

§ 3:2.7   Bank Debt—Term Loans

A typical multi-purpose credit agreement, including any leveraged acquisition credit agreement, will include a term loan portion. The term loans will be drawn down at closing or initial funding, and, once repaid, may not be reborrowed. In contrast, a revolving credit facility need not be drawn down at closing, or ever, and amounts repaid can be reborrowed so long as the commitment is in place.

Term loan tranches may attract different types of lenders from those that want to commit to provide loans on a revolving basis. Term loan lenders are more likely to be institutional investors such as securitization vehicles (CLOs or CDOs), mutual funds and hedge funds, the so-called public-side investors in bank loans. They want an asset to hold or trade and are not set up to meet ongoing borrowing requests. In the leveraged market, bank loans can contain term loan ("B term") tranches that contain some soft-call provisions (early payment can attract a premium or other compensation), or that are in a second lien position on collateral. So this is an area where the old boundaries between bank loans and securities, and between the public versus private spheres, break down.

§ 3:2.8   Private Placement Debt

In the traditional sense, so-called private placement debt refers to the lending by insurance companies direct to companies through the purchase of fixed-rate notes under note purchase agreements. These are heavily negotiated and detailed documents containing covenants often comparable to those in bank loan agreements. This debt is roughly equivalent to bank term loans, except that it is generally fixed-rate and thus contains the normal make-whole protections for fixed-rate lenders.

§ 3:2.9   Public or Rule 144A Debt

Public notes or bonds are registered with the SEC and issued under indentures with corporate trustees, and very similar notes or bonds can be issued without registration to sophisticated investors under Rule 144A promulgated under the 1934 Act (and to overseas investors under Regulation S). Indentures can provide for multiple series, including series consisting of medium-term notes, which are one-off notes with variable maturities longer than maturities in the commercial paper market. Investment grade issuers may run many debt issues off a single shelf indenture and shelf registration.

This debt is nearly always fixed-rate and contains call protections. The terms of the debt are very much ratings-driven, with a wide gulf between what is required of investment grade issuers and what is required in the junk market.

§ 3:3　　Complex Finance

§ 3:3.1　　*Structured Finance*

Modern structured finance developed out of a number of specialized financing concepts and techniques, some of them with a long history. In a nutshell, the development might be traced through the following antecedents, influences and stages:

(1)　the outright purchase of receivables, at a discount representing the time value of money but also allowances for non-collectability and the costs of collection by so-called factors; this has long been a standard arrangement in the garment industry;

(2)　the use of special purpose or single purpose legal entities to isolate ventures in risky industries (film, oil and gas, real estate);

(3)　the development of mortgage securitization by, among others, Salomon Brothers in the 1970s and after; this was the first great wave of credit "disintermediation" between assets (and originating lenders) and investor classes; mortgages, which have certain performance characteristics on an aggregate basis, were bundled into groups, and interests in those groups of mortgages sold into the capital markets;

(4)　the extension of securitization techniques to other asset classes, including revolving or less predictable loans, such as student loans, auto loans and credit card outstandings; these securitizations permitted banks to sponsor consumer finance programs on a large scale but remove the resulting assets from their books;

(5) operating leases, which always represented a form of "off-balance-sheet" financing, and the development of hybrid or synthetic leases accorded different treatment under tax and accounting standards;

(6) the traditional finance subsidiaries of giant consumer companies like General Electric or General Motors, which, because they held relatively secure and diverse consumer receivables, could be stronger credits than the parent or operating companies;

(7) the development of the affiliated but bankruptcy-remote SPV to act as a purchaser of a company's receivables where the SPV might be a better risk than the company itself;

(8) extension of the "asset-based" concept—separating the credit representing receivables from the credit of the originating entity—more generally to, for example, permit emerging markets structured financings, to achieve higher ratings than the country ratings; and

(9) further extension of these concepts to apply to other assets of a company or person, including rights to future cash flows such as royalties.

At step (9), structured finance becomes, potentially, somewhat problematic. A bankruptcy court will generally not give effect to a purported sale by a company of its "core assets" to an affiliated SPV. Another problem is that it can be difficult to value rights to a stream of cash flows, where the timing and amounts are unknown (for example, royalty payments). Even the existence of the future cash flows may be speculative. Lastly, where the cash flow depends on the continuing performance of the selling entity, there seems to be no reason to say that "purchasing" those cash flows is much different from lending to the selling entity directly—except that now the "purchaser" has not only the risk of the seller's performance but also the risk of nonpayment by the party who will owe the payments to the seller in the future; such a structure looks, at best (that is, if there is recourse to the "seller"), like a loan to the seller secured by its rights to receive payments in the future. At worst, the arrangement might be taken to be a non-recourse loan to the seller, repayable solely out of those rights to unknown future cash flows. Attempts to "monetize" such rights through "structured finance" techniques merit close scrutiny.

Having noted that there are risks where the assets to be securitized are core assets or there is risk of non-performance, the structured finance business thrives, and represents a very large and important segment of the capital markets. It continues to provide, in appropriate circumstances, financing alternatives that are both legitimate and salutary, particularly where it permits a well-understood class of assets to be financed by an expanded universe of investors by repackaging cash flows and tailoring tranches of the repackaged cash flows to investor needs. In particular, receivables financings are absolutely commonplace, to the extent that they comprise a standard part of a typical acquisition finance package.

Parties in a structured finance transaction may include:

- The originator or seller of the assets: for example, the company generating receivables in the case of a receivables financing, or the lender where the underlying asset is a loan;

- The obligors on the underlying assets (receivables or loans);

- The sponsor: the bank that is putting together the deal, which may be an affiliate of a lender-type originator;

- One or more special purpose vehicles—usually one of which is not owned and controlled by the originator or seller—to own the assets and to issue securities to the investors;

- Equity investors in any special purpose vehicles not consolidated with the originator or seller, which might include charities or other third parties;

- A trustee, a collateral trustee and, in some cases, a servicer, these being banks or other fiduciaries or financial services providers who actually hold the assets and administer the program;

- A placement agent or underwriter responsible for placing or underwriting the selling of the securities;

- In some cases, a liquidity bank, which for a commitment fee stands by to provide short-term loans to the SPV (particularly if the SPV issues commercial paper), or swap counterparties that bridge interest rate or other mismatches between cash inflows on the assets and cash outflows to security holders;

- In some cases, a financial guarantor or insurer who agrees to purchase the securities from investors in some circumstances; and

- The investors in the securities.

Documentation for securitization transactions tends to be, as you might guess, lengthy and complex. It does not, and generally cannot, contain representations, covenants, and events of default pertaining to the originator or seller's business, but instead the originator or seller is asked only to stand behind the quality (not creditworthiness or collectability, but instead standards of origination, validity and enforceability) of the underlying assets. On the other hand, provisions regarding ongoing asset quality and performance are comprehensive and stringent. Usually if there is a deterioration in the assets, certain protections kick in, such as substitution of assets. There are also detailed provisions regarding how moneys are to be allocated. The principal allocation provision may be called the "waterfall." All of the parties will need to be satisfied that the documents entitle them to the cash and other protections to which they are entitled in the various circumstances that may come to pass. Rating agencies will typically be very much involved in reviewing the assets and the documents before they will give the ratings that are often necessary to place the securities. Orchestrating the documentation and closing for a securitization can be a challenge, and there is a premium on technical drafting of complex provisions.

Coming full circle, some securitization vehicles (CDOs, CBOs, and CLOs) are in the business of buying bank loans and bonds, including in leveraged deals.

§ 3:3.2   Derivatives

Derivatives refer to any class of financial contract under which one party agrees to make payments to another depending on the value of an underlying asset, commodity, rate, price, or index. Like structured finance, the derivatives market as it exists today represents an organic evolution, in this case of several more traditional trading markets— the commodities exchanges, where people traded for delivery of goods in the future; the foreign exchange markets, where the trading included contracts for forward exchange of currencies; and trading in puts and calls on stock. An option can be layered on to any contract for forward delivery against price, of course. The derivatives market permits participants to trade in risks in a far more fluid way than was possible under the traditional finance, currency, or commodity contracts.

And, also like structured finance, the "derivatives" concept is not subject to any predetermined limitations in terms of the circumstances in which it might be applied. Some derivatives are highly standardized and traded on exchanges, while others are custom-designed and sold "over the counter"—for example, among banks or from a bank to a corporate customer. The quantity of the underlying asset is referred to as the "notional value" of the swap or other derivative contract. This means that an interest rate swap on $100 million of debt has a notional value of $100 million, though the payments to be made by the parties will be a small fraction of that amount, and are usually netted.

In terms of purely financial risk, one of the earliest and biggest drivers of the modern derivatives market was the desire to mitigate interest rate risk. For this reason, the swap contract under which two parties could agree effectively to exchange floating rate for fixed-rate obligations became an important financial instrument. With an interest rate swap, a company could fix its cost of loans made by floating rate lenders like banks. ISDA promulgated standard forms for these and other swap transactions. The forms permitted many trades to occur under the umbrella of a master agreement between two parties and provided for netting and unwind arrangements. ISDA constantly seeks to improve derivatives documentation and standards. The simplicity of the contract forms and relatively relaxed documentation practices (enabling trades to be concluded in real time with documentation to follow) have enabled and expanded the derivatives market. Credit derivatives in particular have had a significant impact on the transferability of credit risk and the readiness of market participants to hold assets where they have contracted to lay off the credit risk.

While ISDA provides excellent documentation support for many transactions, some derivative transactions are highly customized and require careful drafting of technical provisions, including equity and options pricing and other quantitative terms. It should go without saying that lawyers need to exercise special diligence in documenting these transactions, making sure that they understand the deal fully, including its financial terms, running numerical examples, and asking their clients and colleagues to review those provisions closely.

§ 3:3.3 *Financial Engineering and Rule Arbitrage; Issues for Lawyers*

Structured finance and derivatives represent "financial engineering" options that go beyond the standard corporate finance menu of debt and equity. Sometimes they may be used in conjunction with or in substitution for one another, and are sometimes used, and expressly so, to effect a sort of rule arbitrage. That is, their use may be driven by regulatory, tax, rating agency/credit/bankruptcy, financial reporting, or accounting considerations, and in most cases this is entirely legitimate. Some transactions fall into the category of "having your cake and eating it too."

Lawyers need to understand the totality of the deal they are working on, and sometimes that can be difficult when the key elements are spread across different documents and embodied in abstract language. It can be useful in these circumstances to make a schematic and to refer to it on an ongoing basis as things develop. Occasionally, lawyers and accountants are asked to consider proposals that are on or may be over the borderline. It is always the right thing to consult colleagues when a particular idea strikes you as potentially compromising you and your firm or possibly involving an improper transaction.

The desire to reconcile competing considerations seems to have been taken to the extreme in the case of Enron. According to the Powers Report (a report rendered to the board of directors in late 2001), management was facing a set of conflicting goals. Enron needed an investment grade rating to participate as a counterparty in the energy trading markets; at the same time it was actively investing in new ventures that required up-front financing but would not generate near-term revenues. Financing those new ventures on the balance sheet would have made maintaining the investment grade rating difficult, if not impossible. Later, maintaining earnings growth and thereby supporting the stock price also became a key driver. Much of the Enron story is about the use of structured finance and derivatives techniques to "arbitrage" among its conflicting and ultimately irreconcilable financial and accounting needs and constraints.

Chapter 4

Accounting Matters

§ 4:1   Financial Statements

The starting point for understanding a company from a corporate finance perspective is to know what it does (how it makes money) and then to get a copy of the company's financial statements, which will include a balance sheet, an income statement, and a statement of cash flows. The balance sheet is often referred to as a "snapshot" because it is a picture of the company's financial condition at a point in time. The income statement calculates the company's profitability for a period—a quarter or a year. Then a balance sheet is prepared at or as of the closing date for the income statement. The statement of cash flows reconciles the company's opening and closing cash positions for a period by showing where cash came from and how it was used. The income statement and statement of cash flows for the period enable you to tie the opening and closing balance sheets together, and see how the financial condition of the company changed from the beginning to the end of the period.

You should be able to relate how the company earns its money to the financial statements. If you have not had the opportunity to take at least an introductory accounting class you should try to do so or otherwise learn how to read a financial statement. This is time well spent; and the longer you put it off, the more time you will waste working in the corporate world without understanding what is going on around you.

In the United States, accounting of companies is according to generally accepted accounting principles (GAAP). Other countries do not necessarily use U.S. GAAP standards, and there is a push to build the underpinnings of more globally consistent reporting under International Accounting Standards. Financial statements for non-U.S. companies are typically prepared using International Financial Reporting Standards (IFRS) accounting principles. The accounting treatment of some financial items can differ significantly under IFRS and under GAAP. Loan agreements sometimes anticipate the fact that U.S. reporting companies may in the future be permitted to use IFRS instead of GAAP for reporting purposes and provide that if the borrower is permitted to and elects to use IFRS instead of GAAP, references to GAAP will be construed to mean IFRS. Because the change may impact the computation of financial covenants, the right to replace GAAP with IFRS is typically subject to an undertaking to renegotiate the covenant levels or definitions to preserve the underlying business agreement after giving effect to this change. Whether or not U.S. reporting companies are permitted to use IFRS in the future (and a borrower elects to do so), there is already an ongoing effort by the Financial Accounting Standards Board (FASB) and the International Accounting Standards Board (IASB) to align financial reporting conducted in accordance with GAAP and IFRS, which could have significant impact on loan agreement terms.[1]

Public companies in the United States file audited annual financial statements as part of their Form 10-K, and quarterly unaudited statements as part of their Form 10-Q. So-called pro forma financial statements are based on historical financial statements but adjust for some assumed event. Likewise, a company may prepare projections. Neither pro forma financial statements nor projections are GAAP financial statements.

---

1.   *See, for example,* Exposure Draft ED/2013/6 Leases, *available at* http://www.ifrs.org/Current-Projects/IASB-Projects/Leases/Exposure-Draft-May-2013/Documents/ED-Leases-Standard-May-2013.pdf.

The starting point for most accounting is "historical." This means that the value ascribed to a certain transaction and the associated assets or liabilities at the time of the transaction is the basis for establishing book value. If a company bought a piece of equipment for $100 a year ago, generally the value of that piece of equipment on the company's books is $100 less deductions for wear and tear or obsolescence (approximated by an associated accumulated depreciation contra-account). The fact that the same piece of equipment is now selling for $85 or $250 is not, generally, something that requires or permits the company to revalue the asset.

One could imagine something totally different. For example, public companies could say that stockholders' equity is the most widely validated figure on the company's balance sheet (through stock price and, thus, total market capitalization) and that everything should thus turn on that figure, but as you can see, given the volatility of stock price, chaos would quickly ensue. So, in general, the book value of accounting entries is based on the actual dollar value ascribed to them in the transaction that gave rise to them. Where no such value is available, methods of estimation are prescribed; and when historical value is patently inappropriate, as determined under GAAP, "mark-to-market" or other fair market value may be substituted for the historical book value.

Nearly all companies use the accrual method of accounting, which attributes items of income and expense to a period based on when the income is in fact earned by performance, and the expense to the period to which it properly relates. The accrual method of accounting is in contrast to the cash method, which simply looks at when cash is received and when it is paid out.

A simple example can illustrate the difference between cash and accrual methods of accounting. Suppose you were to pay real estate taxes of $600 on December 1, 2013, covering the next six months. Under the accrual method of accounting, you have a 2013 calendar year expense of $100 and a year-end asset—"prepaid taxes"—of $500, which you will reduce to $0 by June 1, 2014, resulting in $500 of tax expenses for calendar year 2014. On the cash basis, your expense is $600 of taxes for the year ended December 31, 2013, end of story. For most individual taxpayers, and some businesses, the cash method of accounting yields a good-enough picture of financial performance and condition, but for most businesses it would grossly distort the picture.

This becomes particularly obvious in the case of long-term or capital expenditures. On December 1, 2013, a company buys a factory that will be used for fifteen years. It would be wildly misleading to charge the company's 2013 operations with the entire expense of that factory. 2013 would look like a terrible year, and the years afterwards could look great, until the factory had to be replaced.

In general, companies do not like to present volatile earnings that swing wildly from period to period, since this suggests either that they are in an inherently risky business or that management does not have good control of what the company is doing. You would be right in imagining that, in some cases, businesses might be tempted to look at alternative ways of recording income, expenses, and other financial events across period-ends and over longer time periods.

§ 4:2   The Balance Sheet and What's Not on It

The company's balance sheet provides a basic picture of the company from the corporate finance perspective. The company's assets are shown on the left hand side of the balance sheet, the company's debt and equity will be shown on the right hand side of the balance sheet, and more details can be found in the footnotes. At all times, assets (the accounting concept, corresponding to the final figure on the left hand side of the balance sheet) are equal to liabilities plus stockholders' equity.

$$A = L + SE$$

or

$$SE = A - L$$

Assets include current assets (cash or items expected to be converted into cash within the year, such as accounts receivable); investments (to be held longer than a year); prepaid expenses (which will be charged against and thus reduced in upcoming periods); plant, property, and equipment (which may be referred to as fixed assets); and intangible assets (such as intellectual property and goodwill). When one company acquires another company for an amount greater than the book value of the acquired company's assets, excess purchase price that cannot be allocated to specific assets (through writing up the value of those assets) ends up as "goodwill." As long-term assets are depreciated (in the case of fixed assets) or amortized (in the case of intangibles), their original book value remains on the balance sheet but is offset by accumulated depreciation and accumulated amortization accounts, shown as a deduction, or a figure net of depreciation or amortization may be shown.

Liabilities include current liabilities (such as accounts payable, accrued expenses, accrued interest expense, income tax payable, short-term debt, and the short-term portion of long-term debt) and long-term debt (maturity longer than a year). In some cases, there are reserves for liabilities, and sometimes there is a liability (or contra-asset) representing minority interests (the portion of non-wholly owned subsidiaries that is owned by others).

Shareholders' or stockholders' equity—sometimes referred to as "book equity"—is equal to paid-in capital (original price paid for stock at issuance) plus retained earnings; it increases when the company issues more stock for consideration and when the company has positive net income, and it is reduced when the company loses money (including through the write-down of assets) or pays money out to its stockholders. Stockholders' equity bears no particular relation at all to market capitalization, which is the aggregate value the market places on the outstanding shares of stock. The balance sheet can show the number of shares outstanding, which is used in the calculation of earnings per share. So-called treasury stock is stock that has been authorized under the company's charter documents and issued, but is at the time held by the company itself.

By looking at the balance sheet and any footnotes about debt, you will be able to see how leveraged the company is, that is, how much of its capital structure (debt and equity) is comprised of debt versus equity. In the most extreme case, a disproportionately large amount of debt as against a smaller amount of assets, or negative net worth, would indicate that the company is insolvent on a book basis (liabilities exceed assets). You might also be able to see whether the company has a lot of debt coming due soon, and to spot a timing mismatch between assets and liabilities. This could indicate a problem with liquidity (short-term cash needs exceeding available short-term cash sources). For example, if the company has short-term debt that greatly exceeds its cash and short-term assets plus short-term cash earnings, you might ask how the company is going to be meeting those short-term obligations. If a large chunk of long-term debt is coming due in the near term, how does the company intend to pay it off? There are only a few options—refinance, including by a stretch of the obligations coming due, equity injection, or sale of assets. If you are working on a debt deal, you should understand where the resulting debt fits in, and what the money is going to be used for.

A special aspect of the balance sheet relates to "working capital." This concept refers to the wash of cash in and out in the course of the company's ordinary operations, resulting in changes in current assets and current liabilities. It won't surprise you to hear that most businesses do not take in each day exactly the amount of cash they need to pay out on the next business day. This is especially easy to see in the retail business. Many retail businesses do a large portion of their annual sales in the Christmas season. They can't start that season with empty shelves or they will be out of business by the end of it. This means they need funds to build up inventory in anticipation of Christmas, while over the Christmas season the inventory is sold and starts turning into cash receipts or accounts receivable, which will in time also turn into cash. A buildup in non-cash current assets (receivables and inventory) over a period of time is a use of cash; a reduction in non-cash current assets from the period beginning to period end generates cash over that period.

As informative as a balance sheet can be, it does not always provide an accurate and up-to-date picture of the company's financial obligations and overall health.

You will hear people talk about the "write-down" of assets. This can occur when an asset that is listed as having a certain book value is judged by management in fact as having a much lower real value, to the point that the book value requires adjustment. An example might be where a company has leased out to others a large number of SUVs, and has listed as an asset the residual values of the SUVs as they come off lease. If gasoline prices were suddenly to triple, the residual values of the SUVs might be much less. The "write-down" of assets may go through the income statement as a deduction to net income, but in any case results in a hit to the left side of the balance sheet (assets) and thus must reduce the right-hand side as well, reducing stockholders' equity.

Of course this can go the other way too, where an old asset has been depreciated down to next to nothing on the books, but is worth much more. Rarely are assets "written up," though this can occur when a company is acquired: The acquirer can take the fair market value of the asset onto its post-acquisition consolidated balance sheet at the allocated fair market value at the time of sale.

Valuations of investments are also potentially tricky. Some investments must be "marked to market" (that is, valued at their then-current market value), whereas others are on the books at their historical cost. This distinction has had a significant impact on, for example, the values ascribed to portfolio investments of private equity operations inside banks. Valuations of hedging and derivatives positions in those cases where there isn't an established market value may be difficult, and in some cases those positions appear on a net basis. Foreign currency translations can also have interesting effects on asset valuations period to period.

Not all liabilities on a balance sheet are "debt," and some important types of liabilities are estimated. These might include, for an ordinary company, litigation reserves, which are amounts that the company has estimated ("set aside" in an accounting though not necessarily cash sense) will become payable in respect of pending litigation. The company will expense the litigation reserve when it creates it. When the judgment becomes final and is paid, to the extent it matches the reserve, cash (an asset) is reduced and so is the reserve, with no effect on income for the period. If there is more to pay, then there will be a further expense, but if the judgment is less than the reserve figure, then the reserve is reduced to $0, and there is associated income corresponding to the amount by which the reserve exceeded the final judgment.

Other important categories of liabilities appearing on the balance sheet are also estimates. These include liabilities for warranties, extended service contracts, and other contingent obligations such as for airline frequent flyer miles, and, quite significantly for providers of insurance, reserves for future claims. For companies with defined benefit pension plans ("defined benefit" plans are those where the provider has agreed to provide a certain level of benefits, whereas "defined contribution" plans are those where the provider makes defined payments, but has no obligation with respect to the benefits the accumulated amounts will ultimately provide), or that are obligated to provide retirees with health benefits, these estimated obligations can be enormous, and in some cases have precipitated bankruptcy.

Accounting for pension obligations and reserves calculations for the insurance industry are so complicated that there are specialized accounting rules and practices devoted to them, and companies and accountants rely on actuaries for assistance in determining the amount of reserves. Actuaries are known among the lay population for estimating future life expectancy for life insurance companies, but they do more than this. In the insurance industry, the calculation of claims reserves as well as claims paid actually drives the determination of net income.

Many financial obligations are "off-balance-sheet," meaning that under accounting rules they do not need to be listed as liabilities on the balance sheet. They can nevertheless be real enough. It may even be that the deal you are working on is "off-balance-sheet." Some off-balance-sheet financings are required to be described in footnotes to the financial statements. The fact is, a company has many financial obligations and only some of these constitute "debt" or other liabilities that are required to be reported on the balance sheet.

One of the most significant types of liabilities that do not appear on the balance sheet is a guarantee. As a contingent obligation, it is generally not required to appear on the guarantor's balance sheet, and yet from the perspective of other lenders to the guarantor it is clearly a parity obligation that must be satisfied out of the assets of the guarantor. Obligations to pay liquidated damages for failure to perform under contracts, take-or-pay contracts, indemnification obligations relating to retained liabilities under asset sale agreements, environmental liabilities, reimbursement obligations to sureties for performance obligations, and many other contingent or non-debt obligations may not be revealed anywhere on the balance sheet or in the footnotes to the financial statements.

Furthermore, many businesses engage in financial transactions that are designed to be off-balance-sheet. Why would this be?

Off-balance-sheet financing exists for a couple of reasons. First, it can be very attractive to take a financial obligation off a company's balance sheet! This can be so even where the corresponding assets go as well. Operating leases are leases that take both the assets (no matter how key to the company's operation, such as its hotels, for a hotel business, or its airplanes, for an airline) and the associated amount of long-term obligations off the balance sheet of the company, turning its obligation for accounting purposes into a periodic lease payment, which is an operating expense. Sales and leasebacks have been arranged in this way for decades, and have enabled capital intensive transportation and manufacturing businesses to finance the acquisition of assets on terms favorable to them and advantageous to the financial lessors.

As of 2013, the accounting treatment of a lease under U.S. GAAP and IFRS depended on whether it is classified as an operating lease (not recorded as either an asset or liability on balance sheet but instead treating lease payments as an expense over the lease term) or a capital lease (recorded as debt on balance sheet). Thus the effect of operating leases on financial leverage and earnings of a company is not evident from the face of the balance sheet. To ensure greater transparency and to help users interpret and compare financial statements that account for leases differently, on May 16, 2013, the FASB and IASB published a revised joint proposal relating to lease accounting for financial statements prepared in accordance with U.S. GAAP or IFRS.

Capital adequacy requirements have been another driver of off-balance-sheet financing. Of particular significance for the banking industry have been the Basel requirements applicable to regulated banking institutions. In December 2010, the Basel Committee published Basel III, with implementation beginning in 2013, which, among other things, required banks to hold more and better quality capital and imposed additional and more stringent capital to risk-weighted assets and leverage ratios on banks. Even at the very high leverage or gearing permitted to banks relative to other industries, minimum capital requirements constrain the assets and, thus, the size of the book of business that the bank can write. Securitization used to permit a bank to originate large volumes of financial transactions that it could then remove from its balance sheet and finance on a stand-alone basis, but accounting rules now make this difficult.

At the time of this writing, the amount of leverage in lending activities remains in the U.S. regulatory spotlight. In March 2013, U.S. bank regulatory agencies published joint guidance on leveraged lending setting out high-level principles related to safe and sound leveraged lending activities and the regulators' view on the overall market impact. According to that publication, the guidance was in response to concerns that underwriting practices of regulated banks in the leveraged loan market do not adequately address risks with appropriate allowances for losses and advised those banks to risk-rate loans considering the borrower's ability to delever.

Off-balance-sheet or bankruptcy-remote financing may be attractive when the borrower as a whole is not as creditworthy as some of its assets may be on a stand-alone basis. In this case, the desire is to do as much as possible to isolate healthy and liquid assets such as receivables and to finance them separately, away from the rest of the company. The key test will be whether the owner of the assets is substantively consolidated with the originator of the assets in bankruptcy.[2] Bankruptcy-remote financing is predicated on a "true sale" of the relevant assets to an entity outside the consolidated group or, under current U.S. GAAP, to a special purpose subsidiary that is sufficiently separate from its affiliates that it is considered to be remote from the operating risks of bankruptcy that affect its affiliates. This "true sale" analysis can *support* deconsolidation for accounting purposes but whether such deconsolidation is appropriate will be determined under the accounting rules.

§ 4:3   The Income Statement; LIFO and FIFO

The income statement shows the company's financial activity for a period of time. It is displayed as a running sum, of pluses and minuses, starting with a gross revenue or total sales figure and ending with a figure for net income.

The top line on an income statement (gross revenue or total sales) tells you how much business the company did: the total sale price of coats or computers or airline tickets it sold. Right at that point there might be a "minus" line—for assumed returns, for example—to show a "net sales" figure.

Against this top line figure is charged the cost of goods sold. This is the direct cost of producing the thing that is sold. In a services business, of course, the main comparable item is salaries paid to employees.

Where there is a physical goods inventory, the company must select one of three possible methods of accounting for the cost of goods

---

2.   *See* chapter 5.

sold. The least used option is an average cost method, which uses the average cost of inventory over the reporting period. The other two options are LIFO (last in/first out) and FIFO (first in/first out). Under LIFO, current sales are charged against the most recently produced inventory. In an environment of rising production costs, this results in an arguably more conservative outcome. Current sales are matched to something approximating the current cost of producing the goods sold, and income is, relatively speaking, depressed. When LIFO is used for tax reporting this can result in lower taxable income. LIFO would also result in the unsold inventory being shown at the low historical cost, also arguably a conservative reporting position. FIFO accounting, on the other hand, typically more directly tracks how physical goods are in fact handled and cleared, as businesses like to rotate their inventory outward and move older inventory whenever possible. In an environment of generally increasing costs of production, FIFO will result in higher income and higher reported valuations of inventory.

LIFO accounting can have some interesting implications. Because the inventory on hand is always valued at the earliest historical cost, a run-down of current inventory or liquidation of a line of inventory altogether (in a rising cost environment) results in expensing low-cost historical inventory against current sales, and thus a significant uptick in gross margin (sale price over cost of goods sold). Where this is in connection with a full liquidation of LIFO inventory, this is called LIFO liquidation gain. Obviously, it is a non-recurring event and not a regular part of earnings. Similarly, a change in the method of inventory accounting can result in a one-time accounting event as the change is recognized, and then a lack of comparability between the periods pre- and post-change.

After cost of goods sold (and calculation of the gross operating profits) would come a general overhead expense item—for the costs associated with running the business but not really directly attributable to producing the goods or the services that the company offers. This might be called SG&A, for selling, general and administrative costs. These might include, for example, management salaries, corporate advertising, property and casualty insurance premiums on the company headquarters, or the fees paid to the company's auditors.

A certain category of expenses is of particular interest from the corporate finance perspective, that is, non-cash expenses. Of these, the two most significant are depreciation and amortization. Depreciation is the periodic charge against the value of tangible capital assets acquired in earlier periods. In the example of the factory above, if a factory with an expected life of fifteen years costs $15 million, the company may choose straight-line depreciation, and expense $1 million a year. Or the company might be able to support a more rapid or "accelerated" depreciation schedule. Amortization is the same concept applied to non-tangible assets—in particular, goodwill.

At this point we have reached a figure for net operating income. This tells you what the company's ordinary operations produce in terms of book income. This figure should generally be positive, over time, or the company is not in a sustainable business.

Moving to the next portion of the income statement we see, first of all, the effects of financial activities and corporate structure; second, the effects of unusual events; and third, the effects of taxation. Income and investment earnings are added and interest charges are deducted. There are deductions for the minority interests in consolidated subsidiaries (where a non-wholly owned subsidiary's income has been taken in full into the statements of the parent but a portion of that should be reallocated back out to minority shareholders) and additions for the proportional ownership in companies accounted for on the "equity method" (roughly, 20% to 50% ownership). Gains and losses from asset sales out of the ordinary course and extraordinary gains and losses are included, as are earnings from discontinued operations. Lastly, there is a deduction for taxes payable, and the resulting figure is net income.

§ 4:4   EBITDA

In the debt capital markets, and in particular in the "leveraged" zone, EBITDA is significantly more important a measure than net income. Deals are positioned and marketed based on multiples of debt to EBITDA, not income and not shareholders' equity. It is the standard industry measure for calculating leverage and credit quality, though not a GAAP concept nor, because of the frequency of negotiated adjustments, necessarily calculated in the same way even for similar companies in similar deals.

What is EBITDA and why is it so important in the leveraged finance business? EBITDA (earnings before interest, taxes, depreciation, and amortization) is considered the best indicator of cash debt service capacity. If you go back and look at the running tally that creates the net income figure, you will see the point at which the income statement veers off from the earnings of the regular business, into finance-affected results that might also swing period to period based on out-of-the-ordinary asset sales and other unusual events.

The interest charge, of course, is entirely dependant on the level of debt the business is carrying. Interest is usually tax deductible, and thus tax can be minimized by borrowing. The theory here is that the earning asset should be levered optimally to return the maximum to shareholders and reduce income taxes payable. The debt level and, thus, both interest expense and taxes, are "plug figures" or variables, not intrinsic to the cash flow potential of the business.

Depreciation and amortization are added back to the net income figure for a different and more straightforward reason—they are non-cash expenses.

This much is common to all definitions of EBITDA, but there are variations as you go from deal to deal based on the accounting aspects of each company that may otherwise cause its net income figure to diverge from its cash-generating capacity. These are not necessarily too hard for lawyers to understand; by reading the words of the definition against the company's financial statements, you may find that the logic becomes clear.

§ 4:5   How the Financial Statements Fit Together

It may seem like some sort of miracle that assets should always equal liabilities plus stockholders' equity. In fact this is a function of the rules of accounting, and in particular the rules of "double-entry bookkeeping." Every accounting transaction or entry is taken to have a plus aspect and a minus aspect. If I sell a pair of shoes for $80 cash, cash goes up by $80 and my inventory goes down, let's say by $40— the cost of producing the shoes. This means that my asset position has improved by $40. How does this increase in asset position work its way into the other side of the balance sheet? Assuming no other changes, it should increase stockholders' equity.

In fact the route will be more circuitous. From an income statement perspective, when I sell the shoes I have revenues of $80, I have a matching expense—cost of goods sold of $40, and the remaining $40 will makes its way down through the rest of my operations toward a net income figure for the period, and, all else being equal, the retained earnings portions of stockholders' equity will be increased, from the beginning of the period to the end of the period, by the amount of net income for the period.

The income statement and balance sheet interrelate. Incurring an expense may move assets from one category to another (say from cash to inventory), but otherwise either reduces assets (such as cash, if you pay right away) or increases liabilities (such as accounts payable, if you expect to pay thirty days later). Depreciation and amortization expenses are added to accumulated depreciation and amortization accounts on the balance sheet as reductions to total assets. An item of income increases assets (such as cash or accounts receivable) or might instead correspond to the reduction of a previously booked liability (as would be the case where tax to be paid is eventually lower than the amount booked as a tax payable liability).

The statement of cash flows reconciles the starting cash position for a period to the ending cash position for the period. In the case of cash flows from operations, this can be done either by starting with net income and then making adjustments for all non-cash items (such as depreciation and amortization), or by tracking changes in operations-related assets and liabilities (other than cash itself) from the beginning to the end of the period. As noted, an increase in accounts receivable or inventory is a use of cash, and decreases in these items would represent cash being freed up. Likewise for non-operating or capital activities, changes in balance sheet items indicate whether cash was coming in or going out. A reduction in debt is a use of cash, while an increase in debt represents a source of cash. An increase in plant, property, and equipment is a use of cash, and new equity issuance is a source of cash.

Spending a bit of time to make out how the three principal financial statements interrelate will help you understand financial covenants. In particular, if you understand how net income is converted to cash from operations in the cash flow statement you will have a good grasp of the basic concept of EBITDA.

§ 4:6 Consolidation; Minority Interests; Equity Accounting

Most large businesses are organized and run as a group of affiliated companies, with a parent or holding company at the top. Subsidiaries are formed for a variety of tax, legal, and operational reasons, and in many cases a large corporate group's effective business units do not match up with its corporate structure. In some cases they do, with the financing arms of major automotive companies and conglomerates such as General Electric as a prime example. In the case of Berkshire Hathaway, the corporate structure beneath the parent holding company directly reflects the fact that the parent owns a group of separately functioning, separately managed, and, in many cases, quite dissimilar self-standing businesses acquired by Berkshire Hathaway over the years.

Regardless of the history and the business alignment, GAAP principles provide that a corporate holding company structure be reflected in consolidated financial statements of the parent company. Ownership interest of more than 50% will generally require consolidation, and the principal effect of consolidation is to eliminate the effect of intercompany transactions. That is, within the consolidated group, two subsidiaries can buy and sell from each other as much as they like but these sales will "wash out" in consolidation and will not contribute to consolidated revenue. For accounting purposes, the group is effectively treated as a single entity, with aggregate incomes and expenses calculated across the group for a picture of the group as a whole. It is still possible to break down to the contributing companies by looking at the "consolidating" income statements.

To reiterate, the consolidated revenues of the parent will be equal to the aggregate revenues of the group, less intercompany sales, and net income should equal the aggregate net income of the group, less the effect of intercompany transactions. However, let's say a subsidiary is 80% owned by the parent. In that case if all of the subsidiary's income is included in the income of the parent, this would not be an accurate picture because in fact 20% of that net income belongs to the minority shareholder. Therefore, a further step is taken in the income statement to adjust net income for minority interests.

If a company owns between 20% and 50% of another company, a proportional share of the second company's net income may appear in the net income of the first (investing) company. This proportional treatment is called the equity method of accounting.

§ 4:7   Interplay of Consolidation Concerns and Off-Balance-Sheet Financing

Under the principles of consolidation, a sale of assets by a parent or operating company to a finance affiliate, and a financing of those assets by the finance affiliate, will not achieve off-balance-sheet treatment of the financing for the consolidated group. The intercompany sale is ignored and the debt incurred by the finance affiliate appears as debt of the consolidated group.

One of the goals of many securitizations is to finance a set of assets off-balance-sheet for the originator. For a group of assets to be financed by a company on an off-balance-sheet basis, it must be the case that the assets be transferred (in a "true sale") to a special purpose vehicle, which in turn funds the purchase price it has to pay by a second-step transfer (often not a "true sale") or by borrowing money against the assets. Of course, lenders will not lend 100% of the fair market value purchase price of the assets to the vehicle company, but only the normal percentage of loan value ranging from say 50% to 90%, depending on the characteristics of the assets (realizability or liquidity, and volatility in value). The appropriate treatment of any particular deal requires securitization expertise from accountants as well as lawyers.

§ 4:8   How Financial Statements and Financial Reality Can Diverge

Auditors state that audited financial statements "fairly present the operations and financial condition of the company," but that they do so in accordance with GAAP.

At this point, you can readily see that the picture of the company revealed by its financial statements and the financial reality of its operations and position—defined as the cash-generating ability and/or fair market value of assets and the actual amount and timing of liabilities—can diverge. Accounting, though it deals with numbers instead of words, is a set of rules that, like the practice of law, is perhaps more of an art than a science.

Bankers and their lawyers, thus, must consider how they will draw substantive reality out of the financial statements so that they can monitor the financial health of the companies they finance, and how to design appropriate margins of error in their analysis of, and reliance on, historical financial statements. Companies and their lawyers need to understand and, to the extent possible, anticipate how accounting rules and business events might combine to put them into default.

Particularly from the lender or investor perspective, main areas of indeterminacy or possible divergence from financial reality would include the following:

- Revenue recognition issues, as to timing (for example, anticipating revenues by "channel stuffing" or improper "monetization" of future, speculative cash flows), or as to value (especially as to, say, non-cash or barter consideration), or more broadly as to whether reported revenues are too contingent and uncertain (whether the revenues have in fact been earned) or even artificially inflated (the result of "channel-stuffing," "round-tripping," or other schemes)

- LIFO versus FIFO inventory accounting, and a change from one to the other

- Proper expensing as opposed to capitalization of expenditures

- Appropriate recording of non-cash expenses generally (for example, stock options)

- Historical book values of assets that exceed fair market values

- Valuations of intangibles generally, especially goodwill that is an acknowledged plug figure, and, therefore, amortization, but also including intellectual property

- Asset valuations that are estimated without market benchmarks or that are subject to downward pressure based on external events (asset write-down scenarios)

- Mark-to-market valuations that are likely to exhibit volatility due to external circumstances

- Foreign currency effects likewise subject to volatility

- Proper categorization of debt as long term or short term (possible liquidity problems)

- Estimated liabilities such as reserve figures

- Pensions and retiree benefit figures (and any associated payment obligations)

- Guarantees and other contingent obligations not on the balance sheet

- Off-balance-sheet financings, particularly of key assets and operations

- Timing generally, particularly period-end activities addressed toward "window-dressing" for quarterly disclosure or compliance

- Intercompany transactions with non-consolidated but affiliated entities ("sweetheart" deals, or transactions to create or enhance the appearance of gains or hide losses)

- Stockholders' equity variance from the true value of the company equity

These could be of concern, or, in some cases (such as the last), possible upside interest, where things could be worse, or, in some cases, better than the financial statements would seem to indicate. Financial analysts who work for banks, institutional investors, and private equity are precisely in the business of carefully studying historical financial statements, deconstructing them, and building their own financial models.

Chapter 5

Bankruptcy—Rules of the Endgame

§ 5:1   Priorities of Recovery

The framework for the ranking of corporate finance instruments is defined by the rules that will govern the endgame—the bankruptcy rules of recovery. Bankruptcy is a complex area. The U.S. Bankruptcy Code provides the substantive statutory grounding, elaborated with a quite significant amount of case law. Furthermore, the actual outcomes in bankruptcy are as much a product of negotiation as law, with law and circumstances providing the parameters for the discussion.

Of course it is quite important to involve bankruptcy lawyers in a distressed credit situation, but all corporate finance lawyers need to be familiar with some fundamental concepts. If the company is anything other than a plain vanilla corporate issuer, the corporate finance lawyer needs to understand how bankruptcy would apply to that type of legal entity and, as relevant, to other potential obligors (such as general partners or guarantors).

As for other subjects discussed in this book, we can only provide the most basic introduction, but if you are working on a corporate finance deal that will potentially be subject to the U.S. Bankruptcy Code, you should have a grasp of the following (very simplified) principles:

- The priority rules applicable to the debtor's capital structure are generally: secured debt recovers 100 cents on the dollar before unsecured debt gets anything, but only up to the value of the collateral in which the lender has a perfected security interest; debt recovers 100 cents on the dollar before any kind of equity, including preferred stock; preferred stock recovers 100 cents on the dollar (liquidation preference and accrued dividends) before common equity.

- There is a class of statutory and administrative claims that comes ahead of other claims. These may be significant, including costs of the proceeding itself, tax claims, and certain employee claims.

- *Post-petition interest* (interest accruing after the bankruptcy petition is filed) is recoverable only by secured creditors, and only out of an over-secured position.

- Contractual *subordination* is given effect in the bankruptcy but subject to (and it is a big qualification) the last point below.

- Payments, transfers of assets (including grants of security interests in assets), and the incurrence of obligations, in each case without adequate consideration, may be set aside in certain circumstances under the doctrine of *fraudulent conveyance*, and a payment or transfer of assets (including the granting of security) within ninety days (or in the case of insiders one year) of bankruptcy may be set aside in certain circumstances as a voidable *preference*.

- Separate legal entities will in general be treated as separate in bankruptcy, that is, their separate identities respected, so that the above rules and priorities will apply to each entity in a corporate group individually. This means that claims at the parent company level will be *structurally subordinated*, as to the assets of a subsidiary, to claims at the subsidiary level.

- However, the separate identities of affiliated companies may, in certain exceptional circumstances, be disregarded under the doctrine of *substantive consolidation*, and their assets and liabilities effectively treated as those of a single entity. Some claims (principally tax, ERISA and possibly some environmental claims) attach to all the companies in the affiliated group by statute, effectively ignoring corporate separateness.

- Claims of "controlling" creditors who have acted "inequitably" can be subordinated under the doctrine of *equitable subordination*.

- Almost all of the above may be negotiated and compromised in the course of a bankruptcy proceeding. In particular, subordinated debt may get a percentage recovery even where senior unsecured debt receives less than 100 cents on the dollar—but having a good claim, not subject to fraudulent conveyance or preference attack or other equitable challenge, at the level (that is, owed by the specific legal entity) where the assets are located is a very strong hand, best yet if the debt is secured with a comfortable margin to cover post-petition interest.

§ 5:2 Fraudulent Conveyance

Can you spot a fraudulent conveyance? The classic fraudulent conveyance is the case of the village cobbler who owes the blacksmith a cow; but when the blacksmith comes to collect, he finds that the cobbler has given the cow to his wife, the purpose being, of course, to defeat the claims of his creditor, the blacksmith. The transfer of the cow to the wife for no consideration was a transfer in fraud of creditors and can be set aside (the cow returned to the cobbler and then claimed by his creditor the blacksmith) under the doctrine of fraudulent conveyance. Of course, if the cobbler, instead of giving the cow to his wife, had sold the cow for fair value, he can pay the blacksmith the value of the cow; or if, after giving his wife the cow, he still has other cows and can pay his debt, all is well. So a transfer for fair value is not a fraudulent conveyance. Neither is it a fraudulent conveyance if, after giving affect to the transfer in question, the debtor is solvent (assets exceed liabilities).

It's easy enough then to identify it as a fraudulent conveyance when a person gives his home to his brother-in-law just before declaring bankruptcy.

It is also a fraudulent conveyance when a person takes on a liability—for less than adequate consideration, meaning "reasonably equivalent value" or fair market value (not the "peppercorn"-type consideration)—and is thereby rendered insolvent. So, if parents guarantee their son's home mortgage, and that causes the parents' liabilities to exceed their assets, the parents' own lenders could assert that giving the guarantee was a fraudulent conveyance. The guarantee could be set aside, leaving the son's mortgagee bank empty-handed. Again, if the parents were solvent when the guarantee was given, it should hold up as valid.

Can a person who owns several companies move assets from one that is about to go under to another company that will survive? Or to himself? Can he have a company he owns guarantee his personal debts? How would you advise a bank that is lending him money based on a guarantee from his business?

How about in the purely corporate context? Fraudulent conveyance could be invoked in any situation where a company has transferred assets or incurred liabilities without adequate (dollar-for-dollar) consideration—that is, unless after giving effect to the transfer or to the liabilities incurred the company is still solvent. For this purpose, what matters is the fair value of assets on the one hand and the amount of all liabilities on the other hand. A GAAP balance sheet is not a good measure of fair value solvency because assets are booked at their historical value and many liabilities, including potentially large contingent liabilities, are not listed. Instead, to ascertain solvency for this purpose a fair value appraisal of all assets and an estimation of all liabilities is required.

Declaring an extraordinary dividend that leaves the company without the wherewithal to pay its debts as they become due would be a fraudulent conveyance, and would leave the shareholders vulnerable to an action to require them to return the dividend. Could this, for example, apply to the spin-off of a profitable business while leaving behind a financially troubled company to cope with accumulated liabilities such as mass tort claims? Quite possibly.

What about dividends from a subsidiary to a parent company? What about the guarantee by a subsidiary of its parent company's debt? Or of a sister company's debt? Generally, these are all subject to possible fraudulent conveyance analysis. A guarantee by a parent of a subsidiary company's debt, however, does not generally raise fraudulent conveyance issues because the parent has received the benefit of the debt incurred (the loan proceeds) through its equity interest in the subsidiary, at least where the subsidiary is wholly owned.

Sometimes people will ask whether a guarantee fee (equal, say, to a comparable letter of credit fee) constitutes consideration for giving a guarantee that would otherwise be subject to a potential fraudulent conveyance challenge. Depending on the circumstances, the answer may be no, keeping in mind that consideration must be full consideration with a value equal to the obligation incurred.

Most significant in the leveraged buyout arena: Does the assumption by an acquired company of the debt incurred to finance its own purchase constitute a possible fraudulent conveyance, as a structural matter? The answer is, without a doubt, yes. The company is incurring an obligation for which it received no consideration. All consideration was received by its shareholders. The reason why leveraged buyouts nonetheless proceed is that the acquired company is solvent after giving effect to the debt—if not on the basis of its balance sheet before the transaction, then after giving effect to the write-up in asset value at the point of the acquisition. A "solvency certificate" is usually required at closing expressly to address the fraudulent conveyance issue.

§ 5:3   Preference

And can you spot a preference? Payments and other transfers of assets for the benefit of antecedent creditors within the preference period (ninety days) before bankruptcy can be recovered by the bankruptcy estate. Suppose your law firm renders a bill to a company on January 1, it pays on July 1, and it files bankruptcy on July 15. Is the payment subject to being required to be returned to the company's estate in bankruptcy as a preference? Yes.

Suppose you represent a bank group lending to a troubled company, with the full amount of the facility already drawn and outstanding. The company is in default under a couple of financial covenants, and its trade creditors (for example, vendors) are starting to require cash on delivery. The bank agent wants to require that as a condition to the banks' granting the covenant waiver the company must pledge stock of its subsidiaries, receivables and inventory, and other assets. Is this pledge of assets subject to a preference attack if the company goes into bankruptcy within the preference period? Yes. Should you advise they grant the waiver but not require the collateral? No, if the company gets past the preference period the security arrangements will hold up. Is it better to accelerate the loans and try to make the company pay the loans back instead? That too would be subject to preference attack. Will making the demand for payment or forcing repayment (for example, by setting off against all cash receipts as they come into the bank or by attaching assets) be more likely to force the company into bankruptcy? Quite possibly.

What if someone suggests that the bank loans be paid off by a second bank group, which takes collateral at the time its loans are made, so that the security will not be given for "antecedent" or pre-existing debt? This doesn't work. From the company's perspective, which is the relevant point of view, it is providing collateral to secure a previously outstanding debt. The interposition of a second bank group does not cure the problem, and the first bank group still has a preference risk.

If you are advising the company, and the company gave the collateral, what should you advise when you near the end of the preference period but a bankruptcy filing looks inevitable? You might advise filing before the preference period expires, depriving the banks of their secured position and entering the proceeding with as many unencumbered assets as possible. Or you might advise waiting because the banks are the key to your eventual successful reorganization and will require a secured position to give you financing after bankruptcy.

Suppose you get to a closing for a secured loan, but it is clear that not all the security is in place. The bankers want to go ahead and fund, and will require that the rest of the security be in place within thirty days. Will they be running a preference risk with respect to the security interests that are perfected post-closing? Yes, though hopefully the risk of a bankruptcy filing within the preference period is remote.

What about a credit facility or other extension of credit (for example, a swap agreement) that requires the posting of collateral upon the occurrence of certain conditions, such as a ratings downgrade? Will granting collateral under this arrangement be subject to preference attack? Yes. The fact that there was a covenant to provide collateral does not immunize the arrangement.

In the last two cases, the lenders are making choices that create preference risk, though it may be reasonable to do so. And indeed one can say that taking almost any payment in reduction of debt exposes the recipient to at least a theoretical preference risk. Preference risk is mostly academic outside of a troubled credit scenario, and in a troubled credit scenario it will almost always make sense for creditors to better their position—in a way that does not force immediate bankruptcy—and take the attendant preference risk. The strategic considerations for the troubled company may be more complex.

Where it is critical to avoid preference risk, the interposition of a letter of credit from the outset may be the answer. If bondholders purchase bonds with the benefit of a letter of credit, they really take free of issuer preference risk from the very beginning. Their risk of obligor bankruptcy has shifted from the issuer of the bonds over to the letter of credit issuing bank. If the letter of credit is put on later, however, they may have a preference risk for the preference period running from the letter of credit issue date.

The preference period is significantly longer (one year) if insiders are involved. Lawyers advising insiders need to be aware of this, and lawyers advising non-insiders where insider loans are in the picture should be aware of it as well.

Corporate finance lawyers need not be accomplished bankruptcy/workout lawyers but they do need to be able to spot and analyze bankruptcy-related structural risks, and, to the extent possible, address them. In particular, issue-spotting fraudulent conveyance and preference risks should become second nature. Even where risks cannot be fully mitigated, full discussion and disclosure is required. Experienced bankers, investors, and CFOs are fully versed in these issues and expect their lawyers to be as well.

It is also important to follow case law in the bankruptcy field, as developments there may affect not only your analysis and advice, but drafting. The Bankruptcy Code is perennially under review and is a contested space where competing interests argue for change, or for maintaining the status quo, as benefits their respective positions. Keep abreast of these developments.

Chapter 6

The Issuer and the Obligation: Recourse, Ranking, Rights, and Remedies

§ 6:1   Identify the Obligor

§ 6:1.1   *Who's on the Hook?*

Analyzing any debt, equity, or other corporate finance instrument or interest begins with figuring out the identity of the issuer or borrower (or contract counterparty), and, likewise, what other parties may be involved in the credit and, thus, part of the credit analysis. Except in some markets (such as asset-based lending), corporate finance transactions do not typically rely on joint-and-several borrowers or issuers (comparable to co-signers on a mortgage); instead, there is usually a single primary obligor. There may also be guarantors or other parties that are obligated to support the issuer or borrower's obligation, such as a third party providing a letter of credit, bond insurance, or even a surety bond. A liquidity facility, take-or-pay contracts, and other arrangements may also be relevant to the credit analysis. In each case, it is very important to identify the party with the contractual obligation.

§ 6:1.2   *What's in a Name?*

It is customary for deal lawyers to think of their clients in terms of the client corporate group, and not to worry too much about which entity in the group will ultimately be signing the documents. This is particularly true on the banking side of things. And where the use of single purpose or special purpose entities is common (for example, real estate or oil and gas), the precise vehicle for financing may not be identified until just before closing. However, it is absolutely essential, in the case of an issuer or obligor, that the correct legal entity be identified and its proper name appear on all of the documents. If a pledge of collateral is made by the borrower but the collateral to be pledged is owned by its sister company, then it is likely that the lenders will not end up with the security they were looking for. Putting the wrong counterparty name on a swap document could mean that your client will be owed money by an offshore shell instead of a creditworthy company with real assets. As noted in chapter 5, there is no rule that makes a corporate group generally liable for the debts of its various members; on the contrary, the rule is that debt contracted by one will not be an obligation of any other. Getting it nearly right isn't nearly good enough.

§ 6:1.3 What Type of Legal Entity?

Most of this book is written about corporations. The corporation has been the vehicle of choice for doing business because it offers equity investors the ability to participate in the success of a business venture with limited downside: They can only lose what they put in. This is the miracle of limited liability.

There are costs associated with this benefit, the principal one being that the corporation exists as a entity subject to income tax, so the investors get their return out of after-tax cash and then pay taxes on their dividends and capital gains. This is the so-called double taxation associated with being an investor in a corporation.

On the other hand, sole proprietorships and general partnerships leave their owners exposed to liability, theoretically without limit. Why would anyone do business in this fashion? To avoid paying income tax at the business level. Partnerships are common in real estate and oil and gas finance.

In the last twenty years or so, there has been an increase in the use of other borrowing and issuing entities that usually combine some features of limited liability, at least for most equity investors, with some of the tax benefits more associated with general partnerships. A prime example of this is the limited liability company, or LLC.

Suffice it to say, to work in corporate finance you MUST understand the legal structure of each obligor in order to understand how the particular financial instruments you may be working with fit into the overall picture of the obligor's financial obligations, their relative rank, and the cash flows, assets, and other parties (such as a general partner) to which the lenders or investors will have recourse. The fundamentals of this are defined by the state law under which the legal entity was formed and exists.

§ 6:1.4   *What Is Non-Recourse Financing?*

Unless otherwise agreed, a debt incurred by an entity is full re-course, which means that recourse may be had to all of the assets of the entity and to the assets of parties (such as general partners) who are, by law, also obligated with respect to the liabilities of the entity. However, a lender may agree that a debt is limited recourse to certain assets of the entity or that it will forgo recourse to the general partners of a general partnership.

A typical way to effectively limit recourse with respect to special projects or particular assets is to form a single purpose or special pur-pose entity to be the borrower (without recourse to the parent), which will be the project participant or owner of the asset. For exam-ple, to limit exposure to general partnerships or joint venture liabili-ties, companies may invest through single purpose or special purpose corporations. This structure insulates the parent company from lia-bilities incurred at the partnership or JV level.

§ 6:2   Debt or Equity or Something Else?

The right-hand side of a balance sheet is broken down into liabili-ties and stockholders' equity, or, roughly, between debt (money that is owed to others) and equity (the owners' interest, which, as an ac-counting matter, is what is left when liabilities are subtracted from as-sets). Debt is to be paid in accordance with its terms, regardless of how the company performs. Equity, on the other hand, does not enti-tle the owners to any specific return of what they have invested, but instead represents a share of the business.

In the case of debt, the holder is entitled to a return of the princi-pal and interest, and the failure to pay principal and interest when due is a breach of contract. In the case of common equity, the holder has voting and other rights associated with ownership, but no right to a return of the amount invested or the earnings of the company, ex-cept as determined by the board of directors from time to time or in a liquidation scenario, and then only subject to satisfying prior obliga-tions of the company, including debt. The holder of common equity has (literally) unlimited upside if the company performs well, but can lose everything if it fails. However, if capital has been fully paid up (in a corporation), then the common stockholder has no responsibility to make good any losses, and the worst the holder can do is to lose the investment.

Some investments or instruments have qualities of both debt and equity. For example, a convertible bond not only entitles the holder to payments of principal of and interest on a bond, but also the right to swap out the bond for stock. Preferred stock has a regular dividend that must be paid ahead of returns on common equity, and redeemable preferred stock has a redemption date on which holders expect to receive a return of their investment. Failure to make these payments on preferred stock does not generally result in contractual default, but will block common dividends and may entitle holders to, for example, appoint directors.

Derivatives and other financial contracts are designed to allocate risks, rights to payment, and attributes of ownership to investors in more complex ways. In project finance, venture capital, real estate, oil and gas, film finance, private equity, and other entrepreneurial settings investors may hold loans, partnership interests, preferred equity interests, points, carry and other types of profit participations, and may be subject to cash calls. These arrangements are typically the subject of intense negotiation and result in complex documentation providing for how money is to be invested in the venture and how cash flows will be shared out.

§ 6:3 Secured or Unsecured?

§ 6:3.1 *Benefits of Security*

When debt is secured the debtholder has (unless the debt is nonrecourse) a general claim on the company on a parity with all other unsecured debtholders. In addition, the debtholder has a specific claim on the assets of the company that constitute collateral for that debt. Secured debt enjoys special benefits in bankruptcy in that, vis-à-vis the proceeds or value of the collateral, the secured debtholders come ahead of other creditors of the company, and this priority may include post-petition interest (interest accrued on the debt after bankruptcy), whereas debt claims in bankruptcy do not generally include or accrue post-petition interest.

§ 6:3.2   *Terminology; Negative Pledges; Equitable or Constructive Liens*

Lawyers talk about the grant of security interests in U.C.C. (Uniform Commercial Code) collateral, the pledge of collateral, and, in particular, the pledge of stock, the mortgage of real property (including leasehold interests), chattel mortgages, or, in general, the granting of a lien. All of these refer to the creation of a security interest that is intended to provide for a preferential right to the lender under state or other applicable law and in bankruptcy.

A negative pledge, however, is a covenant not to create liens. It does not create a security interest or lien.

An equitable lien or constructive trust would be an equitable right to certain properties that may be found to exist due to the facts and circumstances, but is not a concept relied upon in corporate finance. Instead, it would generally be the case that companies and banks would want to avoid circumstances that give others the right to assert an equitable lien or constructive trust. For example, a lender would want to avoid having others assert that because the company violated an equal and ratable clause in granting the lender a lien, the debtholders having the benefit of that clause are entitled to share in the lien and the collateral.

§ 6:3.3   *Nothing Short of Perfection Will Do*

To attain secured status in bankruptcy, the particular security interest must be granted (created) and perfected under the relevant law. Other creditors and the debtor's estate may (and can be expected to) attack purported or intended security interests that have not been properly perfected.

Steps required to perfect a security interest are determined by type of collateral and jurisdiction, and the rules are complex. If in doubt about which of several methods is required to perfect a particular security interest, it is always better (to the extent possible) to comply with all of the rules that may apply, rather than to make a close legal judgment about which rules apply and, thus, which method of perfection should apply. For any collateral that is of material value, the opinion of local or foreign counsel versed in the applicable governing law should be obtained. Care must be used in the selection of agents when their services are to be used to assist in perfection, and post-closing check or audit of perfection may be warranted.

Failure to perfect a security interest is one of the most common mistakes by lawyers or their agents that cannot be attributed in any way to the actions or decisions of the principals or other parties, and it also can provide one of the more direct links between the alleged negligence of the lawyers and loss suffered by the intended secured creditors. In addition, the perfection of a security interest is one of the most tedious aspects of finance law practice, and execution tends to be delegated downward. Therefore, lawyer supervision and appropriate checks and cross-checks are especially important in this area.

§ 6:3.4   *Types of Collateral*

In the United States, collateral tends to fall broadly into the following categories:

- U.C.C. collateral, consisting of most types of personal property, including stocks and bonds; accounts receivable and general intangibles; and inventory, tools, and equipment not (generally) constituting fixtures (improvements and equipment attached to the ground and subject to the state real property law);

- real property, including fixtures, and oil, gas and mineral interests; and

- collateral to which special (usually federal) schemes apply, such as airplanes (Federal Aviation Administration rules apply), rolling stock, ships, and federal mineral leases.

There are also rights of set-off (the right of a bank to net amounts payable to a customer, not technically involving a lien because a bank deposit represents an obligation of the bank, not property belonging to the customer) and various statutory liens (mechanic's and materialmen's liens, landlord's liens, vendor's liens on inventory, and the like). In certain cases, analyzing the possible operation of these statutory liens is important to the credit and legal analysis.

Collateral owned by non-U.S. companies or located in non-U.S. jurisdictions should be analyzed and categorized under the applicable non-U.S. laws.

§ 6:3.5   *Which Rules Apply?*

Most rules of perfection are based on either the company's or the collateral's location. This simple statement begs the question of how to analyze situations where the company and its assets are located in multiple (especially if non-U.S.) jurisdictions. The U.C.C. provides answers in many fact patterns, but, of course, difficulties arise when competing jurisdictions apply different and inconsistent analyses.

Choice of law rules and method of perfection should be carefully reviewed on a belts and suspenders basis. For example, in the case of a stock pledge, possession may be the appropriate method of perfection in the jurisdiction of the borrower. But if the stock is of a company formed under the laws of a foreign jurisdiction, then notation on the books and records of the company in that jurisdiction might be required, and it is in that jurisdiction that a purported owner or person stepping into the shoes of the owner of the company would need to exercise remedies. It might even be that another creditor perfects or has perfected in that competing fashion and trumps the possessory interest. Likewise, notwithstanding the U.C.C.'s choice of law rule that would deem certain foreign companies to be located in the District of Columbia, you would not normally rely (solely) on that analysis, but instead would take appropriate steps under the relevant foreign law where the pledgor is a foreign corporation.

§ 6:3.6   *Need for Careful Review; Key Defined Terms*

Security documents often get short shrift in terms of senior lawyer review, which isn't really best practice from a risk-based perspective. The clients are not likely to be combing through these documents, and it is really up to the lawyers to get them right. In particular, the definitions of *secured debt* and of *collateral* bear close and repeated scrutiny, including peer review by a lawyer expert in the technicalities of the U.C.C. or other relevant terminology defining categories of collateral. Lawyers for the company and for the lenders need to be very careful, not only that these are correct for a particular tranche of debt but that they work together among all tranches of secured debt and are not inconsistent. If a bunch of standard form security agreements are used and not harmonized, you may find that different sets of lenders have conflicting claims to the same collateral. The handling of proceeds of collateral, as it is converted into different categories of collateral (for example, as inventory becomes receivables, and receivables become cash, and as cash becomes investments or deposit accounts), can be especially tricky.

§ 6:3.7 A Note on Stock Pledges

Subsidiary stock pledges granted by parent holding companies are a popular form of security on a number of grounds. They, of course, advantage the pledgees vis-à-vis unsecured creditors of the parent holding company, and they tend to be quick and easy to perfect, under relatively short and simple documents—perfection usually being by delivery of the stock certificates (together with the related stock powers) to be held in custody, perhaps with a U.C.C. filing as well. Loans or notes that have a benefit of a stock pledge are indeed "secured" and can be syndicated or sold as such.

But there are some major downsides to reliance on stock pledges. Of most significance, the pledgees are structurally subordinated to all debt and other obligations of the pledged subsidiaries, and in some holding company structures stock pledges by the parent have turned out to be essentially worthless. A second far more mundane issue is that, where perfection is by possession, it is critical for the secured party to keep the stock certificates in safekeeping and be able to produce them to evidence perfection. Lawyers should not hold pledged stock certificates for their clients, and definitely should not hold them in commingled files of closing documents. Stock pledges for the benefit of public bondholders may trigger reporting requirements for the pledged companies. Lastly, as noted above, it is important to make sure that appropriate steps are taken to perfect under the laws of all relevant jurisdictions.

§ 6:3.8 What About Proceeds?

What happens when one type of collateral becomes a different type of collateral, for example, inventory is sold, resulting in an account receivable, which is then liquidated into cash, which, in turn, is then invested in, say, marketable securities? In most cases, security interests should extend to the proceeds of collateral (that is, what is realized upon sale or other liquidation of the collateral). Perfection extends to proceeds to the extent included in the definition of collateral and then further to the extent that perfection is followed through into the proceeds. At some point, the secured lender will no longer be able to assert an interest in proceeds that have been commingled, and invested in other assets.

Can there be competing claims to proceeds? Yes, and, as noted above, it is very important for the lawyers to carefully scrutinize the definitions of collateral granted to different secured lenders.

§ 6:3.9   *Preference Risk*

The grant of security to pre-existing lenders can constitute a preference if it occurs ninety days before a bankruptcy filing (one year for insiders) and is not given for new value. New value really means new value—for example, new loans made, not rolling over existing loans or forbearing to call a default and accelerate. Preference risk cannot be eliminated with new borrowings used to pay off the existing borrowings; the old lenders are still subject to preference risk if they are paid down. While preference risk is a significant consideration for lenders who are contemplating taking security in a troubled credit situation, the rule is that it is better to try to get secured (as fast as possible, of course) than to pass up the opportunity, even though the company may file before the preference period is over.

§ 6:3.10   *In a Troubled Credit Situation*

In a troubled credit scenario, secured lenders are well-advised to audit the collateral and the security interests. Obvious defects should be cured as soon as possible, though a preference risk will run from the point of cure (perfection).

When lenders are unsecured, the granting of security interests is a major issue and bargaining chip. Lenders who are in a position to control liquidity, because they have near-term maturities on their debt or are backstopping near-term maturities, will typically seek to become secured as soon as possible, and by as much collateral as possible. The speed at which liens can be granted and perfected is important.

It is a very big deal for a company to grant one group of lenders a lien on most of its assets. It is likely to mean that all of its ordinary course and miscellaneous counterparties—vendors, letter of credit providers, and hedge counterparties—will also start to demand collateral to do business. Becoming a secured borrower thus has significant operational ramifications that must be considered and provided for. In addition, the company's management has to consider what a possible bankruptcy reorganization will look like if it has hocked its most liquid and valuable assets. It may be, particularly in a liquidity crisis, that it isn't feasible to work through all of these issues quickly enough, or that management decides it is losing too much maneuvering room in a likely subsequent filing, and that it is the better course to seek bankruptcy protection. There are other cases where companies go right to the brink, pledge most of their assets and, after a rough patch, recover and move on.

§ 6:3.11 Roles of Collateral Trustee, Custodian, or Servicer

The role of a collateral trustee (a bank or other financial institution) or custodian is to take effective custody of the collateral on behalf of the secured lenders or debtholders. This role is expected to be principally administrative in that the trustee or custodian does not make credit-related or enforcement decisions; but in the case of some types of collateral the role can be quite significant as an operational matter, involving the management of physical and electronic files pertaining to assets such as loans, purchases and sales of securities, and valuations of mark-to-market-type collateral. Where collateral is in the nature of accounts receivable or loans, there may be servicing, or at least back-up servicing, arrangements. Collateral trustees and similar agents play key roles in securitizations, where the "issuer" is a special purpose vehicle whose only assets consist of collateral (the assets being securitized).

§ 6:3.12 Sharing Collateral

When lenders share collateral they need to agree on how they will act on a collective basis to make decisions and exercise the various rights of a secured creditor. A lead bank agent, trustee, or collateral trustee will typically act for the group based on the instructions of a majority. It may be the case that a percentage lower than 50% can trigger or initiate enforcement, but at the point where an action is to be taken or not taken majority control is required so that the representative is not at risk of receiving inconsistent instructions.

The amount of debt for voting purposes in this as in other contexts should include outstanding loan and letter of credit commitments, as well as agreed-upon amounts with respect to hedging arrangements.

There is one exception to a general rule of majority voting control, which is where certain categories of the secured debt are included on a tag-along or silent basis, pursuant to an equal and ratable clause[1] or a second lien position.[2] This passive aspect of the tag-along lenders can continue even up to the point of the release of collateral for sale where the proceeds are paid directly over to the lead lenders to the exclusion of the tag-along lenders. The way this would work is that the lead lenders release the collateral for sale (with no security interest in the proceeds) and, thus, they and the tag-along lenders are unsecured for a moment in time. Directly afterwards, the proceeds of sale are used to pay down the lead lenders but not the tag-along lenders. In a troubled credit situation this course of action is not without risk of, on the one hand, a preference attack as the lead lenders were momentarily unsecured and, on the other, a claim for sharing from the tag-along lenders, depending of course on the facts and circumstances.

§ 6:3.13　*Consistency with Debt Agreements; Release of Collateral*

It is quite important that security documents be entirely consistent with the principal debt agreements. Except for provisions particular to the security interest itself, they should not contain covenants, events of default, or other provisions of general applicability, but instead cross-reference to the principal debt agreements, as amended from time to time. One important practical reason for this is that the security documents receive relatively little attention during negotiations and are rarely referenced after closing. Lawyers should make

---

1.　*See* chapter 12.
2.　*See* section 6:4.9.

sure their standard forms, as well as security documents produced by local or foreign counsel, do not contain these sorts of substantive or, worse, inconsistent provisions.

A particular concern is that releases of collateral that are permitted under the principal debt documents (for example, for a permitted asset sale) should be clearly permissible under the security agreements. If a bank group has agreed that certain assets may be sold or if they grant a covenant waiver by majority vote to permit the sale of an asset, it is at the least highly embarrassing to have to go to the banks for a separate unanimous consent because the security agreement states that release of collateral requires the consent of all secured parties.

§ 6:4 Senior or Subordinated?

§ 6:4.1 Subordination Is Contractual, Not an Absolute Priority

There are three types of subordination: contractual, structural, and equitable. In all cases the meaning or effect of subordination is that when debtholders line up to be paid, the debt that is subordinated is behind senior debt or senior claims. When people talk about "subordination," without an adjective, they are talking about contractual subordination. When they are talking about structural subordination, they will refer to "structural subordination." Structural subordination is a function of how claims are positioned (at what level) in the corporate structure.[3] Equitable subordination is a doctrine in bankruptcy to the effect that a claim should be subordinated relative to other claims because of the actions of the holder.

This section is about contractual subordination. While the bankruptcy rules of recovery distinguish between equity and other types of claims, and between secured claims and unsecured claims, subordination is a matter of contract. It does not reflect a rule of absolute priority recognized by the Bankruptcy Code.

---

3. *See* chapter 7.

The contractual provisions defining the terms of subordination are contained in the subordinated debt instrument binding the issuer of the debt, but the contract runs from the subordinated debtholders to the senior debtholders, who are third-party beneficiaries and rely on the subordination provisions. As is the general rule under contract law, the provisions cannot be amended to the detriment of senior debtholders who have relied without their consent; the terms of senior debt on the other hand may generally be amended without limitation.

Holders of debt or other claims that are neither senior (as defined) nor subordinated are unaffected by the subordination provisions.

As is expected, subordinated debt generally carries a lower credit rating and higher interest rate than senior debt.

§ 6:4.2   The Payover Provision; Obligations of the Issuer Unaffected

The heart of a set of subordination terms is the payover provision, which says, literally, that what the subordinated debtholder receives in bankruptcy or a similar proceeding it will pay over to the senior debtholder until the senior debtholder has been made whole. There is usually an exception, where subordinated debtholders receive new debt instruments that preserve the quality of subordination vis-à-vis senior debtholders. If there is a payover, the subordinated debtholders are subrogated to the rights of the holders of the senior debt.

That the subordination is an intercreditor agreement only is made clear and emphasized by standard provisions to the effect that the subordination provisions do not affect the obligations between the issuer and the holders of the subordinated debt. In other words, the issuer cannot use the subordination provisions as an excuse not to pay the subordinated debt or to fail to perform its other obligations under the subordinated debt instrument. This provision is critical in defining the reality of the relations between senior and subordinated debtholders. While the subordinated debtholders may not have much leverage over the holders of senior debt, they continue to hold significant rights against and leverage over the issuer.

In the high-yield market, subordination provisions themselves are highly standardized. What is not standardized is how subordinated debt interacts with senior debt, and the exercise of subordinated debtholder rights vis-à-vis the issuer. As one cynical observer stated, "The game in the subordinated debt world is to agree to be subordinated and then claw your way back to pari passu status with the senior debt." So while the subordination provisions in a subordinated debt indenture seem to put the subordinated debtholders in a disadvantaged position, they are far from toothless because the rest of the indenture is full of provisions binding the issuer and giving rights to the subordinated debtholders. Even in the bankruptcy context, where the terms of the payover provisions have direct application, it is often the case that a negotiated outcome in bankruptcy will result in some percentage recovery to subordinated debt even when senior debt has not received 100 cents on the dollar.

§ 6:4.3   *Definition of Senior Debt; Tiers of Subordinated Debt*

This brings us to a second key element of the subordination provisions: the definition of Senior Debt. As we've noted, subordinated debtholders are not agreeing to come in the bankruptcy priority ranking somewhere between unsubordinated debt and preferred equity. Ordinary trade creditors (for example, a vendor of office supplies) are generally not entitled to payover from subordinated debtholders. Instead, subordinated debtholders are making a contract specifically with the holders of Senior Debt, as defined.

The terms of subordinated debt may contemplate other debt that is pari passu with it (subordinated to the same Senior Debt, and under the same terms of subordination), debt that is subordinated to it, or specific debt that is senior to it but still subordinated. When subordinated debt is tiered in this way, the top tier will be referred to as Senior Subordinated Debt and the lower tier Junior Subordinated Debt.

The definition of Senior Debt can contain a number of traps that those aspiring to senior debt status must successfully run. Note that it is to the issuer's benefit to be able to offer lenders senior debt status, so the issuer has a keen interest in the scope and clarity of the Senior Debt definition.

Issues can arise with respect to refinancings. How are revolving credit facilities handled? Can a single facility be refinanced in multiple facilities? Can a new financing be covered as a refinancing under several different clauses of the Senior Debt definition? What if there is a time gap between the old financing and the new one? In that case, could the new financing qualify as a "replacement" of the old one?

Another question might come up when there is a qualification that Senior Debt will not include debt incurred in violation of the indenture. This puts great pressure on the non-contravention representation and opinion—the representation by the company that the new debt does not violate any terms of any contracts binding on it and the opinion of counsel to the same effect. In some cases this will turn upon the question of compliance with a coverage ratio. What would be the result if it were discovered after the fact that the debt incurrence violated the indenture because there was an error in the coverage ratio calculation? There should *not* be a condition to the effect that debt incurred during an event of default or incipient event of default is disqualified as Senior Debt. Any qualifications that are not within the knowledge and control of senior debtholders should probably be stated in such a way that they are entitled to rely definitively on company certificates to the relevant effect.

§ 6:4.4   *The Credit Agreement Debt*

In the typical LBO or other leveraged credit situation, the issuer's main bank facility at the time of issuance of the subordinated debt and successor credit facilities are intended to fall within the definition of Senior Debt without question and are usually defined as the Credit Agreement. The Credit Agreement will be covered under the definition of Designated Senior Debt (see below) and lenders party to the Credit Agreement may have certain other special rights, for example, to provide hedging contracts on a senior debt basis. The lenders to the original Credit Agreement and the company should make sure that the defined term is sufficiently well crafted to enable the company to afford its principal bank lenders, including lenders under a successor credit facility, senior status as Credit Agreement lenders. To consider:

- Is the revolving part of bank debt clearly covered regardless of what is outstanding on the date of issue? Can the revolving facility be increased?

- Can the Credit Agreement amount be increased? Is it forced into a reducing mode by the definition so that if term loans are paid down or revolving commitments reduced the debt capacity is lost for all time?

• Is trade financing provided by the bank group (for example, in the form of letters of credit) covered, notwithstanding any exclusion of trade creditors generally?

• How well are refinancings covered? What is the ability to split or increase the bank facility? To go with new lenders? Could the "Credit Agreement" include a senior note indenture? What about a gap in time in terms of what is actually outstanding?

• What about financing that the bank lenders may provide in the form of interest rate hedging or other derivatives?

§ 6:4.5   *Designated Senior Debt, Payment Blockage and Delay on Acceleration*

In the leveraged acquisition market, Designated Senior Debt, consisting of debt under the Credit Agreement and other senior debt above a threshold level and granted the status by the issuer, has privileges in the form of payment blockage provisions and advance notice of acceleration of the subordinated debt. Payment will be blocked on the subordinated debt during an actual payment default (past any grace period) on Designated Senior Debt or for a period of time (typically up to 179 days) after receiving a Payment Blockage Notice from the representatives of the Designated Senior Debt (based on a default other than payment default). A Payment Blockage Notice can be given only periodically (typically, once every 360 days), so it is not the case that holders of Designated Senior Debt can put the subordinated debt into extended abeyance. Furthermore, subordinated debtholders can still exercise their rights to accelerate their debt, a gun at the head of the Designated Senior Debt as well as the issuer—although they have to give advance notice to the holders of Designated Senior Debt (or to the lenders under the Credit Agreement) presumably allowing them to accelerate first.

The payment blockage provisions are of some use in bringing subordinated debtholders to the table with representatives of Designated Senior Debt before money goes out the door to the subordinated debt, but what happens at the table is far from pre-ordained in favor of the senior debtholders. In many cases the subordinated debthold-ers, who may have purchased debt in the distressed debt market and be purely interested in a short-term return, have significant effective leverage over not only the issuer but also over holders of senior debt, who may be banks with relationships with the issuer or lenders who have significant credit exposures and, perhaps, revolving credit com-mitments.

§ 6:4.6   Anti-Layering

Generally, holders of senior subordinated debt are not keen to per-mit layers of debt between their debt and Senior Debt as defined. They have signed up to an agreed position in the debt structure and want to retain it. And if non-pari passu lenders are paying over to the holders of Senior Debt, subrogation rights will have to be shared. This concern is usually covered by a covenant called an anti-layering provi-sion. (More junior subordinated debtholders may also be interested in preserving their agreed rank, whatever it is.) Also note that "Senior Debt" will not include debt subordinated to any other debt. An un-controlled proliferation of subordination provisions "above" the sub-ordinated lender could obligate it to "pay over" to another debtholder that is, in turn, required to pay over to a third. It would be like guar-anteeing to fill up a sink that is draining from the bottom.

§ 6:4.7   Terms That Can Frustrate Subordination

Typical payover provisions by no means create preferred status for Senior Debt akin to the preferred status that debt has to (perpetual) equity. Subordinated debt is not a permanent part of the capital structure, providing a cushion for Senior Debt. In fact, the simplest way subordinated debt can trump Senior Debt is through maturity date. No matter how deeply subordinated, debt that is due next year is "ahead" of debt that is due the following year, and doesn't provide lower tier capitalization beneath senior debtholders.

Senior debtholders thus have a keen interest in the terms of subor-dinated debt and should approve them initially and have a veto over changes. Other terms that can distort the intended effect of subordi-nation provisions (senior debtholders to be paid out first) are covenants and events of default—events that require or could require mandatory repayment. For example, debt issued under a subordinated debt indenture containing a change of control provision requiring an offer to purchase upon a change in control may effectively "come ahead" of senior investment grade-style notes of the same issuer without that protection. Though there is a lot of standardization in the basic terms of subordination, there is enough play in the definitions of Senior Debt and in the rest of the terms of the indenture, the covenants particularly, for aggressive lawyers to win valuable points off their less diligent and vigilant, or more trusting, counterparts, at the drafting stage and thereafter.

§ 6:4.8 Guarantees of Subordinated Debt

Again, the expectations of senior debtholders can be frustrated if the theme of subordination is not carried through consistently in guarantees and other credit support. If subordinated debt has the benefit of guarantees or other third-party credit support, there should be like guarantees or credit support provided to the holders of Senior Debt, and the subordinated guarantees or credit support must contain subordination provisions that mirror those in the debt instrument between the issuer and the subordinated debtholders. Put another way, the senior-subordinated relationship only makes sense when both Senior Debt and subordinated debt are obligations of the same company.

§ 6:4.9 When Subordinated Debt Is Secured; Second Lien Debt

Things become even more complex in those rare instances where subordinated debtholders have the benefit of security. The fact that holders of subordinated debt could ever be secured emphasizes that subordination is a contract between two groups of creditors, not a rank or tier in the capital structure. Subordinated debtholders who are secured will fare better in bankruptcy than unsecured creditors, if the security has value sufficient to cover their claim.

Much more common is the grant of a second lien on collateral to lenders whose debt is not subordinated to the debt of the first lien holders. In fact this arrangement is sometimes made to create an additional tier of debt, and more debt capacity, without violating an anti-layering covenant, which usually addresses subordination "in right of payment" only.

Second lien term loans in bank facilities are generally placed with non-traditional investors such as hedge funds. Compared to standard term loan facilities, they may contain more relaxed covenants, higher pricing and some limited call protection. Second lien notes approach the same market from the direction of the high-yield bond market, and tend to be slightly more "silent" than the second lien term loans. When second lien debt is in the picture, the company may lose some financial flexibility, as second lien debtholders are naturally keen to limit the amount of first lien debt.

Where subordinated debt is secured (unusual in the U.S.) or there is second lien debt, the relationships of the secured parties would typically be the subject of an intercreditor agreement, as the terms are quite technical and do not concern the company to any great degree (except where there is a concern about not running afoul of an anti-layering covenant). In either case, it is a principal concern of the senior lenders that they remain in the driver's seat in terms of any exercise of rights with respect to collateral.

Secured creditors in large U.S. corporate credits (excluding, for example, real estate mortgages, margin loans and other asset-based financings including securtizations) rarely actually exercise rights against collateral; instead the company will seek the protection of the bankruptcy courts and creditors will be stayed, with their relative rights determined in the outcome of the bankruptcy proceedings. However, once again, the issue is leverage. It would be an unfortunate outcome, from the perspective of both senior lenders and the company, if subordinated debtholders or second lien holders had the right not only to accelerate their debt but to attach company assets and, thus, plunge the company into crisis. Thus, the enforcement rights granted in these circumstances generally let the senior or first lien debt control the collateral and the exercise of remedies. Though holders of senior debt will be at pains to deny it, there are probably limits on their ability to disregard the interests of the subordinated debtholders or second lien holders entirely. For example, a senior debtholder who ran a "fire sale" of the collateral to ensure a fast, full payout without regard to obtaining a fair price for collateral, leaving nothing for the holders of subordinated secured debt or second lien debt, might expect to be challenged. These are issues comparable to those reviewed in connection with "equal and ratable" security arrangements.[4]

What are the key elements defining the relationship of the senior secured debtholders and subordinated secured debtholders, or of the first and second lien holders?

The mechanics of the intercreditor arrangements are typically handled through designated representatives of the two groups.

First priority lien holders often have a right to release collateral for permitted sales of assets or otherwise. They might require, or the company's debt instruments might require, that the asset sale proceeds in such cases are used either to reduce senior debt (it may be the intention of subordinated or second lien debtholders that such reduction be a permanent reduction in senior debt or senior lien capacity) or to reinvest in other earning assets. They also control insurance and condemnation proceedings affecting collateral.

Generally, the first lien holders have the exclusive right to control enforcement until they have been paid in full (including provision for contingent obligations such as with respect to letters of credit), with no risk that payment will have to be returned, at which point the second lien holders take over. Until the first lien holders have been paid in full, the second lien holders are in a standstill position. Proceeds will of course go first to first lien holders until they are paid in full (as defined).

The controlling position of the first lien holders is preserved in bankruptcy with a set of agreements and waivers to that effect running to the benefit of the first lien holders.

Thus, before bankruptcy and in bankruptcy the second lien holders are in a tag-along, "silent," or at least "quiet," position on most issues. There are only a few exceptions to this passive position. They are permitted to file claims in bankruptcy, and it may be that they are to be treated as a separate voting class in bankruptcy for purposes of approving a plan of reorganization.

The intercreditor terms specifically override any countervailing facts or issues, and, thus, apply to any judgment liens that the holders

---

4. See chapter 12 and *supra* section 6:3.12.

of the second lien position may obtain. If second lien holders have collateral that the first lien holders do not have, the intercreditor terms nonetheless should apply. Faults and failures of perfection and the like are also overridden.

The relationship within the security documents is defined to be strictly a matter of lien subordination, not payment subordination. The lien subordination does not affect the company's obligations, or the lenders' rights vis-à-vis the company. Notwithstanding this nice analytical point: it is certainly the far better practice, where subordinated debt is being secured, if senior and subordinated debt are defined consistently in the subordination terms and the intercreditor terms relating to the collateral. This eliminates awkward governance issues, including concerns about violation of the anti-layering provision as well as the difficulties that would arise if Designated Senior Debt (referred to above) ended up holding a second lien position. Therefore, the same issues and concerns about defining the scope of Senior Debt apply to the senior lien position, for example, assuring that refinancing may come within scope, or covering letter of credit and hedging obligations that the company may owe (typically to the senior debt/senior lien lenders). If the subordination and security arrangements are not carefully dovetailed, confusion reigns.

§ 6:4.10   What Conclusions Can Be Drawn?

The chances that the literal terms of subordination provisions will be implemented (for example, in a payover) are small. Negotiated outcomes, including in bankruptcy, are the rule. However, it is critically important to get the terms right. They set the ground rules for the negotiated outcomes. Lawyers who do not provide their clients with the "market" rights and positions will have some explaining to do.

The fact that the subordinated debt is "subordinated" should provide only measured comfort to holders of Senior Debt. If the subordinated indenture is, as is normally the case in the high-yield market, chock-a-block with covenants, even if they are of the "incurrence" variety,[5] subordinated debtholders, particularly those who have purchased significantly under par in the distressed debt market, can find

---

5.   *See* section 10:7.2.

points of "leverage" in unexpected and likely unintended places. "Subordinated" though it may be, it is still debt and it has covenants that can bite.

Chapter 7

Beyond the Issuer: Corporate Structure Issues

§ 7:1   Structural Subordination

§ 7:1.1   *Structural Subordination*

Most businesses of any size operate through a group of affiliated entities. This can be for tax, accounting, legal, historical, or business reasons. Regardless, it is absolutely key in corporate finance to identify the exact legal entity that is the borrower, issuer, or other obligor with respect to the loan, security, or other obligation. It is also nearly always relevant to understand the rest of the company's corporate family—which entities own the assets and generate the cash, which entities have what obligations, and how money moves around the group.

Many companies that are in the leveraged acquisition mode, including companies owned by private equity houses, are financed through multiple-level capital-raising exercises. There may be several tiers of holding companies above even the top holding company in the operating group structure to address various equity, management, and tax considerations, and typically the equity is issued at one of those levels. It is also possible that subordinated debt will be issued at a level above the senior debt. In other words, a multi-tier structure can position the debt, or at least the senior debt, truly "closer to the assets" and structurally senior. Holders of debt and preferred stock of a subsidiary will recover out of the assets of the subsidiary ahead of the creditors of the parent company, whose claim on those assets is derivative through the parent company as holder of the subsidiary's common equity.

The effect of the separateness of corporations in an affiliated corporate group on the relative recoveries of the creditors at different levels results in what is called *structural subordination*: The parent company creditors are structurally subordinated to the claims of subsidiary creditors as to the assets of the subsidiary, and the subsidiary creditors are structurally senior, as to those assets, to the parent company creditors. (Borrowing at the holding company where proceeds are downstreamed as equity to subsidiaries is sometimes referred to as creating "double leverage." The parent company debt can in effect create borrowing capacity (against equity) at the subsidiary level.)

Supposing a lender or investor is satisfied with the assets, cash generating capability, and liability profile of its obligor, it is obviously important to ensure, insofar as this is possible through contract, that the assets and cash flows stay within that company, to limit the claims of others to those assets and cash flows, and especially to limit the claims that might be interposed between (be effectively senior to) those assets and cash flows and the claims of the lender or investor.

In this respect, the way that most large businesses are organized—with a top level holding company and a group of subsidiaries—presents a challenge. On the one hand, the value contained in subsidiaries is presumptively of benefit to the parent, and it is generally agreed that it is fine for companies to form and invest in subsidiaries. The result is likely to be that assets and cash-generating activities may be located in one or more operating subsidiaries, whereas capital-raising activities—unless specific to an asset, such as a mortgage—usually occur at the top level, in the holding company. Furthermore, cash is often moved around the group through intercompany loans or equity investments in order to make the best use of group cash resources. Why should a subsidiary borrow overnight from banks when the parent company or other group companies are sitting with cash? Consolidated cash management makes sense and is efficient, but when the parent company acts as the intragroup banker but has no assets other than claims on its subsidiaries, it can leave parent holding company lenders in a weak position:

- Creditors of subsidiaries, which includes lenders but could also include judgment creditors and other claimants, have a prior claim on the assets of those subsidiaries ahead of the claims of the corporate parent.

- If a subsidiary has issued preferred stock to a third party, that third party will also recover ahead of the parent as common equity holder.

- If a subsidiary is partly owned by a third party, what is left over after the debts and other liabilities and any preferred stock of the subsidiary have been paid in full will be shared ratably by the corporate parent and that third party.

- Even in a wholly owned corporate family that is debt-free at the subsidiary level, certain statutory obligations *of the group* can attach to each corporate entity separately, *on a joint and several basis.*

In sum, there are many potential barriers between lenders to a parent holding company and the assets of its subsidiaries.

§ 7:1.2 *Pledge of Intercompany Loans; Upstream Guarantees*

However, couldn't the parent lend money to its subsidiary and thus itself become a creditor of the subsidiary and pledge the intercompany loans to the parent company lenders? Or can't the subsidiaries guarantee the debt of the parent company? After all, in many cases the subsidiaries do reap the benefit of the parent company borrowings. But not so fast:

- In bankruptcy, loans made by a controlling shareholder, such as a corporate parent, are at risk of recharacterization as equity or quasi-equity under the doctrine of equitable subordination. There is also a longer preference period for insiders.

- Subsidiary guarantees of parent company debt (called "upstream guarantees") and sister company guarantees are subject to challenge as fraudulent conveyances, because it can be argued that the guarantor took on an obligation without receiving a commensurate asset or benefit.

Regardless of the limitations of subsidiary guarantees as a way to "get close to the assets," they are customary in highly leveraged transactions. There is no real downside to having them in place and they can be sustained in the face of a fraudulent conveyance challenge to the extent the guarantor did in fact receive the benefit of the financing, or was solvent after giving effect to the guarantee. Upstream and sister guarantees sometimes contain fraudulent conveyance savings clauses to anticipate the issue. In a deal with subsidiary guarantees the formation or acquisition of new subsidiaries, or the transfer of a material amount of assets into a subsidiary, should trip the requirement for new guarantees.

If there are no subsidiary guarantees in place, it makes no sense to talk about debt at the subsidiary level being "subordinated" to the parent company debt. Remember that subordination is a contractual relationship between lenders and debtholders of the same company. Even subordinated debt of a subsidiary is structurally senior to debt at the parent company level. To carry the concept of subordination through to the subsidiary level, the subsidiaries have to incur, or provide guarantees of, both the senior debt and the subordinated debt.

§ 7:1.3   *Stock and Debt of Subsidiaries*

Ideally, a lender to a parent company would prefer all debt of the group to be only at the parent level and, likewise, to prohibit the issuance of stock, common or preferred, by subsidiaries to third parties. Both subsidiary debt and subsidiary stock held by outsiders are structurally senior on an ongoing basis to the parent's debt to the lender as far as the assets of the subsidiaries are concerned. And while the parent company effectively controls the assets of majority-owned subsidiaries, a parent company lender would nonetheless prefer that all subsidiaries be wholly owned in order to avoid any dilution of the parent's interest in subsidiary assets: Dividends paid by the subsidiary and any proceeds allocated to stock of the subsidiary in a sale or liquidation will have to be shared with other stockholders if there are any.

The company, on the other hand, would like to maintain as much flexibility as possible with respect to its subsidiaries and their financial needs, and would prefer its debt agreements to permit the subsidiaries to finance themselves by way of parent investments, minority stock interests, preferred stock, and third-party debt all without limitation. Inevitably, some middle ground is reached but the global resolution of this set of issues must be reflected across a number of covenants and other provisions within a typical debt agreement. The deal agreed on about the borrower's corporate structure is embodied in, and should be treated consistently across, many provisions of the agreement.

§ 7:2 Subsidiaries—Presumptively Within the Credit Group

§ 7:2.1 *Wholly Owned Versus Non-Wholly Owned Subsidiaries; Preferred Stock*

At this point, it should be apparent that debtholders of a parent company are much less likely to be worried about wholly owned subsidiaries than those subsidiaries where a minority interest or preferred stock is held by third parties. In the case of non-wholly owned subsidiaries, the parent company's interests in the assets and earnings of the subsidiary are diluted by the minority interest, and upstreaming to equity interests will have to be shared.

In the leveraged debt market, preferred stock, particularly preferred stock of subsidiaries, may be treated as debt. Not only does preferred stock represent a call on the equity of the subsidiary ahead of the parent company's common interests, failure to stay current on preferred dividends will block dividends on the common equity and may give preferred stockholders board representation. It is therefore quite likely the subsidiary will keep current on preferred stock dividends, so they are most properly treated as an interest-like charge or fixed charge that must be serviced. A comparable analysis applies, of course, to any redemption terms of redeemable preferred stock.

These are the reasons that debt agreements will give more lenient treatment to wholly owned (as opposed to non-wholly owned) subsidiaries, and will discourage preferred stock at the subsidiary level.

§ 7:2.2   *Restricted Versus Unrestricted Subsidiaries*

Often a debt agreement defines a relevant subset of subsidiaries as being within the credit group for credit analysis and thus covenant purposes. These are called "restricted subsidiaries." For some purposes, the relevant group may be more narrowly limited to the parent and "wholly owned restricted subsidiaries" or "domestic restricted subsidiaries."

Restricted subsidiaries are subject to the covenant structure, but dealings within the group consisting of the parent and restricted subsidiaries (or wholly owned or domestic restricted subsidiaries) may be freely permitted. That is, it may be the case that assets can be transferred and mergers can occur; investments, both debt and equity, can be made; and transactions will not have to be on an arm's-length basis, provided all these things are happening within the restricted group. Tests run on a consolidated basis, such as a restriction regarding the borrower's line of business or a sale of a substantial part of the assets, would normally apply to the restricted group taken as a whole. Covenants in leveraged bank deals routinely distinguish between investments in transactions with guarantors (which are unlimited) and non-guarantor restricted subsidiaries.

On the other hand, "unrestricted subsidiaries" are just like strangers to the credit. They are not subject to the covenants, by and large, but the price paid for their freedom includes limitations on investments in them and other dealings with them, and their exclusion from the consolidated group for purposes of financial covenant compliance. The latter point means that the earnings of unrestricted subsidiaries would be (1) taken into account (a) on the "equity basis" of accounting or (b) only to the extent actually remitted to the parent, or (2) excluded altogether. In the drafting, it is important to make it clear which of these is intended.

§ 7:2.3   *U.S. Versus Non-U.S. Subsidiaries*

In a leveraged financing for a U.S.-domiciled borrower or issuer, it is customary to distinguish between U.S. subsidiaries and non-U.S. subsidiaries. Be careful to define them so that they are mutually exclusive (do not overlap) and together cover all subsidiaries (no "undistributed middle"). Why would foreign subsidiaries merit special treatment?

- The guarantee or pledge by a non-U.S. subsidiary in support of a U.S. parent company's debt, or the pledge of all of its stock, can have adverse tax consequences.

- For commercial or tax reasons foreign subsidiaries may need to self-finance abroad. They have cash management needs, such as payroll, that are wholly local in nature.

- Local laws may require, or local business realities may compel, local equity participation, which might even be, at least nominally, majority equity ownership by locals.

- International tax planning is often the most critical determinant of how non-U.S. operations of a multinational are structured and financed. In particular, there may be significant costs associated with repatriation of earnings.

- Even if the foreign subsidiaries or their assets may be pledged, security interests in foreign stock and assets may be cumbersome and costly, and enforcement in the foreign jurisdiction may be difficult.

For all of these reasons it may be appropriate to make a box around a company's foreign operations, to some extent isolating them from the parent credit and the parent credit from them, leaving them mostly free to go about their business. In other cases (large, multi-facility bank credit agreements for major multinationals), certain non-U.S. subsidiaries are specifically accommodated under the credit facility as separate borrowers; the credit analysis here is usually that a parent guarantee covers all borrowings, and there are sufficient banks in the group willing to extend credit in the relevant foreign country and currency.

§ 7:2.4   *Material or Significant Subsidiaries*

Another category of subsidiary that is sometimes established is that of "material" or "significant" subsidiary. This concept usually defines as material or significant those subsidiaries accounting for more than say 5% or 10% of group assets or revenues, and might be used in cross-default or bankruptcy default clauses. In this way, adverse credit events affecting immaterial subsidiaries become "non-events" so far as the parent company debt is concerned. Sometimes, the defined term incorporates the test from the definition of "significant subsidiary" from the SEC's Regulation S-X. However, be careful about definitions that run off a percentage of consolidated income. In a down or loss year, small subsidiaries may become "material" or "significant."

§ 7:2.5   *Single-Purpose or Special-Purpose Subsidiaries*

Companies sometimes create single-purpose or special-purpose subsidiaries (or other vehicles) for financing or business reasons. The purpose of such structures is to isolate the credit of the subsidiary from the parent or the parent from the debts and other obligations of the subsidiary.

- For example, a company may establish a bankruptcy-remote subsidiary for purposes of a receivables financing. In this case, the subsidiary can finance the receivables of the group on more favorable terms because it is set up under safeguards that are intended to keep it separate from a bankruptcy affecting the parent and protect it from most of the general liabilities associated with the ongoing business of the parent.

- In other cases, the parent wants to avoid the responsibility for the debt and other obligations incurred in a project financing or joint venture, and it establishes a special-purpose subsidiary through which it will own its equity interest in the project or venture. By participating in this fashion, it will limit its risk to whatever investment it has made in the special-purpose subsidiary. Lenders to the project or joint venture for their part want to isolate the project or joint venture assets from the general claims of the parent company or partner creditors.

- Real estate and oil and gas companies finance separate properties or projects on an expressly limited recourse or non-recourse basis. Again, the lender is to look to the property or project to be repaid and has neither the benefit of the general assets of the owner or sponsor to look to nor the risk that the particular asset dedicated to it will be subject to the general claims against the owner or sponsor.

A "plain vanilla" set of covenants affecting all subsidiaries alike will not do a good job of coping with these financial structures, which can legitimately be accommodated, generally by expressly permitting them when covenants would otherwise block them, limiting the restricted group's investment in and exposure to them, and as appropriate through carve-outs from the cross-default.

§ 7:3   Non-Subsidiary Affiliates—Presumptively Outside the Credit Group

§ 7:3.1   *Upstream Affiliates*

Lenders to a company generally have no recourse to or call upon the owners of the company. The only exceptions will be where the parent or other owners have expressly provided guarantees or other credit support, or in the case of recourse to general partners of a partnership. Lenders could benefit from contractual cash calls upon partners or other equity investors in a partnership or joint venture setting, but only indirectly. In the normal corporate context, there is a requirement that stockholders make up shortfalls in paid-in capital up to par value, but this is for the most part a theoretical issue because par value of corporations is typically set at a nominal amount and stock is issued at a price far exceeding par value. The rule is then that lenders cannot, as a legal matter, rely on owners to bail out their companies.

So while the value represented by the subsidiaries of the top-most obligor (from the obligor down) are presumptively of benefit to the obligor's lenders, value in the corporate group upstream of the topmost obligor is not. As a corollary, a downstream guarantee (guarantee by the parent of a subsidiary's debt) is deemed for value and so not generally subject to fraudulent conveyance attack. This does not apply to an upstream guarantee (by a subsidiary of a parent company's debt).

As a further corollary, debt agreements containing a full set of covenants nearly always constrain payment upward to owners (dividends, stock buy-backs, and returns of capital), and otherwise look to restrict payments to parent companies, controlling persons, and other non-subsidiary "affiliates" (through covenants limiting transactions with affiliates). In contrast to investments in subsidiaries, where the parent continues to have, albeit indirectly, the benefit of the invested assets and the corresponding earning power, money once paid out to owners is gone. Upstream affiliates of the topmost guarantor are definitively outsiders to the credit.

§ 7:3.2   *Sisters*

The same is true of sister companies. These may be "affiliates" in that they are under common control with the obligor, but there is no way an obligor or its lenders can tap into the assets of a sister company, short of having a guarantee or another direct obligation issued by the sister company (say pledge of an intercompany loan). Any such guarantee would be subject to fraudulent conveyance analysis. So even sister companies of the topmost obligor are definitively outside the credit group. That means that investments and other transfers of assets to, and transactions with, sisters would generally be controlled.

Sometimes credit situations among an affiliated group of companies develop so that lenders agree to "cross-collateralize" obligations, meaning that the sister companies will pledge assets in support of each other's debts. This arrangement is a way to sweep up any excess assets and equity in the group for the benefit of the lenders of the group, but as to each company's guarantee or pledge in support of a sister company's debts there is a fraudulent conveyance risk. That is why this is viewed as a way to squeeze what is available out of the group as a whole, rather than a rigorous credit structure built up out of clearly enforceable obligations.

§ 7:3.3   *Joint Ventures, Minority Interests, and the Like*

Continuing in the same theme, lenders to a joint venture (JV) cannot assume that they have recourse to the JV partners. A JV may be made up of two or more JV partners who agree to contribute to the JV per contract. They may form a legal entity, such as a partnership, or may operate as an unincorporated JV. Even where the JV is structured as a general partnership with recourse to the general partners, most substantial companies will interpose single-purpose subsidiaries to act as their designated JV partners to insulate them from general claims upon the JV. Likewise the JV will be structured so that its assets will not be available to creditors of the partners. At the point of articulation between any well-structured JV and its partners, there is a clear dividing line regarding assets and liabilities to keep them separate. Thus, a JV in which the obligor participates is also, definitively, outside the credit group.

More generally, if the obligor is a minority shareholder in an entity that is accounted for under the equity method of accounting, which could include joint ventures, those entities are presumptively not within the credit group. We would expect that a full set of covenants on the obligor would limit investments and other transfers of assets to, or transactions with, any of these entities.

Chapter 8

Commitments, Conditions, Pricing, and Risk; Liquidity Support and Credit Support; Credit Derivatives

§ 8:1   Commitments, Conditions, Pricing, and Risk

Providers of finance—lenders and investors, but also providers of liquidity or financial assurance—expect to earn significantly more on funded commitments (actual loans or investments made) than on unfunded commitments. But they generally expect to earn money on unfunded commitments as well. Unfunded commitments represent a potential drain on their balance sheets and, at least for regulated lenders, capital costs. In the ordinary course, bank lenders take on commitments in advance of signing up definitive bank loan documents and then under the definitive documents as well, including after initial funding if there is a revolving credit facility. Underwriters of equity and bond offerings take on funding commitments when they sign the underwriting agreement or purchase agreement, but those com-

125

mitments are usually short-lived and, in the circumstances and under the conditions they are given, usually entail little risk. But in the acquisition context, the providers of committed financings, including bridge loans, may be on the hook for some weeks. And a letter of credit issuer, liquidity provider, or bond insurer will commit for an extended period and, in the worst case, be taking on funded credit exposure just at the time that no one else wants it.

Pricing of financial commitments is directly related to the level of commitment and the conditions to funding. In general, the longer the term of the commitment and the fewer outs to funding, the higher the price. That is, the price of the financing or funding commitment is directly related to risk. This is consistent with the pricing of funded positions, where lenders generally expect to be compensated at a higher rate if their money is going to be locked up for a longer period of time.

Equity and debt underwriting agreements in the United States are of very short duration. Up until the point of signing the underwriting agreement at pricing, the underwriters are essentially uncommitted, and even at that point they do not agree to purchase in the face of all risks, such as disruption of the markets. Since they will not price and sign until they are comfortable, they have placed the offering at the agreed-upon price, and since they are protected from market disruption and other events that might prevent a successful offering, they are not compensated for the commitment.

On the other hand, lending commitments, particularly in an acquisition context, are often agreed-upon in principle well in advance of loan closing, as lining up financing is necessary to planning and going forward. Commitment letters provide fees starting at the date the lenders agree to commit, and conditions to funding are carefully worded.

In the case of a general purpose credit facility, banks reserve a number of customary outs to funding, both before definitive documentation is signed and initial loans are made, and with respect to revolving credit facilities thereafter. The biggest variable is the extent to which lenders may refuse to lend based on material adverse change or material litigation. Depending on the purpose of the facility and who might be relying on it (for example, commercial paper holders and, therefore, rating agencies in rating commercial paper), conditions to lending may be watered down and, for example, for a highly rated credit, might not include a material adverse change after an initial signing date.

In the case of an acquisition financing, especially if the terms of the financing are part of a bid package, the lenders will generally have limited outs to funding beyond those that the bidder is reserving in the purchase agreement. The bidder and the seller do not want lenders to have independent veto rights over a transaction that the bidder is required to proceed with. For example, in today's U.S. market there is very limited conditionality in financings to support auction bids by private equity and other borrowers.

A letter of credit is one of the most expensive forms of undrawn but committed financing. Under a letter of credit, the issuing bank is agreeing in advance, sometimes well in advance, to pay money over to a third party if stipulated documentary requirements are met. In some cases, these requirements may be related to default or non-performance by the account party, and the letter of credit effectively serves as a guarantee.

Commitments and the related conditions allocate the elements of risk between, on the one hand, the company or other parties relying on the funding commitment and, on the other, the providers of the funding commitment. As to those conditions within the company's direct control—such as there being no new debt incurred between the time of commitment and the time of funding, or that past financial statements are accurate—management can be fairly relaxed. Due diligence outs, which mean that the financial provider has not completed its homework analyzing the credit at the time of commitment, are obviously more troubling from the company perspective and would also be problematic from the perspective of another party relying on the commitment, for example, the seller in an auction. Conditions that permit financers to walk away because of material adverse change or material litigation relating to the bidder pose the risk that events outside the company's control will derail the financing or deprive it of funds; these are rarely invoked. "Market outs," which let the financers out of the commitment based on general market disruption, are rarely seen except in certain middle market transactions. Instead, parties will negotiate a "market flex," allowing the banks to adjust pricing and other terms within agreed limits to accommodate changes in the market or uncertainty about syndicate acceptance of particular features of the credit.

It is important to distinguish the quality of the commitment. A true commitment or underwriting means that the lender or underwriter signing the agreement is itself committed to fund, though it may sell down or syndicate to others. A best efforts underwriting or so-called highly confident letter (a letter from a bank stating that in its opinion a financing on the attached terms could be placed under current market conditions) may create a moral obligation to take the deal forward, and there may be substantial commercial embarrassment if the deal cannot be taken forward, but the lender or underwriter is under no obligation to fund. "Market flex" commitments commit the initial lenders to fund, but with flexibility to address changes or unknowns in market conditions, meaning that the terms of the credit set forth in the commitment letter may be altered, within limits, as necessary to bring in additional syndicate lenders.

Commitments and conditions, and managing the associated risks, are highly important to companies and their financial providers. At each stage of the transaction the allocation of risk must be consistent with the overall market, as the financial officer or banker who agrees to off-market commitments and conditions, on the side of the company depriving it of funds when expected or on the side of a banker putting it out of funds in unexpected negative circumstances, can be subject to severe criticism and second-guessing.

Banks that end up holding unwanted and unsalable securities have not judged the market properly, and may take a reputational as well as financial hit. For companies, the failure to manage commitments and conditionality can be even more serious, since it can turn a temporary setback into a general liquidity crisis. Interlocking provisions—notably the cross-default—can have a cascading effect, like an electrical blackout, where a localized problem, instead of being isolated, trips defaults and shuts off funding all across the system. Companies that have not managed their banking relationships in a centralized fashion, but perhaps played banks off against each other and ended up with a multiplicity of uncoordinated debt agreements, may not be able to organize their lenders for timely discussions. Some companies with generally sound operations and solid assets exceeding liabilities (solvency) have been forced into bankruptcy when their normal sources of cash suddenly dried up and an effective response could not be put together in time.

§ 8:2   Beyond the Issuer: Analyzing Levels of Credit Support

From the perspective of the lender to a company, what are the most important aspects of credit support, that is, the commitment of a third party to pay or provide funds?

The first question is, in what circumstances will payment be made? The highest level of support provides for payment of the obligation as and when due from the obligor (including upon acceleration or if the conditions to acceleration are met, even if acceleration is blocked for some reason), with no conditions and a minimum of procedural requirements, limited to, say, notice or demand on the provider. This would be the terms of a typical guarantee, and a letter of credit could be structured to provide a comparable degree of support. But lesser forms of support could still be valuable, such as an agreement to pay per the original scheduled (unaccelerated) maturity (bond insurance) or an agreement to make funds available but subject to certain conditions (a liquidity facility).

A second question is: To whom will payment be made—to the obligor or directly to the lender or other debtholder? Obviously, if cash is made available to the obligor but is paid into its general funds, then the money becomes subject to the demands of other creditors of the obligor. Will the funds instead go directly to a trustee or other earmarked account for the debtholders? If so, will the arrangement hold up against the claims of other creditors? Or, instead, will funds go directly to the debtholders? And in what cases will the payment be preference-proof, so that the take-out financer steps into the shoes of the debtholder and assumes the preference risk?

§ 8:3   Liquidity Support

Liquidity support is intended to constitute a source of funds when the company or issuer is facing a cash flow mismatch or market disruption, providing ready access to cash to meet short-term obligations. Liquidity facilities may be generic (part of a company's regular working capital or cash management arrangements), dedicated (if not in so many words) to support of a commercial paper program, or even more special purpose: established to support bond payments with earmarking arrangements or set up as part of a securitization (again, usually to support the operations of a commercial paper conduit).

In a normal bank revolving credit facility, there are conditions to lending that can include the requirement that there has been no material adverse change and no material litigation since the original commitment date. Whether these conditions have to be met only at initial signing or initial funding, or instead at each cash advance, is a matter of borrower creditworthiness and leverage or a matter of rating agency requirements. Certainly, a revolving credit facility without an ongoing MAC condition is worth more to the company and to those who may be relying on the liquidity as a source of funds for their take-out than a revolving credit facility that includes the condition.

Regardless of its terms, a liquidity facility is not a credit substitution. In the worst case (bankruptcy), or even short of the worst case, where there are tangible events of default, the liquidity facility may not provide funding. Furthermore, though there may be some cash segregation or earmarking, the liquidity facility does not eliminate preference risk for those whose debt is paid off with liquidity facility proceeds.

§ 8:4   Credit Support and Credit Substitution

Credit support or credit substitution involving a third-party obligor can provide significantly higher assurance, as a legal matter—that is, assuming the third-party obligor is creditworthy.

§ 8:4.1   *Guarantees*

The guarantee is the traditional and straightforward contract whereby one party stands behind the obligation of another. Defenses to a properly drafted guarantee are relatively few, but include lack of adequate consideration (fraudulent conveyance), which is why upstream and sister guarantees are considered less reliable than parent guarantees.

§ 8:4.2   *Non-Guarantee Credit Support?*

There are weaker forms of credit support, such as comfort letters and keepwells. These may be relatively strong, as in the case where a parent assures a lender to a subsidiary that the subsidiary will always pay its obligations or will always have positive net worth. Or they may trail off into either moral obligation, or nothingness, depending on your outlook, where, for example, one company agrees merely to continue to own a minimum percentage of another. Agreements to "take or pay" can be used as credit support, as in the case where one party agrees that it will make certain payments to a supplier (for example, a utility) whether or not it accepts delivery of the corresponding goods or services, and the supplier uses that agreement to obtain financing from a third party. Performance bonds have been used to approximate guarantees. In a sense it is also credit support when a purchaser's purchase contracts are assigned over to the seller's lenders.

In all these cases, you need to figure out:

- Why is the party providing the comfort or other support not giving a guarantee? It might be that the party can't give a guarantee without violating covenants in its debt agreements or for other legal reasons, in which case support that too closely approximates a guarantee could also be a problem.

- What exactly is the party giving the comfort or other support agreeing to do? Is there an actual financial undertaking? Is it qualified by or dependent on performance by the borrower?

- How would that party's obligations be enforced? Can they be enforced by lenders to the borrower or would the borrower have to enforce the agreement?

- Does the party know that others are relying on its undertakings? Is that referred to anywhere and acknowledged? Are the lenders explicitly named as third-party beneficiaries? Will moneys go directly to them or, instead, be commingled with the borrower's general assets and subject to the claims of other creditors?

Reliance by lenders or investors on quasi-guarantees or comfort letters is a potential trap for lawyers. Typically, it comes up when there is a reluctance to force the issue of a guarantee or a guarantee is not available for some legal or other reason. Regardless of its possible defects as credit support, bankers will be keen to derive as much comfort from it as possible. In hindsight, they may claim that their lawyers did not adequately explain the difference between what they got and a guarantee.

§ 8:4.3   *Letters of Credit*

A letter of credit can serve as a guarantee and it is a very solid credit substitution mechanism. Provided the letter of credit is issued before the preference period, the beneficiary can take payment under the letter of credit without preference risk associated with the account party (original obligor). Depending on how it is structured, it can be drawn in an acceleration context or even when the debt cannot be accelerated against the original obligor for any reason (including in bankruptcy). When rating agencies are really serious about credit substitution, including on an accelerated basis, they will require a letter of credit, and prospective failure to have a letter of credit in place (that is, notice that a letter of credit will not be renewed) will itself trigger acceleration before the current letter of credit expires.

§ 8:4.4   *Bond Insurance*

Similar (but not identical!) instruments (bond insurance) can be issued by financial insurers who are in the business of guaranteeing bond payments, usually at maturity on an unaccelerated basis. These are customary in the municipal bond and securitization businesses.

§ 8:4.5   *Credit Derivatives?*

What if you were a bank lender or a bondholder and could insure against, or lay off, the risk of payment default by the borrower or issuer? That is, you would keep the earning asset but pay a premium to a third party (hopefully creditworthy) who would agree to pay you if the company defaulted. This is the idea behind credit derivatives, now a huge business where banks and others can trade in the risk of default. The borrower or issuer is not party to these arrangements at all, and neither party needs to hold the underlying debt. Obviously, though, "insurance" is only as good as the "insurer." Relying on a credit derivative as an effective risk-shifting mechanism means being comfortable not only with its terms, but also with the credit worthiness of the counterparty.

Chapter 9

A Deal in Time

§ 9:1   The Deal Life Cycle and the Role of the Lawyer

A deal has a life cycle from inception through closing and post-closing. Eventually it becomes just history, for the participants and for the lawyers. From the perspective of the corporate lawyer, the deal that gets to closing smoothly and expeditiously, that delivers what was anticipated to the parties, and that is not a source of later trouble and contention is a success. However, when a deal goes bad, it engenders angst among the participants. Even if it is through no fault of the lawyers, every aspect of the failed transaction and its accompanying documentation will be scrutinized.

Good lawyering begins with the first phone call from the client. Lawyers typically have little or no involvement in the earliest discussion stages of a deal, but are brought in when it is time to move to documentation and execution. For lawyers in a law firm, the first step will be to make sure that the matter is cleared for acceptance through the firm's intake function. Then you are set to go.

§ 9:2   Understanding the Company and Its Financing Needs

As tempting as it may be to skip this step, it is important for the lawyers to understand the rationale and context of the deal. Senior lawyers on the team have to be well informed of the company's financing needs, and then they, in turn, must inform the entire team. The failure of the team to understand and share information about what is going on can lead to inadvertent breaches of confidentiality and to less serious political missteps that make the lawyer and the team look unprofessional. It is worth pulling up research materials on the parties and on the deal, including SEC filings, financial statements, and analyst reports on the company.

§ 9:3   Defining the Market and Instrument

Next you should have a clear understanding of what security or obligation the company proposes to issue and the market where it is going to be sold or placed, which will give you direction in finding the right forms and precedents. In addition, demonstrating an understanding of the market will help you gain the client's confidence.

§ 9:4   Locating and Using Forms and Precedents

A lawyer almost never creates an entirely new contract without reference to a form (a neutral, generic template, or a standard form provided by the bankers) or precedent (a negotiated document from a prior deal). By using a good form or precedent, the lawyer will start with something nearer to the finished work product and produce a first draft that is along the lines of what the clients expect. Forms and precedents let you see what is customary and piggyback off the thought processes of others, and they provide a checklist of items to be considered. However, even if you have a good form or close precedent, preparing spreadsheets from comparable deals and checklisting against them is worthwhile because it educates you about what is standard, what is variable, and the scope of variation.

Some best practice caveats about using forms and precedents:

- Special care must be exercised when using a precedent instead of a form. The precedent document represents the negotiated outcome for a different deal and may include provisions that could be inappropriate to the new deal or unfavorable to your client.

- When using a precedent instead of a form, be extremely careful to excise all names and words that might identify the source. Serving up leftovers from an old deal can be pretty embarrassing and is a sure sign of haste or carelessness. The "leftovers" might show up in historical metadata attached to a document circulated in electronic form, so you should circulate electronic documents with historical metadata stripped or in a flat and inert form such as a static pdf or other image type file.

- Word-processing can make it easier to check for and correct purely careless errors through global search, but global search and replace also generates errors. Each find-and-replace instance must be carefully checked.

- Computer-based document production, which today means effectively all document production, also creates an error-generating environment. More about this later.

§ 9:5   Preliminary Agreements—Term Sheets and Commitment Letters

The first stage in a financing is the preparation of preliminary agreements between the company and the banks providing or arranging the financing. This is an extremely important step. Lawyers may or may not be heavily involved, although lawyers are typically involved in the leveraged market and for acquisition financings.

The preliminary agreements lay out the terms of the expected financing and how the financing works with any related transaction (such as an acquisition) and other related financings. Signing up these agreements provides a kind of protected space for working toward closing, and the terms included in the preliminary agreements provide the starting point for drafting definitive documentation.

The timing of a preliminary agreement relative to closing or funding varies, but is also market-driven. In the private credit (bank loan) context, the commitment letter with attached term sheet may precede closing and funding by weeks, and syndication usually occurs prior to closing based on the agreed commitment letter. The underwriting agreement for a capital markets transaction is signed only at pricing, when the underwriters are convinced they have lined up ("circled") the accounts that will purchase the securities from the underwriters, but prior to that time the company will have signed an engagement letter, mostly for the benefit of the underwriters to protect them from losing the deal to a competitor.

In addition to laying out the terms of any funding commitments, including conditions and indicative terms, preliminary agreements contain obligations on the part of the company to pay various fees, expenses, and indemnities, and to refrain from working with other banks on a competing deal. There are likely to be provisions about confidentiality and disclosure.

According to their terms, preliminary agreements are binding, and some terms may survive, indeed are especially intended to survive, if no deal is completed—for example, fees required to be paid if a competing deal is done within the exclusivity period, and expense and indemnity provisions (expense provisions being of particular interest to lawyers). Because the parties can be taking on substantial financial and reputational risks, banks do not enter into preliminary agreements without internal approvals, and, likewise, these agreements would be the basis for seeking board approval for the financing at the company. In the acquisition context, these letters are attached to bid papers and may be carefully reviewed by sellers as an element of the bid.

Lawyers tend to focus on preliminary agreements mostly as a guide to drafting definitive documentation. But it is a mistake to lose sight of the client perspective. Bankers and the company are keenly interested in the compensation arrangements, whereas lawyers see the fee amounts as "plug figures" in rather simple clauses. Though there is nothing much that the lawyers have to "do" with the fee arrangements, other than make sure they are accurately documented, it's good to keep in mind how important these are to the clients. Fee arrangements may be confidential even within the larger working group. Sometimes fee arrangements are set out in separate letters so that they do not have to be disclosed in SEC filings or to third parties who need to understand the level of funding commitment, the conditions to funding, and the terms of the financing. The amount of the lead agent's compensation may not be known to all participants in a tiered bank syndication. Lawyers may not always be as sensitive as they might be to these dynamics, and have been known to give away too much information by inadvertently filing or distributing documents containing the confidential fee arrangements.

A second best practice point is that clients who are not familiar with the particular market may not always have a good grasp of what they are getting and what they are committing to under a preliminary agreement. Giving an underwriter exclusivity does not commit the underwriter to provide the financing. A "drop dead" date in a bank commitment letter does not require the bank to fund by that date; instead it permits the bank to walk if the deal has not closed.

§ 9:6   Due Diligence, Detail, and the Preliminary Agreement

It is important to identify the right level of detail for the preliminary agreement and the right amount of due diligence that should be carried out up front. Ideally, a term sheet should contain sufficient detail so that the parties are confident not only that a deal can be done but that getting there will not involve too many unpleasant surprises. Every seasoned lawyer will tell you about instances where late identification of a "showstopper" or near-"showstopper" (major legal, structural, or third-party approval issue or impediment) caused great embarrassment. Less dramatically, if a term sheet is too vague in an area of known sensitivity, subsequent negotiations may be protracted and unpleasant.

Is the answer a long and detailed term sheet? In my experience, people who are inclined to negotiate the details of a lengthy term sheet are quite likely to negotiate hard over the details of the far lengthier definitive documentation.

A term sheet that refers in shorthand to standard, so-called boilerplate provisions but is quite precise about basic structural assumptions and specific deal terms, and anticipates and resolves potential areas of important disagreement, represents an intelligent level of detail. Likewise, a measured amount of legal due diligence to surface any "showstoppers" is sensible. It will help to think about third-party consents as well as the opinions that will likely be required at closing, and to focus especially on those opinions that will require statutory or contractual analysis. Early and frequent consultations with tax and other specialist lawyers are important.

The preliminary agreement phase should not include pre-negotiation of minor or routine points that can be easily compromised when the definitive documents are discussed. On the other hand, "finessing" a known area of likely misunderstanding or conflict in order to sign up a deal can turn out to be very unwise. Lawyers need to understand the pressures that may make their clients want to push through issues or, occasionally, sweep them under the rug, but it is our job to help the overall process along by asserting our best judgment on this type of question and call a halt for investigation and discussion when it is warranted.

§ 9:7   Drafting and Negotiation

§ 9:7.1   *The Drafting Process*

Once a preliminary agreement has been reached, lawyers for one of the parties—almost always the bank or the underwriter, except in the private equity context—will begin to prepare documents. Unless time is very short, these documents will go to the client first, and then start circulating among the larger group for review and negotiation. Unless the lawyer has an exceptionally good understanding of the client's needs and expectations based on prior experience, it is nearly always right to resist client pressure to distribute initial drafts of documents to the other side without client review. There will be no going back from what is out there.

The drafting lawyer keeps the master. Over the course of a series of meetings, conference calls, and exchanges of documents, the documents are revised and the points of disagreement narrowed until the parties finally declare themselves satisfied, at which point execution copies can be prepared and the deal set for closing.

The drafting party generally has an advantage. The first draft sets the baseline for discussion and thereafter agreed-upon changes can be (though should not be) tilted slightly in favor of the drafting party's client. Time pressures and inertia mean that many provisions will be accepted rather than fought over.

§ 9:7.2   *Golden Rules of Document Drafting and Negotiation*

The drafting lawyer is responsible for:

- fairly and responsibly reflecting in the words the agreed-upon outcomes of negotiation; failure to do this reflects badly on the professionalism of the lawyer or, worse, calls into question the good faith of the lawyer or the lawyer's client;

- circulating correct redlines and properly marking or noting open issues;

- proofreading, carefully checking cross-references and the like, and making appropriate conforming changes; and

- working to keep documents as short as possible.

The commenting parties should:

- allow the drafting lawyer sufficient time to draft and, after ne-gotiations, to redraft;

- provide small comments in writing (not in a meeting or over the phone);

- *not* (disingenuously) make important comments or request important changes in the guise of conveying "nits"; and

- exercise restraint in commenting (for example, do not re-write for style).

All parties should allow enough time for everyone to carefully read and analyze documents before meeting or conveying comments. This is particularly true if you are representing a company where officers and employees outside the finance department or general counsel's office may need to review particular parts of the documents. A rush to give initial (and too superficial) comments may be followed up with a second round of heavy comments—better to hold up the first go-round and make sure it is comprehensive. Allowing proper time for review at each stage will save time in the end.

§ 9:7.3   *How to Read a Contract*

Another technique or discipline that will also save you time in the long run is structured reading of contract documents. Whether you are drafting or commenting on documents, working with a contract as a lawyer requires rigor and analysis. I suggest the following steps:

1.   Look at the table of contents and give the document a straight read-through once so that you have a general sense of what it contains and where various provisions are located. Sometimes provisions can turn up in surprising places, so do not rely on headers or assume logical or even customary or-ganization.

2.   Read the contract closely for the important business terms and the substance of the negotiated points to make sure they are accurately reflected, cross-checking against the term sheet

and checking off term sheet items to make sure they are all covered.

3. Analyze each part of the contract closely, keeping in mind how the contract provisions work together. This read should be at a very technical level. If the representations must be repeated at future times, are they written in such a way that they in fact can be?[1] Are related subjects such as litigation, judgment defaults, and judgment liens treated consistently across the conditions precedent, representations, covenants, and events of default? Subject-matter or functional reading, not linear reading, is required to make sure the contract is coherent and consistent.

4. Before finalizing the contract, another straight read-through is advisable, preferably after the dust has settled on redrafting for a day or two. The purpose of the last read is to catch the incorrect cross-references, unclosed loops, and other loose ends that are the inevitable product of multiple piecemeal drafts. It is best yet if a fresh pair of eyes can be enlisted to do a cold read.

This kind of aggressive, structured, and staged reading and analysis is an essential element of successful contract drafting and negotiation.

Occasionally, documents are prepared under enormous time pressure so that there is no time for a "fresh eyes" or even "rested eyes" read before signing. In that case, it is good practice to look at the closing documents very carefully as soon as possible after closing, when the closing sets are being prepared. Parties are likely to be quite amenable to technical corrections of obvious errors, provided they are caught within the first few days. Of course, you will not be able to fix substantive oversights or problems in this way! Even so, were you to discover a problem requiring a quick amendment as a cure, that is better to do than not.

---

1. *See* sections 10:5 and 10:6.

§ 9:7.4   Negotiation and the Lawyer's Role

Good contract drafting is not only a product of but an aid to negotiation.

At a simple level lawyers can help parties reach agreement by softening language, using such formulas as "best efforts"; "reasonable"; "promptly" or "as soon as practicable" rather than "immediately"; consents "not to be unreasonably withheld"; appointment of a third party to make determinations; and so forth. These are all part of a lawyer's toolkit.

Lawyers can also help by listening carefully and by asking probing questions. A discussion between the two sides over a disputed issue may suggest to the resourceful lawyer a more precise and detailed formulation of the provision at issue that would be acceptable to both parties. This sort of probing will also help the lawyer define precisely what each party is interested in and avoid "over-drafting."

Most obviously and significantly, good lawyers add value to negotiations because they can bring to the table solutions they have seen in other similar deals. They are also experienced in negotiation per se—managing meetings and discussions toward fruitful ends. Importantly, lawyers are professional advisors, not principals. As professional advisors they have duties to the client, but also to the integrity and quality of the process. Because lawyers are not principals and can (or should) maintain a disinterested perspective, they can, in the best of circumstances, provide wise counsel, not making business decisions but making sure their clients have considered the situation and alternatives in the most constructive light. Objectivity can help in avoiding some common errors in decision-making.

§ 9:7.5   Common Errors in Decision-Making

There is established literature on the subject of systematic errors in decision-making. A few points are relevant in the negotiation context.

- Availability: The ease of recall of a fact or certain events will cause us to overestimate its importance or frequency. We tend to overweight what we know from recent experience and discount or ignore what isn't familiar to us.

- Representativeness: We tend to put too much emphasis on associations we have noted in the past in making conclusions about the facts before us.

- Anchoring and adjustment: We tend to grab onto any quantitative input and adjust from there, no matter how baseless the input.

In other words, we tend to put too much faith in our own recent experience, no matter how limited; we tend to reason from one example to other situations even though we shouldn't; and we tend to work off what we have in front of us, such as figures presented in the first draft of the document, whether or not it presents a reasonable starting point.

Other processes you will see at work in a typical negotiation:

- People will sometimes pursue a series of "what-if" scenarios to the point of utter remoteness, or to a level of complexity that cannot be resolved in advance.

- In other cases, people making difficult or painful decisions between *x* and *not-x* find themselves debating the pros and cons of these, when in fact *not-x* is clearly a non-starter. The thinking would be better put to use in making sure that the *x/not-x* dichotomy is right in the first place.

- Self-serving biases affect the reading of ambiguous language and sometimes make even spotting a potential ambiguity difficult.

- The perception of risk can be significantly influenced by how the risk is presented. Studies indicate that people tend to be risk-averse when looking at potential gain (a sure gain of $100 is better than a 50% chance of $200 gain) and risk-tolerant when they are looking at potential loss (a sure loss of $100 is worse than a 50% chance of $200 loss).

- People assign real, if non-rational, value to getting a good deal. As a corollary: After the fact, people prefer to avoid confronting that they have overpaid or left money on the table.

- Perceptions of value may be skewed by context and timing. The example frequently cited is that while you might walk three blocks to save $10 on a $25 calculator, you would be less likely to walk the same three blocks to save $10 on a $200 television. You would typically demand more to part with something you already own than the price you would pay to buy it. We ascribe more value to money paid or received now than money to be paid or received in the future, over and above the time value of money.

- You can sometimes maximize perceived value by unbundling—serving up the same consideration or negotiating concessions piecemeal over time or in the form of a generous-looking list. This is the reason that you will often find a negotiator's list of "points conceded" containing a number of easy gives, or maybe the same basic point conceded in a number of ways. Of course, one of the lawyer's jobs is to see through this sort of thing.

- People respect a norm of fairness and expect it to be observed in the short term and over time. People who push for the absolute last advantage when they have the upper hand can expect no mercy when the tables are turned. People in the financial world move around a lot, and no one can say exactly what the future will bring. This is why experienced business people often want to feel that they have left a little something on the table for the other side.

- Team dynamics tend to bind the members together and to make each team discredit the abilities, even the motives, of the other team. This unrealistically negative view of the other side is generally not constructive and may well blind us, to an even dangerous degree, to our own relative weaknesses and vulnerabilities.

- A major motivator in decision-making is the avoidance of regret; the impulse to critical hindsight (second-guessing) is nearly irresistible. And people tend to regret results of actions they affirmatively take more than they regret the results of inaction or even neglect. So people often take one path because they could not bear the reproach (including self-reproach) associated with possible outcomes of taking the other.

- Negotiations, especially in the bidding context, frequently feature "non-rational escalation of commitment," where the decision maker has too much invested to stop or reverse course. Another version of this is the "sunk costs" dynamic: You have spent $100 on ballet tickets, but when the night of the performance rolls around you would rather do something else. Do you have too much invested in the ballet to skip it? Or should you look at it this way instead: You've spent the money and it's gone. That decision is in the past. Now what is the best expenditure of your time and energy tonight? Time and again, people throw good money after bad, prop up previous investment decisions with additional questionable investments, and overbid in bidding contests. We do it to save face and to avoid recognizing our earlier wrong decision. (Banks move bad loans from the customer relationship officer who made the loans to a special department expert in dealing with troubled credits in part to deal with this dynamic.)

• People frequently devote disproportionate time in negotiations to haggling over variables such as dollar amounts and time periods, and to pet subjects—topics that are inherently intriguing, current, or of particular interest to the negotiating parties though perhaps not that relevant to the deal. When this gets out of hand, lawyers should help the parties manage their time and attention more appropriately.

§ 9:8 Closings

§ 9:8.1 *Good Closings*

A closing represents the real-world satisfaction of the conditions precedent in a contract. At the closing, the transaction that is the subject of the contract is consummated, so the last event to occur will be the filing of the merger certificate in the case of a merger, or the exchange of funds against the issuance of securities in a securities offering, or the funding of the term loan under a credit agreement. A closing under a revolving credit agreement means that the conditions to effectiveness have been met; there may be a shorter list of conditions to be met at the time of each borrowing.

The closing may be as simple as obtaining relevant physical or electronic signatures and confirming that these have been received and are in good order, so that you are "closed." At the other end of the spectrum, a closing may involve so many parties, documents, and actions that it is scheduled well in advance and takes place in many rooms over a number of days or in stages.

Focusing on the nuts and bolts of a closing is important because a realistic appreciation of the relative difficulty of meeting various conditions will both sharpen your precision in defining these conditions early on and make you think about the logistics of reaching the clients' shared goal of consummation or effectiveness of the deal. More pragmatically, clients recognize that a smooth and professionally executed closing is a mark of competent, organized, and considerate lawyering. A botched, sloppy, or overly emoted closing, with the clients on pins and needles, is neither appreciated nor easily forgotten.

The key to a successful closing is preparation, teamwork, and more preparation. In any complex closing, it is inevitable that one or more unforeseen last-minute hitches will require all of your attention to untangle. If you have reduced everything that could possibly have been foreseen to the mechanics of a checklist item, your mind is free to deal with the unexpected and to tend to clients. That unexpected phone call, delay, or overlooked detail will seem like a major crisis instead of an ordinary glitch if you are busy fooling around with routine matters that have been left to the last minute.

Advance preparation includes a closing memo or list. Early on, the drafting lawyer or, if the drafting lawyer cannot or will not do it, the commenting lawyer must put together and circulate a closing memorandum corresponding to the conditions precedent in the contract. The closing list must be detailed: it should have a column for status and a corresponding column identifying the person responsible for each item. The closing list should be the subject of early and frequent meetings or phone calls; it should be annotated, updated and recirculated often. Potential problems (for example, third-party consents, surveys, appraisals, or delinquency in circulating draft certificates for comment) should be identified and dealt with firmly.

A client relations tip: Do not assume that authorized signatories for the agreements (client officers) will make themselves available for signing at the lawyers' convenience. Clients do not like being tracked down at the airport or being paged on the beach to sign documents. Advance planning is required and it may be a good solution to hold pre-signed signature pages so long as you use them only as clearly instructed (the instruction memorialized in writing) by the client.

§ 9:8.2 *Typical Documentary Requirements*

Beyond execution and delivery of the principal documents, the company (if a corporation) will be expected to deliver documentation evidencing corporate existence (through evidence of good standing from the secretary of state of the jurisdiction of incorporation), certified copies of the articles or certificate of incorporation (certified by the secretary of state or, providing a lesser level of comfort, the corporate secretary), copies of the bylaws certified by the corporate secretary, and copies of board resolutions approving the transaction and certified by the corporate secretary. The authorizing resolutions might be general (for example, approving borrowings not to exceed $50 million for working capital purposes), but significant transactions should have specific authorizing resolutions (likely referring to the preliminary agreement terms).

Documents to be certified by a secretary of state or other government official need to be ordered in advance. Certification by a corporate secretary involves nothing more than obtaining the corporate secretary's signature to a statement that "The attached is certified to be a true and correct copy of the [specify document] as in effect on [relevant date or dates—for example, including the date board resolutions were adopted through the date of closing]," with possibly the corporate seal affixed by the secretary. Affixation of the corporate seal has become relatively unimportant in modern practice, but some bylaws still require it for some documents.

For legal entities that are not corporations, such as LLCs and partnerships, lawyers must understand the legal structure and authorization procedures (for example, by action of the general partner in the case of a limited partnership) and, as necessary, trace the chain of authorization up through as many entities as necessary to establish due authorization and execution, performing this analysis at each level. This requires looking at the state or other law under which the entity was organized, and the organizational documents. Particularly with respect to private equity, ownership may be through a series of limited partnerships, whose general partners are themselves limited partnerships, or other legal entities. Foreign entities are likely to have their own formalities and authorization arrangements, which should be respected so long as foreign lawyers advise they are sufficient.

It is also important to identify the person actually signing the relevant documents on behalf of the corporation or other legal entity. In an incumbency certificate, the corporate secretary attests that the person signing is the duly elected officer of the corporation and is duly authorized to execute the documents on behalf of the corporation, and further attests to a specimen signature of the person. Institutions such as banks keep books of signatures of persons authorized to sign on behalf of the institution. The relevant book may be inspected by counsel for the other side or the page may be photocopied and certified as a true and correct copy. Likewise, foreign companies may present evidence that the signing person is a managing director, which may be sufficient to authorize the person to bind the company.

In more formal closings, the secretary's signature would itself be certified through a so-called cross-incumbency certificate (provided by another corporate officer), which states that the secretary is the duly elected secretary of the company and the specimen signature of the secretary (on the cross-incumbency certificate) is true and correct. The value of a cross-incumbency certificate is greatly reduced if the secretary certifies as to the signing officer, and then the signing officer certifies as to the secretary! The better practice is for a third officer to certify as to the secretary.

Banks and other financial institutions do not generally produce documents evidencing corporate authority, exceptions being where the bank is taking on obligations to investors (acting as corporate trustee, providing a liquidity facility to support bonds, or providing a letter of credit).

§ 9:8.3   *Potential Documentation Problems*

Even relatively simple documentary requirements may yield up problems that can generate serious nail-biting and worse, if discovered on the eve of closing. It is far better to identify these problems and cure them in advance.

- Once in a while, though rarely, you will find that an issuer's charter limits the powers of the corporation in a way that affects your deal. This problem has become practically extinct, given the use of generic form charters and the broad powers language in state business corporation statutes. However, it is still an issue in the municipal finance, governmental agency, and non-profit sectors. Special purpose vehicles may have very limited powers, perhaps designed for just a specific deal, so recycling a special purpose vehicle for a new or expanded deal may turn out to be problematic.

- The review of bylaws occasionally turns up a problem. Some require the affixation of a corporate seal to certain types of legal documents. Some require two officers to sign certain types of agreements. Some do not specify any standing authority for officers, leaving their ability to bind the corporation absent board action open to question.

- If you are in charge of making sure that a resolution was duly adopted, you need to track the state law, charter, and bylaw provisions regarding board action and make sure of compliance. In the case of subsidiaries, you may find that shareholders have not acted to elect directors in some time, that the board has not met to select officers, or that board members have resigned without replacements, etc. It may take time to get the corporate house in order for closing.

- Upon close inspection, many "standing" resolutions fall short: Poorly drafted resolutions or resolutions drafted far in advance may turn out to raise questions. A typical dilemma faced by outside lawyers is where the company's standing resolutions authorize "aggregate working capital borrowings not in excess of $50 million." Does this permit a particular credit agreement? Possibly. How can outside lawyers know in advance and opine that borrowings under that credit agreement and other working capital borrowings in total won't exceed $50 million? The answer is that they cannot, so some combination of officer certifications, conditions to borrowing, covenants, and assumptions in the opinion will have to plug the gap. A resolution specifically authorizing borrowings under the relevant credit agreement, appropriately defined to include amendments and extensions, is preferable. But in-house counsel and financial officers are understandably reluctant to approach their boards for new resolutions, especially if it requires scheduling a special meeting. For this reason, early review (in time to cure problems at a regularly scheduled board meeting) is recommended.

- State statutes, corporate charters, and bylaws may impact directly on execution of a transaction. To leave review of these to closing (while preparing the legal opinion, for example!) can be a potentially fatal error. Delaware General Corporation Law section 203 imposes limitations on certain transactions with interested shareholders; replacing a board or holding a board meeting may be difficult; preferred stock terms, which are contained in charter documents, may include covenant-like terms or mandatory redemption requirements triggered by your deal; or the number of shares of stock that can be issued is limited. These types of issues, if they affect your deal, really come under the heading of due diligence—discovering them at closing will be too late.

§ 9:8.4   Requirements in the International Context

Signatures of non-U.S. persons can be attested by their consulates or by notaries in their countries, whose notarial certificates are then consularized. Embassy websites can provide information on these procedures.

In some countries, notaries have a role closer to that of an American lawyer and unlike that of an American notary public. Both their prestige and their remuneration (including notarial fees, which might be imposed on an ad valorem basis) are significant, and they may provide advice of a legal nature that must be heeded.

In some countries, stamp taxes (taxes imposed for the formalization of certain contracts) apply, and these can be significant as well.

§ 9:8.5   Related Transactions and Simultaneous Closings

If a deal is tied to the consummation of a related transaction, such as a merger or acquisition, the availability of other financings, exit from bankruptcy or the pay-off of financings that are being retired, then the closings of these individual transactions will be linked and cross-dependent.

This is the "chicken and egg" problem. All the closings are conditions precedent to each other. But if a new financing is dependent on the release of collateral pledged under an old financing, which is to be repaid with the proceeds of the new financing, how do you ever get there? If somebody takes the first step on trust, what are the chances that things will get stuck in the middle? Although a theoretically difficult problem, here is how it works: Everybody relevant to the final sign-off on each piece of the deal stands by. They acknowledge they are about ready to go, and the first steps involving third parties—filings and payments—are initiated. People, or maybe just some of the people, hang around to make sure that all the other steps fall into place.

Keep a close eye on funding deadlines and the time of day. The reason that most financing transactions "preclose" a day early is to permit funding (wire transfers) to commence early in the day and complete well before day's end. In a complex matter, lawyers will need to take time out to help their clients map funding instructions or, if these are prepared by others, to make sure they are in order. If you don't meet the funding deadline, you may come up to the moment of closing and be stalled out. A closing that "hangs" overnight on payment delays can require parties to make adjustments among themselves to compensate for the overnight loss of funds, but, in the odd case, could raise difficult issues as to whether or when the deal has closed.

§ 9:9   Opinions

§ 9:9.1   *Opinions Are Hard; Not Just a Word-Processing Exercise*

It is customary in the United States for legal opinions to be given as part of the closing of corporate finance transactions. Legal opinions represent the opinion giver's conclusions as to legal issues and facts of a legal nature. When a law firm renders an opinion, it is stating that it has reached certain conclusions on the basis of a review of relevant facts and law, and is taking on the associated liability. It is fair to say that giving a legal opinion heightens the level of due diligence or scrutiny of the matters covered. In addition to opinions required from the principal lawyers running the deal and in-house counsel, a transaction might merit opinions from local, foreign, or special expert counsel.

Sometimes a difficult legal issue merits a supplemental opinion or memorandum of law, and the conclusions in the opinion or memorandum might be qualified or "reasoned," not "clean" or "flat." Other times, parties decide that it is in everyone's best interest to deal with the issue orally and informally, rather than creating a written record of the pros, cons, uncertainties, and vulnerabilities that a reasoned opinion or memorandum of law will lay out.

Though opinions are closing items, they require early attention. It is not just a question of producing a document to be signed. Opinions are not and should not be aspects of deal execution that engage the client's attention in the ordinary course. If there is a problem with an opinion at closing, then it is almost always a clear indication that the lawyers fell down on the job earlier on.

Lawyers have come to recognize that, while opinions serve the valid purpose of encouraging close scrutiny of legal issues, neither the profession nor business clients have been well-served by historical opinion practice. Practices and standards on even the simplest issues can vary greatly. In particular, a schism developed between the so-called California style of opinion, chock-full of exceptions and qualifiers, and the so-called New York style of opinion, kept short on the basis that the common exceptions and qualifiers are understood by the presumptively well-informed and well-advised recipient. (This may be in accordance with the New York courts' strict construction of contracts and their general disinclination for inferring or creating protections for which the parties haven't bargained.) Now that firms operate in multiple jurisdictions, the style differences can arise within a single firm, with the offices in the various states rendering differing opinions on comparable issues in comparable situations.

Lawyers have also expressed concern regarding the extent to which knowledge might be imputed from one lawyer to another in a large firm with branch offices, or the extent to which general language in an opinion might be read to cover specialized legal issues beyond the competence of the general corporate or finance practitioner. Clashes between firms that are really about different opinion practice can become high-visibility showstoppers at closings, in front of the clients and to the credit of none of the lawyers involved. For these reasons, the profession has tried to progress standards of opinion practice, but these efforts have fallen short of establishing a uniform opinion practice.

§ 9:9.2   *The Basic Opinion*

The standard opinion for a corporate finance transaction is given by counsel to the company, but delivered to and relied upon by the banks, underwriters, or purchasers (the "buy side"). (Lawyers for the "buy side" often give a basic opinion as well.) The basic opinion usually covers:

- the existence and good standing of the company and its corporate power and authority to enter into the transaction;

- due authorization, execution, and delivery of the agreements; and

- the validity, binding effect, and enforceability of the agreements (this is the "enforceability opinion").

Due diligence for the first point consists of a review of recent evidence of good standing (a certificate from the relevant state authority for the jurisdiction of incorporation) and of the charter and bylaws; for the second, review of authorizing resolutions, incumbency certificates, and signatures on the executed documents; and, for the third, the review of the substance of the agreement for possible problems of enforceability under the stipulated governing law.

Corporate existence and power, as well as due authorization, are governed by the laws of the jurisdiction of incorporation. Execution and delivery is a question of both the laws of the jurisdiction of incorporation and the governing law, while the "enforceability" opinion is a matter of stipulated governing law.

Opinion practice would generally be that a lawyer admitted to practice in any state can review the good standing issue, since the opinion is given in reliance on the certificate of a government official. Many firms not admitted in those states give opinions on the corporate law of Delaware or, in the Western United States, Nevada. The enforceability opinion is more difficult to deal with if the opining lawyer is not admitted in the state of the governing law. This can sometimes be finessed by giving the opinion as if the governing law were the law of the state in which the counsel is admitted, or with an assumption that the governing law is in all relevant respects identical to the law of the state in which the counsel is admitted; depending on the circumstances, this approach may not be acceptable and other lawyers, qualified in the relevant jurisdiction, will have to be engaged to give the opinion.

§ 9:9.3   Conclusions About Legal Facts

A second set of opinions might be characterized as conclusions about legal facts:

- that the borrower and its subsidiaries are qualified to do business in the relevant jurisdictions;

- that the current deal does not violate applicable law, judgments, or other contracts;

- that there is no material litigation affecting the borrower or the deal (which has not been disclosed); and

- that a related transaction (such as a merger) has been consummated.

The first and third of these opinions are most properly the province of the in-house counsel, or of outside counsel only if outside counsel provides ongoing general representation of the borrower. Outside counsel could opine as to no violation of applicable law, limited to the law of the jurisdiction in which counsel is admitted. Outside counsel could also, given sufficient notice, cover non-contravention of specified contracts after a review of them, and could properly cover consummation of related transactions in which it is acting. Otherwise, these matters will likely fall to in-house counsel to cover.

§ 9:9.4   Security Interest Opinions

Special legal opinions are usually required if there are mortgages or other security interests or pledges. Again, the governing law issues are tricky. It is customary for mortgages to be governed by the law of the jurisdiction in which the real property is located. Security agreements usually specify as governing law the law that governs the principal credit document. In any event, U.C.C. perfection is most commonly governed by the law where the borrower is incorporated (for a domestic corporation). Federal law impacts security interests in some types of collateral; foreign law is relevant to perfection of pledges by foreign companies and to pledges of stock of foreign companies and other foreign assets. The point to take away from this is that there may be numerous difficult choice of law questions implicated in a simple opinion that "the security interests are perfected." Dealing with them properly and lining up outside counsel as necessary are long lead-time items.

§ 9:9.5   True Sale and 10b-5 Opinions

Other opinions that may actually shape a deal or drive its execution are "true sale" opinions in the securitization context and, of course, "10b-5 opinions," which cover the adequacy and accuracy of disclosure (and opinions on compliance as to form in the securities offering context). Suffice it to say that a last-minute request for an opinion of this type would be considered out of bounds, professionally speaking.

§ 9:9.6   Rules to Opine By

Rules of professional courtesy should dominate opinion practice. Opinion practice is hard, and many lawyers find it tedious as well. In truth, it is one of the more scholarly exercises that a corporate lawyer must perform and is a long way from the excitement of cutting a deal. For these reasons, opinion practice tends to get short shrift as a matter of overall attention and timing; and when lawyers finally turn to the opinions, at or just prior to closing, it is easy for tempers to flair. Everybody feels put-upon. Even worse, every so often the opinion exercise does in fact turn up a show-stopping or stomach-churning legal problem that did not, as the parlance goes, get focused on up front.

- The first rule of opinion practice is: Get the opinion request or proposed draft on the table right away, and get it out of the way, that is, every jot and tittle of the wording agreed to, well in advance of the closing. This requires the cooperative effort of both sides of a deal. In the end, it does the deal no good if the opinion request goes out with the first draft of the document, but the first response back is the opinion that shows up on the closing table. The greatest sin, though, is the last-minute demand for an opinion that cannot be given without extensive research or due diligence, such as a 10b-5 opinion in a Rule 144A offering or private placement, or a non-contra-vention opinion.

- The second rule lawyers should observe is the "golden rule" of opinion practice. A firm should not ask for or require an opinion, within its general area of competence, of a sort that it itself, would not be able and willing to give.

- The third rule is the more substantive corollary to the "golden rule": You cannot fix a known legal problem by getting an opinion that there isn't one. If you know there is an uncertainty as to a legal issue, not only is it unfair to ask for a "flat" or "clean" opinion that ignores the uncertainty, but, more substantively, the opinion does not make the uncertainty go away. If you receive an opinion that is not supported by the facts and the law, you might, at best, be able to sue the opinion giver for malpractice, which is not really much of a fix for financial loss or legal liability, and further assumes that you, as recipient, were not aware of the issue and relied on the inaccurate legal opinion. Hence, it is inappropriate for a firm or a client to pressure a lawyer to give a flat legal opinion in order to paper over an underlying legal problem or uncertainty.

- It is appropriate to make an opining lawyer do the necessary work to give an opinion that is in fact important for the deal. Opinion practice requires a cost-benefit analysis that should be addressed early on. The most common problem that arises is the resolution of the proper scope of the opinion and the determination of who will be responsible for the different parts of the opinion. If an opinion request legitimately covers perfection of security interests in collateral having material value, and if the borrower's counsel is not a U.C.C. expert in the relevant states, then supplemental opinions will have to be obtained. If there is U.C.C. collateral in fifty states and three foreign countries but 95% of the value of the collateral is pledged by obligors "located" in two states, then it would be unreasonable, in most deals, to require U.S. local counsel opinions for more than those two states. On the other hand, if perfection is sought in foreign jurisdictions, advice, if not opinions, of foreign counsel will be required. The lawyers need to work this sort of thing out well in advance of closing and since incremental legal costs are involved, it is certainly a business issue as well as a lawyer's issue. (Note that, even though lawyers not qualified in Delaware may give basic Delaware corporate law opinions, they generally will not give Delaware U.C.C. opinions.)

- The other common scope problem is the coverage of the non-contravention opinion (and to a lesser extent, other corporate housekeeping opinions, such as qualification to do business in multiple jurisdictions). Giving a non-contravention opinion, to the effect that the instant deal does not violate the terms of other deals, requires documentary review and analysis of the type explained in this book. It is time-consuming and hard for outside lawyers and, thus, costly for clients, except in the case where those same outside lawyers have recently worked on the contract being reviewed for compliance. Scope questions like this usually get resolved by asking in-house counsel to cover this and other matters that they should be monitoring in the ordinary course.

- Opinions given must not be misleading. If an opinion is technically correct but, in the totality of the circumstances, fails to put the recipient on notice of a problem or anomaly, then the opinion giver has not acted properly. Likewise, it is not appropriate to disingenuously request an opinion that looks ordinary and simple on its face but, as a technical matter, covers or may be read to cover a point that is known by the requesting party to be problematic or questionable.

§ 9:10   Post-Closing

§ 9:10.1   *Final Documents and Closing Sets*

After the closing, the lawyers should scrutinize the final documentation, distribute it to the parties, and prepare the closing set for the firm's own record. Preparing correct reference versions of final documents is especially important. These are the versions that parties and lawyers will rely upon later to understand the parties' rights and obligations and, in the case of the lawyers, to give advice.

The exercise of creating a final record of the matter has become more challenging in the era of electronic documents and records. In particular, lawyers may rely upon electronic versions of documents that reside in their document management system without being properly locked down. These documents might be inadvertently altered after closing. Another problem is that hand-written changes made at closing might not be made in the electronic version of the document, once again making the electronic version unreliable. Unfortunately, it is not unheard of for lawyers to give incorrect advice on contract questions because they pulled up a document on their computer systems, instead of looking at a reliable copy (either paper or a locked-down and fully conformed electronic version) of the document as executed.

§ 9:10.2   Post-Closing: Amendments, Waivers, and Questions of Interpretation (When to Call a Lawyer)

After the closing, clients may call with questions about how to interpret the documents or with other questions about the deal. Sometimes they will have a question about whether something is permitted under the agreement, they may have news of an impending default, or they may say that they need to amend or refinance the deal. Requests for amendments, waivers, and proposed refinancings present rather straightforward tasks for corporate finance lawyers. Difficult questions of interpretation and issues that may lead to declaration of a default or taking remedies should be handled in consultation with other lawyers, including, as appropriate, litigators or bankruptcy/workout specialists. If there are indications that a company is entering into the troubled credit zone, an audit of any collateral security arrangements to assure perfection may be called for. In other cases, such as securitizations, it may be appropriate to review other aspects of compliance with documentation with collateral trustees and administrators. In all cases where interpretation of language is at issue, lawyers should consider whether, in hindsight, their own work and advice could be questioned, and consult with risk management colleagues where that might be the case.

Chapter 10

Contract Structure and Key Elements

§ 10:1   Overview

Contract structure is similar across many contract types. Once you start reading and analyzing many contracts, you will quickly note the following common structural features:

- The contract is given a title, it is dated, and the parties are identified.

- The contract may or may not contain recitals—"whereas" clauses. These are the introductory descriptive paragraphs (often beginning with "WHEREAS") at the beginning of the contract that orient the reader. They may, for example, describe how the contract fits with other contracts or within a larger transaction. These provisions are not binding. They can in some cases provide helpful background (for example, explaining the history of a settlement agreement), but should be left out if no useful purpose is served.

- The contract will contain the basic terms of the agreement— the lease, the loan, the merger, the sale, the settlement. For a finance contract, the key terms are all about money—the conditions on which money will be made available and how the investors or lenders will get it back with the agreed return.

- There may be conditions precedent; for a financing, there almost surely will be.

- The contract may contain representations and warranties upon which the other party relies; in finance, these are required from the borrower or issuer.

- One or both parties may agree to covenants mandating or restricting certain actions in support of performance of the basic terms; in the case of a financing, it is the company, of course, that agrees to covenants.

- The contract may set forth defaults or termination events and remedies. In finance, there are defaults that can lead to acceleration of outstanding debt and the termination of commitments.

- A contract of any length or complexity will have a set of defined terms and definitions.

- The contract will usually contain rules of construction and other miscellaneous terms.

- The companions to the listing of parties at the beginning of the contract are the signature blocks at the end. These should match up, precisely.

It is important to understand the way the parts of a contract operate and work together. A contract is not like a newspaper article, a memo, or a pleading. A contract is more like a computer program, a set of rules and procedures, or a machine.

§ 10:2   Title, Date, and Parties; References to Other Contracts

The title ("Indenture" or "Credit Agreement"), the parties, and the date together identify the contract.

Correct identification of the parties is of paramount importance. The parties that are named on and sign the contract, and no others, are obligated to perform under the contract. At closing, evidence of the existence and authority of the obligors will be required.

Given the logistics of execution and delivery, and the need to "pre-close" any complex transaction, the "as of" date is a useful and customary convention. This practice should be distinguished from the back-dating of contracts where that has substantive and inappropriate consequences.

When a contract is referred to in other agreements, the formulation of the reference can be important. If the reference is to the contract "as amended from time to time," then the parties to that contract are free to amend it, and the referring agreement will tag along. If the reference is to the contract "as in effect on the date of its execution," "as in effect on the date hereof," or "as amended by Amendment No. 1 dated as of the date hereof," then the contract reference is frozen. Changes made to the contract not captured by the reference will not be picked up in the referring amendment. Whether this is important or not is something that the lawyers need to figure out.

Sometimes an agreement will refer to another contract "as amended from time to time in accordance with the terms hereof." This formulation may make sense where the referring (controlling) agreement piggybacks on terms contained in the second (controlled) contract (for example, where the referring contract permits payments to be made pursuant to the second contract), and where the intent really is to "freeze" the controlled contract with original approved terms and only such changes as are approved under (or otherwise don't contravene) the controlling agreement. In all other cases, and even though the phrase has a nice comforting ring to it, it probably doesn't make sense, may even generate some odd outcomes (would acceleration under an unauthorized amendment to another debt agreement not give rise to a cross-default?), and would be an example of overdrafting. If the parties to the "controlling" agreement really mean to have a veto over changes to the other contract, then they should have a covenant that gives them that right in a straightforward fashion.

§ 10:3   Successors and Assigns?

Parties to a finance contract are usually defined to include successors and permitted assigns, but the related provisions in the contract are not symmetrical.

Obviously the holders of debt are not going to permit the obligor to assign away its rights and obligations to another party. This is consistent with the general rule under contract law, where a party cannot be relieved of its obligations through a unilateral assignment of such obligations not agreed to by the party to whom they are owed.

However, if a party is a corporation and merges into another corporation, the merged entity becomes, by operation of law, the successor entity bound by contracts to which the two separate corporations have been party. To control an effective change in the obligor through succession by merger, the debt contract should address the issue of succession in the case of a merger.

On the other side of the coin, investors and lenders are very interested in maintaining liquidity in their portfolio—that is, their ability to sell their assets. A public bond indenture is set up from the very beginning to allow bonds to be freely traded. Holders of debt issued in private placements and holders of bank loans are also keen to preserve as much liquidity as possible, but may live with some restrictions on their ability to sell their debt. These restrictions are driven by legal requirements (in particular, compliance with the securities laws, which is an important issue, but beyond the scope of this book) and by the desire of the company and other members of a lending group to restrict membership in the group.

Where a bank or lending group has ongoing funding commitments, the company, other members of the lending group, and third parties who may be relying on the commitments have a strong interest in the identity of the bank or other group members. In these cases there may well be limitations on the ability of credit providers to assign their obligations. This is relevant to syndicated letter of credit facilities and to revolving credit and liquidity arrangements, generally including "swing-line" subfacilities.

There are other considerations that may limit free transferability of bank loans. Companies are reluctant to allow competitors to hold their loans. Coming up to an acquisition, the bidder may want the lead banks to stay on the hook to the point of funding the initial loans. And the composition of the bank group can have a significant effect on requests for waivers and amendments, or in the restructuring or workout context. Companies that find themselves in trouble may find that their agent banks have mostly sold down their positions to other institutions including strategic purchasers in the distressed debt market.

Bank loan agreements also have rather complex provisions permitting the sale of loan participations. Under these arrangements, lenders that are party to the agreement remain in privity with the borrower and retain their lending commitments, but they sell participating interests in the loans against funding by the participants. Participants have some limited voting rights by pass-through, so that their fundamental rights and obligations cannot be changed without their say-so.

§ 10:4 Conditions Precedent

The conditions precedent section of a financing contract contains the checklist of preconditions to availability of funds. If funds are made available in a single closing or drawdown, then they have to be met only once. Conditions precedent to a single funding or to the initial funding under a revolving credit facility will include: documentary requirements and legal preconditions (effectiveness of a merger, filing of security documents), possible third-party consents, representations and warranties being true and correct, and no default (or incipient event of default). In a revolving credit a subset of conditions precedent applies to each subsequent borrowing after the initial borrowing. These are focused on the company's continued financial health and compliance with the agreement—representations and warranties being true and correct, and no default (or incipient default).

§ 10:5   The MAC Clause, Material Litigation, and Incipient Events of Default

By incorporation of representations and warranties, the conditions precedent usually include a material adverse change (MAC) clause, to the effect that there has been no material adverse change (from a certain date, usually a fiscal period end for which there are financial statements on which the lenders or investors relied), and a condition that there is no material litigation other than as disclosed at the time of the funding commitment. Another customary condition is that there be no event of default (entitling debtholders to terminate commitments and accelerate outstanding debt) under the debt agreement, but under most bank credit agreements this condition would also block borrowing of new funds (but not rollovers) if there is an event that, with the giving of notice or passage of time, would constitute an event of default.

No material adverse change, no material litigation, and no default or incipient default are customary factual conditions precedents that can be quite problematic, not to draft, but to interpret. The first two in particular represent a risk for the company that events outside its control can block its access to cash.

The concept of material adverse change, and the related concept of material adverse effect as a materiality qualifier, run throughout financial documentation, but MAC has the most potentially dramatic effect in conditions precedent, including those in commitment letters and underwriting agreements. MAC rarely appears as an event of default, but instead as a condition to the making of loans or other extensions of credit, where a MAC gives the banks an out and excuses them from funding.

Notwithstanding their structural significance to the credit, the MAC and no material litigation clauses are, in fact, rarely formally invoked in the finance context. The MAC and material litigation clauses are *not* good protection for investors or lenders with respect to long-term financial deterioration or accumulating lawsuits. That is, they are not effective substitutes for good covenant construction, including financial covenants that will trip "on the way down." An event that would be considered as a potential material adverse change tends to be sudden, quite exceptionally adverse, and particular to the company, not to the world at large, the general economy, the markets, or the company's industry. There have been attempts to define material adverse change to create a bit more clarity:

> "**Material Adverse Change**" means any event, circumstance, development, change or effect that, individually or in the aggregate with all other events, circumstances, developments, changes and effects, (x) is materially adverse to the business, operations, assets, condition (financial or otherwise) or results of operations of the Company and its Subsidiaries, taken as a whole, (y) has arisen out of the operations or relates directly to the assets of the Company or its Subsidiaries (and not the industry generally) and would reasonably be likely to be materially adverse to the business, operations, assets, condition (financial or otherwise) or results of operations of the Company and its Subsidiaries, taken as a whole, or (z) would reasonably be expected to prevent the consummation of the Merger or prevent the Company from performing its obligations under the Merger Agreement; *provided*, that in no event would any of the following, alone or in combination, be deemed to constitute, nor shall any of the following be taken into account in determining whether there has been, or will be, a "Material Adverse Change": any event, circumstance, change or effect resulting from or relating to (i) a change in general economic or financial market conditions, (ii) any acts of terrorism or war (except, in the case of clauses (i) and (ii), to the extent such event, circumstance, change or effect has had a disproportionate effect on the Company and its Subsidiaries, taken as a whole, as compared to other persons in the industry in which the Company and its Subsidiaries conduct their business), (iii) the announcement of the execution of the Merger Agreement or the pendency or consummation of the Merger, or (iv) compliance with the terms of, or the taking of any action required by, the Merger Agreement.

> **"Material Adverse Effect"** means (a) a material adverse ef-
> fect on the business, operations, assets, liabilities (actual or
> contingent) or financial condition of the Company and its
> Subsidiaries, taken as a whole, (b) a material adverse effect
> on the ability of the Borrowers or the Loan Parties (taken as
> a whole) to perform their respective payment obligations
> under any Loan Document to which any Borrower or any of
> the Loan Parties is a party or (c) a material adverse effect on
> the rights and remedies of the Lenders under any Loan Doc-
> ument.[1]

At the end of the day, though, MAC is more of a "know it when
you see it" type of concept. It is easier to add some concreteness to the
no material litigation test, where a dollar amount of damages
(claimed) can be included. In either case, when there is a "material
adverse change" or litigation of a magnitude sufficient to raise questions under these clauses, the company's need for funds—to post
bond, to secure trade credit—is often quite pressing. What the MAC
or material litigation clause tends to do in these circumstances is
bring the parties to the table to address the new credit situation.

Bank credit agreements usually provide that an incipient event of
default ("an event that with the passage of time or giving of notice
would constitute an event of default") will block funding. This too
can be difficult to interpret, particularly in the case of a typical judgment default such as: "a judgment is entered against the company or a
subsidiary in the amount of $500,000 or more and such judgment is
not paid or stayed pending appeal within ten days." Is there an incipi-

---

1.   CREDIT AGREEMENT, dated as of August 11, 2005 among Solar Capital
Corp. and The Overseas Borrowers Party Thereto, as Borrowers, Sungard
Holdco LLC, Sungard Data Systems Inc., J.P. Morgan Chase Bank, N.A., as
Administrative Agent, Swing Line Lender and L/C Issuer, The Other
Lenders Party Thereto, Citigroup Global Markets Inc. and Deutsche Bank
Securities Inc., as Co-Syndication Agents, and Barclays Bank PLC and The
Royal Bank of Canada, as Co-Documentation Agents, and J.P. Morgan Se-
curities Inc. and Citigroup Global Markets Inc., as Co-Lead Arrangers,
and J.P. Morgan Securities Inc., Citigroup Global Markets Inc. and Deutsche Bank Securities Inc., as Joint Bookrunners, at 35–36, *available at*
www.sec.gov/Archives/edgar/data/789388/000119312505221637/
dex101.htm.

ent event of default, blocking funding, during the ten-day period? I would say the better argument is that there is not, but it is not entirely clear, and if a company intends to borrow solely to satisfy that large judgment, the lender may wish to discuss the matter further. Best practice is to review all events of default as drafted and see whether elements of grace and notice (procedural elements) can be clearly distinguished from the substantive elements of the default.

§ 10:6   Representations and Warranties

Representations and warranties are made by one party to another party that relies upon them. They are made *as of* a certain date and are not ongoing promises or requirements to do or refrain from doing certain things.

In a finance contract, representations are not symmetrical but, instead, fall mostly upon the company as obligor. The company represents as to its existence, due authorization, execution, enforceability of the contract, and non-contravention (that the contract does not violate law or other contracts, or require the imposition of a lien (under an equal and ratable clause)). It will typically represent as to the accuracy of financial statements on which the investors or lenders have relied, and there may be other representations as well.

§ 10:6.1   *Representations As "Hidden Covenants"*

Occasionally a representation may be over-drafted in such a way that it becomes a "hidden covenant." For example, a representation may say that the borrower represents that X is *and at all times will be* true. This construction should be avoided (by drafters) and resisted (by companies) because representations are focused on at certain times and not understood to contain ongoing compliance requirements. A requirement of this type may be easily overlooked in the future.

Another type of hidden (and unintended) covenant is a representation that is true at contract signing but, though required to be repeated at future borrowings, has not been drafted broadly enough to take into account changes in facts permitted by the contract. An example would be "All subsidiaries of the borrower are listed on Schedule I." The formation or acquisition of additional subsidiaries may be permitted or not prohibited under the agreement, and yet, if there were new subsidiaries, then the representation could not be repeated at ("brought down" to) a future date. Technical fixes would be: to qualify the representation by adding "at the Closing Date," to permit or require Schedule I to be updated, or to add "or were formed or acquired after the Closing Date in compliance with the terms of this agreement."

These may seem like subtle points, but to an experienced finance lawyer these "hidden covenants" will all but literally leap off the page.

§ 10:6.2   Representations About the Unknown: Who Bears the Risk?

A representing party may object that it is not in a position to make a requested representation because it cannot know or, if the representation has to be repeated in the future, cannot control all of the relevant facts. Sometimes the scope or strength of representation can be limited by inserting materiality qualifiers (such as "except as would not in the aggregate have a Material Adverse Effect") or the knowledge qualifier "to the best of its knowledge."

In other cases, under an "allocation of risk" theory of representation, it may be appropriate to put the burden of untruth upon a party regardless of the ultimate knowability of all relevant facts. This rough justice may be good enough where there is only a small risk of a misrepresentation having serious consequences or when it really is fair for the representing party to hold the other harmless for the unknown elements.

But a party that knowingly makes false representations to induce the relying party to act to its detriment is subject to claims of fraud, and counsel can be implicated as well. If the party being asked to represent something it does not and cannot know is uncomfortable with the idea of possible misrepresentation but is willing to underwrite the risk of the unknown, then an alternative is to recast the untruth of the relevant facts as either a default or a predicate for indemnification or other remedy. This bypasses the characterization of the untruth as a "misrepresentation" and goes straight to the agreed-upon consequences.

§ 10:6.3 Misrepresentation Versus Inability to Make a Representation

Misrepresentation may give rise to claims for damages under general contract law and in equity, but under most debt contracts the principal effect of a material misrepresentation is a default, permitting the credit to be accelerated and any lending commitments to be terminated. Misrepresentation is a failure of a representation to be true *when made (or deemed made)*, and in most corporate finance settings, it would be a drafting error to list as a default "a representation ceases to be true and correct in all material respects."

If a representation is untrue at the time a company needs money and must be made as a condition to funding, then the company cannot borrow without a waiver from its lenders. This dynamic can lead a company from an adverse event directly into a liquidity crisis. For example, if a large judgment is entered against the company and it must represent as to no material litigation, then it may not be able to borrow the money to pay the judgment or post bond to appeal. As we've noted, the principal exposure is under the material adverse change and material litigation representations, although the absence of default or incipient event of default can also be a problematic condition.

§ 10:7 Covenants

Covenants are promises to take or refrain from taking certain actions, or to maintain or prevent certain conditions or events. There is a tension in coming to terms over covenants. Investors or lenders are trying to preserve the world as it stands today, maybe improved, but generally with only such changes as are both likely over the life of the agreement and benign from the creditor's perspective. The company, on the other hand, wants sufficient flexibility to react to a world that is certain to change in unpredictable ways.

§ 10:7.1 Affirmative Covenants, Negative Covenants, and Financial Covenants

Covenants can be described as either affirmative covenants (the company promising to do something), negative covenants (the company promising *not* to do certain things), and financial covenants.

171

Breaches of negative covenants and financial covenants tend to be more clear-cut and more serious than alleged or possible breaches of affirmative covenants such as "good housekeeping" covenants and information covenants, which tend to be either vaguely drawn or easily curable. There is usually no grace period before a breach of a negative covenant or financial covenant ripens into a fully actionable default. Otherwise, in practice, the distinction among these types of covenants rarely matters.

§ 10:7.2   *Maintenance Versus Incurrence Tests*

Covenant design and analysis requires careful attention to time and valuation. What is measured, and when is compliance tested? To a casual reader, the following two covenants appear the same:

- The Company will not incur any Debt if after giving effect to such incurrence Total Debt would exceed 200% of stockholder's equity.

- At no time will Total Debt exceed 200% of stockholders' equity.

But the difference is significant. Stockholders' equity can be eroded through losses. If this occurred and as a result Total Debt already outstanding exceeded 200% of stockholders' equity, there would be a default under the second (maintenance) test, but not under the first (incurrence) test. The second (maintenance) test might appear in a bank loan agreement but, as a rule, public or quasi-public debt agreements contain incurrence tests only and not maintenance tests. If you are representing an issuer in a high-yield bond deal, then you would normally be expected to object strongly to any covenant that was not an incurrence test, and the bankers would generally not offer up documents containing maintenance tests. In general, private (senior) debt is supposed to "trip" before public or quasi-public debt (especially subordinated debt).

§ 10:7.3   *Principles of Covenant Design and Analysis*

A covenant package should permit credit-neutral (or favorable) transactions, restrict credit-dilutive transactions, and treat transactions that are substantially identical from a credit-effect perspective on a consistent basis.

For example, in principle covenants should not restrict refinancings that take place at the same level in the capital structure (subordinated debt refinances subordinated debt) or at a level more junior (preferred stock refinances subordinated debt), and do not have terms (such as shorter maturities) that, taken together, do not disadvantage the lender.

On the other hand, lenders at a holding company may legitimately restrict subsidiary borrowings, and lenders to the subsidiary may, for their part, legitimately object to a merger up into the parent. (Can you sum up the reason why, in two words?)

The question in each case is whether the lender is made worse off by the transaction.

The covenant package should be blind to the form of a transaction, and instead should focus, from a credit perspective, on its substance and its effect. A covenant that permits the company to acquire a building with the proceeds of a $10 million mortgage loan but prohibits the company from buying the same building subject to an existing mortgage loan of $10 million (which might be more favorable than the mortgage the company can obtain) is not well-constructed. Or, if a borrower can make an equity contribution to a subsidiary, why not a loan?

§ 10:7.4 Related Definitions: How Important Are They?

Fully understanding the meaning of a contract, including the covenants, requires close reading of the related definitions. (By "close," I mean very close, as in printed out and sitting side by side on your desk so that you can cross-refer to the definition at each instance where it used in the operative provisions.)

There may be some important subtleties to consider, and these are easier to identify through this close, side-by-side reading. For example, many of the concepts in financial covenants will derive from the company's financial statements and can be calculated with certainty. But because GAAP does not capture all the concepts of importance to lenders, some of the adjustments may not. This is even more pervasive with negative covenants that restrict activities that go beyond terms reflected in financial statements. For example, a definition of "debt" for negative covenant purposes may include liabilities (such as guarantees or other contingent financial obligations) that do not appear on the company's balance sheet, do not generate "interest expense" on the company's income statement, may be indeterminate in amount and may not count for financial covenant purposes. Someone who does not understand the difference between how a financial covenant works and how a negative covenant works might not understand how "debt" should be defined in each case, or why the terms used might differ.

§ 10:8   Defaults

§ 10:8.1   *Default Versus Event of Default*

Corporate finance documents, except for very short-term instruments, contain a list of defaults. Upon default, the debtholders can accelerate the debt, demanding immediate repayment in full, and terminate lending commitments. Defaults typically include failure to pay when due, covenant default, failure of a representation or warranty to have been untrue when made, cross-default (default under another debt agreement) or cross-acceleration, and bankruptcy, and may also include other events that mark a material deterioration affecting the company or the credit. Change of control can be treated as a default or, alternatively, as a trigger for mandatory redemption or put.

Many defaults contain a grace period or a period for cure after notice. After the grace period or notice period has lapsed, the incipient event of default becomes an Event of Default, or predicate for immediate acceleration. A "Default" typically means an Event of Default *or* "an event or condition that with the passage of time or giving of notice would constitute an Event of Default." For example, a failure to make a payment of principal may be an Event of Default, whereas failure to make an interest payment may not be an Event of Default until five days after the due date with continued non-payment; three days after the due date, there is a Default but not an Event of Default.

§ 10:8.2   Acceleration; the "Ipso Facto" Clause

How often does debt become accelerated under default provisions? In the corporate finance world, it is not all that often. For a company in a troubled credit situation there are generally two states—workout and bankruptcy. In a workout situation, the company is in discussions with its lenders. Some may have declared a default or they may have agreed among themselves to a standstill (all agreeing to hold back from the exercise of remedies for a period in the hopes of arriving at an agreement on a plan of restructuring), but it is fairly rare in the U.S. for a company of any substantial size to have its lenders declare default, accelerate debt, and then attach assets. Normally, a company will have sought the protection of bankruptcy courts before too much of this sort of thing is allowed. The first thing that will happen in bankruptcy is that all will be put back on an even footing (for example, by recapturing preferential transfers) and allowed a claim in the amount of their debt.

In the case of bankruptcy, the debt is usually said to become immediately due and payable, without action by debtholders. This "ipso facto" clause is included because the bankruptcy code stays action by creditors, and acceleration by the lenders could be deemed to violate the stay. So long as they are allowed their full claim in bankruptcy, acceleration is academic.

Regardless of how rarely the default provisions result in actual acceleration and exercise of remedies, they are 100% standard and do of course set the baseline for leverage and strategy. As with other customary provisions (such as material adverse change), these terms are what will bring the parties to the table for necessary discussion and only rarely be given literal effect.

§ 10:8.3   Cross-Defaults

Any business with multiple debt agreements needs to manage its cross-default provisions. There are different types of cross-defaults. The strictest type trips if there is any event of default under another debt agreement *or any event that with the passage of time or giving of notice would constitute an event of default under another debt agreement.* This second phrase eliminates, vis-à-vis *this* lender, the grace periods and notice requirements that the company has negotiated with other lenders. This strictest version of a cross-default might appear in bank and other private credit documents with senior lenders, and does in fact afford them a senior or preferred position over other debtholders: They will *always* be the first to trip.

A public bond indenture would not contain a cross-default per se but would include as a default the acceleration of a material amount of other debt or the failure to pay a material amount of debt when due. This might be referred to as a cross-acceleration provision, in contrast to a cross-default.

An intermediate ground would be a cross-default that is tripped if the defaulted debt is subject to immediate acceleration, that is, all notice requirements have been met and all grace periods elapsed so that an Event of Default exists.

A tricky and unintended problem can occur when two senior credit facilities both contain the first, hair-trigger form of cross-default. The result can be that, in the case of an incipient default under either, both will trip prior to negotiated notice and grace provisions by virtue of the circular cross-default. This can even occur when only one of two senior credit facilities has a hair-trigger cross-default, where the incipient default under the other effectively trips full default under both. In either case, this can be a conceptually interesting result, but is unlikely to be what the parties bargained for.

§ 10:8.4   *Judgment and Lien Defaults*

The default provisions relating to judgments and liens are another tricky area. A typical judgment default might say that it is an Event of Default if a judgment in excess of $10 million is entered and not either paid or stayed pending appeal within ten days. Let's say, as would also be typical, that it is an immediate Event of Default if a negative covenant, including the negative pledge (covenant restricting liens), is breached. The negative pledge has an exception for judgment liens, but there is no capacity for secured debt.

Suppose that a judgment in excess of $10 million is rendered against the company, one that it intends to appeal. Under state law, the company must bond the judgment in order to appeal and prevent levy against its assets. The bondsman requires a letter of credit. Banks might be willing to provide the letter of credit, but only on a secured basis. In the meantime, the company's revolving credit agreement says that no loans will be made so long as there is a "Default" under the credit agreement. Can the company borrow under the credit agreement? How can it appeal the judgment? What's *your* verdict?

§ 10:9   General or "Miscellaneous" Terms

At the back of the agreements you will find the general or "miscellaneous" terms. These might normally include or cover: a merger or integration clause that states that the contract constitutes the entire agreement between the parties; governing law; submission to jurisdiction and waiver of forum non conveniens; notice provisions; provisions regarding amendment, transferability and assignment; counterpart signatures; governing language (in the international context); survival; and a "no waiver and severability" clause.

In terms of drafting, these terms tend to be "boilerplate"—part of a standard form or copied from another agreement. That doesn't mean the lawyers can be asleep at the wheel, though. Each of these provisions has a meaning, purpose, and history, and you should make sure you know what they say and why they are included. If you don't understand why something is included or find the language unclear, ask! Occasionally a piece of "boilerplate" contains a mistake that is carried over from deal to deal because no one has bothered to read it carefully. While you do not want to spend a lot of time laboring over these provisions, they do merit a good close read, and some of them can turn out to be quite important after the fact—in particular, the amendment and notice provisions.

§ 10:10 Definitions

In financial contracts of any length, the definitions are set out in a separate section. When you are drafting or reading and analyzing a contract, it is, as we've noted, critical to look at the definition at each place where the defined term is used. If you find yourself having to flip pages or screens too much, print out the definitions so that you can refer to them separately. One reason to require the side-by-side reading is that it is, unfortunately, not unheard of for a definition to be left out of an agreement altogether or (less harmfully) a defined term to be included that is not actually used in the document. Another problem is that sometimes a defined term (such as Debt or Lien or

Investment or Guarantee) is used in a place where the common meaning of the word is intended. This can have pernicious effect or be circular.

If a lengthy definition is used exclusively or principally in one operative provision, it is good practice to put the definition in the operative provision, where it will be easy to read in conjunction with the operative terms. In that case, the definition section will say that the term "has the meaning set forth in Section X [the operative provision]."

Definitions should *not* contain non-intuitive elements or substantive operative content, which can turn them into "hidden covenants." Occasionally a lawyer will overload a definition with substantive requirements and qualifications. This is not good practice, because people using the document in the future will read the operative provisions and will not in every instance diligently flip back to the definition of each defined term. Jamming out-of-the-ordinary stuff into a definition where it won't be easily found or focused on can even be just plain devious.

§ 10:11 Who's Covered?

When down in the trenches laboring over particular wording, it is easy to lose sight of the agreement's overall philosophy and approach as to which companies are obligated, bound, restricted, or covered. What is the general scope of representation? Which companies are covered by the covenants? Which companies are the subject of cross-default, bankruptcy, and other defaults? Are the provisions consistent? On this point alone, it is worth at least one careful look through the agreement. For example, an omission of the word "Restricted" in front of one instance of "Subsidiary" could have far-reaching and unintended effect.

§ 10:12 How Do the Provisions Work Together?

In brief:

- Representations are statements by the company made at a point in time—when the funds are first made available or, in the case of a revolving credit, when loans are made or rolled over later.

- Covenants are promises to do certain things, not to do certain other things, and to meet or maintain certain financial performance standards.

- Defaults enable debtholders to accelerate loans and to terminate any unfunded commitments. They include failure of a representation to have been (materially) true and correct when made, and breach of covenants (grace periods may apply).

- Conditions precedent control the access to funds—the initial purchase of bonds, the making of loans, etc. A reduced set of conditions usually apply in a revolving credit to loans made after the initial loans or after an effective date. A further reduced set of conditions may control rollovers. Conditions precedent normally incorporate by reference the representations, which may include a MAC clause, as well as require that there be no default (including an incipient default?), which in turn means that there be no breach of covenant.

The interlocking is most complex within the four corners of a typical credit agreement. In the case of a one-time issue of public or quasi-public debt, the conditions precedent and representations live in the underwriting or initial purchase agreement and have limited applicability after the issuance of the debt, at which point the covenants and the defaults take over.

This interlocking of representations, covenants, defaults, and conditions precedent becomes second nature to finance lawyers, but is not immediately apparent from the sequential reading of the credit documents. The good news is that these basic contract mechanisms are more or less standard in corporate finance practice.

Chapter 11

Housekeeping, Insurance, and Information Covenants

§ 11:1   Good Housekeeping

"Housekeeping" covenants are those customary contractual provisions that require a company to maintain its "corporate household" in good order. They typically include requirements to maintain corporate existence and qualifications to do business, to maintain assets in good working order, to comply with laws, and to pay taxes and other claims in due course, particularly those that might, by statute, "prime" the company's debt to the lender or give rise to liens. These provisions are almost always included in either short or long version and rarely generate any controversy that cannot be resolved by the insertion of some concept of materiality (for example, "except as would not in the aggregate have a Material Adverse Effect"), though there may be some back and forth in a credit agreement discussion about lender rights to review records, talk with accountants, and visit borrower premises and facilities. It would be the rare situation where a lender would be prepared to declare a default based on breach of such general provisions; defaults regarding these provisions typically provide for a period of cure after notice in any case.

§ 11:2 Insurance Covenants

The insurance covenant is one type of covenant that might be only a "housekeeping" covenant or might be considerably more substantive in effect, and bears special mention. The insurance covenant may range from something quite innocuous, really just a requirement to do what other prudent people in the same business do, to something quite elaborate and specific, with the benefits of certain types of insurance, such as property and casualty insurance, running to the lenders as additional insureds, or loss payees.

You would expect the more substantial requirements in a secured credit, where the lenders are looking to the value of pledged assets to support the general credit of the company. Clearly, if those assets are destroyed or damaged, the value received should be part of the lenders' security. It follows that where assets are pledged, and sometimes even when they are not, the lenders may require either repayment of their loans (to the extent of the proceeds, or perhaps, in the case of total loss, in full), or the escrow of insurance proceeds pending repair or replacement. Usually insurance proceeds (and condemnation awards) are treated as if they were proceeds of asset sales under any provisions of the agreement requiring prepayment from the proceeds of asset sales.

A common error is to include insurance and condemnation provisions relating to real property in a (standard form) mortgage and to omit any references to those provisions in the basic credit agreement. When the provisions are in an ancillary agreement, such as a mortgage, but not in the principal agreement, it is more likely that parties will fail to focus on them during negotiations and will overlook them in the future.

Another common error is for insurance and condemnation provisions in a mortgage to be actually inconsistent with those in the credit agreement or other principal debt document. "How does this happen?" you might reasonably ask. The answer is: A banking lawyer drafts the credit agreement, a real estate lawyer drafts the mortgage, and neither looks at the other's work. To reduce the chances of inconsistencies, lawyers should use mortgage forms within a coordinated suite of credit documents, and most substantive provisions should be reserved to the principal debt document, with cross-references from the mortgage. Where the mortgage contains substantive provisions for default or paydowns, the principal debt document should cross-reference to those so that they are not overlooked in the future.

§ 11:3 Information Covenants

Information covenants are intended to assure a flow of information to the lender or investor that will keep the lender apprised of developments in the company's business and provide a basis for checking covenant compliance. In the private credit context, the submission of information by the company to the lender or investor under these covenants also prompts a dialogue regarding financial performance and outlook, provides the occasion for relationship-building, and meets the lender's prudent lending due diligence and record-keeping needs.

Holders of debt are usually entitled to get annual audited and quarterly unaudited financial statements (accompanied by certificates regarding covenant compliance), public communications to stockholders, and most SEC filings. If the company is a public company its 10-K and 10-Q reports will fulfill most of the financial reporting requirements. In the public or quasi-public debt markets, the information covenants are crafted so that the debtholders are not burdened with inside information. Credit agreements may require that the audited financials are not qualified as to scope of audit (meaning that the auditors were limited in carrying out their audit) or going concern (meaning that there is substantial doubt the company can remain in business—for example, because all its debt is in default and accelerable!).

In the private bank lending market, lenders are usually entitled to request additional information on some reasonable basis; in the leveraged context, borrowers are generally required to provide much more on a regular basis, such as budgets, notices of material litigation, and notices of default under other debt agreements. How much the lenders want and the company will agree to depends largely on the type of deal and on the creditworthiness of the company and its consequent bargaining leverage. As we've already noted, non-traditional participants in bank credit facilities may receive different and more limited information packages, to ensure that they will not be tainted with potential inside information.

Historically, one would say that failure to meet information requirements was unlikely to lead to an actionable default. In the private credit context, bank lenders would be in communication with the company, find out what was going on, and agree to delays in the delivery of information. In the public context, many would have thought that the debtholders were entitled to piggyback on SEC filings, as and when made, and that was it; if the company was not or ceased to be an SEC reporting company, debtholders were entitled to information comparable to what would be required if the SEC reporting requirements did apply. This seems rather straightforward.

However, in 2006, bondholders of BearingPoint called a default on the basis that the company had failed to make its SEC filings within the specified time periods due to accounting reviews and possible restatements required to take account of backdated stock options. BearingPoint was in good company in its predicament, as there was a veritable rash of stock-option back-dating reviews. As troubling as the underlying problem might have been, the company most likely did not expect the problem to be compounded by its bondholders calling a default under an information covenant.

This case illustrates how wording that appears to be "bland" and "inconsequential" can have possibly unintended consequences. It is also a good example of how a small difference in wording can have a big effect. There could be a significant difference in outcome depending on which of the following formulations was used: "as and when filed with the SEC" versus "as and when required to be filed with the SEC" versus "within X days of the end of each fiscal quarter/within Y days of the end of each fiscal year." Lastly, it is indicative of the willingness of some players in the debt capital markets to go sleuthing for defaults in unexpected places, to look for unforeseen, if arguably not unintended, consequences of contract language, and to place sometimes profitable bets on document interpretation.

Chapter 12

Debt and Liens (Negative Pledges)

Debt and lien covenants are the key credit protection covenants. Lenders are very interested in making sure that their borrowers do not take on more debt than they can repay. It is bad for a lender to find out its borrower is over-leveraged. But it is even worse if the other debt has a priority. This can occur in one of two ways. The other debt may have the benefit of collateral security or it may have been incurred at a subsidiary level. In either case it has an effective prior position. If the other debt is secured, it has a first claim on the collateral; if the other debt was incurred at a subsidiary level, it has a first claim on the assets of the subsidiary.

Debt and lien covenants address these concerns.

§ 12:1   The Negative Pledge (Restriction on Liens)

A negative pledge is a restriction on the ability of the borrower to create liens. If a credit facility or indenture has only one covenant, it is likely to be a negative pledge. A negative pledge, together with a minimum net worth test, provides bare bones credit protection.

A negative pledge protects the lender from finding itself unsecured while other lenders have security but, notwithstanding the name, is not itself a pledge of any kind and does not provide any security or collateral to that lender. This is not always clearly understood. Some people erroneously think that a negative pledge is a sort of quick and dirty way to get security—not so!

§ 12:2   The Construction of Negative Covenants

The structure of negative covenants is generally the same across all subject matters. For example, in a negative pledge:

1.   the concept of "lien" is defined;

2.   the creation or existence of "liens" is prohibited, though the prohibition might be limited in its coverage to liens securing "debt" as defined or to liens on certain assets; and

3.   there is a list of exceptions, or a basket limitation, or the last item in a list of exceptions will be a basket ("other liens securing amounts not in excess of $10 million in aggregate at any time").

The list of exceptions will be different based not only on the substantive agreement about the company's needs, but also on the scope of prohibition. For example, if the negative pledge only limits liens securing debt, exceptions should all relate to liens securing debt, as defined. The list of exceptions does not need to include other types of liens, and a list of exceptions that is appropriate for one negative pledge may be overinclusive or may fall short if used in another negative pledge. As another example, a basket for liens securing debt would not be available to cover liens securing obligations that don't constitute debt as defined. So generally, a basket clause should correspond to the original prohibition.

This structure—definition, prohibition, and exceptions—is common across all negative covenants. If you read the text of the covenant without studying the definitions or make up the list of exceptions without looking carefully at the scope of the prohibition, then you are likely to end up with a covenant that does not make sense.

§ 12:3   Equal and Ratable Clauses

In credit agreements, negative pledges flat out prohibit the creation of liens or liens securing debt, with certain exceptions or subject to a certain overall limit, or basket. In the public or quasi-public debt markets, though, it is standard for the negative pledge to include a so-called equal and ratable clause. This clause says that the company may create liens not otherwise permitted under the covenant, provided it equally and ratably secures the debt issued under the indenture or other agreement containing the clause.

A non-contravention representation for a particular financing will frequently contain a statement to the effect that the financing does not require the creation of a lien under another agreement. This means that no equal and ratable clause will be triggered by the financing. In addition, a lawyer for the company may be required to give an opinion to this effect; if you are giving an opinion of this type, be sure to limit its scope to clearly identified other agreements (that you have carefully reviewed!).

Authoritative interpretation of equal and ratable clauses is frustratingly sparse. There is a fair amount of commentary on such subjects as whether a particular clause provides the basis for an equitable lien and when the equitable lien might arise.

There are much more interesting practical issues and questions that come up with some frequency, such as:

- Who is most interested in making sure that there is full compliance with equal and ratable clauses? The secured lenders taking the security that triggers the requirement—because in any case they are subject to having to share! There are no odds for lenders in playing too fast and loose with the covenant. This is another case (compare the concern of senior lenders regarding the terms of subordination) where credit providers have a strong interest in the interpretation of agreements to which they are not a party.

- What collateral is subject to the requirement? The simplest way to comply is to share one pool of collateral. However:

    1. If the equal and ratable clause appears in a negative pledge that in the first instance only restricts liens on asset class A, and the triggering lien is on asset classes A

and B, then it seems appropriate to restrict the sharing to asset class A. The lenders having the benefit of the triggering lien should study the words carefully and, if there is doubt, could consider a savings clause (obliquely worded so as not to give up the issue), and should also consider the credit aspect of having to share class B, if it comes to that.

2. If it is not possible to share the collateral, then a comparable pool of collateral should be identified. This was the path taken with respect to the Mexican "Brady bonds" issued in the 1980s. New bonds then issued were collateralized by U.S. treasuries as to payment of principal at scheduled maturity only; outstanding bonds had the benefit of equal and ratable clauses. Of course the value of the collateral as against the face amount of the bonds varied directly as a function of the maturity date. Could Mexico have provided collateral for the outstanding bonds based on the percentage of face value secured for the newly issued bonds? Possibly. Or should they have collateralized the outstanding bonds, most with shorter maturities, with treasuries covering payment of principal at scheduled maturity? The latter course was more conservative on the facts, and it was not courting controversy.

• Does the equal and ratable clause implicate paydown schedules and requirements, requiring them to be proportional? To say yes would seem to read far too much into a piece of boilerplate intended generally to get the parties who bargained for it into a secured status when a borrower they have lent to on an unsecured basis becomes a secured borrower.

• To what extent can the lenders having the benefit of the "triggering" lien control, first, the decision to take recourse to the shared collateral, and, thereafter, the remedies? This is comparable to dealing with a second position lien,[1] but without the benefit of having the "second position" lenders at the table negotiating the terms that will be acceptable to them.

----

1. *See* section 6:4.9.

Generally, however, it seems appropriate to reserve to the lenders having the benefit of the "triggering" lien both the ability to commence any remedial action and to direct its course, so long as they understand that they cannot do either of these things in a way that directly or demonstrably adversely affects the sharing of the benefits of the collateral.

- As a further elaboration on the point, can the lenders who bargained for the benefit of the "triggering" lien release the lien without regard to the rights of the "equal and ratable" claimants? There are almost certainly limits on their ability to do so. For example, if a company is in distress, then the release of a lien on the shared collateral against payment of proceeds of sale of that collateral to the one group of lenders but not the others is quite likely to be questioned. This sequence of events has to create a preference risk for the lenders who are being paid, as they have to assert that the shared lien was extinguished, at least momentarily, in order to avoid the duty to share the proceeds. This is a very tricky business.

There seems to be little reason to grant the "equal and ratable" group express contractual rights they did not bargain for, in terms of control of remedies or the release of the lien. What they bargained for was to be along for the ride. To the extent necessary to have assurance that the equal and ratable clause has been complied with, and in view of the paucity of useful case authority, it seems more attractive, in a close case, to include a savings clause rather than give up too much to the tag-alongs.

§ 12:4   Restrictions on Sale-Leasebacks

Sale-leaseback covenants are intended to capture "end-runs" around a negative pledge, where the company uses a sale-leaseback to finance an asset it owns without creating a lien. In a sale-leaseback, the asset is sold to a third party and (usually) goes off the balance sheet of the seller, but is leased back to the seller under (usually) an operating lease.

Exceptions for sale-leaseback covenants tend to be of the following types:

(1) leases of short duration (say, less than three years);

(2) sale-leasebacks permitted to be incurred up to a dollar limitation;

(3) sale-leasebacks where the sale of the asset is permitted under the asset sale covenant and the sale proceeds are used to reduce debt;

(4) sale-leasebacks where the corresponding secured debt could have been incurred;

(5) a combination requiring *either* (3) or (4); and

(6) a combination requiring *both* (3) and (4).

Viewing a sale-leaseback as an alternative form of secured financing, (4) makes sense, whereas (3) may or may not. Thus, (5) is workable and (6) often is not. A fair number of high-yield indentures nevertheless have followed the approach in (6), even though the comparable secured debt—a substantially identical transaction in a different form—would not be treated as an asset sale.

§ 12:5   Restrictions on Negative Pledges

A lender, secured or not, may want to make sure that no other lenders have the ability to stop it from getting collateral or additional collateral. This is accomplished through a covenant that prohibits other negative pledges.

§ 12:6   Debt Covenants

Covenants restricting debt are of basically two types. Some rely on a financial test alone. Though they may use a definition of debt that is not entirely GAAP-based, the elements of the defined term "debt" used in these covenants must be susceptible of exact valuation.

Others are negative covenants:

1.   "debt" is defined; it almost always includes some obligations that would not appear as indebtedness on a GAAP balance sheet;

2.   then "debt" as defined is prohibited; and

3.   lastly, a list of enumerated exceptions and/or a quantitative test or basket will qualify the prohibition.

In a negative covenant of this type, neither the elements of the debt definition nor the exceptions need be susceptible of exact valuation, except for the purposes of quantitative exceptions. In high-yield bonds, the debt limitation is an incurrence test, and the principal quantitative exception is based on a pro-forma coverage test, using historical numbers but giving effect to the debt to be incurred. There is also a list of permitted debt exceptions.

Again, the exceptions should not only reflect the parties' substantive agreement but should dovetail technically with the prohibition. For example, to list in the exceptions "obligations in respect of surety bonds incurred in the ordinary course of business and consistent with past practice," where the definition of "debt" does not include obligations in respect of surety bonds, can only muddy the waters. More technically speaking, this sort of construction raises a possible "negative implication" that the parties intended to prohibit obligations in respect of surety bonds incurred other than in the ordinary course of business and consistent with past practice.

§ 12:7   Restrictions on Debt of Subsidiaries

Whether or not there is an overall debt limitation at the company level, there is likely to be a restriction on the debt of subsidiaries—again, because that debt is structurally senior. Preferred stock might be considered debt for this purpose, and this would be typical in a high-yield indenture. Note that, while there might be a list of exceptions for permitted debt at the subsidiary level, a general ability to incur subsidiary debt provided a coverage test is met on a pro forma basis would not be available.

§ 12:8   The Priority Debt Package

Investment grade bond indentures have often included a cluster of three covenants that together limit priority debt, by limiting:

- the amount of debt that can be secured by the issuer without "equally and ratably" securing the subject debt;

- sale and leaseback transactions; and

- debt incurred or guaranteed at a subsidiary level.

The three covenants typically work together and jointly tap a single "basket," such as 10% of Consolidated Net Tangible Assets. This sort of "priority debt" limitation may appear in indentures that place no restriction on total debt for the consolidated entity.

Chapter 13

General Business Covenants

§ 13:1   Purposes

General business covenants impose restrictions on the business activities and corporate structure of the company. The purpose of these covenants from the point of view of the lender or investor is to preserve to a lesser or greater degree the status quo of the company. But the company needs the flexibility to run its business and cannot foresee, or at least cannot foresee in detail, the various transactions and activities that it might want to engage in or pursue. These are the conflicting perspectives that need to be worked out through negotiation.

A further constraint will be the need to provide a covenant package that will be sufficient to market or place the debt and, if the debt is to be rated, to satisfy rating agency requirements. In some cases lenders and investors, or the rating agency, may have a "check the box" approach, meaning that a certain type of covenant needs to be included even if there is a long list of exceptions.

The "easiest" approach that a lender or underwriter might take in designing these general business covenants is to start by saying that the company cannot do anything that it is not currently doing, and cannot do anything in a way different from the way it is doing it now, except in accordance with plans it expressly describes prior to finalizing the debt documentation. In certain situations, this "easy" approach may be justified—for example, where the credit is of very short duration or where the lender wants to force an early refinancing. A small "club" of banks lending to a company in financial distress may be justified in taking this approach, and say "come to us if you need a waiver." However, in more ordinary circumstances, the easy road proves to be unnecessarily burdensome to the company and generates the need for many waivers and amendments. Having to get waivers and amendments is costly and time-consuming, and it does not reflect well on either the company or the responsible financial institution if they are constantly having to fix up their agreement. So it is better for the lawyer, whether representing the company or the lenders or underwriter, to instead take the high road and to figure out whether a more conceptual or scaled-back approach can work, protecting the debtholders but permitting the company a reasonable amount of operational and even strategic flexibility.

§ 13:1.1　Preserving the Identity of the Obligor and the Source of Repayment

Stepping back to first principles for a moment: general business covenants are intended to preserve the company's existence and the business and asset base from which repayment will be made. Preserving the borrower's existence and business and asset base is the focus of merger and asset sale covenants. "Restricted payments" covenants, which limit dividends and other payments to shareholders, and covenants that directly or indirectly prohibit or disadvantage partially owned subsidiaries trap assets within the borrower group. Transactions with affiliate covenants are intended to prevent "sweetheart" deals with affiliates that might circumvent "restricted payments" covenants. Covenants that restrict the company's line of business, capital expenditures, "investments" and "acquisitions" control expenses but also control expansion beyond the "known" of the status quo.

§ 13:1.2 Reducing Risk

General business covenants may also limit specific activities that are thought to be risky (for example, derivatives), provide inadequate return (the incurrence of guarantees), or represent unknown or unquantifiable exposure (the incurrence of "contingent obligations").

§ 13:1.3 Controlling the Use of Cash

Covenants that restrict possible uses of cash can indirectly force debt reduction: to the extent that distributions to stockholders, investment in the business, and business expansion are limited, reduction of debt turns out to be the only permitted use of cash. In some cases, this de facto "squeeze" of excess cash toward paydown of debt is exactly what is intended. Covenants may also directly force reductions in debt, so that, for example, proceeds of asset sales are required to be applied to prepayment of debt.

Conversely, a covenant package may provide that excess cash flow not required to pay down debt may be used to build a kitty to pay stockholders or to finance expansion.

Viewed as a package, the general business covenants govern the allocation of the company's cash resources. Keeping this in mind as you analyze the various types of covenants—many of them overlapping in coverage or conceptually muddy—should help you make sense of their intended scope and effect.

§ 13:2 By Type of Transaction or Activity

§ 13:2.1 Mergers and Asset Sales

Merger and asset sale covenants appear in many forms, from weak versions you would find in a public debt indenture for a highly rated issuer, to a strong version you would find in a credit agreement or indenture for a non-investment grade company.

In the case of an investment grade public debt indenture, the principal purpose of the merger covenant is to provide for a continuity of the debt obligation over to the successor merged entity or to the purchaser of "all or substantially all" the assets of the issuer. There is a significant amount of gloss on "all or substantially all."[1] In any transfer of a significant amount of assets, measured either by value of the assets or by value of the income they produce, the "all or substantially all" question is relevant and needs to be analyzed. Under governing precedent, the test kicks in far below the level that a first-time general reader of the phrase would assume. Would you guess 90%? In fact, assets that constitute a majority of assets or provide over half of revenues or income should be scrutinized. This could apply, for example, to a spinoff of a significant business unit. A series of transactions that result in substantial assets in aggregate going out of the company also needs a careful look.

The merger provisions in a public indenture are typically not listed as a covenant, but instead stand alone. Again, the principal thrust of the provisions, as traditionally written, is to define transactions that will cause the debt to be assumed by a successor or transferee corporation. Only indirectly do the provisions effectively block a sale of substantially all the assets, by potentially burdening the transferee with the debt obligation when that isn't the deal.

Suppose that a company's bonds are rated AA (investment grade) and are trading at par, and the bond indenture freely permits mergers provided the successor assumes the debt. That is, the indenture contains a standard, traditional merger clause focused on identifying the successor obligor, but with no other tests on the transaction. What is to prevent the company from merging into a company with lots of debt and its bonds being downgraded (to, say, BB to trade at 92 cents on the dollar)? The answer is, unless there is some other protection in the indenture, nothing! This happens upon occasion, and bondholders are naturally unhappy when it does. To address this concern, some indentures include so-called event risk protection that tests the debt level, post-merger, or the rating of the post-merger entity (or both).

---

1.   *See* section 16:4.

For a lower-rated company, the covenant may prohibit mergers and sales of "all or any substantial part of" the consolidated group taken as a whole, with possibly some exceptions, including perhaps an exception for a successor entity that assumes the debt and subject to a creditworthiness test, for example, that the successor entity "be able to incur $1 of debt" under the debt covenant. This somewhat odd construction is used in many indentures. When you first come across it, it's natural to ask what's so great about a dollar of debt? This classic piece of obscure drafting is a way to invoke the debt incurrence financial test (whatever it may be) without having to repeat it word for word.

Covenant packages for non-investment grade companies may go further to prohibit all sales of assets (including inventory), subject to exceptions (including inventory in the ordinary course of business). Sales of assets outside the ordinary course of business, to the extent permitted, may require debt paydown, first to (permanently?) reduce senior debt and then subordinated debt.

Some important caveats:

- Provisions regarding mergers and sales of "all or substantially all" or "all or any substantial part" of the company's assets should apply to the obligor company (in the case of a merger), or the obligor company and subsidiaries taken as a whole (with respect to sales of assets). Applying a test like this at the subsidiary level is far too unwieldy and unnecessary.

- If assets have been pledged but are permitted to be sold, the release for sale ought to occur automatically and not require a separate consent or waiver under the security documents.

- There is substantial content overlap between the merger covenant and the "change of control" provision, if there is one. It is, of course, very important to make sure the two are consistent.

- Where asset sale proceeds are dedicated to debt reduction, it is important that the paydown provisions in all relevant debt agreements be consistent.

§ 13:2.2   *Restricted Payments*

The "restricted payments" covenant puts a cap on dividends and other payments to equity holders, but may also limit payments to subordinated debtholders and, in some versions, investments, or at least investments in "affiliates," which are entities under common control with the company. A significant structural question is whether the restriction on dividends applies solely at the parent company level or also applies to each subsidiary. If the latter, you need to think about the implications for non-wholly owned subsidiaries—usually minority shareholders will expect to be able to get money out of the subsidiary on a ratable basis, and this will need to be accommodated. Of course, payments from subsidiaries to the parent company obligor should be permitted.

It is easy to see why a holder of debt would want to limit payments to the equity holders ahead of debt repayment. Too much of this sort of thing turns the expectations associated with being a debtholder, as opposed to an equity holder, topsy-turvy. Equity is supposed to provide a "cushion" for debt.

Since payments to equity holders could take different forms, even the most limited version of a "restricted payments" covenant is not just a matter of limiting dividends but also covers stock redemptions and repurchases.

Many restricted payments covenants go on to prohibit voluntary prepayments to subordinated debtholders, or these payments may be prohibited in a separate covenant. Again, the reason is the same: the subordinated debt is supposed to provide cushion in the capital structure and the holders of the subordinated debt are compensated accordingly with a higher return.

Lastly, primarily in high-yield (or "junk") bonds, the "restricted payments" covenant may include a restriction on investments. The provision essentially creates a combined basket for payments in respect of lower tiers in the capital structure (equity and subordinated debt) and investments outside the "family."

Note: Dividends and other payments on stock can be effectively limited by net worth covenants.[2]

---

2.   *See* chapter 14.

§ 13:2.3   Investments

Outside the junk bond context, restrictions on investments have traditionally appeared only in private credit facilities and treated in a covenant separate from the restricted payments covenant. The structure of a stand-alone investments covenant is the standard negative covenant construction: "Investments" are defined, and then prohibited, subject to listed exceptions or a basket carve-out.

"Investment" for purposes of this covenant does not have the commonly understood meaning. An "investment" in this case refers to investing *in another legal entity*; purchasing an asset directly, even one that is expected to last or yield a return, is not an "investment." The interposition of the other legal entity means, presumptively, that the assets the company has invested are beyond its control and subject to the control of another. What the company once owned directly, cash or otherwise, and that was therefore subject to the direct claim by the company's creditors has been converted into a right against a third party, and the assets in the hands of the third party are subject to the prior claims of its creditors.

A simple household analogy would be this: Adding a garage to your home would not be an "investment" as defined, whereas buying a thirty-day treasury bill would be, even though both of these things might be thought of as investments as the term is commonly used. In the case of the treasury bill, you are exposed to the risk (de minimis to be sure) associated with the U.S. government's ability to repay, whereas no third party is in control of or able to sell or pledge your new garage. Note, in this case the garage is probably a capital expenditure and long-term asset, while the T-bill is a short-term money market investment, something to do with a bit of spare cash.

Suppose you run a small business and build a warehouse that you then own. That is a capital expenditure but not an "investment." Suppose you instead purchase a company whose sole asset is a warehouse and you end up owning shares in that company instead of taking direct title to the warehouse. That is both a capital expenditure *and* an "investment."

For a company to own assets through a wholly owned subsidiary, for tax or other reasons, would seem to raise no issues for its lenders. But that is not quite true.

Remember that the parent company lender is subject to the structurally senior claims that may be imposed at the subsidiary level, including not only debt and trade credit, but also tax and ERISA obligations of the group. This means that the parent company's claim on the assets now lodged in the subsidiary is derivative, through its interest as equity holder, and subject to all the debt-type, statutory, and other claims that can be interposed at that level.

Note: A guarantee is an indirect investment in the primary obligor whose debt is being guaranteed.

§ 13:2.4   *Line of Business*

Typical in leveraged finance, these covenants have a simple and straightforward purpose, which is to require that the essential nature of the company's business does not change. There are many variations, but the differences are all in the nuances.

§ 13:2.5   *Capital Expenditures*

Limitations on capital expenditures may appear in non-investment grade private credit agreements but not generally in public (including Rule 144A) indentures. A capital expenditure limitation is intended to restrict both cash outlays and business expansion. Indirectly, it can force debt reduction by closing off the most likely alternative use of cash, which is reinvestment in the business. Capital expenditure covenants are usually constructed based on the company's "capex" program, allowing for some leeway in timing (by permitting (limited?) carryforward of unused capacity to subsequent periods), and maybe some good performance freeboard out of excess cash flow. Insurance proceeds and condemnation awards used to repair or replace should not count against the basket since the company is not going out of pocket and only getting back to square one.

Two common problems in definitions of capital expenditures are (1) overbreadth (for example, picking up all "investments"),[3] and (2) double-counting from period to period because the wording would include, within a given fiscal period, both capital expenditures incurred (that is, booked under GAAP) and paid during that period. The GAAP statement of cash flows typically features a line item repre-

---

3.   For the T-bill example, see *supra* section 13:2.3.

senting capital expenditures or investment in plant, property, and equipment, so it is questionable whether the wordy and muddy definitions mixing cash and accrual concepts serve a useful purpose. A reference to the line item might well suffice.

Another common error is to misstate the deal on carryover of permitted amounts from one period to another, or, more generally, to make the carryover provisions too complicated.

A last point worth noting is that capital expenditures—as a use of cash that has been blessed—are a proper deduction in the formula for excess cash flow in an excess cash flow sweep,[4] but it is also possible to discipline capex indirectly through that mechanism by limiting the amount of the deduction.

§ 13:2.6   Acquisitions?

Another type of covenant occasionally found in non-investment grade credit agreements attempts to define and limit "acquisitions." This construction is usually not too successful, as an analytical matter, and if the proposed transaction is permitted by the capital expenditure limitation, the investments covenant, and the line of business covenant it is hard to see what purpose is served by limiting the ability of the company to, for example, acquire a facility or line of business from someone else instead of starting from scratch.

The limitation on acquisitions may be somewhat obscurely drafted into the middle of a covenant that is mostly about sales of assets, but wherever it appears it is likely to be a trap for the unwary. A different approach is to limit, by amount and type, the consideration used in expansion of the business through acquisition of existing businesses: so much debt, so much cash, and maybe an unlimited amount of parent company common stock.

§ 13:2.7   Leases

Some private credit transactions contain covenants restricting leases, though this covenant can usually be dispensed with if there are proper financial covenants limiting debt (including capital leases) and

---

4.   *See* chapter 14.

measuring operating results (which would be net of operating lease expense). Sometimes lease covenants only relate to operating leases, because capital leases would typically be captured by the debt covenant.

Note: Some forms of "fixed charge coverage ratio"[5] cover rental payments.

§ 13:2.8   *Guarantees and Contingent Obligations*

Limitations on guarantees or "contingent obligations" restrict the guarantee of third parties' obligations or, more broadly, the incurrence of off-balance-sheet liabilities for which the obligor has not received dollar-for-dollar consideration. A common problem is that the definition of "contingent obligations" is a grab-bag, including guarantees, comfort letters, some but not all take-or-pay arrangements, letter of credit arrangements, and hedging arrangements, and the covenant is not analytically coherent. Most of what the definition covers is already sufficiently covered under the debt covenant (as guarantees) or investment covenant, or both. Letters of credit can support all sorts of business obligations, including trade payables. Hedging transactions, if they present a serious issue in the credit, merit clearer treatment than what they typically receive here. Lastly, there is a strong tendency of drafters to forget their defined term and to use "contingent obligations" with its ordinary meaning, that is, obligations that are contingent and not fixed in nature. Notwithstanding these issues, the covenant is very common in the non-investment grade context.

§ 13:2.9   *Assignment of Receivables*

Some credit documents flatly prohibit the assignment of receivables. This prevents the company from entering into any kind of receivables financing or factoring arrangement, whether treated as on-balance-sheet secured debt or off-balance-sheet sale. In a more typical covenant package, the asset sale covenant applies if the receivables financing is a sale, whereas the debt and lien covenants apply if the fi-

---

5.   *See* chapter 14.

nancing is in the form of secured debt. Unfortunately, the characterization of a receivables financing as either a pledge or a nonrecourse sale for purposes of a standard covenant package is not always clear. The financing may be a hybrid, leading to odd results. The accounting treatment of receivables financings depends on factors not necessarily relevant to covenant design. Therefore, if a company expects to do receivables financings, then it is best to address the issue head on in a way that does not depend on accounting treatment, but instead describes the parameters of a permitted receivables sale or securitization.

§ 13:2.10   Transactions with Affiliates

Transactions-with-affiliates covenants are intended to prevent "sweetheart" deals with controlling or influential stockholders or with entities they control, which constitute a loss of value for the obligor comparable to a restricted payment.

Conceptually, there are two types of "affiliate" definitions. The first definition is based on the concept of control, and it is fair to consider all the entities under common control as acting in concert. This sort of definition goes up to some ultimate control point, and then spreads out to capture the entities below the control point. Unless you specify otherwise, it will capture the obligor and its subsidiaries, so these need to be excluded to permit intercompany transactions within the obligor group (top-most obligor and below).

A second type of definition is more difficult to work with. It treats 5% or 10% shareholders and possibly officers and directors of the top-most obligor, and entities they control, as affiliates subject to scrutiny. This is fair. However, if you use 5% or 10% ownership and officer or director positions to define "control," and define "affiliates" to mean entities under common control, the scope of the covenant becomes unwieldy and, possibly, unfair. Cross-ownership, or a chain of ownership upwards and then downwards again at a 5% level, or common directorships should not necessarily bring entities into the sensitive zone.

There is a question as to whether a transactions with affiliates covenant is appropriate at all in the public company context, where there are other corporate governance schemes intended to rein in abuses of this type. Regrettably, the experiences of the last few decades, and, in particular, the Enron collapse, suggest that improper affiliate transactions can be an issue even for a public company.

§ 13:2.11   *Other*

We wind up this survey of general business covenants by noting a few other types of covenants you may see in private credit transactions for non-investment grade companies.

- Covenants may limit the ability of the company to make changes in the terms applicable to other parts of its capital structure or the terms of key agreements. For example, if a management agreement is a permitted "transaction with affiliates" and payments under the management agreement permitted "Restricted Payments," then the credit agreement would probably prohibit changes in the management agreement without bank consent. It is easy for these types of covenants to go overboard and it would be better if the control is targeted in a more sophisticated way at the relevant provisions only.

- There may be a covenant prohibiting the company from changing its fiscal year. Why would lenders care about this? Presumably they are concerned about preserving the integrity of its financial tests. But changing fiscal years is a highly unusual event in the life of a company so, on the one hand, it is probably overworrying to protect against its happening and, on the other hand, no big deal for the company to agree. If the company desires flexibility (or just resents the intrusion), it is easy to provide that if the fiscal year is changed, then appropriate adjustments in the covenants and other necessary changes will be made in the agreement.

- A lender wanting to keep a very tight rein on cash might prohibit the company from having bank accounts with other banks, or may limit cash balances to force paydowns, even temporary ones.

§ 13:3 Constructing a Multi-Covenant Basket

Sometimes a multi-covenant basket is constructed, so that the company can build up out of excess cash flow a kitty available for any combination of dividends, prepayments of subordinated debt, investments, and capital expenditures that would not otherwise be permitted. This creates an incentive for owners and management because they get to reward themselves for better-than-expected performance by taking money out of the business or having more financing, expansion, and reinvestment options.

Note: Make sure you do not end up charging the basket twice for the same item because of overlapping covenants or definitions.

§ 13:4 Cross-References to Ensure Consistent Treatment

As you've probably figured out by now, a particular proposed transaction might have to be analyzed under multiple covenants—a guarantee would constitute debt, a contingent obligation, and an investment; a letter of credit obligation can constitute debt, as well as a contingent obligation; and so forth. You should comb through all of the negative covenants—*after* the substantive agreement on exceptions and so forth—and make conforming edits (adding any exceptions with cross-references) so that activities and transactions expressly permitted under one covenant would not be unintentionally blocked by operation of another covenant.

§ 13:5 Change of Control Provisions and Definitions

The change of control concept in corporate finance is designed to protect lenders and investors from a change in ownership of the borrower or issuer—a takeover of a public company or, where the borrower or issuer is controlled by a private equity group or other known and acceptable entity, loss or change of that control to another. A change of control may be a default (typical in a credit agreement—majority lender action required), may create a put right for holders of bonds through a requirement by the issuer to make an Offer to Purchase (bondholder by bondholder determination), or be a mandatory prepayment or redemption event. It is important in "change of control" scenarios to analyze other covenants, including, of course, any merger covenants.

In a holding company structure, where the borrower is a subsidiary, the existence of the parent holding company and intermediate holding companies must be taken into account in crafting the change of control definition. It is at a level above the borrower where changes in equity ownership would occur. In these cases, there is usually a requirement that there be 100% ownership up to the top company where private equity, public, or other beneficial owners participate. Then there is a change of control test run at that higher level.

For public companies, the change of control test runs off the concentration of a percentage of shares (30% or 40%, say) in the hands of a person or group of persons acting in concert. It may also be triggered if there is a turnover in board composition (as a result of a proxy fight, for example). The latter type of test can be a bit overreaching and needs to avoid treating the "directors die in a helicopter crash" scenario as a change of control.

For private equity portfolio or other privately held companies, the test runs off a continuity of control in the hands of "Permitted Holders," defined to mean the private equity sponsor or other principals including management. Typically these definitions contemplate a later stage in the company's life after the private owners have taken it public. So a second prong of the definition addresses the post-IPO world, though one where the private owners may retain voting control.

Chapter 14

Financial Covenants

§ 14:1   Lawyers Should Not Be Afraid of Financial Covenants

At the business level, financial covenants receive and deserve a lot of attention. They are not subjective, or are less subjective than other parts of the agreement. In the private credit context, financial covenants serve as reliable tripwires alerting lenders to financial deterioration. In the public context where financial tests feature in incurrence-type covenants, they act as governors.

Lawyers won't be asked to develop financial covenants and don't need to analyze the bankers' spreadsheets and base case, and downside and upside cases. But with just a basic understanding of financial statements, and the company's financial statements before you, you should be able to make sense of the financial covenants you are asked to draft. This is important. The lawyers will be held responsible for the document. If there are mistakes, the fact that the lawyers did not understand what they were writing is not a particularly strong defense.

§ 14:2   Correcting Toward Cash and Fair Value

Note: In general, financial covenant adjustments to generally accepted accounting principles are toward cash and away from accrual accounting, and toward realizable value, instead of book value.

§ 14:3   Maintenance Versus Incurrence Tests (Again); Historical Versus Adjusted or Pro Forma

Remember the distinction between maintenance and incurrence tests.[1] This distinction is particularly relevant in analyzing the operation of financial covenants. Remember too that maintenance tests (requiring a certain level of financial health to be maintained) appear only in private credit agreements, whereas public or quasi-public indentures or other debt agreements should contain only incurrence tests (where an affirmative action of the obligor is being tested).

Maintenance tests run on historical or actual results with such adjustments off the financial statements as are prescribed in the test. However, incurrence tests are based on historical figures adjusted for events after the end of the test fiscal period, and then further pro forma calculations are made to show the effect of the proposed transaction, for example, merger or incurrence of debt. Even preparing the pro forma calculations for an incurrence type covenant could be a substantial exercise. For these provisions, you may see special defined terms of "Incur" and "Acquired Debt."

In so-called "covenant-lite" loan agreements, the parties may have negotiated to have incurrence tests only—no maintenance tests. The frequency of this sort of loan agreement tends to increase with bor-

---

1.   *See* chapter 10.

rower-friendly conditions in the leveraged loan market. It is rarely seen in the investment grade market except, possibly, for the highest rated borrowers.

§ 14:4   Coverage Versus Balance Sheet Tests; Timing Questions

Financial covenants are generally either coverage tests or balance sheet tests.

Coverage tests measure operating performance over some period of time—a fiscal quarter, a fiscal year, or a period of four consecutive (or "rolling") fiscal quarters. The income or cash flow concepts that are used to construct a coverage test should be found on the company's income statement or statement of cash flows.

Balance sheet concepts, such as net worth or total debt, are based on a "snapshot" of the company's financial condition at a certain time. These snapshots are usually only taken at fiscal quarter ends.

A covenant can also measure cash flow available for debt service over a period of time—a measure of debt repayment capabilities—against total debt, a balance sheet concept. The most common financial covenant is a measure of leverage in the form of total debt to EBITDA[2]—a balance sheet concept as related to an income statement concept.

Compliance is usually tested quarterly, but in some bank credit agreements a balance sheet ratio may be required to be maintained at all times.

These conventions raise some interesting questions:

- If total debt and net worth are measured only at quarter end, how can a lender make sure that the company does not engage in impermissible transactions mid-quarter, with a quarter end "balance sheet cleanup"? This is a legitimate question; there is no easy answer.

- Since actual net worth would fluctuate daily based on operating results, how can a company be assured that it will not in-

---

2.   *See* section 14:5.2.

advertently and unknowingly trip a minimum net worth test mid-quarter? The practical answer is that if the company truly doesn't know, then it is likely that its lenders will never know either. However, if something happens that results in a clear hit to net worth mid-quarter, bringing it below the minimum, then there is a breach under the covenant.

- It takes some days after a quarter end or year end to finalize figures and prepare financial statements. How do lenders and the company deal with this period of uncertainty when a financial covenant default is expected "as of" the period end date? The answer is that they communicate and, if necessary, arrange for waivers as of the period end to be in place before the final numbers are released.

It helps that all of these questions arise in connection with maintenance covenants, that is, in the private credit agreement context.

§ 14:5   Coverage Tests

Coverage tests look at the company's ability to service its debt (and meet its other obligations) out of its income or cash flow. More abstractly, they focus on the health of the company's ongoing operations. These tests are constructed with a numerator, which is some measure of income or cash flow, and a denominator, which is a set of expenses and charges that are to be covered.

For example, a ratio of Consolidated Cash Flow to Consolidated Fixed Charges compares the company's net cash generated from operations (for example, excluding cash proceeds from non-ordinary course asset sales) against its regular financing costs, and possibly rental payments and/or capital expenditures. A ratio that exceeds 1:1 indicates that the operations of the business are throwing off enough cash to keep the business going, with extra cash available for that significant use of cash that isn't listed—the reduction of debt.

Most coverage tests contemplate improving coverage over time. This may reflect expected reductions in the debt level, hoped-for improvements in performance (for example, through rationalization of operations after an acquisition or other leveraged transaction), or just the lender's desire to keep a tight rein on the credit. Often it is a combination of all of these factors.

§ 14:5.1   The Numerator

The numerator—cash flow or "free cash flow" (almost always EBITDA)—is typically constructed from net income with a set of add-backs toward cash. In many cases you should be able to track the adjustments from net income to cash flow by looking at the company's statement of cash flows.

Coverage tests can adjust for gains and losses from out-of-the-ordinary asset sales and other extraordinary or non-recurring events affecting income period to period. This makes sense if you are trying to focus on ordinary operating income. Some lenders and underwriters will exclude gain but include losses. This is the conservative approach, but it does deviate from measuring the success of operations.

§ 14:5.2   EBITDA

EBITDA (Earnings Before Interest, Taxes, Depreciation, and Amortization) is the touchstone for the leveraged market and, in particular, for high-yield (junk) bonds, since it is a rough-and-ready approximation of the issuer's capacity to pay debt. The additional add-backs in this case are, of course, those potentially significant non-cash charges depreciation and amortization, the latter being particularly relevant when there is an ongoing amortization of goodwill after an acquisition.[3]

§ 14:5.3   The Denominator

The denominator of the coverage ratio can be equal to principal plus interest, or interest only, or cash interest only. In some cases, the "fixed charges" to be covered include rental expense (lease payments) as well as capital expenditures. Preferred stock dividends may also be included.

Coverage of debt reduction (principal payments) out of operating income would make sense:

- for a conservatively run or mature enterprise where you want to see an ability to actually reduce debt over time;

---

3.   *See* section 4:4.

- for a public or quasi-public (regulated) enterprise where managing regular payments on large amounts of long-term debt is part of the ordinary course of doing business;

- where a large capital expenditure program up-front is expected to produce cash to pay for itself; or

- where the lenders otherwise want and expect to see overall debt come down over a period of time.

Covering interest only is an appropriate test for a shorter-term credit or where it is expected that debt will be refinanced and not retired out of earnings during the life of the agreement.

Cash-only interest coverage is a feature of leveraged deals, where there may be discount debt accreting interest or payment-in-kind (PIK) debt (interest is paid by issuing more debt).

Note: A "bullet" or "balloon" repayment—where a big amount of debt is due at one time (often on the assumption that it will be refinanced or extended)—can make a forward-looking test covering scheduled principal repayments trip in advance of the bullet maturity.

§ 14:5.4   *Depreciation and Capital Expenditures*

Remember that depreciation is a non-cash charge to income and represents a way of expensing over time, for accounting purposes, the up-front costs of long-term assets. When a factory is built in year one to last for thirty years, expensing the total cost in year one grossly distorts income as a measure of financial performance. Earnings look worse than they should in year one and better than they should in each of the following years. Instead, the cost is expensed, that is, run through the income statement to reduce current earnings, over some number of years by way of depreciation. There is a use of cash in the first year and a corresponding set of non-cash charges in the form of depreciation over the life of the asset.

A steady pace of capital expenditures would, theoretically, generate a rough identity between current use of cash and the depreciation charge. The depreciation relating to past capital expenditures would generate cash, in a notional sense relative to GAAP net income, for current capital expenditures or for repayment of associated purchase money debt. (Related concepts appear in the sinking fund and "additions and betterments" provisions in industrial or railroad mortgage bond indentures.) A mature business might well be doing maintenance capex that more or less funds itself out of depreciation, roughly speaking. For that kind of company, a fixed charge coverage ratio that incorporates capex spending would be a good indication of the business's ability to finance normal operations out of earnings.

What happens when you apply a traditional fixed charge coverage test to a company that is in significant growth mode and borrowing for expansion? It does not work very well. Cash expenditures for "PP&E" (plant, property, and equipment) are high, and corresponding depreciation charges—add-backs to net income—at the beginning of the expansion cycle do not balance out those expenditures, which are in fact financed with debt. That is why, for a business in a start-up or expansion mode, you are likely to find coverage tests that focus only on interest coverage and, in the private lending context, a separate covenant that restricts capital expenditures.

Capital expenditures can be deducted from the numerator (cash flow) or included as an element of the fixed charges to be covered, in the denominator of the ratio. Note that if capital expenditures are deducted from the numerator instead of included as an element in the denominator, capital expenditures will be covered once in the test, not at a multiple over one. If included in the denominator, the ratio requires them to be covered at the multiple level prescribed by the ratio. They should not be both deducted from the numerator and included in the denominator!

§ 14:6 Leverage Ratio of Debt to Cash Flow

A ratio of total debt to cash flow (or EBITDA) tells you about how long it would take the company to amortize (in the sense of repay) its debt out of operating cash flow. It is a good measure of how leveraged the company is. For example, a ratio of debt to EBITDA of five to one would indicate (very roughly) that the debt could be repaid in five years. A rough equivalent in the consumer world is a rule of thumb that you should take on a mortgage that is no more than X times your salary.

Averages vary from industry to industry. This is probably a more practical and realistic measure of debt capacity than a ratio that compares debt to assets, since balance sheet asset valuation may be way off in either direction. For this reason, the leveraged market, which is all about cash flow, is constructed around multiples of EBITDA.

§ 14:7 Balance Sheet Tests

Balance sheet tests limit the amount of leverage in the capital structure or otherwise police the company's equity, restricting dividends, and setting a tripwire for excessive losses or liabilities.

§ 14:7.1 Net Worth

Net worth covenants can run directly off stockholders' equity per the balance sheet or, more commonly, a tangible net worth figure calculated by deducting the value of intangible assets.

Net worth covenants, running from the most simple and weakest net worth covenant to the tighter and then more sophisticated provisions, include these:

- A simple requirement that consolidated stockholders' equity not fall below a certain figure puts indirect limits on continuing or catastrophic losses and on large stockholder distributions.

- A minimum consolidated tangible net worth test eliminates intangible assets, assets whose valuation or even existence (in the case of goodwill) may be ephemeral. This is a more conservative test.

- A more demanding test requires tangible net worth to step up over time. Putting aside significant issuances of equity, which are infrequent, stockholders' equity grows through retained earnings. So in this case growth is expected through earnings over the period that are kept in the business and not distributed to shareholders. This kind of covenant is not very forgiving.

- A variation starts with a baseline tangible net worth and ratchets up by 50% of positive income fiscal years. Years of large losses would cause tangible net worth to drop below a minimum previously built up by positive years' results, so the covenant punishes big losses. By upping the ante to take growth into account it is more sophisticated than a flat and unchanging minimum net worth test, but less rigid than a prescribed step-up.

•   An even more finely calibrated and forgiving version might, first of all, increase the floor by the amount of equity issued and, second, by forcing the ratchet upward only when cumulative positive net income exceeds previously accumulated losses.

Obviously these formulations are maintenance tests, of the type you would find in private bank credit agreements. It is possible to design an incurrence test off a minimum net worth, but the standard in the leveraged market is to use an EBITDA (cash flow) test instead.

§ 14:7.2   Balance Sheet Leverage Test

A second type of balance sheet test looks at the amount of debt as a percentage of

(i)   total capital (debt plus stockholders' equity),

(ii)   stockholders' equity, or

(iii) tangible net worth.

All of these are algebraic variations on a single theme and limit the relative portion of the company's capitalization that can be comprised of debt. (Other algebraic equivalents not customarily used would be debt as a percentage of total assets or total tangible assets.)

§ 14:8   Minimum Operating Results

A private credit agreement might include minimum income, cash flow, or EBITDA targets on a period by period or cumulative basis. However, this type of covenant is quite unforgiving of business cycles and changes in the business plan. Companies that have to agree to this sort of covenant are on a very short leash indeed!

§ 14:9   Liquidity and Working Capital Tests

Covenants that test liquidity are far less common today but do remain important in some industries where cash flow management is critical. These tests are focused on the borrower's ability to meet its near-term obligations with liquid or near-liquid assets (cash and cash equivalents, receivables, and inventory). An example would be a working capital test that requires a minimum of working capital, a current ratio that requires that current assets exceed current liabilities by a prescribed percentage margin, or a quick ratio that requires a minimum ratio of cash, cash equivalents, and receivables to current liabilities. Other tests important to certain industries might relate, for example, to inventory turnover (for example, a days sales outstanding test).

Current assets and current liabilities translate well directly from GAAP for testing liquidity, though you may see prepaid expenses excluded from current assets, and the current portion of long-term debt excluded from current liabilities. Cash and cash equivalents, which might be transitory proceeds of long-term debt or non-inventory asset sales, may be excluded from current assets in cases where the real focus of the covenant is on receivables and inventory.

§ 14:10 Excess Cash Flow Sweeps

Financial definitions are also used in designing excess cash flow sweeps, which direct a portion of better-than-expected cash earnings, or excess cash on hand, to reduction of debt. This provision can interrelate with other covenants in complex ways, which presents a tricky design problem. One very practical concern is that the "sweep" cannot siphon off cash that needs to be put aside for regularly scheduled debt reduction or budgeted capital expenditures. Particularly for a test based on actual cash in hand, the provision should provide a reserve for upcoming expenses or normal cash needs.

Chapter 15

Amendments, Waivers, and Control Provisions

§ 15:1   Amendments and Waivers

§ 15:1.1   Level of Consent Required

Amendments and waivers are an ordinary part of working with corporate finance documents. The normal rule of contracts would say that the consent of all of the parties is required to amend a contract, and the statute of frauds, as well as business practice, would require the amendment to be in writing. But in the corporate finance context, where there are usually multiple debtholders under a single agreement, amendments can be effected with the consent of less than all of the lenders or investors. A typical syndicated bank credit agreement can be amended with the consent of the borrower and of lenders holding (historically, 66 2/3%, but now) a simple majority in principal amount of the loans. In a public indenture, it is usually holders of

217

a majority of the outstanding principal amount of the series of bonds or notes affected that can amend. The general amendment section will state that its rules apply "unless otherwise expressly provided." This means, for example, that a particular covenant could contain a super-majority (for example, 75%) consent requirement that would override the lower general amendment requirement.

These majority or super-majority requirements do not apply to the amendment of key "money terms" that define the basic deal—maturity, interest rate, currency of repayment, and the like—which instead requires either 100% (unanimity) or the consent of each lender or noteholder affected. These are two different standards. The first standard means that, for instance, the maturity of the loans or notes cannot be extended unless each and every holder agrees (or is bought out by someone who will agree). In the second formulation, half the noteholders could agree to the extension, while the rest do not. If that happens, the extension would be effective as to the consenting noteholders and would not be effective as to those who withhold their consent. The second formulation permits substantial changes in key terms, like pricing and maturity in a troubled situation like a workout, even if there are a few lenders who refuse to go along—an attractive feature from the perspective of flexibility; however, it likewise means that the lending group as a whole and the borrower have lost the necessary club to bring uncooperative hold-outs into the fold. The uncooperative hold-outs are rewarded, and if there are too many of them (for example, in an exchange offer) the entire benefit of the re-structuring may be lost. These few words can have a major impact on the course of negotiations in a deteriorating credit situation.

The provisions that set out the required votes for amendments and waivers cannot be amended without unanimous consent. If this were not the case, the lower voting percentage of holders could reduce a unanimous or super-majority voting requirement.

Is isn't always clear whether a particular amendment requires unanimous consent. Suppose the amendment provision states that any change in the maturity of the notes requires unanimous consent. Does the waiver of a covenant default, which if unwaived could then trigger an acceleration, require unanimous consent? The generally accepted answer is no. Suppose the same agreement requires mandatory paydowns from asset sale proceeds. Does a waiver of that provision require unanimous consent? It is unclear, though if the reference in the unanimous consent provision is to "stated maturity" or "scheduled maturity," the answer should be no. It is best practice to be clear one way or the other about this sort of early but contingent and unscheduled paydown provision; sometimes a super-majority requirement (75% or 80%) applies.

There is another category of amendments provided for in public indentures, which are amendments that effect technical corrections or that add to the obligations of the issuer, that may be agreed to between the trustee and the issuer without bondholder consent.

§ 15:1.2   Can the Obligor Vote?

Under standard indenture terms, bonds owned by the issuer cannot be voted, unless they have been pledged, in which case the pledgee can vote. Credit agreements were traditionally silent on this point, but with the growth of loan trading some credit agreements have started to be explicit that loans acquired by the company or its affiliates are not entitled to vote.

§ 15:1.3   Multi-Series or Multi-Tranche Agreements

Managing voting requirements under an agreement that covers lenders or bondholders with disparate interests can be tricky. Before plunging into the wording, answer these questions:

- How should the voting class be defined, and in what circumstances will it act?

- What actions might the voting class appropriately take based on the particular vote, considering the impact on those who aren't in the voting class or who are in the voting class but don't go along?

- How can the agent or trustee be protected from receiving conflicting instructions?

A shelf indenture (a single indenture providing for multiple series of debt to be issued off the same basic indenture, pursuant to supplemental indentures) provides for series-by-series voting on series-related issues and for acceleration on a series-by-series basis for some types of defaults. On the other hand, some actions make sense only if they apply to all the series under the indenture. And in all cases, the trustee cannot be subject to conflicting instructions. So, for example, while 25% of a series on which there is a payment default might be able to accelerate that series, and the trustees might be able to act on majority instruction from that series in distributing cash in a reserve account dedicated to that series, a majority of all holders under the indenture should instruct before the trustee can take action against collateral shared among all the series outstanding under the indenture.

Note: In a series indenture, be careful about how so-called medium-term notes—one-off small issuances—are treated for voting and control purposes.

The different interests of revolving banks and term lenders under a multi-facility credit agreement are easy to see. Suppose there is a "simple" rule that says that holders of a majority of aggregate outstanding loans and outstanding commitments can waive or amend. Term lenders have already made their loans. The making of further revolving credit loans is, of course, subject to there being no default and no incipient event of default. Now suppose we are in a troubled credit scenario, where there is a default (or incipient event of default) and the borrower needs cash. It may need cash to pay other maturing debt, including, in the most pointed case, the term loans. The term lenders are already fully exposed and stuck in the deal. They may very well want to see the company have access to new funds. Revolving lenders, depending on their funded exposure at the time, might just as soon walk from the credit if they can. So how will the term lenders and the revolving credit banks vote on a waiver of the default? Will the borrower be able to obtain the waiver and borrow? The "simple" rule can have very different outcomes depending on the relative sizes of the two facilities. Early on in the deal, term loans might be larger than the revolver, but late in the deal after term loans have been paid down they might be smaller than the revolver. And what if the revolver banks have the unilateral right to terminate the revolving facility upon default?

If we can obtain fact-based variations on the results that are so inconsistent, the superficially "simple" rule is not simple at all in operation but, instead, is widely off the mark of what is needed. Instead, you might require the separate affirmative vote of each class to waive.

In some cases, the facilities might be syndicated and, thereafter, transfers restricted so that there is substantial overlap between the revolver and the terms loans. Or, in some cases, there might be mandatory sharing of credit exposures to equalize the interests of the two groups.

§ 15:1.4 Banks and Bondholders That Do Not Go Along

Banks or bondholders that do not cooperate in granting requested waiver relief or amendments can keep the group from reaching closure and moving on to the next stage. Even more aggravating is the case where the non-cooperating debtholders get the benefit of the stabilized situation but still keep their old debt terms. The "hold-out" or "free-rider" problem can present a serious obstacle to a restructuring or refinancing.

In the public debt indenture context, this is dealt with by making money terms (for example, maturity) not amendable except by the particular debtholder, and most other terms amendable by majority vote. In a tender offer to restructure or refinance, there is a minimum acceptance required, usually well over the majority level but not at 100%. The accepting debtholders agree to the new terms or exchanged debt, but amend the old indenture (on the way out) to make it toothless, in a so-called exit consent. The tiny sliver of holders remaining under the "stub" have their old money terms, but no covenant protection. Bankers help structure the consideration paid to bondholders so that the necessary take-up is achieved and the residual bondholders on the old terms are not too problematic going forward.

The bank market has historically been more of a unanimous-voting market on money terms, with a lot of pressure brought to bear on the hold-outs. A couple of innovations in the leveraged market soften this position somewhat. The "snooze you lose" provisions say that a non-responding lender is knocked out of the voting group for calculation purposes, and "yank the bank" provisions say that, where a unanimous consent is required, a bank that does not want to go along has to be bought out at par if another lender makes the offer. Both are intended to reduce the "market value" of a non-cooperating or hold-out position.

One might ask why these borrower-friendly provisions developed out of the leveraged market, where one would have thought the borrowers had the least leverage. There are two reasons. The first reason is that non-investment grade agreements are jammed full of covenants and need to be amended or refinanced on a regular basis. It is both in the borrower's and lending group's interests that they be able to carry on doing this as necessary. Second, while the borrowers in this market may not be too creditworthy, the financial sponsors have been very powerful and controlled deal flow. So equity interests behind the weak companies have been able to exercise quite a bit of leverage in negotiations with the banks.

§ 15:2   Amendment Versus Waiver; Form of Amendment

Substantively, there is no difference between an amendment and a waiver, and no difference between an amendment embodied in an amendment agreement or supplement, and an amendment and restatement of the entire agreement. But certain rules of thumb apply.

An ongoing change in the deal, such as new covenant levels or pricing, is usually reflected in an amendment or, in the case of an indenture, in a supplemental indenture. A waiver is usually reserved for circumstances that are one-shot or short-lived, such as a one-time delay in the delivery of financial statements.

Amendments are sometimes so extensive that it is easier to produce an amendment and restatement of the entire document, incorporating all changes, than an amendment agreement.

An amendment and restatement is a single coherent document, which is easier to work with than a mass of technical wording changes collected in an amendment agreement. It is also possible to prepare a so-called composite document that incorporates a series of amendments into a single, as-amended, but unofficial working document.

When preparing amendment agreements, in any form, you need to make sure that:

- the transition from the old document to the new is dealt with in a clear and unambiguous fashion;

- there is no overlap in time periods for accruals and the like;

- conditions to effectiveness of the amendment are properly set out; and

- the document properly distinguishes between those terms that apply pre-amendment and those that apply post-amendment.

If an amendment and restatement contains changes that require the unanimous consent of all lenders under the old agreement (as would be the case for changes in pricing or term), then all lenders under the old agreement must consent even if they are not going forward under the new agreement. This consent can be in the form of signature blocks for "exiting Lenders" to sign the new agreement or in a simple self-standing consent to the new agreement. Some bank agreements anticipate this issue with special provisions permitting a different group of lenders to take the facility forward without unanimous consent of the original group, so long as a particular lender cannot be bound to an increased or extended commitment without its consent.

Why amend and restate an agreement rather than start anew? It might be that security interest filings will carry over for an amended agreement. Other agreements may accord special treatment to the original agreement, as amended, but not to de novo replacements or refinancings.

The amendment of a public bond indenture will be requested through a consent solicitation, which may or may not accompany a tender offer for outstanding bonds. To get the consent, the issuer will generally pay a fee; its bankers will help determine how much of a fee is required. As already noted, it is typical for an issuer that wants to refinance outstanding bonds through a tender offer to obtain a so-called exit consent from tendering bondholders to change or eliminate the covenants in the indenture. If this were not done, those bondholders that did not tender for whatever reason would have the continuing protection of the original covenant package and the related "hold up" value if a future waiver or amendment were needed.

Most indentures provide that the consent of the bondholders need not be to the exact form of the proposed amendment; instead the consent may be to its substance. After the consent of the necessary bondholder is obtained, the issuer and trustee would execute a supplemental indenture containing the technical amendment.

§ 15:3   Shared Collateral; Intercreditor Agreements; Standstill Agreements

In shared collateral agreements it is customary to permit the affected class of secured creditors to "trigger" the commencement of steps to take remedies. They might also be able to require that additional protective measures be taken, such as establishing cash collateral arrangements, if the measures benefit all the secured parties alike and cannot harm any of them. But attachment of assets and foreclosure are serious steps, which are likely to immediately and adversely affect the borrower's business and, possibly, precipitate a bankruptcy. Because the consequences of this type of remedy are so severe, shared collateral arrangements usually provide that once the affected class gives the "triggering" notice, control of remedies of this serious, irreversible type shifts over to the majority of all secured creditors taken as a single voting class, except for those in a passive status because they are second lien holders, holders of subordinated debt, or tag-along secured debtholders under an equal and ratable clause.

However, suppose that it is in the interests of a group in a blocking position to sit on their hands. A well-crafted collateral trust agreement may anticipate a second stage where if the controlling lenders decline to take action for an extended period, then the triggering or affected lenders take over again until the larger group of secured parties comes to the table to give the trustee affirmative instructions on remedies.

Intercreditor agreements can be entered into in the ordinary course of putting together a complex financing or when a company is in workout. In either case, the very purpose of these agreements is to define how control will be shared and exercised among the interested creditors. In a troubled credit situation, a standstill agreement among creditors is an agreement that all will forgo the exercise of remedies long enough to see if a deal can be worked out. Both types of agreements are beyond the scope of this book, but the principles we have discussed here apply to those agreements.

§ 15:4   Analyzing Control Provisions

§ 15:4.1   A Common Apparent Anomaly

An apparent anomaly is that while majority or super-majority holders may waive a default or amend a covenant, it may be the case that a different and lower percentage may accelerate. A waiver or amendment curing the default is often effective to rescind the acceleration, so that the larger group can act to override the smaller group. Another scenario is that lenders or bondholders may decline to accelerate, but still be unable to garner sufficient votes to amend or waive. So it is possible to have an uncured, unwaived default that likewise has not been the predicate for acceleration.

Acceleration is rare because it so dramatically alters the dynamics. It can trigger cross-acceleration provisions, so that the accelerating group loses control of the situation, and the borrower may take quick recourse to bankruptcy. More profoundly, accelerating the debt of a borrower does not necessarily help get you paid.

On the other hand, an uncured and unwaived default is not that sustainable. For the company it means that the debt, if by its terms long term, may have to be characterized as short term for accounting purposes. So long as the aggrieved debtholders do not waive or amend, they have leverage over the company and, indirectly, its other lenders.

In sum, it can be in the interest of bondholders or lenders wanting to extract concessions to neither waive nor accelerate.

§ 15:4.2   Trading of Loans and Bonds, and the Relevance to Control

Notes and bonds issued under an indenture are, of course, designed to trade. Bank loans, though not designed to trade in the same way, do in fact trade and end up in the hands of non-traditional investors such as hedge funds.

This means that, when control provisions in agreements become relevant, the obligor may be looking at investors and lenders very different from those that were there at the beginning. Some of them may have bought debt at below par in order to repayment at par (by threatening acceleration) to make a profit. Hedge funds or other strategic investors may have bought a controlling block to extract the maximum value out of a default or alleged default position. They may be willing to capitalize on drafting errors or assert unusual legal positions to carve out a position of leverage not generally recognized by the market. Or they may be positioning themselves for an exchange of debt into equity.

Control provisions in indentures were originally drafted to enable and protect collective action by holders of publicly and widely held bonds. Credit agreement control provisions were originally drafted assuming and to facilitate close relations between a company and its relationship banks. Neither contemplated strategic purchasers of debt at below par who might concentrate holdings expressly to accumulate control positions for short-term profit or, in the rarer case, to end up with control of equity.

The strategic acquisition of debt ups the ante considerably in terms of document drafting, the giving of opinions, the importance of control provisions, and, in the case of bank loans, assignability. All elements have much more strategic importance and, for the company and the lawyers on both sides, represent significantly more potential downside vulnerability than in the past.

§ 15:4.3   *How to Review Control Provisions*

The amendment and all other collective action or control provisions, such as provisions relating to notices, acceleration, enforcement against collateral, and release of collateral, both in the main agreement and in collateral documents, should be carefully reviewed and tested for consistency. You need to do scenario analysis and take into account how the provisions will work when bonds and loans have traded hands and, perhaps, have even been concentrated for strategic control purposes.

To avoid conflicts and lack of clarity, don't get lost in the wording of the form or precedent you are working with. Instead write out the rules you intend to live by. Also keep in mind any requirements dictated by law (for example, sections 315 and 316 of the Trust Indenture Act, or rules of relevant stock exchanges). Make sure the relevant provisions, whether in the remedies section, the amendment section, or elsewhere say exactly what they are supposed to.

This sort of balancing of the parties' interests through admittedly technical aspects of the agreement is important. Perhaps counter-intuitively, the provisions of the contract that define its operational aspects in the technical sense—who controls and how they act on their control—turn out to be of critical importance in bad times. Their relative sterility in terms of apparent business content tends to make them invisible at the drafting and negotiation stage. Don't be fooled!

Chapter 16

Risk-Based Review; Transactions Analysis

§ 16:1 Spend Your Time Wisely

Lawyers are responsible for every word in the contracts they draft or review on behalf of their clients. That being said, grinding away through many flat sequential readings of the documents for a deal, particularly if you are tired or are interrupted by phone calls and emails, does not guarantee a good work product. Instead, break your review and analysis up into specific tasks, make a list of them, and tackle them one by one. The more difficult analytical exercises should be scheduled for when you are rested and can think clearly, without distractions.

Pay special attention to and ask for colleague review of:

- provisions that are most likely to be relevant after closing if things go well;

- provisions that are most likely to be relevant after closing if things go badly;

- dollars and cents items (where mistakes could cost big money); and

- contract provisions and related work that are otherwise the most likely to generate claims of attorney negligence (actual damages directly caused by attorney error).

To address the first category, think ahead to that client call: "This is what we want to do. Is it permitted under the agreement? If not, what do we have to do to amend it or get a waiver? If we can't amend the agreement, is there a way to pay off the debt early and get rid of it?" What can you anticipate about the likely needs and the future of the company—including possible changes in corporate or financial structure, such as acquisitions, IPOs, and refinancings? Some of these (for example, a takeover by another company) should probably be prohibited, but then the question becomes, how will the company need to proceed in the face of the prohibition? Will it be able to amend its agreements, and if it cannot how will it be able to get rid of them? If other exit strategies or refinancings are clearly contemplated, it is going to look bad if the documents don't permit them. More ordinary course questions of interpretation may also come up with respect to how covenant wording might apply to business or operational changes or events.

More toward the downside, the questions are likely to be about conditions to lending (including questions about material adverse change and material litigation), possible defaults, and the operational aspects of the agreement, in particular notice and control (amendment, acceleration, and remedies) provisions.

It is commonplace in corporate finance law practice that morning-after questions may take you to places in the documents such as notice requirements and amendment provisions where you haven't spent much time before and, occasionally, you can come across some unpleasant surprises when you have a close look. Better before the closing than afterward.

The third question relates principally to the issue of drafting. Drafting errors do occasionally cost clients money. Nearly always there is some confusion about what was really intended, who saw what drafts, and what was in fact agreed to by the clients, but a little prevention in the form of a second review of the key provisions, ideally by a lawyer not involved in the day-to-day negotiation, can help tremendously in identifying a lack of clarity or apparent "slippage" off the term sheet. Needless to say, these sorts of errors, ambiguities, or alleged errors are very hard for the drafting lawyer to catch.

The fourth issue relates to things that attorneys are clearly most responsible for and the clients most clearly are not, such as the perfection of security interests, legal opinions, or giving advice about notice periods that turns out to be wrong.

§ 16:2   How to Deal with Boilerplate and Other Standard Provisions

May you tune out on boilerplate provisions? Definitely not, especially if changes are requested and made during negotiation. However, review of boilerplate can be kept within bounds if:

- You know the purpose and meaning of the provisions, and, importantly, where they come from (for example, a client policy).

- You carefully read and compare the boilerplate provisions against a standard form that has been blessed by firm experts or against the relevant client policy, if that is the source of the provision.

- You also read the boilerplate once for sense and meaning. Sometimes a mistake can creep in and, due to computer-based word-processing, will proliferate in documents before someone actually reads the words and sees the error.

- You are extremely careful about making any changes in these provisions. In the case of pricing terms, yield protection or make-whole provisions, tax provisions, indemnities, and the like, client policy may not permit any deviation from the pre-scribed wording without internal client approval. And in many cases, a very small change in wording can have a significant effect; this is especially so with respect to tax provisions.

§ 16:3 Recommendations and Questions for Risk-Based Review

Certain issues tend to cause problems for lawyers (and their clients). It is worth bearing down on these throughout your work on a deal, and then taking another look at them as you approach closing. Don't be afraid to ask colleagues to review the more technical or more important pieces of language, or to discuss any other concerns or uncertainties you may have.

§ 16:3.1 *Party and Client Identification*

Though this may seem like a silly or obvious point: Do you know who your client is? Many malpractice claims arise because there is confusion about precisely whose interests the lawyer was looking out for. In the case of a private equity deal, are you representing the sponsor, the target, or both? What if their interests conflict? Are there minority shareholders who might say that they got the short end of the stick? If you are representing both senior and subordinated lenders, how are you making sure that their interests vis-à-vis each other are being aired? This is a knotty subject and merits discussion among the team members at the outset of the assignment. You also need to keep an eye on emerging issues as you go along. If anyone you think is not your client suggests they are relying on your representation, or if a client suggests that you are not really looking out for their interests but instead for someone else's, it should be discussed with senior lawyers right away.

At a more technical level, have you made sure that all the party names in the documents are correct and match up precisely to the identified parties? This is definitely worth a good check as part of the initial drafting and at closing.

§ 16:3.2 Correspondence to Term Sheet

Do the documents correspond precisely to the term sheet? If not, can you document that the changes came from the clients or were agreed to by them? When signed documents do not match up with the term sheets, clients have sometimes claimed that the lawyers were negligent in drafting or failed to keep them properly informed of changes made during the course of negotiations.

§ 16:3.3 Closing Documents; Disclosure Schedules; Side Agreements; the Closing Set

Are the corporate documents in good order, with a clear chain of authorization running from the person signing to the party being bound? Are closing documents generally in accordance with the conditions precedent, and if they are not, are the gaps documented and agreed upon? Every so often (fortunately not too often), there is a substantive problem with a deal that turns out to relate to, or that can be tied to, a closing condition. Clients generally rely on their lawyers to check off closing conditions. If a client agrees to waive a closing condition or to accept something a bit different from what was required, then the client instruction should be memorialized in writing. If an agent or trustee is doing this on behalf of a syndicate or noteholders, be sure that the discretion properly lies with the agent or trustee to give the instruction.

This might come up, for example, where there are complex security arrangements that are not all fully in place at closing and yet the parties agree that the deal is substantially completed and do not want to delay consummation of the transaction. In this case, it might be agreed that some conditions precedent become post-closing conditions (for example, must be completed within thirty days). If there are post-closing conditions agreed to, do the credit providers understand the risks—for example, preference risk with respect to post-closing perfection of security interests? It is likely that they do, but it is not hard to inform them in writing in the course of working out the post-closing conditions.

If there are disclosure-type documents (for example, schedules, certificates, or calculations) surfaced at the closing and not much before, do the clients receiving them have a chance to review them? If you just attach them to documents without client review, and they contain something material in hindsight, there could be some explaining to do. You should make sure all substantive items receive client attention, including, as necessary, by walking the client around the closing table to review the final documentation.

Side agreements that are put together at closing can be innocuous, stitching up a loose end or bridging over a non-material gap in the closing conditions. However, side agreements that are secret from some of the parties, or that seem to cut away from or run counter to the main thrust of what is going on, should be discussed with senior lawyers. Side agreements also tend to be put together hastily, and it is easy to skip the careful and considered review with the client that should occur.

The closing is not finished until the final documents, as executed, including any handwritten changes, side agreements, and so forth, are incorporated into the final closing sets and, in any electronic versions, locked down to ensure document integrity. Too often this is put off until it is hard to do the compilation accurately, and it is delegated downward to people who will not necessarily know of, or understand the implications of, handwritten changes or side agreements.

§ 16:3.4   *Opinions*

Opinions should not "gloss over" or "finesse" known problems. Could anyone take the view that the scope of an opinion is broader than it is meant to be? Is anyone relying on the words of an opinion that could be broadly read but which the giver of the opinion does not intend to be read in that broad fashion? Are any lawyers giving opinions that they are being pressured to give but that you would not give? All of these are warning signs of something that might well turn out to be a substantive problem.

§ 16:3.5 Timing, Risk, Commitments, and Conditions; Continuing or Repeating Representations

It's a good idea to map out the provisions of the agreements relating to timing, commitment, risk, and conditions (including interactions by way of conditions to representations, and by way of conditions to defaults to covenants). Do these accord with the clients' understanding and other parties' reliance on the availability of funds?

Make sure that there are no representations that purport to speak on a continuing basis. Representations that need to be brought down and other conditions for future borrowings merit a specific review. Inability to meet these conditions can stop the flow of funds to the company.

§ 16:3.6 Complex Calculations and Tax Provisions

Complex calculations and tax provisions should be looked at very closely (ideally by "fresh eyes") and in the case of tax provisions blessed by tax lawyers at each stage of negotiation and at closing. Anti-dilution formulas deserve special attention. (In the 1987 defensive leveraged recapitalization of Harcourt Brace Jovanovich, anti-dilution provisions in a series of convertible bonds resulted (if read literally) in a negative conversion price because the per-share amount of the special dividend being declared was in excess of the benchmark stock market price.)

§ 16:3.7 Security

As we have noted, defects in collateral security are hard for lawyers to explain and defend. Further, in the unfortunate case where the company goes into bankruptcy, it will be in the interest of the estate and the unsecured creditors to find technical problems with the security. This is an area that can merit careful review by a second lawyer.

Make sure the definitions of collateral are complete and correct. Pay special attention to the definitions when there are different collateral packages pledged to different lenders—that there is no overlap and that proceeds (for example, as inventory generates proceeds from sale, or as accounts receivable generate cash that is invested in temporary cash investments) are handled properly, and not pledged to two different sets of lenders.

Are the definitions of secured debt complete and correct, covering as appropriate amendments, extensions, refinancings, and replacements? If there is a problem in the future, the definitions of secured obligations and the collateral will be looked at very carefully.

In the case of permitted transactions (for example, permitted asset sales) involving collateral, is the collateral automatically released without further action from the lenders? Again, this is a provision that is likely to be referred to in the future. Better to anticipate the questions before the documents are finalized and signed.

Is the security interest in each case granted by the right party? A pledge of assets by a non-owner is not worth too much.

If you are not getting local counsel opinions or not requiring title insurance, is the client aware of the risks (informed in writing)? What seems like a sensible business decision when things are going well can look less sensible in hindsight, and it may be that the bankers who made the call are not around to explain it.

Most importantly, are the security interests perfected at closing? Sometimes bankers will allow more time to perfect on some of the security or, where perfection is onerous, be willing to give it up. To the extent security interests are not perfected, you should make sure clients understand the risks (failure of perfection; preference if later perfection) by documenting what is agreed upon and noting the consequences.

Before the closing files are put away, set up robust and redundant tickler systems so that U.C.C. filings (and any other perfection requirements) will be renewed on a timely basis and not lapse. You need to provide for the fact that personnel turn over at companies, banks, and law firms. Even if the company has the obligation to keep perfection in place, it is the lenders who will suffer if perfection lapses.

§ 16:3.8　　*Interrelatedness and Consistency Generally Within the Financing*

If there is a suite of credit documents, carve out some "quality time" to make sure they are consistent with one another, looking at the provisions where there is an overlap or intersection of subject matter coverage—for example, default and remedies. Definitions of the secured obligations or guaranteed obligations should be exact and consistent from one agreement to another.

Stepping back a bit and taking all provisions together, is there subject matter consistency? Do all provisions relating to liens match up? Or letters of credit? If a transaction is expressly permitted under one negative covenant, could it be blocked by operation of another negative covenant? More generally, are transactions that have been carved out as permitted exceptions in the covenants carved out in each relevant covenant? If a transaction is prohibited under a single covenant even though clearly permitted under others, it is prohibited. For example, suppose a $10 million basket has been agreed upon for joint venture investments under the restriction on investments. These investments might be straightforward infusions of equity, but they might alternatively be in the form of guarantees, providing letters of credit or pledging deposits, which might trip restrictions on debt, contingent obligations, and liens. In a case like this the agreed-upon exception should flow through all these covenants. The easiest way to do this is to include in the other covenants an exception for "Investments permitted under [the restriction on investments]." Be careful though to study the definitions. Sometimes a transaction is excluded from the definition of "Investment" (or "Debt" or "Contingent Obligations"), so that a cross-reference to "Investments" permitted under the investments covenants will not pick up the excluded transaction! (Other common examples: Contingent Obligations may constitute Debt and also Investments; intercompany debt must be permitted for both lender and borrower; restricted payments may also be asset dispositions and transactions with affiliates.)

§ 16:3.9 How Different Financings Work Together

If there are multiple debt instruments, review the interplay closely.

Look at the cross-references (including relevant defined terms) and make sure they are correct. They should not contain unclear or possibly suspect language such as "as amended from time to time in accordance with the terms of this agreement."

Looking at all the documents together, at a high level, make sure the relative priority (including by structural subordination) is what is intended and what is described in any disclosure documents. Shifts or restructurings of the deal can occasionally cause things to drift from the original plan.

Though this will probably be covered under the company counsel's non-contravention opinion, make sure the debt to be incurred under your agreement is clearly permitted under any other debt agreements being signed or which are known to you. If there are any conditions you need to meet to make sure that the debt to be incurred is permitted (for example, a coverage ratio), these should be documented. Likewise, the debt agreement for which you are responsible should clearly permit the other debt agreements of which you are on notice. You should determine that any relevant equal and ratable clauses are not applicable, or that compliance is complete.

Whomever you represent, you need to take a very close look at the definition of "Senior Debt" to make sure it is fully satisfactory. The downside risk is especially high for the senior lenders but also for the company.

Look carefully at all the concepts of debt refinancing to make sure that they provide the intended refinancing flexibility and to give the refinancing lenders the intended status and benefits. Again, this question is critical to the company and to holders of debt that might want to be taken out in the future.

§ 16:3.10   *Credit Support or Liquidity Support?*

If your client is relying on credit or liquidity support (guarantees, letters of credit, liquidity facilities), you will need to make sure it is signed up and in place at closing. There should be safeguards so that the appropriate level of credit or liquidity support remains in place (for example, requiring guarantees from future subsidiaries when they are acquired or formed) over the life of your deal. If third-party credit or liquidity support could expire before the terms of your client's facility, there should be a protective mechanism for ensuring that your client will be able to draw or force a draw before the expiry.

§ 16:3.11   *Covenants Dealing with Securitization and Derivatives*

Covenants dealing with securitization transactions and derivatives transactions need to be handled with sophistication and flexibility, particularly because so many covenants might potentially touch on them. The best approach is to define the permitted scope of these financings and then to make sure they are carved out of all covenants that might otherwise limit or prohibit them.

§ 16:3.12   Definition of the Corporate Group; Definitions of Affiliates and Control

The handling of the corporate group and, in particular, subsidiaries of the primary obligor should be consistent across all provisions (representations, covenants, and defaults). How would you, generally, describe the intended scope of the agreement in this regard? Having defined the intended scope, read carefully all relevant provisions to test for consistency with the intent. A possibly inadvertent inconsistency—referring to Restricted Subsidiaries in one place, but to Subsidiaries in another—has to be interpreted later on, and there are sometimes peculiar results.

If transactions with affiliates are covered, be very careful of an overly broad definition of "affiliate" (running a definition of "control" that can pick up chains of minority shareholdings) or one that accidentally covers the obligor and subsidiaries (which should be carved out).

§ 16:3.13   Adverse Developments—Stress Testing

Think through various "adverse development" scenarios. How will they be treated under the various provisions, and is the handling consistent? Consider such events as a write-down of assets or increase of reserves; a major judgment; a ratings downgrade (or going onto credit watch with negative implications); inability to roll commercial paper; inability to deal with vendors or counterparties except on a secured basis; a major change in commodities or other prices that could generate a loss on fixed price or take-or-pay positions; large mark-to-market adjustments; or a major accident or catastrophe. What are likely cash needs in these events and what is the effect on liquidity through operation of conditions precedent or events of default? Consider, in particular, incipient events of default and cross-defaults, and the interplay of the provisions relating to litigation, judgments, and liens.

§ 16:3.14   M&A Scenarios

The change in control and related provisions should be appropriate to the transaction. If the obligor is a public company, do they sweep too broadly (for example, capturing a case where a majority of the board of directors is killed in a plane crash)? If the obligor is a private company, are exit strategies covered, including an IPO (with appropriate public company provisions kicking in at that point), or other sales of interests so long as the original sponsors remain in control?

Think through various M&A scenarios. Are the transactions that should be permitted in fact permitted under change of control provisions, merger covenants (including sale of all or substantially all assets), asset sale provisions, and investment provisions? If particular transactions are negotiated as permitted exceptions or carve-outs under one of these provisions, cross-references should be included so that other provisions do not inadvertently prohibit them.

§ 16:3.15   Maintaining Flexibility: Amendments, Waivers, and Refinancing Options

What is the ability of the borrower to seek amendments and waivers? These provisions should be consistent.

What is the ability of the company to pay off the debt out of different sources of cash, such as equity proceeds, asset sales, or refinancings? Some bond indentures permit early redemption of bonds only from certain sources (for example, an IPO), only in limited amounts, or only from sources other than lower cost financing (the so-called clean-money call provision). There is also a significant difference between an ability to call (issuer has control) and having to make an offer to purchase (issuer must make the offer but has no control as to whether it is accepted).

§ 16:4   Transactions Analysis at the Margin

Regardless of how carefully a contract is written and how customary its provisions are, clients will have questions of interpretation at the margin. Many of these queries relate to proposed corporate or financial transactions that were not contemplated by the lenders or investors and that may not be in their interest—mergers, spin-offs and corporate restructurings, or refinancings to take advantage of lower interest rates or to get rid of troublesome covenants.

We have already noted that many investment grade bonds typically do not protect bondholders from dramatic corporate transformations like leveraged acquisitions that may leave them with a substantially worse credit. Spin-offs or other dispositions of key businesses and assets are also problematic from a bondholder perspective. And bondholders do not like being paid out when they thought they had call protection. There is a fair amount of case law on these recurring themes. Some of the cases date back decades. There is a certain continuity in corporate finance—along with the new, the same old questions (and same old tricks) come round and round again.

Sharon Steel[1] is a basic source for interpreting the meaning of "all or substantially all" in merger clauses. *Associated Gas & Electric*[2] is cited for the proposition that "you can't do indirectly what you can't do directly" (in that case, evasion of (equal and ratable) negative pledge and merger ("all or substantially all") covenants): "What cannot be done legally in one act does not necessarily become legal when the act is split up into various steps, all seeking and attempting to do in final result, what the one act might have accomplished." Can issuers avoid non-call provisions or the payment of premiums through intentional default? Cases say no.

Though Second Circuit (New York City-based) courts are famous for strict interpretation of contracts and not reading into them protections that the parties didn't bargain for, there are judicial interpretations placing limits on corporate action. Bondholder activism will result in new law being made. Before you give advice about whether a particular proposed transaction is permitted under the company's debt agreements, make sure you have looked at any governing case law and consulted with your colleagues.

---

1. Sharon Steel Corp. v. Chase Manhattan Bank, N.A., 691 F.2d 1039 (2d Cir. 1982).

2. *In re* Associated Gas & Elec. Co., 61 F. Supp. 11 (S.D.N.Y. 1944), *aff'd*, 149 F.2d 996 (2d Cir. 1945).

Chapter 17

Best Practices

§ 17:1 Drafting As a Professional Skill

Most technical errors in drafting fall within easy-to-define categories. Technical errors—as opposed to drafting that does not correctly reflect the intent of the parties or the real-world facts—are "bugs," or mistakes in design or execution of the work product. They can yield results that neither party intends or even knows about until after the fact.

§ 17:1.1   Cross-References

In order for a contract to be more than a mass of disjointed, even conflicting provisions, proper connections among the provisions must be established through the use of cross-references, together with prioritizing and linking words such as "subject to," "provided that," "notwithstanding," "pursuant to," and "in accordance with." Cross-references make critical ties between contract provisions within the same document or to other documents.

Incorrect cross-references are mistakes and are, for the most part and for better or worse, quite clear mistakes. For better because sometimes the error is so obvious that parties can later agree to fix it; for worse because it is obvious that the person whose job it was to make sure the cross-references were right did not catch the mistake. Errors can be reduced through automatic cross-reference features in word-processing applications (which save the junior lawyer the less-than-stimulating task of mechanically changing cross-references as the draft goes through sequential revisions and can reduce the use of the inelegant "[intentionally omitted]"). But these tools cannot tell if the cross-reference is substantively incorrect.

Cross-referencing, useful and necessary as it is, can get out of hand, sometimes in a creeping fashion over the course of multiple revisions. For example, a new concept might be introduced and then turn out to have many more uses than originally envisioned. When you see yourself constantly repeating a cross-reference, maybe a well-crafted definition is in order instead. More significantly, if cross-references are piled on willy-nilly, with "subject to sections . . . but in accordance with sections . . ." all over the place, the drafter needs to go back to the drawing board and reorganize the document. Similar subjects are being treated in too many different places, making the document difficult to work with and creating a fertile breeding ground for inconsistency. Lastly, a cross-reference that is overly oblique may be disingenuous or even deceitful in its operation—for example, where the "subject to section . . ." clause all but guts the qualified provision.

§ 17:1.2   Consequential and Conforming Changes

It is absolutely the job of the drafting and commenting lawyers, and no one else, to study the document thoroughly to make sure that an agreed-upon item is reflected in each and every place where it needs to be reflected. Clear organization can make it less likely that the document will say the same thing, or nearly the same thing, repeatedly. If organization meets this test, checks for conforming changes are easy.

§ 17:1.3   *Working with Precedent*

Lawyers need to assess the appropriateness of language inherited from a form or precedent. If it isn't right for your deal, it needs to be fixed or eliminated.

Several things make this harder to do than it sounds. First, the profession is traditionalist in its orientation. Risk-averse lawyers, which is to say nearly all lawyers, tend to be wedded to the tried and true and are most comfortable sticking to the old formulas. Many feel that this is the best way to avoid both liability and criticism. In addition, because they are used to reading "legalese," they are not always sensitive to formulaic language but tend to focus on the key business variables in a situation. To a certain extent this makes sense. If the language has worked in the past and has an established meaning in the legal and business community, and furthermore addresses a point that the clients are not too interested in, service to the client and efficiency demand that the lawyers direct their attention to places other than the "boilerplate."

However, there are some traps here for the time-pressed lawyer. It is very easy to read language as it ought to read, based on the lawyer's experience, and not see how it in fact appears on the page and might be read by others. Over time, just as your ability to quickly digest and analyze whole pages of text greatly increases, your ability to slow down long enough to take in the actual words in front of you diminishes. Even if you can take the time to read carefully, if the language is generally familiar you may have a hard time stepping back and asking the question whether it really applies or should apply in this situation.

Consider an easy example: many lawyers like to toss in "in the ordinary course of business in accordance with past practice" as a sort of ho-hum qualifier, to let the borrower have some leeway so long as it does not do anything too outrageous. "Ordinary course of business" may be ho-hum, but "in accordance with past practice" certainly is not. All successful businesses mark themselves by responding appropriately to change, and this requirement could keep them from doing that in a sensible fashion.

In other cases thoughtless markup of precedent indentures can, for example, result in the retention of legalistic-sounding clauses designed for secured indentures but having no meaning in the unsecured indentures where they appear.

Properly eliminating unnecessary wording—tossing out the bath water while keeping the baby—requires knowledge of the legal substance underpinning the words, their purpose, and their provenance. All too frequently a lawyer cannot explain why certain language needs to be in the contract, but likewise refuses to take it out or change it because it must be there for some important reason (unknown to that lawyer). If the lawyer does not know the purpose of a provision, then that lawyer cannot know whether it should be in or out, or whether or how it can be altered. Likewise, a lawyer who does not know the history of a provision nor understand its scope can easily include it or agree to its inclusion even when inappropriate. If you find yourself in this situation (completely normal for a new lawyer), don't be afraid to ask your seniors for guidance.

§ 17:1.4   Excessive Generality and Too Much Specificity; Over-Engineering

Unintended scope ("but we didn't mean to [cover/prohibit] that") can result from too high a level of generality or too much specificity. You can help define what the clients really want, by questioning them about specific what-if scenarios, and then writing exactly what is required, no more, no less.

For example, a provision that restricts all dividends by non-wholly owned subsidiaries, subject to a cap, may do a good job of discouraging non-wholly owned subsidiaries, but it also restricts money going up to the parent obligor, which is not really in the interest of parent company debtholders. A covenant that says that subsidiaries may not agree to any restrictions on their ability to pay dividends will probably have the effect of limiting the ability of subsidiaries to borrow money. Is that really what is intended? Ferreting out unintended scope is hard because a reader generally tries to make the most sense of words as giving effect to their intended purpose. Here, though, the critical reader/lawyer must instead become almost stupidly literal, to think not about what was intended but how the words might be interpreted by a neutral third party. If the words cover situations that neither party is thinking about in ways they would not intend, the language is probably struck at too high a level of generality.

On the other end is the over-engineered and, thus, too limited exception. Describing a permitted securitization with a lot of particularity off a specific term sheet for a proposed deal is likely to be problematic—who cares whether the vehicle is a Delaware LLC or an offshore trust? Instead, you should focus on the aspects of the proposed deal that are relevant, from a credit perspective, to the obligor's lenders and describe the permitted deal at that level of abstraction.

In either case the goal is *precision as to the appropriate level of generality.* They say that anyone can design a bridge to carry a specified weight, but the challenge is to build the bridge elegantly and efficiently to meet, but not greatly exceed, the specifications. It takes real skill to design and build a bridge that is not over-engineered. Many lawyers routinely produce documents that are their work product equivalent of the over-engineered bridge.

§ 17:1.5 Identifying and Correcting Ambiguity; Vagueness

Lawyers use the word "ambiguous" a lot—often when they are asked to interpret language in a contract, to mean that the language isn't clear.

True syntactical ambiguity, when language can be read to mean two different things (as in "debt of subsidiaries existing on the date hereof"), can usually be fixed by rewriting or by inserting logical markers (as in "if (x)(i) or (ii) and (y)(i) or (ii), then . . ."), so long as it is spotted in the first place.

Vagueness or lack of clarity is another story. Sometimes it is simply unclear from reading the words what was meant. A read of documents by "fresh eyes" can help reduce the instances of unclear wording, but any experienced lawyer will know that it is impossible to eliminate lack of clarity (judged in hindsight) entirely. Sometimes wording is just too general for a lawyer to be able to speak to definitively—for example, whether a proposed transaction is "in the ordinary course of business." Perhaps the lack of specificity is intended. Language like this can be a good way to reach agreement or to finesse disagreement, but neither party is going to be able to take any comfort from it in close cases, either (in the case of the company) to proceed in reliance on it or (in the case of debtholders) to call a default.

§ 17:1.6   *Logical Completeness and Correctness; Speculative Worlds?*

A contract should be logically complete but cannot define and anticipate all possible worlds. Lawyers should keep their feet solidly grounded in logical construction and their heads well above the treetops, but not so high that they are in the clouds. At the technical level, if a formal structure has been established in the contract that is meant to cover all possibilities—for example, a pricing grid—it should be tested for logical correctness and completeness, that is, no gaps and no overlaps. But more generally, in covenant design, for example, when has enough "contingency planning" been done? At this level of hypotheticals and contingencies, the lawyer should cover the universe of likely possibilities over the life of the contract, prescribe rules about how unexpected eventualities will be dealt with (for example, amendment provisions), and move on.

Take the pricing grid example. Suppose pricing is based on S&P ratings of the borrower's long-term unsecured debt. Leaving out the BBB rating altogether is a pretty obvious error and would be spotted, but people do make more subtle errors in these pricing grids, especially in *and/or* and *lesser than/greater than/equal to* constructions. But should there be an elaborate alternative pricing grid for the situation where S&P goes out of business? For a three year loan agreement, the answer is no. Pricing on a thirty-year public debt issue, though, should not depend on the S&P rating. Do credit documents have to take into account that the Federal Reserve System is no longer operating? What if a country's currency is going to change? What if the company's computer system is down for three days? For a month? Not knowing when to shut off speculation about hypotheticals is one of the things that give lawyers a bad name.

§ 17:1.7   *Over-Drafting*

Over-drafting is another fast route to unpopularity. Once they are on to a subject, sometimes lawyers just do not know when to quit writing, and overdraft. They "see ghosts." One example might be the (often overreaching) inclusion in the definition of "lien" of "the filing of any financing statement under the Uniform Commercial Code." This has a nice, protective ring to it, but financing statements are required to be filed in circumstances that do not involve a lien, for example, with respect to operating leases. So perhaps during negotiations an exception is added to cover "protective filings associated with operating leases." After signing, the borrower wants to sell some receivables to a factor (a specialized financial intermediary that purchases accounts receivable at a discount), which also requires the filing of a UCC financing statement, but does not give rise to a lien or secured obligation, and . . . you need a waiver. All this bother over language that was overbroad to begin with and has to be whittled away exception by exception is not a good expenditure of time.

§ 17:1.8   *Too Many Words*

Traditionalism in law and computer-based word processing are constantly pushing towards length; people tend to add language but rarely do they feel as confident in striking out. Too often they do not have time to collapse and combine provisions that substantially overlap or substantially repeat each other. And so the form grows.

It is up to the lawyers to push back. Brevity enhances readability and makes error, especially inconsistency, less likely and easier to spot and fix as you go along. Short, concise documents are easier to analyze after the fact, and to amend. Brevity is considerate and makes clients think well of lawyers.

Pushing for brevity consists of, at the simplest level, deciding whether "if any" and "as the case may be" are always necessary; then thinking about when and where the "laundry list" approach is worth the extra words; more dramatically, converting archaic formulations to simpler, more modern usage; and, finally, keeping a ruthless eye on organization. As the contract develops in more whole-cloth drafting, it needs reshaping; and wherever a lawyer sees overlap in content—parsing, outlining, or diagramming as necessary—words can be cut.

§ 17:1.9   *Good Definitions*

Definitions make sure that important concepts stay rigidly fixed through the entire contract, particularize the meaning of words that have vague or multiple meanings in general use, and let drafters reuse concepts without having to repeat words (perhaps inconsistently!).

Notwithstanding their non-normal usage in contracts, however, defined terms should have definitions that are not too different from the meanings of the same terms in ordinary usage and, thus, are in accord with the readers' expectations. It is too much to expect people to work with defined terms that have been assigned strained and/or non-intuitive meanings.

Also taboo are artificial or misleading definitions ("Loans" in a security agreement defined to include loans made in the future to any company in the affiliated group) and definitions that include operational provisions ("Bank Loan Agreement means the loan agreement dated today between [bank] and [company], which shall not be amended without the prior consent of [insurance company lender].").

There should be no more definitions than are necessary to make the contract easier to read and use. There is no need to define obvious concepts, and if a complex concept is used only once, then its definition can be contained in the provision where it is used (easy to find) and need not appear in an alphabetical listing at the front or the back of the agreement (making the reader flip pages). On the other hand, if you find yourself repeating some long formula or provisions word for word, or constantly invoking it with a cross-reference, it is time to create a defined term. And then once a term has been defined it should be used everywhere it properly applies.

Definitions should logically build one on top of another—for example, a single concept of subsidiary used in constructing definitions of foreign subsidiary, consolidated subsidiary, and so forth. They should not be circular. A definition can properly say "x means y, including a and b"; but "x includes y" is only a gloss on a meaning and not a definition; and "x means and includes y" is contradictory.

A final review of the document should include frequent looks back from the body of the contract to each related definition to make sure that some aspect of the definition does not have unintended operational effect. This is a common structural problem when, first, a definition features exclusions ("provided that [defined term A] does not include [a-4]" and, second, the defined term is used in an exception in the body of the contract ("provided that the foregoing does not apply to [A]" will not exempt [a-4] from coverage).

§ 17:1.10   Provisions in Related Documents

Security documents must accurately refer to the obligations intended to be secured. Guarantees should provide complete coverage of the obligations intended to be guaranteed. Whenever there are back-to-back, dependent, or co-extensive provisions among agreements, all the agreements should fit together so that the parties have the desired level of protection and the mechanics work. This is of particular relevance in the securitization area, where the issuer/SPV really exists as nothing other than a bundle of contractual rights and obligations.

§ 17:1.11   Lists

A few notes about lists: They should feature parallel construction, and have the right lead-in language. It is easy to slip from this standard over the course of periodic redrafts.

Likewise, as you make changes in lists, adding and deleting, you need to make correcting and conforming changes so that the list as a whole is still right. A common mistake for a beginner is to add new items at the end of a list, whereas the last item in a list is often "in addition to the foregoing, . . . ," defined in reference to all of the other items in the list.

§ 17:2   Drafting Disclosure of Contract Terms

§ 17:2.1   Where the Contract Is Relevant but Is Not the Main Event

When a proposed financing contract is relevant to, say, a tender offer, the disclosure about the terms of the financing may be only a paragraph or two long. Generally the audience for a cash tender offer document is interested in knowing whether there are conditions to funding that affect the viability of the tender offer, and that's about it. For a stock tender offer or other disclosure document where the readers will have to live with the terms of the agreement, they are interested in knowing about conditionality (to the deal), pricing, and other terms of the document that may impact the company or, particularly, shareholders—such as change of control or restricted payments provisions.

§ 17:2.2   For the Selling Document for the Debt

By and large these documents contain large chunks of text precisely corresponding to the language of the definitive document, with only introductory changes such as "The indenture provides that . . .". In the high-yield market it is customary to negotiate off the prospectus and prepare the indenture just before closing. This practice creates a risk of inadvertent discrepancy between the selling document and the definitive documentation, and it would be better to simply attach the relevant portions of the definitive document as part of the prospectus so that there is no possibility of mismatch.

Wholesale incorporation of portions of the document seems to work reasonably well in the sophisticated market where these bonds are sold, though one could argue that it does not constitute helpful disclosure in the sense of highlighting risks or issues.

§ 17:2.3   In Regular Disclosure for Public Companies?

After Enron, corporate finance lawyers would do well to keep an eye on the issue of disclosure of their deals in regular disclosure documents for a public company. The quality of disclosure of the company's many "structured finance" deals has been subject to criticism.

§ 17:3   Levering Technology—Possibilities and Pitfalls; Documents Handling and Retention

In general, lawyers are still discovering how information technology can make the practice of law easier (or at least faster) and riskier.

When contracts had to be laboriously typed, the incentives were first, to include only the necessary provisions, and second, to make each turn of the document, from first draft to last revision, really count. Lawyers learned to husband words and to be painstaking, careful, and precise in drafting revisions.

Computer technology has changed the incentives, and not, in this case, all for the better. The fastest and cheapest product can be generated by finding a contract from another deal that is more or less on point, and making the fewest number of changes to it to fit the current deal. I have seen what should have been a two-page term sheet sent out as a forty-page term sheet, and what should have been a six-page promissory note distributed as a 100-page indenture, in each case because there was a ready precedent. The production and internal review of documents generated in this fashion tend to get short shrift in the interests of fast initial distribution. This approach to addressing client demands for quick response is both short-sighted and, in my view, less than professional. The working group assumes the lawyers have chosen a good precedent or scrubbed the basic form, they ignore all but the key business points, and . . . *voilà*, the signed agreement has provisions drafted for some other deal that have never been carefully read by either the parties or their lawyers. Eventually, lawyers will make good use of computer-based drafting capabilities, but in the short term the pressures are all in the wrong direction.

Thus, computers "cause" lawyers to make errors—by encouraging lawyers to copy documents and language, and make minimal changes without thinking and reading through the document. It is easy to incorporate inappropriate wording or substantive language with missing or incorrect definitions. "Find," "find and replace," or other "global" text features are a great boon to lawyers (ask any lawyer who practiced before these were available), but also create embarrassing errors due to incorrect substitutions. It is far too easy to make errors in blacklining/redlining, particularly as the software tools for these processes become more complex and with usually less-than-perfect version control as documents are exchanged by email. Nonetheless, parties generally rely exclusively on blacklines for their document review. Email or posting allows for near-instantaneous distribution of changes but does not guarantee sufficient time for reading and review.

The electronic document environment creates other pitfalls for lawyers. Lawyers may refer to a "final" version of a contract on their computer system and give incorrect advice, not realizing that hand-marked changes were made on the execution copy at closing. Or the document may have been (unintentionally) altered because it was not locked down.

Rules about the use of metadata that is inadvertently disclosed are not yet fully clear and consistent. Safe practice (unless otherwise relevant or agreed, for example, if ordered in discovery) is to scrub all documents going outside the firm of historical metadata (history of editing, comments, etc.).

Defining and creating the "record" of a matter is more difficult than it used to be; this is particularly true of email. The old practice of some firms to throw away all drafts and notes, and rely upon the final document as the sole and definitive record of what was agreed, is not very meaningful when an entire record of the exchange of drafts as well as informal commentary exists. Indeed, it is difficult to get rid of anything with any confidence.

Clearly, email sent outside the firm constitutes part of the "record" of the matter, and all emails are potentially discoverable, including emails in the nature of "chat." Working on documents from home is more likely to make your home PC discoverable. Writing and receiving personal emails through your work email address makes your personal life more vulnerable.

Lawyers should resuscitate their old (pre-blogging) habits of discretion, leaving sensitive items for (unrecorded) phone or in-person conversation. They should consider what records a client will be able to call for, and how difficult it would be to go through emails and other electronic records in detail after the fact.

On the upside: The profession has barely scratched the surface of what is possible to achieve with more creative use of standard documentation and computer-assisted contracting systems. Though the downside, near term, may be a reduction in billable hours, the eventual upside should be more interesting and valuable work to be done. Certainly, if the lawyers do not embrace the possibilities here, their clients will.

§ 17:4   Lessons of Enron

What can corporate finance lawyers learn from the Enron case?

Though the Enron story has many chapters and many morals, the Powers Report produced on the instructions of the board of directors before Enron filed for bankruptcy relief is a good description of the prototypical "structured finance" deals that brought Enron down. In brief, assets that were subject to unfavorable mark-to-market adjustments (downward), speculative future cash flows, and other assets of questionable value or quality were, when deemed necessary to meet accounting goals, sold, "securitized," or "monetized" through sale to special purpose vehicles that were classified as "off-balance-sheet" to Enron. Where did the funds come from for these sales? For the most part, the sales were financed by bank lending to the special purpose vehicles. The required equity portion of the capitalization of the special purpose vehicles typically consisted of Enron stock or debt. Enron, in some cases, seems to have provided extra levels of comfort (credit support) to the bank lenders. Through transactions of this type, Enron seems to have recorded as income (gain) funds that more accurately represent moneys borrowed.

In addition, other special purpose vehicles entered into hedging transactions that accomplished the desired accounting goal—for example, by selling a put to Enron (the SPV standing by to purchase the assets at a floor fixed price). But for these arrangements to be given effect, the counterparties had to be deemed creditworthy themselves. Typically, they too were capitalized with Enron stock and debt.

Debt that Enron owed or that the vehicles owed contained triggers related to Enron's stock price and/or credit ratings.

Enron's outside lending arrangements had typical material adverse change conditions to funding.

With the interlocking arrangements all ultimately dependent on Enron's stock price and credit rating, the stage was set for a spectacular liquidity crisis, and when the dust settled there was not much by way of hard assets to be found. Notwithstanding the scope of the debacle, it is all but certain that the professionals involved did not view their work for Enron as unsound or questionable. This did not save Arthur Andersen, though the firm was brought down not on accounting judgments, but on alleged document destruction practices.

Enron and subsequent financial scandals suggest that finance lawyers would be well-advised, to the extent possible, to:

- Understand and be comfortable with the context, purpose, and disclosure aspects of the deal, particularly if it is tax- or accounting-driven.

- Understand the accounting issues.

- Consider whether exclusively defensive disclosure, technically accurate so as to withstand shareholder lawsuits but perhaps not actually very meaningful or revealing, should not give way to disclosure writing that is more transparent and informative, and that might incorporate appropriate levels of editorial shape, clarity, and emphasis.

- Ask questions about "side agreements," "as of" dates, and transactions with company officers or other insiders.

- Consider document retention practices—beyond the scope of this book but a subject of active best practice development, as well as rapidly evolving standards in the law.

- Review law firm and client reliance on information barriers; even if they "work" in that the activities on each side of the wall, judged separately, may be defensible, what both sides together are doing may make the firm as a whole look foolish.

- Exercise some scepticism about the efficacy of the system of checks and balances in corporate finance (public shareholders, independent directors, outside auditors) that have served well for so many years but appear to be less than reliable today.

Enron reminds us both of the power of the written word in contract and how, in the end, reality will overwhelm a construction of mere words.

For Enron, words in contracts had potent effect. The construction of triggers, conditions, and cross-defaults with which the complex financings had been put together worked as written—in this case, to bring the proverbial house of cards down. Jeffrey Skilling, the former CEO, has made comments likening the events of fall 2001 to a classic run on the bank, a panicky stampede precipitating a crisis that could have been avoided if investors had been more patient, and remarking on the cascading effect of material adverse change clauses. Certainly, these and other triggers—notably ratings downgrade and stock price triggers—kicked in together and made things quite difficult for the company when it got into trouble. But they operated in fact just as customarily intended.

On the other hand, the case of Enron also points to the fact that artificial legal structures can go only so far in substitution of real cash-generating business activities. Managerial and accounting professionals were only delaying the end when they worked to prop up structures to preserve a favorable accounting treatment. Third parties that were not real third parties were used to give substance to deals that could not have been done with real third parties, and in the end these were undone. Arrangements that seemed to let Enron take into income increases in its own stock price—a result not possible under accounting principles—came apart. Contracts and legal entities were used to accelerate and recognize speculative future income, but at the end of the day there was a reckoning after all.

§ 17:5 Stay Informed, Be Engaged, Live Long, and Prosper

Corporate finance practice is hard, and it can be scary, but it can also be lots of fun. The more you know, the more engaging it is. Make the time to read the financial press and to stay informed about deals, legal developments, and how companies and their lawyers got into trouble, or avoided scrapes and did well instead. The more informed you are, the more meaningful your work, the less likely you are to make a mistake, and the more you will impress your seniors and your clients. With all the continuing changes in the field of corporate finance, you will not run out of new developments to stay on top of, and new areas of practice to learn, for a very long time.

Appendix A

Notes, Resources and Sample Language

Foreword to the Second Edition

The financial crisis has been widely covered and is the subject of many scholarly, popular and governmental publications, with no doubt many more to come. The following are just a few selected books and articles that readers might find of interest, some providing a historical perspective and some concerning the relationship of technology and finance.

AMIR SUFI, *Bernanke's failed mortgage application exposes the flaw in banking*, FIN. TIMES, Oct. 14, 2014.

ARJUN APPADURAI (ed.), THE SOCIAL LIFE OF THINGS: COMMODITIES IN CULTURAL PERSPECTIVE (Cambridge University Press 1986).

ATIF MIAN AND AMIR SUFI, HOUSE OF DEBT: HOW THEY (AND YOU) CAUSED THE GREAT RECESSION, AND HOW WE CAN PREVENT IT FROM HAPPENING AGAIN, (University of Chicago 2014).

BEN BERNANKE, ESSAYS ON THE GREAT DEPRESSION (Princeton University Press 2000), especially Nonmonetary Effects of the Financial Crisis in the Propagation of the Great Depression, available as National Bureau of Economic Research Working Paper 1054, http://www.nber.org/papers/w1054.

CARMEN REINHART AND KENNETH ROGOFF, THIS TIME IS DIFFERENT: EIGHT CENTURIES OF FINANCIAL FOLLY (Princeton University Press 2009).

CARRICK MOLLENKAMP, SERENA NG, LIAM PLEVEN AND RANDALL SMITH, *Behind AIG's Fall, Risk Models Failed to Pass Real-World Test*, WALL ST. J., Oct. 31 2008.

CHARLES PERROW, NORMAL ACCIDENTS: LIVING WITH HIGH RISK TECHNOLOGIES (Basic Books 1984).

DONALD MACKENZIE, *How a Superportfolio Emerges: Long Term Capital Management and the Sociology of Arbitrage*, in KARIN KNORR CETINA AND ALEX PREDA (EDS.), THE SOCIOLOGY OF FINANCIAL MARKETS (Oxford University Press 2005).

DONALD MACKENZIE, *Be Grateful for Drizzle: Donald MacKenzie on High Frequency Trading*, LONDON REV. OF BOOKS, Sept. 11, 2014.

GILLIAN TETT, FOOL'S GOLD: HOW UNRESTRAINED GREED CORRUPTED A DREAM, SHATTERED GLOBAL MARKETS AND UNLEASHED A CATASTROPHE (Little Brown 2009).

IAIN HARDIE AND DONALD MACKENZIE, THE LEMON SQUEEZING PROBLEM: ANALYTICAL AND COMPUTATIONAL LIMITATIONS IN CDO EVALUATION (University of Edinburgh 2014), *available at* http://www.sps.ed.ac.uk/__ data/assets/pdf_file/0007/152809/LemonSqueezingFinalComplete2.pdf.

JAMES SUROWIECKI, *High on Speed, a review of* Flash Boys *by Michael Lewis*, N.Y. REV. OF BOOKS, July 10, 2014.

JAMIE MARTIN, *Better Off in a Stocking, a review of* Saving the City: The Great Financial Crisis of 1914 *by Richard Roberts* (Oxford University Press 2013), LONDON REV. OF BOOKS 36:10, May 22, 2014.

JENS CHRISTIANSEN, HAVE THE FED LIQUIDITY FACILITIES HAD AN EFFECT ON LIBOR?, Federal Reserve Bank of San Francisco Economic Letter, Aug. 10, 2009, http://www.frbsf.org/economic-research/publications/ economic-letter/2009/august/fed-liquidity-libor/.

JOHN PLENDER, *Big bond fund outflows are risks for banks*, FIN. TIMES, Oct. 14, 2014.

JUDITH BUTLER, PERFORMATIVE AGENCY, J. OF CULTURAL ECON., 3, 147-161 (2010).

MARK CARNEY, *The Need to Focus a Light on Shadow Banking is Nigh*, FIN. TIMES, June 15, 2014.

MICHAEL LEWIS, THE BIG SHORT: INSIDE THE DOOMSDAY MACHINE (Penguin 2010).

PATRICK JENKINS, *Private Equity Needs Less of a Shadowy Existence*, FIN. TIMES, Mar. 31 2014.

PAUL MCCULLEY, *Make Shadow Banks Safe and Private Money Sound*, FIN. TIMES, June 16, 2014.

PHILIP MIROWSKI, MACHINE DREAMS: ECONOMICS BECOMES A CYBORG SCIENCE (Cambridge University Press 2002).

R. J. O'HARROW AND B. DENNIS, *A Crack in the System*, WASH. POST, Dec. 30 2008.

R. J. SHILLER, THE NEW FINANCIAL ORDER: RISK IN THE 21ST CENTURY (Princeton University Press, 2003).

SCOTT PATTERSON, DARK POOLS: THE RISE OF A.I. TRADING MACHINES AND THE LOOMING THREAT TO WALL STREET (Random House 2013).

THE FINANCIAL CRISIS INQUIRY REPORT, FINAL REPORT OF THE NATIONAL COMMISSION ON THE CAUSES OF THE FINANCIAL AND ECONOMIC CRISIS IN THE UNITED STATES (Public Affairs 2011).

WALTER BAGEHOT, LOMBARD STREET: A DESCRIPTION OF THE MONEY MARKET (various editions, original 1873).

Chapter 1: Introduction

The author's *How to Draft for Corporate Finance* (PLI 2006, now out of print), contains sample language, supplemental readings and references, and exercises. In these notes we include some portions of *How to Draft for Corporate Finance*, especially sample language. The sample language comes from many documents produced over the years and should not be taken as exemplary or as reflecting current market practice.

Other useful sources include:

COMMENTARIES ON MODEL DEBENTURE INDENTURE PROVISIONS 1965, MODEL DEBENTURE INDENTURE PROVISIONS—ALL REGISTERED ISSUES 1967 AND CERTAIN NEGOTIABLE PROVISIONS WHICH MAY BE INCLUDED IN A PARTICULAR INCORPORATING INDENTURE (Am. Bar Found. 1971) (for indenture provisions).

LEE C. BUCHHEIT, HOW TO NEGOTIATE EUROCURRENCY LOAN AGREEMENTS (Euromoney Institutional Investor 2000) (covering eurodollar credit agreements generally).

CHARLES M. FOX, WORKING WITH CONTRACTS (PLI 2013).

THOMAS S. HEMMENDINGER, HILLMAN ON COMMERCIAL LOAN DOCUMENTATION (PLI 2013).

Basic law relevant to the subjects discussed in this book:

Securities Act of 1933
Securities Exchange Act of 1934
Sarbanes-Oxley Act of 2002
Dodd-Frank Wall Street Reform and Consumer Protection Act 2010
Investment Company Act of 1940
Investment Advisers Act of 1940
Trust Indenture Act of 1939
Bankruptcy Code (Title 11 of the U.S. Code)
Uniform Commercial Code (as adopted in the relevant jurisdiction)

Useful websites:

www.sec.gov
www.finra.org
www.naic.org
www.isda.org
www.lma.cu.com
www.lsta.org
www.loanpricing.com

Chapter 2:   The Players

Useful sources include:

Robert C. Higgins, Analysis for Financial Management (McGraw Hill 2012) (an excellent basic text on corporate finance).

Christopher Stoakes, All You Need to Know About the City: Who Does What and Why in London's Financial Markets (Longtail Publishing 2011) (a good introduction to the London financial markets, although nearly all of it is relevant to New York and the United States).

Regarding the cost of debt versus equity, and the effect of leverage:

The general formula for the cost of capital shows how debt is "cheaper" than equity. *See* Robert C. Higgins, Analysis for Financial Management 280–81, reprinted here, in part, by permission. (See facing page.)

Sale of the century: Companies are buying back their own shares at a record rate, Economist, Apr. 28, 2007 ("If business conditions are getting more difficult, a bit of financial engineering can help. Buying back shares with borrowed money boosts earnings per share, so profit growth can continue to look healthy. That was an important driver in the final stages of the 1990s bull market. In the long run, this is not sustainable.").

How the bank loan market has changed:

The evolution of the bank loan market—up through 2004 and thus before the full participation of hedge funds as bank loan investors—is described in Glenn Yago & Donald McCarthy, Milken Institute Research Report, The U.S. Leveraged Loan Market: A Primer (Oct. 2004) (supported by the Loan Syndications and Trading Association).

The following excerpts are reprinted with permission.

What rate of return must the company earn on existing assets to meet the expectations of creditors and owners?

A total of $300 is invested in XYZ on which the company must earn $45, so the required rate of return is 15 percent ($45/$300). This is XYZ's cost of capital.

Let's repeat the above reasoning using symbols. The money XYZ must earn annually on existing capital is

$$(1-t)K_D D + K_E E$$

where t is the tax rate, K_D is the expected return on debt or the cost of debt, D is the amount of interest-bearing debt in XYZ's capital structure, K_E is the expected return on equity or the cost of equity, and E is the amount of equity in XYZ's capital structure. Similarly, the annual return XYZ must earn on existing capital is

$$K_W = \frac{(1-t)K_D D + K_E E}{D+E}$$

where K_W is the cost of capital.

From the preceding example,

$$15\% = \frac{(1-50\%)10\% \times \$100 + 20\% \times \$200}{\$100 + \$200}$$

In words, a company's cost of capital is the cost of the individual sources of capital, weighted by their importance in the firm's capital structure. The subscript W appears in the expression to denote that the cost of capital is a weighted-average cost. This is also why the cost of capital is often denoted by the acronym WACC for weighted-average cost of capital. To demonstrate that K_W is a weighted-average cost, note that one-third of XYZ's capital is debt and two-thirds is equity, so its WACC is one-third the cost of debt plus two-thirds the cost of equity:

$$15\% = (1/3 \times 5\%) + (2/3 \times 20\%)$$

The Cost of Capital and Stock Price

An important tie exists between a company's cost of capital and its stock price. To see the linkage, ask yourself what happens when XYZ Corporation earns a return on existing assets greater than its cost of capital. Because the return to creditors is fixed by contract, the excess return accrues entirely to shareholders. And because the company can earn more than shareholders' opportunity cost of capital, XYZ's stock price will rise as new investors are attracted by the excess return. Conversely, if XYZ earns a return below its cost of capital on existing assets, shareholders will not receive their expected return, and its stock price will fall. The price will continue falling until the prospective return to new buyers again equals equity investors' opportunity cost of capital. Another definition of the cost of capital, therefore, is *the return a firm must earn on existing assets to keep its stock price constant.* Finally, from a shareholder value perspective, we can say that management creates value when it earns returns above the firm's cost of capital and destroys value when it earns below this target.

Robert C. Higgins, *Analysis for Financial Management* (McGraw-Hill 2003). Reproduced with permission of The McGraw-Hill Companies.

Developments in the Market for Syndicated Loans

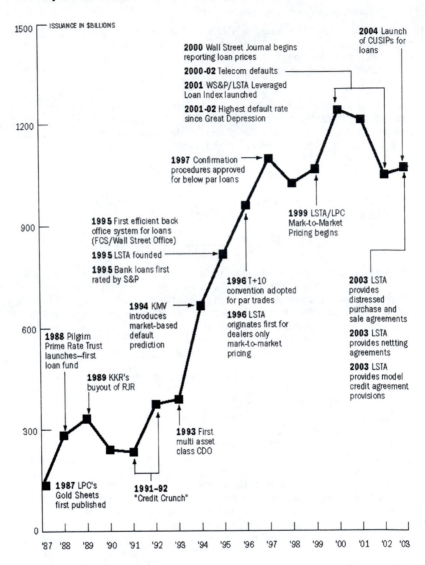

Source: LPC and Thompson Financial

Classifying Leveraged Loans

- Loan Pricing Corporation: Loans with BB, BB/B, and B or lower, bank loan ratings.

- Bloomberg: Loans with a spread over LIBOR of 250 basis points or more.

- Standard & Poor's: Loans with spreads of 125–499 basis points; wide-margin loans are loans with a spread over LIBOR of 500 basis points or more.

- Thompson Financial: Loans with an initial spread of 150 basis points or more before June 30, 2002 or 175 basis points or more after July 1, 2002. Highly leveraged loans are loans funded before June 30, 2002 with an initial spread of 250 basis points and loans funded after July 1, 2002 as highly leveraged if they have spreads of 275 basis points or more.

A Typology of Syndicated Loans

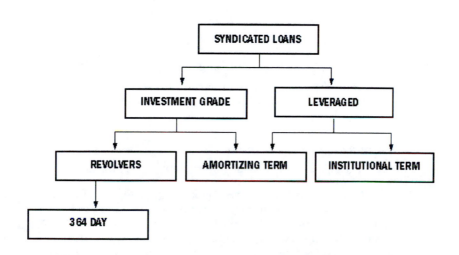

Sample CLO Transaction Structure

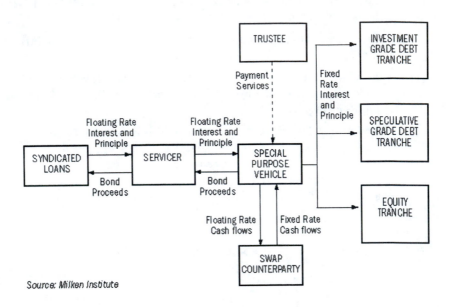

Source: Milken Institute

Regarding the evolution of investment banking:

Changes in Wall Street have been reviewed in JONATHAN KNEE, THE ACCI-
DENTAL BANKER: INSIDE THE DECADE THAT TRANSFORMED WALL STREET (Oxford
University Press 2006).

Regarding rating agencies:

Rating agencies: measuring the measurers, ECONOMIST, June 2, 2007:

> Moody's and S&P have a combined market share of 80%. . . . The big-
> gest concern is structured finance, where the agencies now depend on a
> few large investment banks for much of their revenue. A recent study
> found that the two now work so closely together on complex products
> such as collateralised debt obligations (CDOs)—tranched pools of debt
> from different sources—that the agencies could be seen as helping to
> underwrite them. . . . Janet Tavakoli, a consultant, believes that stan-
> dards have slipped as business has boomed. In subprime lending, she
> says, the models misread the level of correlation between different types
> of assets—a crucial variable—and ignored signs that risks were greater
> than historical data suggested. Securitised assets using this flawed meth-
> odology were used as collateral in other deals, compounding the error.

As an example of the strategic purchase of debt:

Goldman Sachs buy Focus' debt to gain leverage, TELEGRAPH, Oct. 25, 2006
(purchase of distressed debt as "fulcrum investing").

Regarding cyclicality in the debt-financed M&A business—summer of 2007:

A bid too far: How to spot the top of the takeover boom, ECONOMIST, May 12,
2007:

> [A] better place to look [for comparability to today's conditions] is the
> merger boom of the 1980s. Then, as now, many deals were leveraged
> buy-outs (LBOs)—bids financed by private-equity groups such as
> Blackstone, using a large amount of borrowed money. The best-remem-
> bered battle was the takeover of RJR Nabisco, immortalised in the book
> "Barbarians At The Gate", but the top of the market was marked by the
> failed bid for UAL, the parent company of United Airlines, in October
> 1989. The UAL breakdown, which was caused by bankers saying no, sig-
> nalled that the sums behind LBOs no longer added up. A combination
> of high interest rates and the early 1990s recession meant that several of
> that era's LBOs went bust. Returns from the RJR deal proved extremely
> disappointing.

*Behind Buyout Surge, A Debt Market Booms: CLOs Spark Worries of Volatility
and Risk; Loan Standards Loosen,* WALL ST. J., June 26, 2007:

> The corporate buyout boom of the 1980s was funded in large part by
> high-yield "junk" bonds. This time around, another financial product is
> supplying much of the fuel—collateralized loan obligations.
>
> CLOs, as they're called, are giant pools of bank loans bundled together
> by Wall Street and sold off to investors in slices. They aim to spread de-
> fault risk an inch deep and a mile wide. Last year, more than half of the
> loans behind the record wave of buyouts were parceled out to investors
> as CLOs, bankers say.
>
> As corporate borrowing soars, however, concerns are growing that CLOs
> have made it too easy for shaky or debt-laden companies to borrow
> money. If economic conditions deteriorate, those loans could sour and
> investors in the riskiest CLO slices could face large losses. That, in turn,
> could make it harder for buyout firms to borrow money.
>
> "We are witnessing a loan market rife with liquidity and disproportion-
> ate power in the hands of borrowers, arrangers and financial sponsors,"
> said credit-rating firm Standard & Poor's in a June 13 report. S&P ex-
> pressed concern that loans without strong covenants to protect lenders
> are showing up in CLOs. . . .

The companies behind many of these loans aren't the only ones loaded with debt. Many investors who put money into the CLOs use borrowed money to magnify their returns. And the financial professionals who create CLOs use borrowed money when getting them started.

"CLOs are the equivalent of the savings and loans in this cycle," says Kenneth Buckfire of Miller, Buckfire & Co., a restructuring advisory firm. Savings-and-loan institutions gobbled up a mountain of junk bonds issued to fund the 1980s buyout boom. A spike in corporate defaults during the recession of the early 1990s, coupled with a sharp downturn in real-estate markets, caused many S&Ls to fail. . . .

More than a thousand U.S. companies were acquired in leveraged buy-outs in 2006—a record $194 billion of deals, according to data provider Dealogic. . . .

The $11.4 billion acquisition of Sungard Data Systems in 2005 by Kohlberg Kravis Roberts & Co. illustrates how quickly and efficiently Wall Street can parcel out debt.

KKR's banks arranged $5 billion in loans to fund the buyout. Within two weeks, they lined up 150 buyers for loans. CLO managers bought about $3 billion of the loans, according to someone familiar with the financing. Within days, the Sungard loan exposure was spread over thousands of different institutions around the globe, this person says. . . .

Contrast that with KKR's landmark $25 billion purchase of Nabisco in 1988, which required $13.7 billion in loan financing. In that case, four U.S. banks each committed between $600 million and $750 million of their own funds. "We had to scurry around the world ourselves to get 40 other banks to commit to between $250 million and $600 million each," recalls James H. Green, Jr., a partner at KKR. "That only got us to $11 billion. We then had to go looking for smaller commitments."

The Coming Credit Meltdown, WALL ST. J., June 18, 2007 (notes that junk bonds have been trading at historically low premium levels to treasuries—2.63% as opposed to 5.42% average over the last twenty years; also noting laxity in covenants, PIK notes and large payments to sponsor-shareholders paid for with debt; "Perhaps the mispricing of high-yield debt has been exacerbated by the surge in derivatives, a generally useful lubricant of the financial markets. Banks hold far fewer loans these days; mostly, they resell them, often to hedge funds, which frequently layer on still more leverage, thereby exacerbating the risks. Another popular destination is in new classes of securities where the loans have been resliced to (theoretically) tailor the risk to specific investor tastes.").

Goldman, JPMorgan Saddled With Debt They Can't Sell, BLOOMBERG, July 17, 2007:

> Goldman Sachs Group Inc., JPMorgan Chase & Co. and the rest of Wall Street are stuck with at least $11 billion of loans and bonds they can't readily sell. . . .
>
> Bankers, who just a few months ago boasted that demand for high-yield assets was so great that they would have no problem raising debt for a $100 billion LBO, are now paying for their overconfidence. The cost of tying up their own capital may curb earnings and stem the flood of LBOs, which generated a record $8.4 billion in fees during the first half of 2007, according to Brad Hintz, the former chief financial officer at New York-based Lehman Brothers Holdings Inc. . . . "What they've committed to is not current trading rates in the market. If I have a problem it doesn't mean I can't place the problem, but it's going to cause a mark-to-market loss."
>
> The extra yield investors demanded to own junk bonds rather than Treasuries shrank to a record low of 2.41 percentage points in June [2007], according to index data from New York-based Merrill Lynch & Co. The spread has since widened to 3.07 percentage points. . . .
>
> For loans rated four or five levels below investment grade, the spread over the London interbank offered rate shrank to 2.12 percentage points in February from more than 4 percentage points in 2003. It has since widened to 2.72 percentage points. . . .
>
> Just three of the 40 biggest pending LBOs have an escape clause that lets the buyer off the hook if funding can't be arranged, said Mike Belin, U.S. head of equity derivatives strategy at Deutsche Bank AG in New York. A couple of years ago, a majority of deals included a financing contingency, Belin said, based on his research. . . .
>
> Junk bonds lost 1.61 percent last month, the most since March 2005, when General Motors Corp. forecast its biggest quarterly loss since 1992 and the debt lost 2.73 percent, according to Merrill Lynch. . . .
>
> JPMorgan failed to sell $1.15 billion of bonds for Memphis, Tennessee-based ServiceMaster on July 3. The banks provided ServiceMaster, the maker of TruGreen and Terminix lawn-care products, with a bridge loan to make up for the failed bond sale. . . .
>
> In 1989, First Boston Corp., now part of Credit Suisse, made a bridge loan for a buyout of Ohio Mattress Co., the predecessor to Sealy Corp. The junk bond market collapsed before First Boston could refinance the

loan, and the securities firm ended up owning a big stake in the bedding manufacturer. The deal became known as "Burning Bed."

Chapter 3:　The Instruments

Regarding derivatives:

Contracts So Complex They Imperil the System, N.Y. TIMES, Feb. 24, 2002 (according to Henry T.C. Hu, a law and finance professor at the University of Texas, Enron demonstrates that beyond the concerns about systemic risks generated by "daisy chain" effects created by links among derivative contracts, complex financing structures also seem to offer opportunities for financial improprieties by helping the actors cover up what they are doing. "In June, according to the Bank for International Settlements, the over-the-counter market for derivatives consisted of contracts based on $100 trillion in underlying assets—about twice the value of all goods and services produced by the entire world in a year, and a 38 percent increase in size since 1998. . . . Michael Darby, a finance professor at UCLA, puts it this way, 'Do the products have the ability to offset risk through a true hedge? Yes. Do they have a potential for accounting abuses or trading abuses? Yes.'" Hu noted that bells and whistles tend to increase the fees paid to investment bankers who structure these deals, but the article points out that the complexity makes it hard for boards of directors and even professional financial managers of companies to understand what risks they have taken on.).

Regarding the Long-Term Capital crisis:

Michael Lewis, *How the Eggheads Cracked*, N.Y. TIMES, Jan. 24, 1999.

Regarding models used in securitizations and funds:

Gretchen Morgenson, *When Models Misbehave*, N.Y. TIMES, June 24, 2007:

> [M]arking illiquid securities to a model that makes certain assumptions about their future behavior is not the same thing as marking to an honest-to-goodness market of buyers and sellers. . . . In worst-case scenarios, such models may reflect the fantasy that a firm's principals prefer, not the reality of a security's likely value. And yet, investors and financial firms everywhere are relying heavily on these models and building their balance sheets accordingly. . . . That brings us to our second lesson. . . : the rating agencies, which investors rely on to be prescient cops on the beat, are stunningly behind on downgrading mortgage-based securities and the pools that own them. . . . Another bit of reality is setting in now that Bear Stearns has taken action: values higher up in the capital structure of these asset pools [funds investing in subprime

mortgages] will likely take a hit. The Bear funds unwound as quickly as they did partly because of a surprisingly close correlation between lower-rated slices of these pools and higher-rated ones, according to people who have seen the portfolio. The bad performance is bleeding upward.

Floyd Norris, *Market Shock: AAA Rating May Be Junk*, N.Y. TIMES, July 20, 2007.

Chapter 4:   Accounting Matters

See JOHN A. TRACY AND TAGE C. TRACY, HOW TO READ A FINANCIAL REPORT (Wiley 2014).

Regarding improper revenue recognition:

Ex-Chief of Aspen Technology Accused of Inflating Revenue, N.Y. TIMES, Jan. 9, 2007 (a typical allegation of reporting false revenue figures: "by entering into side agreements with a customer when certain revenue would be counted, by backdating software sales agreements into earlier financial quarters and by providing false information to auditors").

Accounting Said to Hide Lender Losses, N.Y. TIMES, May 1, 2007 (subprime mortgage lender adopted "gain on sale" accounting, anticipating profits from sales of loans it originated: "The use of gain on sale was a factor in the collapse of Enron in 2001 and of major specialty lenders in the late 1990s through this decade. Conseco, a large insurance and finance company that made loans to subprime home buyers, filed for bankruptcy protection in 2002, one of the largest corporate bankruptcies ever." As reported in the article, the accounting treatment permitted the company to accelerate its profits, recognizing the entire profit on the sale of loans to banks or into securitizations even though it remained liable to buy back the loans if homeowners did not pay. There are further allegations in the article that when the company was required to buy the loans back it did not account for the fact that the loans now had a lower market value, so there were unrecognized losses on the booked asset values.).

Real-time accounting and reporting?

Opening the books, ECONOMIST, Nov. 11, 2006 (reports on a proposal by accounting firms for near-real time accounting, based on direct access to a company's databases and derived reports. Under this approach, investors would have access to what is basically a portal into the company's accounting databases. Developments in information technology make such a concept realistic but not in the near term. And of course this direct access doesn't help if the information in the company's systems is inaccurate in any way. The role of the auditor would shift from review of financial statements to review of the integrity of the company's information systems.).

Chapter 6: The Issuer and the Obligation: Recourse, Ranking, Rights, and Remedies

See generally CAROLYN E.C. PARIS, HOW TO DRAFT FOR CORPORATE FINANCE, ch. 6 (PLI 2006).

The following are sample key subordination provisions. These do not include provisions relating to the Trustee, notices, representatives, trust funds and the like.

Sample 6-A *Subordination Provisions*

Agreement to Subordinate. The Issuer agrees, and each Holder by accepting a Note agrees, that the Indebtedness evidenced by the Notes is subordinated in right of payment, to the extent and in the manner provided in this Article, to the prior payment in full of all existing and future Senior Debt of the Issuer and that the subordination is for the benefit of and enforceable by the holders of such Senior Debt. The Notes shall in all respects rank *pari passu* in right of payment with all existing and future Pari Passu Indebtedness of the Issuer and shall rank senior in right of payment to all existing and future Subordinated Indebtedness of the Issuer; and only Indebtedness of the Issuer that is Senior Debt of the Issuer shall rank senior to the Notes in accordance with the provisions set forth herein.

Liquidation, Dissolution, Bankruptcy. Holders of Senior Debt will be entitled to receive payment in full of all Obligations due in respect of Senior Debt (including interest after the commencement of any bankruptcy proceeding at the rate specified in the applicable Senior Debt, whether or not such interest is an allowed or allowable claim under applicable law) before the holders of Notes will be entitled to receive any Subordinated Note Payments (other than Permitted Junior Securities) with respect to the Notes, in the event of any distribution to creditors of the Issuer:

(a)   in a total or partial liquidation or total or partial dissolution of the Issuer;

(b)   in a bankruptcy, reorganization, insolvency, receivership or similar proceeding relating to the Issuer or its property;

(c)   in an assignment for the benefit of creditors of the Issuer; or

(d)   in any marshaling of the Issuer's assets and liabilities.

Default on Designated Senior Debt. (a) The Issuer shall not make any Subordinated Note Payments (other than Permitted Junior Securities) in respect of the Notes if:

(1)   a payment default on Designated Senior Debt occurs and is continuing beyond any applicable grace period; or

(2)   any other default occurs and is continuing on any series of Designated Senior Debt that permits holders of that series of Designated Senior Debt to accelerate its maturity and the Trustee receives a notice of such default (a "Payment Blockage Notice") from the holders of any Designated Senior Debt.

(b)   Subordinated Note Payments may and will be resumed:

(1)   in the case of a payment default, upon the date on which such default is cured or waived; and

(2)   in the case of a nonpayment default, upon the earlier of the date on which such nonpayment default is cured or waived or 179 days after the date on which the applicable Payment Blockage Notice is received, unless the maturity of any Designated Senior Debt has been accelerated.

(c)   No new Payment Blockage Notice may be delivered unless and until:

(1)   360 days have elapsed since the delivery of the immediately prior Payment Blockage Notice; and

(2)   all scheduled payments of principal, interest and premium and Liquidated Damages, if any, on the Notes that have come due have been paid in full in cash.

No nonpayment default that existed or was continuing on the date of delivery of any Payment Blockage Notice to the Trustee will be, or be made, the basis for a subsequent Payment Blockage Notice unless such default has been cured or waived for a period of not less than 90 days.

(d)   If the Trustee or any holder of the Notes receives a Subordinated Note Payment when (i) the payment is prohibited by these subordination provisions and (ii) the Trustee or the holder has actual knowledge that the payment is prohibited, the Trustee or the holder, as the case may be, will hold such Subordinated Note Payment in trust for the benefit of the holders of Senior Debt. Upon the proper written request of the holders of Senior Debt, the Trustee or the holder, as the case may be, will deliver the Subordinated Note Payment in trust to the holders of Senior Debt or their proper Representative.

Acceleration of Payment of Notes. If payment of the Notes is accelerated because of an Event of Default, the Issuer or the Trustee (*provided,* that the Trustee shall have received written notice from the Issuer, on which notice the Trustee shall be entitled to conclusively rely) shall promptly notify the holders of the Designated Senior Debt of the Issuer (or their Representative) of the acceleration.

When Distribution Must be Paid Over. If a distribution is made to the Holders that because of this Article should not have been made to them, the Holders who receive the distribution shall hold it in trust for holders of Senior Debt of the Issuer and pay it over to them as their interests may appear.

Subrogation. After all the Senior Debt of the Issuer is paid in full and until the Notes are paid in full, the Holders shall be subrogated to the rights of holders of such Senior Debt to receive distributions applicable to Senior Debt of the Issuer. A distribution made under this Article to holders of such Senior Debt which otherwise would have been made to the Holders is not, as between the Issuer and the Holders, a payment by the Issuer on the Senior Debt.

Relative Rights. This article defines the relative rights of the Holders and holders of Senior Debt of the Issuer. Nothing in this Indenture shall:

(a)   impair, as between the Issuer and the Holders, the obligation of the Issuer, which is absolute and unconditional, to pay principal of and interest on the Notes in accordance with their terms; or

(b)   prevent the Trustee or any Holder from exercising its available remedies upon a Default, subject to the rights of holders of Senior Debt of the Issuer to receive distributions otherwise payable to the Holders.

This Article Not to Prevent Events of Default or Limit Right to Accelerate. The failure to make a payment pursuant to the Notes by reason of any provision in this Article shall not be construed as preventing the occurrence of a Default. Nothing in this Article shall have any effect on the right of the Holders or the Trustee to accelerate the maturity of the Notes.

Subordination May Not be Impaired by Issuer. No right of any holder of Senior Debt of the Issuer to enforce the subordination of the Indebtedness evidenced by the Notes shall be impaired by any act or failure to act by the Issuer or by its failure to comply with the Indenture.

Reliance by Holders of Senior Debt on Subordination Provisions. Each Holder by accepting a Note acknowledges and agrees that the foregoing subordination provisions are, and are intended to be, an inducement and a consideration to each holder of any Senior Debt of the Issuer, whether such Senior Debt was created or acquired before or after the issuance of the Notes, to acquire and continue to hold, or to continue to hold, such Senior Debt and such holder of such Senior Debt shall be deemed conclusively to have relied on such subordination provisions in acquiring and continuing to hold, or in continuing to hold, such Senior Debt.

Without in any way limiting the generality of the foregoing paragraph, the holders of Senior Debt of the Issuer may, at any time and from time to time, without the consent of or notice to the Trustee or the Holders, without incurring responsibility to the Trustee or the Holders and without impairing or releasing the subordination provided in this Article, or the obligations hereunder of the Holders to the holders of the Senior Debt of the Issuer, do any one or more of the following:

(i)   change the manner, place or terms of payment or extend the time of payment of, or renew or alter, Senior Debt of the Issuer, or otherwise amend or supplement in any manner Senior Debt of the Issuer, or any instrument evidencing the same or any agreement under which Senior Debt of the Issuer is outstanding;

(ii)   sell, exchange, release or otherwise deal with any property pledged, mortgaged or otherwise securing Senior Debt of the Issuer;

(iii)   release any Person liable in any manner for the payment or collection of Senior Debt of the Issuer; and

(iv)   exercise or refrain from exercising any rights against the Issuer and any other Person.

Limitation on Other Senior Subordinated Indebtedness [anti-layering covenant]. The Issuer will not, and will not permit any Restricted Subsidiary that is a Guarantor to, directly or indirectly, incur any Indebtedness that is or purports to be by its terms (or by the terms of any agreement governing such Indebtedness) contractually subordinated or junior in right of payment to any Senior Debt (including Acquired Debt) of the Issuer or such Restricted Subsidiary, as the case may be, unless such Indebtedness is either:

(a)   *pari passu* in right of payment with the Notes or such Guarantor's Guarantee (as applicable); or

(b)   subordinate in right of payment to the Notes or such Guarantor's Guarantee (as applicable).

"Senior Debt" means the principal of, premium, if any, and interest (including any interest accruing subsequent to the filing of a petition of bankruptcy at the rate provided for in the documentation with respect thereto, whether or not such interest is an allowed claim under applicable law) on any Indebtedness of the Issuer (or, if specified, of any Guarantor), whether outstanding on the Issue Date or thereafter created, incurred or assumed, unless, in the case of any particular obligation, the instrument creating or evidencing the same or pursuant to which the same is outstanding expressly provides that such obligation shall not be senior in right of payment to the Notes.

Without limiting the generality of the foregoing, "Senior Debt" shall also include the principal of, premium, if any, interest (including any interest accruing subsequent to the filing of a petition of bankruptcy at the rate provided for in the documentation with respect thereto, whether or not such interest is an allowed claim under applicable law) on, and all other amounts owing in respect of (including guarantees of the foregoing obligations):

(1) all monetary obligations of every nature of the Issuer under, or with respect to, the Credit Agreement, including, without limitation, obligations to pay principal, premium and interest, reimbursement obligations under letters of credit, fees, expenses and indemnities (and guarantees thereof); and

(2) all Hedging Obligations (and guarantees thereof);

in each case whether outstanding on the Issue Date or thereafter incurred.

Notwithstanding the foregoing, "Senior Debt" shall not include:

(1) any Indebtedness of the Issuer to the Parent Guarantor or a Subsidiary of the Parent Guarantor;

(2) Indebtedness to, or guaranteed on behalf of, any shareholder, director, officer or employee of the Issuer or any Subsidiary of the Issuer other than the guarantees provided under the Credit Agreement;

(3) Indebtedness to trade creditors and other amounts incurred in connection with obtaining goods, materials or services (including guarantees thereof or instruments evidencing such liabilities other than letters of credit provided under the Credit Agreement);

(4) Indebtedness represented by Capital Stock;

(5) any liability for federal, state, local or other taxes owed or owing by the Issuer;

(6) that portion of any Indebtedness incurred in violation of Section [debt covenant] of this Indenture;

(7) Indebtedness which, when incurred and without respect to any election under Section 1111 (b) of Title 11, United States Code, is without recourse to the Issuer; and

(8) any Indebtedness which is, by its express terms, subordinated in right of payment to any other Indebtedness of the Issuer.

"Credit Agreement" means that certain Credit Agreement, dated as of DATE, among the Parent Guarantor, the Issuer, certain subsidiaries of the Issuer from time to time party thereto, the Lenders party thereto, and AGENT, as Agent, including any related notes, guarantees, collateral documents, instruments and agreements executed in connection therewith, and in each case as amended, restated, supplemented, modified, renewed, refunded, replaced or refinanced from time to time in one or more agreements or indentures (in each case with the same or new lenders or institutional investors), including any agreement or indenture extending the maturity thereof or otherwise restructuring all or any portion of the Indebtedness thereunder or increasing the amount loaned or issued thereunder or altering the maturity thereof.

"Designated Senior Debt" means:

(1)   any Indebtedness outstanding under the Credit Agreement; and

(2)   any other Senior Debt permitted under this Indenture the principal amount of which is $10.0 million or more and that has been designated by the Issuer in the instrument evidencing that Senior Debt as "Designated Senior Debt."

Chapter 7:   Beyond the Issuer: Corporate Structure Issues

See generally CAROLYN E.C. PARIS, HOW TO DRAFT FOR CORPORATE FINANCE ch. 9 (PLI 2006).

Examples of provisions intended to protect against structural subordination:

Sample 7-A *Limitation on Issuances of Guarantees of Indebtedness*

(a)   The Company will not permit any Subsidiary, directly or indirectly, to guarantee, assume, or in any other manner become liable with respect to any Indebtedness of the Company unless such Subsidiary simultaneously executes and delivers a supplemental indenture to this Indenture providing for a Guarantee of the Securities, on the same terms as the guarantee of such Indebtedness except that (A) such guarantee need not be secured unless required pursuant to [negative pledge], (B) if the Securities are subordinated in right of payment to such Indebtedness, the Guarantee under the supplemental indenture shall be subordinated to the guarantee of such Indebtedness to the same extent as the Securities are subordinated to such Indebtedness under this Indenture, and (C) if such Indebtedness is by its terms expressly subordinated to the Securities, any such assumption, guarantee or other liability of such Subsidiary with respect to such Indebtedness shall be subordinated to such Subsidiary's Guarantee of the Securities at least to the same extent as such Indebtedness is subordinated to the Securities.

(b)   Notwithstanding the foregoing, any Guarantee by a Subsidiary of the Securities shall provide by its terms that it (and all Liens securing the same) shall be automatically and unconditionally released and discharged upon any sale, exchange or transfer, to any Person not an Affiliate of the Company, of all of the Company's Capital Stock in such Subsidiary, which is in compliance with the terms of this Indenture.

Sample 7-B *Restriction on Transfer of Assets*

The Company will not sell, convey, transfer, or otherwise dispose of its assets or property to any of its Subsidiaries, except for sales, conveyances, transfers or other dispositions (a) made in the ordinary course of business, or (b) to any Subsidiary if such Subsidiary simultaneously executes and delivers a supplemental indenture to this Indenture providing for a Guarantee of the payment of the Securities by such Subsidiary. For purposes of this provision, any sale, conveyance, transfer, lease, or other disposition of property or assets shall be deemed to be made in the ordinary course of business if, after giving effect to such sale, conveyance, transfer, lease or disposition, the Consolidated Tangible Assets of the Company's Subsidiaries do not exceed 15% of the Consolidated Tangible Assets of the Company.

Sample 7-C *Guaranties by Restricted Subsidiaries*

If the Company or any of its Restricted Subsidiaries acquires or creates a [Domestic] Restricted Subsidiary [(other than a Securitization Subsidiary)] [other than a Finance Subsidiary)] after the date of the Indenture, the new Restricted Subsidiary must provide a Note Guaranty.

A Restricted Subsidiary required to provide a Note Guaranty shall execute a supplemental indenture in the form of Exhibit B, and deliver an Opinion of Counsel to the Trustee to the effect that the supplemental indenture has been duly authorized, executed and delivered by the Restricted Subsidiary and constitutes a valid and binding obligation of the Restricted Subsidiary, enforceable against the Restricted Subsidiary in accordance with its terms (subject to customary exceptions).

Sample 7-D *Savings Clause*

Notwithstanding the foregoing, the Guarantor's obligations hereunder shall not exceed the maximum amount that would not be subject to avoidance under fraudulent conveyance, fraudulent transfer, and other similar laws.

Sample 7-E *Limitation on Issuances and Sales of Capital Stock of Restricted Subsidiaries*

The Company (i) will not permit any Restricted Subsidiary to issue or sell any Capital Stock (other than to the Company or a Wholly-Owned Restricted Subsidiary), and (ii) will not permit any Person (other than the Company or a Wholly-Owned Restricted Subsidiary) to own any Capital Stock of any Restricted Subsidiary, *provided, however,* that this covenant shall not prohibit any issuance or sale of the Capital Stock of any Restricted Subsidiary if, immediately after giving effect to such issuance or sale, such Restricted Subsidiary would no longer constitute a Restricted Subsidiary and any Investment in such Person remaining after giving effect to such issuance or sale would have been permitted to be made under the "Limitation on Restricted Payments" covenant if made on the date of such issuance or sale.

Sample 7-F *Wholly-Owned Subsidiary—Version 1*

"*Wholly-Owned*" means, with respect to any Subsidiary of any Person, such Subsidiary if all of the outstanding Capital Stock or other similar equity ownership interests (other than Preferred Stock) in such Subsidiary (other than any director's qualifying shares or Investments by foreign Persons mandated by applicable law) is owned directly or indirectly by such Person.

Sample 7-G *Wholly-Owned Subsidiary—Version 2*

"*Wholly-Owned Subsidiary*" of any Person means a Restricted Subsidiary of such Person all of the outstanding Capital Stock or other ownership interests of which (other than directors' qualifying shares) shall at the time be owned by such Person or by one or more Wholly-Owned Subsidiaries of such Person or by such Person and one or more Wholly-Owned Subsidiaries of such Person.

Sample 7-H *Limitation on Restrictions Affecting Subsidiaries*

Neither the Borrower nor any of its Subsidiaries will enter into, or suffer to exist, any agreement with any Person, other than this Agreement, the Indenture and the Seller Notes, which prohibits or limits the ability of any Subsidiary to (a) pay dividends or make other distributions or pay any Debt owed to Borrower or any Subsidiary, (b) make loans or advances to Borrower or any Subsidiary, (c) transfer any of its properties or assets to Borrower or any Subsidiary or (d) create, incur, assume, or suffer to exist any Lien upon any of its property, assets, or revenues, whether now owned or hereafter acquired (other than with respect to assets subject to consensual liens permitted under [lien covenant]); *provided* that the foregoing shall not apply to restrictions in effect on the date of this Agreement contained in agreements governing Debt outstanding on the date of this Agreement and, if such Debt is renewed, extended, or refinanced, restrictions in the agreements governing the renewed, extended, or refinancing Debt (and successive renewals, extensions, and refinancings thereof) if such restrictions are no more restrictive than those contained in the agreements governing the Debt being renewed, extended, or refinanced.

Sample 7-1 *Permitted Refinancing Concept—Version 1*

Limitation on Indebtedness

The Company will not, and will not permit any of its Restricted Subsidiaries to, Incur any Indebtedness (other than Permitted Indebtedness); provided that the Company may Incur Indebtedness if, on the date of such Incurrence, after giving effect to the Incurrence of such Indebtedness and the receipt and application of the proceeds therefrom, the Fixed Charge Coverage Ratio exceeds 2.5 to 1.

Notwithstanding the foregoing, the Company and, to the extent provided below, any Restricted Subsidiary may Incur the following Indebtedness ("Permitted Indebtedness"):

(i)   Indebtedness of the Company and any Restricted Subsidiary pursuant to the Bank Credit Facility in an aggregate principal amount at any time outstanding not to exceed (A) $100.0 million under the Term Loan Facility (less the amount thereof which has been permanently repaid as provided under [asset sales covenant]), and (B) the greater of (1) $200 million (less the amount of net proceeds which have been received in connection with a Permitted Receivables Financing; *provided* that, such reduction shall apply only for so long as a Permitted Receivables Financing is in effect) and (2) the aggregate Borrowing Base under the Revolving Loan Facility;

(ii)   Indebtedness of the Company or any Restricted Subsidiary to the Company or any Wholly-Owned Restricted Subsidiary as long as such Indebtedness continues to be owed to the Company or any Wholly-Owned Restricted Subsidiary;

(iii)   Indebtedness of the Company pursuant to the Notes and Indebtedness of any Guarantor pursuant to a Subsidiary Guarantee of the Notes;

(iv)   Indebtedness ("Permitted Refinancing Indebtedness") issued in exchange for, or the net proceeds of which are used to refinance or refund, then outstanding Indebtedness (Incurred under the first paragraph of this covenant or under clauses (iii), (vi), (vii), (viii), or (xii) of this paragraph) and any refinancings thereof in an amount not to exceed the amount so refinanced or refunded (plus premiums, accrued interest, fees and expenses); *provided* that Indebtedness the proceeds of which are used to refinance or refund the Notes or Indebtedness that is pari passu with, or subordinated in right of payment to, the Notes shall only be permitted under this clause (iv) if (A) in case the Notes are refinanced in part or the Indebtedness to be refinanced is pari passu with the Notes, such new Indebtedness, by its terms or by the terms of any agreement or instrument pursuant to which such new Indebtedness is outstanding, is expressly made pari passu with, or subordinate in right of payment to, the remaining Notes, (B) in case the Indebtedness to be refinanced is subordinated in right of payment to the Notes, such new Indebtedness, by its terms or by the terms of any agreement or instrument pursuant to which such new Indebtedness is outstanding, is expressly made subordinate in right of payment to the Notes at least to the extent that the Indebtedness to be refinanced is subordinated to the Notes, and (C) such new Indebtedness, determined as of the date of Incurrence of such new Indebtedness, does not mature prior to the Stated Maturity of the Indebtedness to be refinanced or refunded, and the Average Life of such new Indebtedness is at least equal to the remaining Average Life of the Indebtedness to be refinanced or refunded; and *provided further* that in no event may Indebtedness of the Company be refinanced pursuant to this clause (iv) by means of any Indebtedness of any Restricted Subsidiary;

(v)   Indebtedness of the Company or any Restricted Subsidiary in respect of performance bonds, letters of credit, bankers' acceptances and surety or appeal bonds issued in the ordinary course of business;

(vi)   Acquired Indebtedness of any Restricted Subsidiary; provided that, with respect to this clause (vi), after giving effect to the Incurrence thereof, the Company could incur at least $1.00 of Indebtedness (other than Permitted Indebtedness);

(vii) Indebtedness of the Company or any Restricted Subsidiary outstanding on the Issue Date (other than Indebtedness described in clause (i), (ii) or (iii) of this paragraph);

(viii) Indebtedness of the Company or any Restricted Subsidiary represented by Capital Lease Obligations, mortgage financings or purchase money obligations, in each case Incurred for this purpose of financing not more than 80% of the purchase price or cost of construction or improvement of property used in the Business or Incurred to refinance any such purchase price or cost of construction or improvement, in each case Incurred no later than 365 days after the date of such acquisition or the date of completion of such construction or improvements; provided that the aggregate principal amount of any Indebtedness Incurred pursuant to this clause (viii) and any refinancing thereof at any one time outstanding shall not exceed $40.0 million;

(ix) Indebtedness of a Securitization Subsidiary pursuant to a Permitted Receivables Financing; provided that after giving effect to the Incurrence thereof, the Company could Incur at least $1.00 of Indebtedness under the first paragraph of this covenant or clause (i) of this paragraph;

(x) Indebtedness of the Company or any Restricted Subsidiary under Hedging Contracts entered into in the ordinary course of business for the purpose of limiting risks to the Company or any Restricted Subsidiary of changes in prices for commodities relating to the Business;

(xi) Indebtedness consisting of Interest Rate Agreements directly related to Indebtedness permitted to be Incurred by the Company or any Restricted Subsidiary pursuant to the Indenture;

(xii) Indebtedness of the Company or any Restricted Subsidiary represented by any industrial revenue bonds, pollution control bonds or other tax exempt financing; provided, that the aggregate amount of any Indebtedness Incurred pursuant to this clause (xii) and any refinancing thereof at any one time outstanding shall not exceed $10 million;

(xiii) Guarantees by any Restricted Subsidiary of Indebtedness Incurred by the Company in compliance with the provisions set forth under the first paragraph of this covenant or clause (xiv) of this paragraph may be guaranteed pursuant to this clause (xiii); and

(xiv) Indebtedness of the Company or any Restricted Subsidiary in an aggregate principal amount at any time outstanding not to exceed $25.0 million.

For purposes of determining compliance with the "Limitation on Indebtedness" covenant described in the two preceding paragraphs, (i) in the event that an item of Indebtedness meets the criteria of more than one of the types of Indebtedness described in the clauses of the preceding paragraph, the Company, in its sole discretion, shall classify such item of Indebtedness and only be required to include the amount and type of such Indebtedness in one of such clauses, (ii) an item of Indebtedness may be divided and classified in more than one of the types of Indebtedness described above and (iii) the amount of Indebtedness issued at a price that is less than the principal amount thereof shall be equal to the amount of the liability in respect thereof determined in conformity with GAAP.

"Bank Credit Facility" means the Credit Agreement dated on the Issue Date among the Company, certain Subsidiaries of the Company, the Lenders party thereto, and Friendly Bank, as agent for such Lenders, together with any related documents thereto (including, without limitation, any security documents and guarantee agreements), in each case as such agreements may be amended, supplemented, modified, extended, renewed or restated from time to time, including, without limitation, by adding additional parties thereto or increasing the commitment thereunder; *provided* that there may not be more than one Bank Credit Facility at any one time, which shall be designated by the Company.

Sample 7-J *Permitted Refinancing Concept—Version 2*

"Permitted Indebtedness" means:

(i)   Indebtedness of the Company under the Bank Credit Facility in an aggregate principal amount at any one time outstanding not to exceed (a) $200 million under any term loans made pursuant thereto, minus all principal payments made in respect of any term loans and (b) $100 million under any revolving credit facility or in respect of letters of credit thereunder minus the amount by which any commitments thereunder are permanently reduced;

(ii)   Indebtedness of the Company pursuant to the Securities and Indebtedness of any Guarantor pursuant to a Guarantee of the Securities;

(iii)   Indebtedness of the Company or any Subsidiary outstanding on the date of this Indenture and listed on Schedule I hereto;

(iv)   Indebtedness of the Company owing to a Subsidiary; provided that any Indebtedness of the Company owing to a Subsidiary is made pursuant to an intercompany note in the form attached to this Indenture and is subordinated in right of payment from and after such time as the Securities shall become due and payable (whether at Stated Maturity, acceleration or otherwise) to the payment and performance of the Company's obligations under the Securities; provided, further, that any disposition, pledge or transfer of any such Indebtedness to a Person (other than a disposition, pledge or transfer to a Subsidiary) shall be deemed to be an incurrence of such Indebtedness by the Company not permitted by this clause (iv);

(v)   Indebtedness of a Wholly-Owned Subsidiary owing to the Company or another Wholly-Owned Subsidiary; provided that any such Indebtedness is made pursuant to an intercompany note in the form attached to this Indenture; provided, further, that (a) any disposition, pledge or transfer of any such Indebtedness to a Person (other than a disposition, pledge or transfer to (I) the Company or a Wholly-Owned Subsidiary or (II) the Banks as security for obligations under the Bank Credit Facility by the Company or a Wholly-Owned Subsidiary which is a Guarantor) shall be deemed to be an incurrence of such Indebtedness by the obligor not permitted by this clause (v), and (b) any transaction pursuant to which any Wholly-Owned Subsidiary, which has Indebtedness owing to the Company or any other Wholly-Owned Subsidiary, ceases to be a Wholly-Owned Subsidiary shall be deemed to be the incurrence of Indebtedness by such Wholly-Owned Subsidiary that is not permitted by this clause (v);

(vi)   obligations of the Company entered into in the ordinary course of business (a) pursuant to Interest Rate Agreements designed to protect the Company or any Subsidiary against fluctuations in interest rates in respect of Indebtedness of the Company or any Subsidiary as long as such obligations do not exceed the aggregate principal amount of such Indebtedness then outstanding, (b) under any Currency Hedging Arrangements, or (c) under any Commodity Hedging Agreements;

(vii)   Indebtedness of the Company represented by Capital Lease Obligations, mortgage financings, Purchase Money Obligations, or other Indebtedness incurred or assumed in connection with the acquisition or development of real or personal, movable or immovable, property in each case incurred for the purpose of financing or refinancing all or any part of the purchase price or cost of construction or improvement of property used in the business of the Company, in an aggregate principal amount pursuant to this clause (vii) not to exceed $50 million outstanding at any time; provided that the principal amount of any Indebtedness permitted under this clause (vii) did not in each case at the time of incurrence exceed the Fair Market Value, as determined by the Company in good faith, of the acquired or constructed asset or improvement so financed;

(viii) any renewals, extensions, substitutions, refundings, refinancings or replacements (collectively, a "refinancing") of any Indebtedness described in clauses (ii) and (iii) of this definition of "Permitted Indebtedness," including any successive refinancings so long as the aggregate principal amount of Indebtedness represented thereby is not increased by such refinancing plus the lesser of (I) the stated amount of any premium or other payment required to be paid in connection with such a refinancing pursuant to the terms of the Indebtedness being refinanced, or (II) the amount of premium or other payment actually paid at such time to refinance the Indebtedness, plus, in either case, the amount of expenses of the Company incurred in connection with such refinancing and (A) in the case of any refinancing of Indebtedness that is Subordinated Indebtedness, such new Indebtedness is made subordinated to the Securities at least to the same extent as the Indebtedness being refinanced, and (B) in the case of Pari Passu Indebtedness or Subordinated Indebtedness, as the case may be, such refinancing does not reduce the Average Life to Stated Maturity or the Stated Maturity of such Indebtedness; and

(ix) Indebtedness of the Company in addition to that described in clauses (i) through (viii) above, and any renewals, extensions, substitutions, refinancings, or replacements of such Indebtedness, so long as the aggregate principal amount of all such Indebtedness shall not exceed $75 million outstanding at any one time in the aggregate.

"Bank Credit Facility" means the Bank Credit Facility, dated as of the date of this Indenture, among the Company, the Banks and Prudent Bank, as agent, as such agreement, in whole or in part, may be amended, renewed, extended, substituted, refinanced, restructured, replaced, supplemented or otherwise modified from time to time (including, without limitation, any successive amendments, renewals, extensions, substitutions, refinancings, restructurings, replacements, supplementations, or other modifications of the foregoing; provided that in determining whether any repayments have been made under the term loan under the Bank Credit Facility for the purpose of clause (i)(a) of the definition of "Permitted Indebtedness," such repayments shall not include any repayments or refinancings of any term loan made from the proceeds of a simultaneous refinancing or replacement of the Bank Credit Facility to the extent that the aggregate principal amount of Indebtedness under the term loans outstanding under the Bank Credit Facility at the time of such repayment or refinancing does not increase as a result of such repayment or refinancing).

Sample 7-K *Subsidiary and Voting Stock Definitions—Version 1*

"*Subsidiary*" means, with respect to any Person, any corporation, association, or other business entity of which more than 50% of the outstanding Voting Stock is owned, directly or indirectly, by (i) such Person, (ii) such Person and one or more other Subsidiaries of such person, or (iii) one or more Subsidiaries of such Person. Unless otherwise specified, "Subsidiary" means a Subsidiary of the Company.

"*Voting Stock*" means, with respect to any Person, Capital Stock of any class or kind ordinarily having the power to vote for the election of directors, managers, or other voting members of the governing body of such Person.

Sample 7-L *Subsidiary and Voting Stock Definitions—Version 2*

"*Subsidiary*" of any Person means (i) a corporation more than 50% of the outstanding Voting Stock of which is owned, directly or indirectly, by such Person or by one or more other Subsidiaries of such Person or by such Person and one or more other Subsidiaries thereof, or (ii) any other Person (other than a corporation) in which such Person, or one or more other Subsidiaries of such Person, or such Person and one or more other Subsidiaries thereof, directly or indirectly, has at least a majority ownership and voting power relating to the policies, management and affairs thereof.

"*Voting Stock*" of any Person means the Capital Stock of such Person which ordinarily has voting power for the election of directors (or persons performing similar functions) of such Person, whether at all times or only so long as no senior class of securities has such voting power by reason of any contingency.

Sample 7-M   *Subsidiary and Voting Stock Definitions—Version 3*

"*Subsidiary*" means any Person, a majority of the equity ownership or the Voting Stock of which is at the time owned, directly or indirectly, by the Company or by one or more other Subsidiaries, or by the Company and one or more other Subsidiaries.

"*Voting Stock*" means Capital Stock of the class or classes pursuant to which the holders thereof have the general voting power under ordinary circumstances to elect at least a majority of the board of directors, managers or trustees of a corporation (irrespective of whether or not at the time Capital Stock of any other class or classes shall have or might have voting power by reason of the happening of any contingency).

Examples of definitions relating to subsidiaries:

Sample 7-N   *Restricted Subsidiary and Unrestricted Subsidiary— Version 1*

"*Restricted Subsidiary*" means any Subsidiary of the Company other than an Unrestricted Subsidiary.

"*Unrestricted Subsidiary*" means (1) any Subsidiary of the Company that at the time of determination shall be designated as an Unrestricted Subsidiary by the board of directors of the Company in the manner provided below and (2) any Subsidiary of an Unrestricted Subsidiary. The board of directors of the Company may designate any Restricted Subsidiary of the Company (including any newly acquired or newly formed Subsidiary of the Company) to be an Unrestricted Subsidiary unless such Subsidiary owns any Capital Stock of, or holds any Lien on any property of, the Company or any Restricted Subsidiary; *provided* that either (1) the Subsidiary to be so designated has total assets of $1,000 or less, or (2) if such Subsidiary has assets greater than $1,000, such designation would be permitted under [investment covenant]. The board of directors of the Company may designate any Unrestricted Subsidiary to be a Restricted Subsidiary of the Company; *provided* that immediately after giving effect to such designation (1) the Company could Incur $1.00 of additional Indebtedness under [debt incurrence coverage test] and (2) no Default shall have occurred and be continuing. Any such designation by the board of directors of the Company shall be evidenced to the Trustee by promptly filing with the Trustee a copy of the board resolution giving effect to such designation and an Officers' Certificate certifying that such designation complied with the foregoing provisions.

Sample 7-O   *Restricted Subsidiary*

"*Restricted Subsidiary*" means (1) any Subsidiary organized and existing under the laws of the United States of America and the principal business of which is carried on within the United States of America that owns or is a lessee pursuant to a capital lease of any Principal Manufacturing Facility Property, and in which the investment of the Issuer and all its Subsidiaries exceeds 10% of Consolidated Net Worth, and (2) any Subsidiary that owns any Capital Stock issued by a Restricted Subsidiary as of the date of such determination other than:

(x)   each Subsidiary the major part of whose business consists of finance, banking, credit, leasing, insurance, financial services or other similar operations, or any combination thereof; and

(y)   each Subsidiary formed or acquired after the date hereof for the purpose of acquiring the business or assets of another Person and which does not acquire all or any substantial part of the business or assets of the Issuer or any Restricted Subsidiary;

provided, however, that the Board of Directors of the Issuer may by Board Resolution declare any such Subsidiary referred to in clause (x) or (y) to be a Restricted Subsidiary, effective as of the date such resolution is adopted.

Sample 7-P   *Restricted Subsidiary and Unrestricted Subsidiary— Version 2*

"*Restricted Subsidiary*" means (i) any Subsidiary of the Issuer other than an Unrestricted Subsidiary and (ii) any successor to a substantial portion of the assets of any Subsidiary other than an Unrestricted Subsidiary.

"*Unrestricted Subsidiary*" means (i) any Subsidiary of the Issuer formed or acquired after the Issue Date that at the time of determination is designated an Unrestricted Subsidiary by the Board of Directors in the manner provided below and (ii) any Subsidiary of an Unrestricted Subsidiary. Any such designation by the Board of Directors will be evidenced to the Trustee by promptly filing with the Trustee a copy of the board resolution giving effect to such designation and an officer's certificate certifying that such designation complied with the following provisions. The Board of Directors of the Issuer may not designate any Subsidiary of the Issuer to be an Unrestricted Subsidiary if, after such designation, (a) the Issuer or any Restricted Subsidiary (i) provides credit support for, or a guarantee of, any Indebtedness of such Subsidiary or (ii) is directly or indirectly liable for any Indebtedness of such Subsidiary, (b) a default with respect to any Indebtedness of such Subsidiary (including any right which the holders thereof may have to take enforcement action against such Subsidiary) would permit (upon notice, lapse of time or both) any holder of any other Indebtedness of the Issuer or any Restricted Subsidiary to declare a default on such other Indebtedness or cause the payment thereof to be accelerated or payable prior to its final scheduled maturity, or (c) such Subsidiary owns any Capital Stock of, or owns or holds any Lien on any property of, any Restricted Subsidiary that is not a Subsidiary of the Subsidiary to be so designated.

Sample 7-Q *Restricted Subsidiary and Unrestricted Subsidiary— Version 3*

"*Restricted Subsidiary*" means any Subsidiary other than an Unrestricted Subsidiary. "*Unrestricted Subsidiary*" means (i) any Subsidiary that at the time of determination shall be designated an Unrestricted Subsidiary by the Board of Directors in the manner provided below and (ii) any Subsidiary of an Unrestricted Subsidiary. The Board of Directors may designate any Restricted Subsidiary (including any newly acquired or newly formed Subsidiary) to be an Unrestricted Subsidiary unless such Subsidiary owns any Redeemable Stock of the Company or any Capital Stock of any Restricted Subsidiary, or owns or holds any Lien on any property of the Company or any Restricted Subsidiary; *provided* that (1) such designation would be permitted under the [restricted payments covenant], (2) no portion of the Indebtedness or any other obligation (contingent or otherwise) of such Subsidiary (A) is Guaranteed by the Company or any Restricted Subsidiary, (B) is with recourse to the Company or any Restricted Subsidiary, or (C) subjects any property or asset of the Company or any Restricted Subsidiary, directly or indirectly, contingent or otherwise, to the satisfaction thereof, and (3) no default or event of default with respect to any Indebtedness of such Subsidiary would permit any holder of any Indebtedness of the Company or any Restricted Subsidiary to declare such Indebtedness of the Company or any Restricted Subsidiary due and payable prior to its maturity. The Board of Directors may designate any Unrestricted Subsidiary to be a Restricted Subsidiary; *provided* that immediately after giving effect to such designation (x) the Company could Incur $1.00 of additional Indebtedness (other than Permitted Indebtedness) and (y) no Default or Event of Default shall have occurred and be continuing. Any such designation by the Board of Directors shall be evidenced to the Trustee by promptly filing with the Trustee a copy of the Board Resolution giving effect to such designation and an officer's certificate certifying that such designation complied with the foregoing provisions.

Sample 7-R *Foreign Subsidiary—Version 1*

"*Foreign Subsidiary*" means a Subsidiary formed and existing under the laws of a jurisdiction outside the United States, for the purpose of doing business outside of the United States.

Sample 7-S *Domestic Subsidiary—Version 1*

"*Domestic Subsidiary*" means a Subsidiary formed and existing under the laws of a jurisdiction within the United States.

Sample 7-T *Foreign Subsidiary—Version 2*

"*Foreign Subsidiary*" means any Subsidiary (i) which is incorporated under the laws of a jurisdiction other than the United States of America or one of the states thereof or the District of Columbia; or (ii) the major portion of whose business is carried on or the major portion of whose property or assets is located outside the United States of America; or (iii) the major portion of whose assets consists of securities of any other Foreign Subsidiary.

Sample 7-U *Domestic Subsidiary—Version 2*

"*Domestic Subsidiary*" means any Subsidiary organized under the laws of the United States of America or any state thereof, and having substantially all its assets located within, and operating substantially entirely within, the continental limits of the United States of America.

Sample 7-V *Significant Subsidiary—Version 1*

"*Significant Subsidiary*" means, at any date of determination, any Restricted Subsidiary that, together with its Subsidiaries, accounted for more than 10% of the consolidated revenues of the Company and its Restricted Subsidiaries for the then most recent four fiscal quarters prior to such date of determination for which financial information is available at such date of determination or (ii) was the owner of more than 10% of the consolidated assets of the Company and its Restricted Subsidiaries as of such date of determination.

Sample 7-W *Significant Subsidiary—Version 2*

"*Significant Subsidiary*" means any Subsidiary that qualifies as a "significant subsidiary" under Rule 1-02(w) of the SEC's Regulation S-X.

Sample 7-X   *High-Yield Provisions That Accommodate a Receivables Subsidiary*

"Asset Disposition" means any sale, transfer, or other disposition (including, without limitation, by merger, consolidation or sale-and-leaseback transaction) of (i) shares of Capital Stock of a Subsidiary of the Issuer (other than directors' qualifying shares), or (ii) property or assets of the Issuer or any Subsidiary of the Issuer; *provided, however,* that an Asset Disposition shall not include (a) any sale, transfer, or other disposition of shares of Capital Stock, property, or assets by a Restricted Subsidiary of the Issuer to the Issuer or to any Wholly-Owned Subsidiary of the Issuer, (b) any sale, transfer, or other disposition of defaulted receivables for collection or any sale, transfer or other disposition of property or assets in the ordinary course of business, (c) any individual isolated sale, transfer, or other disposition that does not involve aggregate consideration in excess of $2 million, (d) the grant in the ordinary course of any nonexclusive license of patents, trademarks, registrations therefor, and other similar intellectual property, (e) any Lien (or foreclosure thereon) securing Indebtedness to the extent that such Lien is granted in compliance with [lien covenant], (f) any Restricted Payment permitted by [restricted payments covenant], (g) the sale, lease, conveyance, or disposition or other transfer of all or substantially all of the assets of the Issuer as permitted under [merger and asset sale covenant]; *provided* that the assets not so sold, leased, conveyed, disposed of, or otherwise transferred shall be deemed an Asset Disposition, (h) any disposition that constitutes a Change of Control, or (i) any Permitted Receivables Financing.

"Permitted Investments" means (i) Investments in marketable, direct obligations issued or guaranteed by the United States of America, or any governmental entity or agency or political subdivision thereof (*provided* that the full faith and credit of the United States of America is pledged in support thereof), maturing within one year of the date of purchase; (ii) Investments in commercial paper issued by corporations or financial institutions maturing within 180 days from the date of the original issue thereof, and rated "P-1" or better by Moody's Investors Service or "A-1" or better by Standard & Poor's Corporation or an equivalent rating or better by any other nationally recognized securities rating agency; (iii) Investments in time deposits and certificates of deposit issued or acceptances accepted by or guaranteed by any bank or trust company organized under the laws of the United States of America or any state thereof or the District of Columbia, or incorporated in a foreign jurisdiction and having a branch office in the United States (each, an "Approved Bank"), in each case having capital, surplus, and undivided profits totaling more than $500 million, maturing within one year of the date of purchase; (iv) Investments representing Capital Stock or obliga-

tions issued to the Issuer or any of its Restricted Subsidiaries in the course of the good faith settlement of claims against any other Person or by reason of a composition or readjustment of debt or a reorganization of any debtor of the Issuer or any of its Restricted Subsidiaries; (v) deposits, including interest-bearing deposits, maintained in the ordinary course of business in banks; (vi) repurchase obligations of an Approved Bank for government obligations with a term of not more than seven days; (vii) Investments in money market mutual funds having assets in excess of $2.5 billion, all of whose assets are comprised of government obligations; (viii) any acquisition of the Capital Stock of any Person; *provided, however,* that after giving effect to any such acquisition such Person shall become a Wholly-Owned Restricted Subsidiary of the Issuer; (ix) trade receivables and prepaid expenses, in each case arising in the ordinary course of business; *provided, however,* that such receivables and prepaid expenses would be recorded as assets of such Person in accordance with GAAP; (x) endorsements for collection or deposit in the ordinary course of business by such Person of bank drafts and similar negotiable instruments of such other Person received as payment for ordinary course of business trade receivables; (xi) any interest swap or hedging obligation with an unaffiliated Person otherwise permitted by the Indenture; (xii) Investments received as consideration for an Asset Disposition in compliance with [asset sale covenant]; (xiii) Investments in Wholly-Owned Restricted Subsidiaries or by virtue of which a Person becomes a Wholly-Owned Restricted Subsidiary; (xiv) loans and advances to employees made in the ordinary course of business; (xv) Investments the sole consideration for which consists of Capital Stock of the Issuer; and (xvi) Investments required in connection with any Permitted Receivables Financing to the extent that such Investments are customary in respect of transactions of such nature.

"*Permitted Receivables Financing*" means a transaction or series of transactions (including amendments, supplements, extensions, renewals, replacements, refinancings or modifications thereof) pursuant to which (a) a Securitization Subsidiary purchases Receivables and Related Assets from the Issuer or any Restricted Subsidiary and finances such Receivables and Related Assets through the issuance of indebtedness or equity interests or through the sale of the Receivables and Related Assets or a fractional undivided interest in the Receivables and Related Assets or (b) the Issuer or a Restricted Subsidiary finances Receivables and Related Assets through the sale of the Receivables and Related Assets or fractional undivided interests therein; *provided* that (i) the Board of Directors shall have determined in good faith that such Permitted Receivables Financing is economically fair and reasonable to the Issuer and the Securitization Subsidiary, (ii) all sales of Receivables and Related Assets to the Securitization Subsidiary are made at fair market value (as determined in good faith by the Board of Directors), (iii) the financing terms, covenants, termination events, and other provisions thereof shall be market terms (as determined in good faith by the Board of Directors), (iv) no portion of the Indebtedness of a Securitization Subsidiary is guaranteed by or is recourse to the Issuer or any Restricted Subsidiary (other than recourse for customary representations, warranties, covenants, and indemnities, none of which shall relate to the collectability of the Receivables and Related Assets), and (v) neither the Issuer nor any Subsidiary has any obligation to maintain or preserve the Securitization Subsidiary's financial condition.

"*Receivables and Related Assets*" means accounts receivable and instruments, chattel paper, obligations, general intangibles, and other similar assets, in each case, relating to such receivables, including interests in merchandise or goods, the sale or lease of which gave rise to such receivable, related contractual rights, guarantees, insurance proceeds, collections, other related assets, and proceeds of all of the foregoing.

"*Securitization Subsidiary*" means a Wholly Owned Subsidiary of the Issuer, which is established for the limited purpose of acquiring and financing Receivables and Related Assets and engaging in activities ancillary thereto.

Limitation on Indebtedness

The Issuer will not, and will not permit any of the Restricted Subsidiaries to, directly or indirectly, Incur any Indebtedness (including Acquired Indebtedness), except: (i) Indebtedness of the Issuer or any of the Restricted Subsidiaries, if immediately after giving effect to the Incurrence of such Indebtedness and the receipt and application of the net proceeds thereof, the Fixed Charge Coverage Ratio of the Issuer for the four full fiscal quarters for which quarterly or annual financial statements are available next preceding the Incurrence of such Indebtedness, calculated on a pro forma basis as if such Indebtedness had been Incurred, and such net proceeds received and applied, on the first day of such four full fiscal quarters, would be greater than 2.0 to 1.00; (ii) Indebtedness of the Issuer and its Restricted Subsidiaries Incurred under the Credit Agreement in an amount not to exceed $50.0 million; (iii) Indebtedness owed by the Issuer to any direct or indirect Wholly-Owned Subsidiary of the Issuer; *provided, however,* upon either (I) the transfer or other disposition by such direct or indirect Wholly-Owned Subsidiary of the Issuer of any Indebtedness so permitted under this clause (3) to a Person other than the Issuer or another direct or indirect Wholly-Owned Subsidiary of the Issuer, or (II) the issuance (other than directors' qualifying shares), sale, transfer, or other disposition of shares of Capital Stock or other ownership interests (including by consolidation or merger) of such direct or indirect Wholly-Owned Subsidiary to a Person other than the Issuer or another such Wholly-Owned Subsidiary of the Issuer, the provisions of this clause (iii) shall no longer be applicable to such Indebtedness, and such Indebtedness shall be deemed to have been Incurred at the time of any such issuance, sale, transfer, or other disposition, as the case may be; (iv) Indebtedness of the Issuer or any Restricted Subsidiary under any interest rate agreement to the extent entered into to hedge any other Indebtedness permitted under the Indenture (including the Notes); (v) Indebtedness Incurred to renew, extend, refinance, or refund (collectively for purposes of this clause (v) to "refund") any Indebtedness outstanding on the Issue Date, any Indebtedness Incurred under the prior clause (i) above or the Notes and the Subsidiary Guarantee; *provided, however,* that (I) such Indebtedness does not exceed the principal amount (or accreted amount, if less) of Indebtedness so refunded (plus unused commitments under revolving credit facilities) plus the amount of any premium required to be paid in connection with such refunding pursuant to the terms of the Indebtedness refunded, or the amount of any premium reasonably determined by the issuer of such Indebtedness as necessary to accomplish such refunding by means of a tender offer, exchange offer, or privately negotiated repurchase, plus the expenses of such issuer reasonably incurred in connection therewith, and (II) (A) in the case of any refunding of Indebtedness that is pari passu with the Notes, such refunding Indebtedness is made pari passu with or subordinate in right of payment to the Notes, and, in the case of any refunding of Indebtedness that is subordinate in right of payment to the Notes, such refunding Indebtedness is subordinate in right of payment to the Notes on terms no less favorable to the holders of the Notes than those contained in the Indebtedness being refunded, (B) in either case, the refunding Indebtedness by its terms, or by the terms of any agreement or instrument pursuant to which such Indebtedness is issued, does not have an Average Life that is less than the remaining Average Life of the Indebtedness being refunded and does not permit redemption or other retirement (including pursuant to any required offer to purchase to be made by the Issuer or a Restricted Subsidiary of the Issuer) of such Indebtedness at the option of the holder thereof prior to the final stated maturity of the Indebtedness being refunded, other than a redemption or other retirement at the option of the holder of such Indebtedness (including pursuant to a required offer to purchase made by the Issuer or a Restricted Subsidiary of the Issuer) which is conditioned upon a change of control of the Issuer pursuant to provisions substantially similar to those contained in [change of control provision] and (C) any Indebtedness Incurred to refund any Indebtedness is Incurred by the obligor of the Indebtedness being refunded or by the Issuer; (vi) Indebtedness of the Issuer or its Subsidiaries not otherwise permitted to be Incurred pursuant to clauses (i) through (v) above which, together with any other outstanding Indebtedness Incurred pursuant to this clause (vi), has an aggregate principal amount not in excess of $5.0 million at any time outstanding, which Indebtedness may be incurred under the Credit Agreement or otherwise; (vii) Indebtedness of the Issuer under the Notes incurred in accordance with the Indenture; (viii) Indebtedness outstanding on the Issue Date; (ix) Indebtedness incurred by the Issuer or any of its Restricted Subsidiaries constituting reimbursement obligations with respect to letters of credit issued in the ordinary course of business, including, without limitation, letters of credit in respect of workers' compensation claims or self-insurance, and obligations in respect of performance and surety bonds and completion guarantees provided by the Issuer or any Restricted Subsidiary of the Issuer in the ordinary course of business; (x) Guarantees by the Issuer or its Restricted Subsidiaries of Indebtedness otherwise permitted to be incurred hereunder; (xi) Indebtedness pursuant to a Permitted Receivables Financing; *provided, however,* that Indebtedness Incurred under such Permitted Receivables Financing and Indebtedness Incurred pursuant to clause (ii) above shall not exceed $50.0 million in the aggregate at any time outstanding; and (xii) Indebtedness (including Capitalized Lease Obligations) Incurred by the Issuer or any of its Restricted Subsidiaries to finance the purchase, lease or improvement of property (real or personal) or equipment (whether through the direct purchase of assets or the Capital Stock of any Person owning such assets) in an aggregate principal amount outstanding not to exceed 10% of Consolidated Tangible Assets at any time provided that the principal amount of such Indebtedness does not exceed the fair market value of such property or equipment at the time of Incurrence thereof.

Limitation on Restricted Payments

The Issuer will not, and will not permit any of its Restricted Subsidiaries to, directly or indirectly, (i) declare or pay any dividend, or make any distribution of any kind or character (whether in cash, property or securities), in respect of any class of the Capital Stock of the Issuer or any of its Restricted Subsidiaries or to the holders thereof, excluding any (x) dividend or distribution payable solely in shares of Capital Stock of the Issuer (other than Disqualified Stock) or in options, warrants or other rights to acquire Capital Stock of the Issuer (other than Disqualified Stock), or (y) in the case of any Restricted Subsidiary of the Issuer, dividends or distributions payable to the Issuer or a Restricted Subsidiary of the Issuer, (ii) purchase, redeem, or otherwise acquire or retire for value shares of Capital Stock of the Issuer or any of its Restricted Subsidiaries, any options, warrants, or rights to purchase or acquire shares of Capital Stock of the Issuer or any of its Restricted Subsidiaries or any securities convertible or exchangeable into shares of Capital Stock of the Issuer or any of its Restricted Subsidiaries, excluding any such shares of Capital Stock, options, warrants, rights or securities which are owned by the Issuer or a Restricted Subsidiary of the Issuer, (iii) make any Investment in (other than a Permitted Investment), or payment on a guarantee of any obligation of, any Person, other than the Issuer or a direct or indirect Wholly-Owned Subsidiary of the Issuer, or (iv) redeem, defease, repurchase, retire, or otherwise acquire or retire for value, prior to any scheduled maturity, repayment or sinking fund payment, Subordinated Indebtedness (each of the transactions described in clauses (i) through (iv) (other than any exception to any such clause) being a "Restricted Payment")) if at the time thereof, (1) a Default or an Event of Default shall have occurred and be continuing, or (2) upon giving effect to such Restricted Payment, the Issuer could not Incur at least $1.00 of additional Indebtedness pursuant to [debt incurrence coverage test], or (3) upon giving effect to such Restricted Payment, the aggregate of all Restricted Payments made on or after the Issue Date exceeds the sum of: (a) 50% of cumulative Consolidated Income of the Issuer (or, in the case cumulative Consolidated Net Income of the Issuer shall be negative, less 100% of such deficit) since the end of the fiscal quarter in which the Issue Date occurs through the last day of the fiscal quarter for which financial statements are available, plus (b) 100% of the aggregate net proceeds received after the Issue Date, including the fair market value of the property other than cash (determined in good faith by the Board of Directors of the Issuer as evidenced by a resolution of such Board of Directors filed with the Trustee), from the issuance of, or equity contribution with respect to, Capital Stock (other than Disqualified Stock) of the Issuer and warrants, rights or options on Capital Stock (other than Disqualified Stock) of the Issuer (other than in respect of any such issuance to a Restricted Subsidiary of the Issuer) and the principal amount of Indebtedness of the Issuer or any of its Restricted Subsidiaries that has been converted into or exchanged for Capital Stock of the Issuer which Indebtedness was Incurred after the Issue Date; plus (c) 100% of the aggregate after-tax proceeds, including the fair market value of property other than cash (determined in good faith by the Board of Directors of the Issuer as evidenced by a resolution of such Board of Directors filed with the Trustee) of the sale or other disposition of any Investment constituting a Restricted Payment made after the Issue Date; *provided* that any gain on the sale or disposition included in such after-tax net proceeds shall not be included in determining Consolidated Net Income for purposes of clause (a) above. The foregoing provisions will not be violated by (i) any dividend on any class of Capital Stock of the Issuer or any of its Restricted Subsidiaries paid within sixty days after the declaration thereof if, on the date when the dividend was declared, the Issuer or such Restricted Subsidiary, as the case may be, could have paid such dividend in accordance with the provisions of the Indenture, (ii) the renewal, extension, refunding, or refinancing of any Indebtedness otherwise permitted pursuant to [debt covenant], (iii) the exchange or conversion of any Indebtedness of the Issuer or any of its Restricted Subsidiaries for or into Capital Stock of the Issuer (other than Disqualified Stock), (iv) the redemption, repurchase, retirement or other acquisition of any Capital Stock of the Issuer in exchange for or out of the net cash proceeds of the substantially concurrent sale (other than a Restricted Subsidiary of the Issuer) of Capital Stock of the Issuer (other to than Disqualified Stock); *provided, however,* that the proceeds of such sale of Capital Stock shall not be (and have not been) included in clause (3) of the preceding paragraph and (v) other Restricted Payments of up to $5.0 million in the aggregate. For purposes of this covenant, (a) an "Investment" shall be deemed to have been made at the time any Restricted Subsidiary is designated as an Unrestricted Subsidiary in an amount (proportionate to the Issuer's equity interest in such Subsidiary) equal to the net worth of such Restricted Subsidiary at the time that such Restricted Subsidiary is designated as an Unrestricted Subsidiary; (b) at any date the aggregate of all Restricted Payments made as Investments since the Issue Date shall exclude and be reduced by an amount (proportionate to the Issuer's equity interest in such Subsidiary) equal to the net worth of an Unrestricted Subsidiary at the time that such Unrestricted Subsidiary is designated a Restricted Subsidiary, not to exceed, in the case of any such redesignation of an Unrestricted Subsidiary as a Restricted Subsidiary, the amount of Investments previously made by the Issuer and the Restricted Subsidiaries in such Unrestricted Subsidiary (in each case (a) and (b) "net worth" to be calculated based upon the fair market value of the assets of such Subsidiary as of any such date of designation which shall, in no event, be less than zero), and (c) any property transferred to or from an Unrestricted Subsidiary shall be valued at its fair market at the time of such transfer.

Limitation Concerning Distributions and Transfers by Restricted Subsidiaries

The Issuer will not, and will not permit any of its Restricted Subsidiaries to, directly or indirectly, create or otherwise cause or suffer to exist any consensual encumbrance or restriction on the ability of any Restricted Subsidiary of the Issuer to (i) pay, directly or indirectly, dividends or make any other distributions in respect of its Capital Stock or pay any Indebtedness or other obligations owed to the Issuer or any Restricted Subsidiary of the Issuer, (ii) make loans or advances to the Issuer or any Restricted Subsidiary of the Issuer or (iii) transfer any of its property or assets to the Issuer or any Restricted Subsidiary of the Issuer, except for such encumbrance or restrictions existing under or by reason of (a) any agreement in effect on the Issue Date as any such agreement is in effect on such date, (b) the Credit Agreement, (c) any agreement relating to any Indebtedness Incurred by such Restricted Subsidiary prior to the date on which such Restricted Subsidiary was acquired by the Issuer and outstanding on such date and not Incurred in anticipation or contemplation of becoming a Restricted Subsidiary and provided such encumbrance or restriction shall not apply to any assets of the Issuer or its Restricted Subsidiaries other than such Restricted Subsidiary, (d) customary provisions contained in an agreement which has been entered into for the sale or disposition of all or substantially all of the Capital Stock or assets of a Restricted Subsidiary; *provided, however,* that such encumbrance or restriction is applicable only to such Restricted Subsidiary, (e) customary net worth and other financial covenants in an agreement relating to Indebtedness Incurred in compliance with [debt covenant], (f) the Indenture, (g) applicable law, (h) customary provisions restricting subletting or assignment of any lease governing any leasehold interest of any Restricted Subsidiary or the Issuer, (i) purchase money obligations for property acquired in the ordinary course of business that impose restrictions of the type referred to in clause (iii) of this covenant, (j) restrictions of the type referred to in clause (iii) of this covenant contained in security agreements securing Indebtedness of a Restricted Subsidiary of the Issuer to the extent that such Liens were otherwise incurred in accordance with [lien covenant] and restrict the transfer of property subject to such agreements, or (k) any agreement relating to a Permitted Receivables Financing.

Limitation on Liens

The Issuer will not, and will not permit any of its Restricted Subsidiaries to, incur any Lien on or with respect to any property or assets of the Issuer or such Restricted Subsidiary owned on the Issue Date or thereafter acquired or on the income or profits thereof, which Lien secures Indebtedness, without making, or causing any such Restricted Subsidiary to make effective provision for securing the Notes and all other amounts due under the Indenture (and, if the Issuer shall so determine, any other Indebtedness of the Issuer or such Restricted Subsidiary, including Subordinated Indebtedness; *provided, however,* that Liens securing the Notes and any Indebtedness pari passu with the Notes are senior to such Liens securing such Subordinated Indebtedness) equally and ratably with such Indebtedness or, in the event such Indebtedness is subordinate in right of payment to the Notes or the Subsidiary Guarantee prior to such Indebtedness, as to such property or assets for so long as such Indebtedness shall be so secured. The foregoing restrictions shall not apply to (i) Liens existing on the Issue Date securing Indebtedness existing on the Issue Date; (ii) Liens securing Indebtedness outstanding under the

Credit Agreement and any guarantees thereof to the extent that the Indebtedness secured thereby is permitted to be incurred under [debt covenant]; (iii) Liens securing only the Notes and the Subsidiary Guarantees; (iv) Liens in favor of the Issuer or a Subsidiary Guarantor; (v) Liens to secure Indebtedness Incurred for the purpose of financing all or any part of the purchase price or the cost of construction or improvement of the property (or any other capital expenditure financing) subject to such Liens; *provided, however,* that (a) the aggregate principal amount of any Indebtedness secured by such a Lien does not exceed 100% of such purchase price or cost, (b) such Lien does not extend to or cover any other property other than such item of property and any improvements on such item, (c) the Indebtedness secured by such Lien is Incurred by the Issuer within 180 days of the acquisition, construction or improvement of such property and (d) the Incurrence of such Indebtedness is permitted by [debt covenant]; (vi) Liens on property existing immediately prior to the time of acquisition thereof (and not created in anticipation or contemplation of the financing of such acquisition); (vii) Liens on property of a Person existing at the time such Person is acquired or merged with or into or consolidated with the Issuer or any such Restricted Subsidiary (and not created in anticipation or contemplation thereof); (viii) Liens to secure Indebtedness Incurred to extend, renew, refinance, or refund (or successive extensions, renewals, refinancings or refundings) in whole or in part, any Indebtedness secured by the Liens referred to in the foregoing clauses (i) through (vii) so long as such Liens do not extend to any other property and the principal amount of Indebtedness so secured is not increased except for the amount of any premium required to be paid in connection with such extension, renewal, refinancing, or refunding pursuant to the terms of the Indebtedness extended, renewed, refinanced, or refunded by means of a tender offer, exchange offer, or private negotiation plus the expenses of the issuer of such Indebtedness reasonably incurred in connection with such extension, renewal, refinancing or refunding, (ix) Liens in favor of the Trustee as provided for in the Indenture; (x) Liens incurred in the ordinary course of business securing obligations not in excess of $250,000; and (xi) Liens incurred in connection with a Permitted Receivables Financing.

Limitation on Transactions with Affiliates and Related Persons

The Issuer will not, and will not permit any of its Restricted Subsidiaries to, enter into, directly or indirectly, any transaction with any of their respective Affiliates or Related Persons (other than the Issuer or a Wholly-Owned Restricted Subsidiary of the Issuer), including, without limitation, the purchase, sale, lease, or exchange of property, the rendering of any service, or the making of any guarantee, loan, advance or Investment, either directly or indirectly, involving aggregate consideration in excess of $1 million unless a majority of the disinterested directors of the Board of Directors of the Issuer determines, in its good faith judgment evidenced by a resolution of such Board of Directors filed with the Trustee, that the terms of such transaction are at least as favorable as the terms that could be obtained by the Issuer or such Restricted Subsidiary, as the case may be, in a comparable transaction made on an arm's-length basis between unaffiliated parties, *provided, however*, that if the aggregate consideration is in excess of $5 million the Issuer shall also obtain, prior to the consummation of the transaction, the favorable opinion as to the fairness of the transaction to the Issuer or such Restricted Subsidiary, from a financial point of view from an independent financial advisor. The provisions of this covenant shall not apply to (i) transactions permitted by [restricted payments covenant], (ii) reasonable fees and compensation paid to, and indemnity provided on behalf of, officers, directors and employees of the Issuer and its Restricted Subsidiaries as determined in good faith by the Board of Directors of the Issuer, (iii) loans to employees in the ordinary course of business which are approved in good faith by the Board of Directors of the Issuer and (iv) transactions in connection with a Permitted Receivables Financing.

Future Subsidiary Guarantors

The Issuer will not create or acquire, nor permit any of its Restricted Subsidiaries to create or acquire, any Restricted Subsidiary after the Issue Date (other than a Securitization Subsidiary) unless, at the time such Restricted Subsidiary has either assets or stockholder's equity in excess of $500,000, such Restricted Subsidiary executes and delivers to the Trustee a supplemental indenture in form reasonably satisfactory to the Trustee pursuant to which such Restricted Subsidiary shall unconditionally guarantee all of the Issuer's obligations under the Notes and the Indenture on the terms set forth in the Indenture.

Sample 7-Y *Nonrecourse Debt*

"*Nonrecourse Debt*" means Indebtedness (i) as to which neither the Company nor any of its Restricted Subsidiaries (a) provides direct credit support (including any undertaking, agreement or instrument that would constitute Indebtedness), or (b) is directly or indirectly liable (as a guarantor or otherwise); and (ii) as to which the lenders have been notified in writing that they will not have any recourse to the stock or assets of the Company or any of its Restricted Subsidiaries.

Chapter 9:   A Deal in Time

Regarding preliminary agreements, see generally:

CAROLYN E.C. PARIS, HOW TO DRAFT FOR CORPORATE FINANCE ch. 4 (PLI 2006).

Regarding closings, and for examples of relevant documents, see generally:

CAROLYN E.C. PARIS, HOW TO DRAFT FOR CORPORATE FINANCE ch. 15 (PLI 2006).

Regarding opinions, see:

A.N. FIELD & J.M. SMITH, LEGAL OPINIONS IN CORPORATE TRANSACTIONS (PLI 2010).

FITZGIBBON & GLAZER ON LEGAL OPINIONS: DRAFTING, INTERPRETING AND SUPPORTING CLOSING OPINIONS IN BUSINESS TRANSACTIONS (Aspen 2013).

M. JOHN STERBA, JR., DRAFTING LEGAL OPINION LETTERS (Aspen 2013).

THOMAS S. HEMMERDINGER, HILLMAN ON COMMERCIAL LOAN DOCUMENTS, ch. 7 (PLI 2000).

The ABA, with TriBar, keeps a site of relevant guidance at http://apps.americanbar.org/buslaw/tribar/. Additionally, there are several articles on opinions in Volume 9, Number 3 of The Business Lawyer (May 2014).

Sources regarding decision making:

MAX H. BAZERMAN AND DON A. MOORE, JUDGMENT IN MANAGERIAL DECISION MAKING (Wiley 2012).

GARY KLEIN, SOURCES OF POWER: HOW PEOPLE MAKE DECISIONS (MIT Press 1999).

Examples of termsheets:

Sample 9-A *Termsheet for a Credit Agreement*

For Discussion Purposes Only

INDICATIVE TERMS AND CONDITIONS

These are indicative terms and conditions only and do not constitute and shall not be construed as a commitment to provide any of the financing described herein.

Borrower:	La Luna Corporation (the "Borrower").
Guarantor:	Parent of Borrower (the "Guarantor"), to be a company whose only assets consist of stock of the Borrower.
Amount:	Up to $115 million comprised of the two facilities as described below.
Facilities:	Term loan facility of up to $100 million. Revolving credit facility of up to $15 million. There will be swingline and letter of credit subfacilities in amounts to be agreed.
Purpose:	Term loan facility to finance the purchase of Le Soleil barbershops and for other general corporate purposes. Revolving credit facility: to provide working capital and for other general corporate purposes.
Administrative Agent:	Friendly Bank.
Co-Agents:	Friendly Bank and Congenial Bank.
Lenders:	Syndicate of banks and other lending institutions acceptable to Borrower and Co-Agents (the "Lenders").
Commitment Fee:	50 basis points, applied to the unused portion of the revolving credit facility, commencing on the closing date, payable quarterly in arrears and upon termination of the revolving credit commitments.
Interest Rates:	Base rate, or .75% over reserve-adjusted LIBOR. Base rate is the higher of the Administrative Agent's prime rate and 50 basis points over the federal funds rate. The credit agreement will contain customary provisions protecting the Lenders in the event of unavailability, illegality, increased capital and other costs and funding losses.
Interest Periods:	Base rate loans: 30 days. Euro-dollar loans: 1, 3 or 6 months.
Letter of Credit Fee:	.75% p.a.

Amortization:	Term loan amortization to be $10 million in each of years 1 and 2; $20 million in each of years 3, 4 and 5; and $10 million at 6 years and $10 million at 7 years with a final maturity date 7 years after closing.
	Revolving credit facility—seven years after closing.
Optional Prepayments:	Base rate loans may be repaid at any time on three business days' notice. Euro-dollar loans may not be prepaid except at the end of interest periods.
Drawdowns:	In minimum amounts of $3 million. Drawdowns are at the Borrower's option with one business day's notice for base rate loans and three business days' notice for Euro-dollar loans.
Termination or Reduction of Commitments:	The Borrower may terminate the revolving credit commitments or reduce the revolving credit commitments in amounts of at least $3 million at any time on three business days' notice.
Representations and Warranties:	Customary for transactions of this type, or otherwise appropriate for this transaction, to include corporate authority, noncontravention, no material adverse change, no material litigation or environmental liabilities, financial information, compliance with laws, payment of taxes and other obligations, and full disclosure.
Conditions to Closing and Funding:	To include:

1. Consummation of the purchase of Le Soleil barbershops.
2. Absence of default and accuracy of representations and warranties.
3. Other customary closing documentation, including legal opinions.

Covenants:	Customary for transactions of this type, or otherwise appropriate for this transaction, to include corporate existence, furnishing of information, maintenance of property, insurance coverage, compliance with laws, restrictions on liens and debt, restrictions on dividends, restrictions on investments, restrictions on mergers and asset sales, and a minimum tangible net worth covenant ($175 million).

Events of Default:	Customary for transactions of this type, or otherwise appropriate for this transaction, to include failure to pay principal, interest or other amounts, breach of covenant (with grace periods when appropriate), representations or warranties false in any material respect when made, cross-default ($5 million threshold), judgment default ($5 million in aggregate), change of control and other usual defaults, including bankruptcy and ERISA.
Required Lenders:	66 2/3%
Transfers and Participations:	Lenders will have the right to sell participations in their loans and/or their commitments and, with the consent of the Borrower and the Administrative Agent, to assign their note and their commitment.
Indemnifications:	The Borrower will indemnify the Co-Agents and Lenders against all third-party liabilities, claims, damages or expenses relating to the loans, the credit agreement, the Borrower's use of loan proceeds or the commitments, including, but not limited to attorneys' fees and settlement costs.
Governing Law:	State of New York.
Expenses:	The Borrower will pay all legal and out-of-pocket expenses of the Co-Agents.

Sample 9-B *Termsheet for an Indenture*

THE CALIPER COMPANY

Offering of Senior Notes—Preliminary Summary of Terms

Issuer	The Caliper Company (the "Company")
Issue	Senior Notes due 2024 (the "Notes")
Maturity	10 years
Size	$350 million–$400 million
Coupon	_____%
Ranking	The Notes will be senior unsecured obligations of the Company, senior in respect of payment of principal and interest to all subordinated Indebtedness existing or created in the future. The Notes will rank pari passu with all senior unsecured indebtedness existing or created in the future.
Optional Redemption	The Notes will be noncallable for seven years and will be callable at a premium of ___% starting at the end of the seventh year, declining to par at the end of year ten. However, at any time prior to _____, 2016, the Company may redeem up to 35% of the aggregate principal amount of the Notes with the proceeds of a Public Equity Offering (as defined) at a redemption price of 100% plus the coupon.
Mandatory Redemption	The Notes are not subject to mandatory redemption or sinking fund provisions.
Change of Control	In the event of a Change of Control, the holders of the Notes will have the right to require redemption of the Notes by the Company at a redemption price of 101% plus accrued interest.

Limitation on Indebtedness

Neither the Company nor any Restricted Subsidiary will incur any Indebtedness unless, after giving effect to the incurrence of such Indebtedness and the receipt and application of proceeds therefrom, the Interest Coverage Ratio for the Company and its Restricted Subsidiaries shall be at least 2.25:1.

Notwithstanding the foregoing, the Company and its Restricted Subsidiaries may incur any and all of the following Indebtedness:

(i)   the Notes;

(ii)   up to $400 million under the Credit Agreements and refinancings thereof;

(iii)   Indebtedness issued in exchange for or the proceeds of which are used to exchange, refinance, or refund outstanding Indebtedness so long as (a) the principal amount of the Indebtedness issued does not exceed the principal amount of, premium, if any and accrued interest on the Indebtedness so exchanged, refinanced or refunded, (b) the Indebtedness issued does not mature prior to the stated maturity, and does not have an average life shorter than the average life, of the Indebtedness being so exchanged, refinanced, or refunded, and (c) where the Indebtedness to be exchanged, refinanced or refunded is subordinated to the Notes, the Indebtedness is subordinated to the Notes in right of payment; and

(iv)   other carveouts and basket, as required;

less, as applicable, any amount of Indebtedness permanently repaid as provided under "Limitation on Asset Sales."

Limitation on Liens

Neither the Company nor any Restricted Subsidiary will create, assume, incur or suffer to exist any lien, mortgage, pledge, security interest, conditional sale or title retention agreement on any property or asset, except for Permitted Liens.

Limitation on Restricted Payments

Neither the Company nor any of its Restricted Subsidiaries will:

(i) pay dividends (either in cash or property) or make distributions on, or redeem, repurchase, retire or otherwise acquire, Capital Stock of the Company or any Restricted Subsidiary (including warrants, rights or options to purchase shares of Capital Stock);

(ii) make any payments or prepayments of principal or redemption premium, or repurchase, acquire or retire for value prior to the scheduled maturity, Indebtedness subordinated to the Notes (except if refunded with Indebtedness which (a) is subordinated to the Notes to the same extent as the Indebtedness refunded, (b) does not mature prior to the stated maturity of the Indebtedness refunded and (c) has an average life at least equal to the remaining average life of the Indebtedness refunded); or

(iii) make any investment (other than a Permitted Investment) in any Person;

(the foregoing being called "Restricted Payments"), except that the Company may declare and pay dividends on its Capital Stock or make other Restricted Payments up to an aggregate amount of the sum of (a) 50% of Consolidated Net Income (less 100% of Consolidated Net Losses), beginning on the closing date, plus (b) the net cash proceeds from the issuance and sale of the Company's Capital Stock, plus (c) $35 million;

provided, however, that if at the time of any such Restricted Payment or after giving effect thereto, an Event of Default, or an event that through the passage of time or the giving of notice, or both, would become an Event of Default, shall have occurred or be continuing, then no such Restricted Payment shall be made;

provided further, that if immediately after giving effect to such Restricted Payment, on a pro forma basis, the Company could not incur at least $1 of additional Indebtedness under the first paragraph of "Limitation on Indebtedness," then no such Restricted Payment shall be made.

307

Limitation on Dividends and Other Payment Restrictions Affecting Restricted Subsidiaries	Subject to exceptions to be agreed, the Company will not, and will not permit any Restricted Subsidiary to create, cause or suffer to exist, any encumbrance or restriction on the ability of any Restricted Subsidiary to:

(i)   pay dividends or other distributions on its Capital Stock owned by, or pay any Indebtedness owed to, the Company or any Restricted Subsidiary;

(ii)   make loans or advances to the Company or any Restricted Subsidiary; or

(iii)   transfer any of its properties or assets to the Company or any Restricted Subsidiary.

Restriction on Issuance of Restricted Subsidiary Stock	The Company will not permit any Restricted Subsidiary to issue any shares of its Capital Stock (including warrants, rights or options to purchase shares of Capital Stock) except to the Company or a wholly-owned Restricted Subsidiary of the Company.
Transactions with Affiliates	The Company will not and will not permit any Restricted Subsidiary to enter into a transaction with any Affiliate unless such transaction is completed on terms no less favorable to the Company than would occur in a similar transaction completed on an arm's-length basis with a person who is not an Affiliate.
Limitation on Asset Sales	The Company and its Restricted Subsidiaries may not sell or otherwise dispose of assets (including Capital Stock of Restricted Subsidiaries) in any transaction or series of related transactions during any twelve month period in excess of $25 million unless the Company shall (a) apply the excess amount of net proceeds from such sale over $25 million to repay and permanently retire recourse Senior Indebtedness of the Company or a Restricted Subsidiary, or (b) invest an equal amount not so used in clause (a) in properties or assets of related businesses within 180 days, or (c) make a Net Proceeds Offer to purchase the Notes at a price of 100% with the proceeds not so used in accordance with (a) or (b) above.

Limitation on Sale and Lease-back Transaction	Neither the Company nor any Restricted Subsidiary will enter into any arrangement, directly or indirectly, with any person whereby the Company or such Restricted Subsidiary shall sell or transfer any property whether now owned or hereafter acquired, and then or thereafter rent or lease as lessee such property or any part thereof or any other property which the Company or such Restricted Subsidiary, as the case may be, intends to use for substantially the same purpose or purposes as the property being sold or transferred unless an Attributable Amount of secured Indebtedness could instead be incurred.

Limitation on Merger, Consolidation

The Company will not consolidate with or merge with or into or sell, transfer or lease all or substantially all of its properties and assets to any person, unless:

(i) the surviving entity (if other than the Company) shall be organized under the laws of the United States and shall assume in writing all the obligations of the Company under the Notes;

(ii) no Event of Default shall exist or be continuing;

(iii) immediately after giving effect to such transaction, on a pro forma basis, Consolidated Net Worth of the surviving entity is at least equal to the Consolidated Net Worth of the Company immediately before such transaction; and

(iv) immediately after giving effect to such transaction, on a pro forma basis, the surviving entity could incur at least $1 of additional Indebtedness under "Limitation on Indebtedness,"—and would be in compliance with the "Limitation on Liens" covenant.

Financial Information

Whether or not required to do so by the SEC rules, the Company will file and make available to holders annual and quarterly reports and such other documents as the Company would be filing with the SEC if so required.

Events of Default The following shall be Events of Default under the Notes:

(i) default in payment of interest within thirty days of when due;

(ii) default in payment of principal or premium, if any, on the Notes when due and payable at maturity, upon redemption, mandatory repurchase, acceleration or otherwise;

(iii) failure by the Company to comply with any of its covenants or agreements under the Notes, and such default shall continue for forty-five days;

(iv) with respect to any other Indebtedness of the Company or any Restricted Subsidiary having an aggregate amount outstanding in excess of $10 million, (a) an event of default which has caused the holders thereof to declare such Indebtedness due and payable in advance of its scheduled maturity or (b) a failure to make a principal payment at the final (but not interim) fixed maturity, and in each case such accelerated or defaulted payment shall not have been made, waived or extended within thirty days of such acceleration or payment default;

(v) the Company or any Restricted Subsidiary commences a voluntary or involuntary case of bankruptcy, consents to the appointment of a custodian of the Company or any Restricted Subsidiary or all or substantially all of its assets, makes a general assignment for the benefit of its creditors or is generally unable to pay its debts when due;

(vi) a court having jurisdiction in any involuntary case or proceeding enters a bankruptcy order against the Company or any Restricted Subsidiary, and such order shall remain unstayed for a period of sixty days; or

(vii) final judgments for the payments of money that in the aggregate exceed $10 million shall be rendered against the Company or any Restricted Subsidiary by a court shall remain undischarged for a period of sixty days.

If an Event of Default occurs and is continuing with respect to the Indenture, the Trustee or the holders of 25% in principal amount of the outstanding Notes may declare the principal of and accrued but unpaid interest on all the Notes to be due and payable. Upon such a declaration, such principal and interest shall be due and payable immediately. In the event of bankruptcy default affecting the Company, principal of and interest on the Notes shall be immediately due and payable.

Supplements and Amendments	Subject to customary exceptions by majority.
Defeasance	Customary defeasance provisions.

You can find up-to-date versions of commitment letters by looking at the SEC filings for announced deals, often as an attachment to a Schedule 14D-1.

Some examples of closing documents:

Sample 9-C *Closing Memorandum*

MEMORANDUM OF CLOSING

July 1, 2015

Definitions

Agent	Cordial Bank as Agent for the Banks under the Credit Agreement
Banks	The banks listed on the signature pages of the Credit Agreement
Borrower	Ambergris Co., a Delaware corporation
Closing Date	July 1, 2015, the date of closing under the Credit Agreement
Credit Agreement	Credit Agreement dated as of July 1, 2015, among the Borrower, the Banks and the Agent
L, D&H	Levi, Devi and Heavy, counsel for the Borrower
Notes	Promissory notes of the Borrower in substantially the form of Exhibit A to the Credit Agreement
WB&N	Winken, Blinken & Nod, special counsel for the Agent

Distribution Codes

A — one executed original for each of Agent and Borrower and their counsel

B — one original for the Agent

C — original for each Bank, payable to that Bank

D — photocopy for each Bank

E   —   photocopy for Agent (if Agent does not hold original) and Borrower and their counsel

F   —   filing or recording copy

G   —   title company copy

SCHEDULE B

Documents delivered on or before the Closing Date

		Person Responsible	Status
A.	**Principal Documents:**		
	1. Credit Agreement [A, D]		
	2. Security Agreement [A]		
	3. Trademark Security Agreement [A, F]		
	4. Mortgages [B, E, F, G]		
	(a) Maryland		
	(b) Virginia		
	(c) Texas		
B.	**To be delivered by the Borrower:**		
	5. Executed Notes [C, E]		
	6. Certificate of Incorporation of the Borrower and all amendments thereto, certified as of a recent date by the Secretary of State of Delaware [B, E]		
	7. Long-form certificate of the Secretary of State of Delaware dated as of a recent date, as to the Borrower's good standing and tax status and listing all charter documents of the Borrower [B, E]		
	8. Long-form good standing telegram dated as of the close of business on the day prior to the Closing Date [B, E]		

    (a)   Delaware

    (b)   Maryland

    (c)   Virginia

    (d)   Texas

9. Certificate of Secretary of the Borrower dated as of the Closing Date as to no amendments to Certificate of Incorporation of the Borrower since the date of the last amendment; no liquidation or dissolution proceedings; attached copy of Bylaws; attached copy of resolutions adopted by the Board of Directors of the Borrower authorizing the execution, delivery and performance of the Credit Agreement; and incumbency and signatures of officers [A]

10. Opinion of L, D&H [A, D]

11. Opinions of local counsel [A, D]

    (a)   Maryland

    (b)   Virginia

    (c)   Texas

12. Opinion of Trademark Counsel [A, D]

13. Certificates of Insurance [B, E]

14. UCC Lien Searches [B, E]

15. UCC Filings [B, E, F]

    (a)   Maryland

    (b)   Virginia

    (c)   Texas

C. **To be delivered by WB&N:**

16. Opinion of WB&N [A, D]

Sample 9-D *Certificate of Secretary of Borrower*

I, Stephen Leslie, Secretary of Ambergris Co. (the "Borrower"), a Delaware corporation, DO HEREBY CERTIFY as follows:

1. No amendment to the Certificate of Incorporation of the Borrower has been authorized or become effective since July 1, 2013, no amendment or other document relating to or affecting the Certificate of Incorporation, as amended, has been filed in the office of the Secretary of State of the State of Delaware since July 1, 2013, and no action has been taken by the Borrower, its shareholders, directors or officers in contemplation of the filing of such amendment or other document or in contemplation of the liquidation or dissolution of the Borrower.

2. Attached hereto as Exhibit A is a true, complete and correct copy of the Bylaws of the Borrower as in full force and effect on the date hereof and at all times since July 1, 2013.

3. Attached hereto as Exhibit B is a true, complete and correct copy of resolutions duly adopted by the Board of Directors of the Borrower on June 15, 2015. All such resolutions are in full force and effect on the date hereof in the form in which adopted and no other resolutions have been adopted by the Board of Directors of the Borrower or any committee thereof relating to the Credit Agreement referred to below and the transactions referred to in such resolutions.

4. The following persons are, and have been at all times since a date prior to June 15, 2015, duly qualified and acting officers of the Borrower duly elected or appointed to the offices set forth opposite their respective names and signatures below, and each such person who, as an officer of the Borrower, signed documents delivered prior hereto or on the date hereof in connection with the any borrowings under the Credit Agreement, was duly elected or appointed, qualified and acting as such officer at the respective times of such signing and delivery, and the signatures of such persons appearing on such documents are their genuine signatures.

Office   **Name**

_____   _____

IN WITNESS WHEREOF, I have hereunto set my hand and affixed the seal of the Borrower.

Dated: July 1, 2015

_____

Stephen Leslie

I, Nobelle Preis, Assistant Secretary of Ambergris Co., hereby certify that Stephen Leslie is, and has been at all times since a date prior to June 15, 2015, the duly elected, qualified and acting Secretary of Ambergris Co. and that the signature set forth above is his true and correct signature.

Dated: July 1, 2015

_____

Nobelle Preis

Sample 9-E *Board Resolutions*

RESOLVED, that there are hereby approved the form and the terms and provisions of (a) the Credit Agreement dated as of July 1, 2015 (the "Credit Agreement"), a draft of which dated June 10, 2015, has been presented to this meeting, among this Corporation, the Banks listed on the signature pages of the Credit Agreement (the "Banks") and Cordial Bank, as Agent (the "Agent"), which provides for loans to this Corporation by the Banks in the aggregate principal amount of up to $15 million upon the terms and conditions therein set forth; and further

RESOLVED, that any officer of this Corporation be, and they and each of them, acting alone, hereby is, authorized and empowered, in the name and on behalf of this Corporation, to execute and deliver the Credit Agreement, and each and every other instrument and document the execution and delivery of which in the name and on behalf of this Corporation is therein contemplated, with such changes therein from the draft presented to this meeting, if any, as the officer executing the same may approve, such approval to be conclusively evidenced by such execution; and further

RESOLVED, that any officer be, and they and each of them, acting alone, hereby is, authorized and empowered in the name and on behalf of this Corporation from time to time to execute and deliver to the Banks or the Agent such other and further agreements, certificates, notices, instruments and documents, and do and perform such acts and things, as any of them, in his or her discretion, may deem necessary or advisable in connection with the Credit Agreement.

Sample 9-F *Board Resolutions—Example of Vague Resolution*

RESOLVED, that the Corporation be and hereby is authorized to borrow, and/or cause letters of credit to be issued for its account, in an aggregate amount of up to $75 million in any combination under commercial paper programs or pursuant to loan agreements or otherwise;

RESOLVED, that any officer be, and they and each of them, acting alone, hereby is, authorized and empowered in the name and on behalf of this Corporation from time to time to execute and deliver to the lenders or other parties such agreements, certificates, notices, instruments and documents, and do and perform such acts and things, as any of them, in his or her discretion, may deem necessary or advisable to give effect to the foregoing resolution.

Chapter 10:   Contract Structure and Key Elements

Regarding contract structure generally, and for references to different types of contracts for review and comparison, see:

Carolyn E.C. Paris, How to Draft for Corporate Finance, ch. 3 (PLI 2006).

Regarding MAC clauses in the M&A context, see:

MAC clauses have been more often invoked in the M&A context:

Coho Sues Hicks Muse Units on $250 Million Deal Pullout, Wall St. J., May 28, 1999.

Left at the Altar: Jilted Merger Partners Increasingly Turn to the Courts, N.Y. Times, July 14, 2001 (quoting the then co-chair of M&A practice at Brobeck Phleger & Harrison: "What a 'material adverse effect' is—well, to describe it as an art rather than science is to be charitable.").

There were several disputes and a few cases involving MACs in 2008 and thereafter, the one best known involving the Hexion-Huntsman transaction. In all of these disputes and cases the sellers invoked *In re* IBP, Inc. Shareholders Litigation, 789 A.2d. 14 (Del. Ch. 2001) (IBP v. Tyson). For a summary of the current law, see http://www.mondaq.com/x/140706/Corporate+Company+Law/Material+Adverse+Change+Clauses+Do+They+Hold+Any+Water. In general it is fair to say that a buyer looking to exit a deal on the basis of MAC carries a very heavy burden of proof.

Regarding MAC clauses in finance, see:

MAC Clauses: Subjective by Nature, Vague by Design and a Potential Source of Liquidity Risk, Fitch Ratings Credit Market Research, Jan. 30, 2006, *available at* www.fitchratings.com/corporate/reports/report_frame.cfm?rpt_id=263578 (registration required).

> CP [commercial paper] investors, in particular, need to be aware of the existence of MAC language within credit facilities, since these facilities often serve as an anticipated secondary source of repayment for CP. Generally, should crisis or unforeseen circumstance occur and one of these clauses be violated, a borrower's access to funding may be restricted. At the very least, the violation may force a borrower to renegotiate terms in order to maintain its credit facility when access to capital is needed most. Corporate events involving extensive litigation or fraud generate an entirely new set of potential consequences by possibly triggering a MAC clause specific to litigation or compliance with laws. . . .

> [In the case of Marsh & McLennan in 2004,] a legal probe enveloped the firm. The company's ability to access its credit facility was called into question due to the presence of a MAC clause within its credit agreement that concerned litigation.

> A recent review of CP backup facilities conducted by Fitch revealed that MAC concepts appear in a significant portion of credit agreements. Among the 80 investment-grade issuers sampled, a form of the language surfaced in the vast majority, or more than 90%, with more than 50% of agreements containing ongoing MAC language within the representations and warranties. [The most common form of MAC, running from recent financials to the closing date, were in the majority (more than 90%) of the deals. In about 50%, MAC provisions also applied to subsequent borrowings.]. . . .

> MAC clauses are seldom invoked; more often, a breach of these clauses leads to a waiver of the breach agreed on by the bank group. Ultimately, a waiver and subsequent amendment maintain the facility at increased cost for the borrower, not only in facility fees and interest rates paid on borrowings, but in potentially tighter terms or covenants. . . .

> The circumstances surrounding the complaint filed against Marsh & McLennan by the New York State Attorney General regarding collusion and price-fixing illustrate how an unforeseen situation can trigger a MAC clause within a credit facility and affect borrower access to liquidity. Marsh & McLennan's bank group, as a direct result of the allegations, was in a position to invoke MAC provisions regarding the existence of litigation (R&Ws) and compliance with laws (Affirmative Covenants), either of which could mean its CP backup liquidity would be unavail-

able. As a result, Marsh & McLennan worked quickly to renegotiate the terms of its facility with its bank group, securing a waiver of the MAC language in order to maintain its backup liquidity.

As a result of legal matters confronting Marsh & McLennan, the company received downgrades in both its long- and short-term ratings; consequently, the company's CP ratings fell to Tier 2 from Tier 1. The resulting downgrades presented a considerable problem for Marsh & McLennan, who was at the time heavily dependent on short-term funding due to its acquisition of Kroll Inc. According to Marsh & McLennan's SEC filings, CP outstanding in October 2004 totaled $2.1 billion. The company needed access to its credit facilities, as rolling over its CP would be problematic following the ratings downgrades. (Tier 2 CP is not as commonly purchased as Tier 1, due to SEC rule 2a7, which limits money market fund holdings of Tier 2 paper.) As evidence of how critical the facility was to Marsh & McLennan's liquidity, the facility was ultimately drawn upon during the last quarter of 2004 for approximately $1.7 billion to cover maturing CP.

Regarding cross-defaults, see:

Floyd Norris, *A Tempting 13% Yield, But Is It Secure?* N.Y. TIMES, Oct. 11, 2002: TXU, the former Texas Utilities, bought a utility from the U.K. government in 1998. It suffered financial reversals, and in 2002 TXU decided to put it into insolvency proceedings. However, executives had to stay their hands while they figured out whether there were cross-defaults from the U.K. utility back to the parent company in the United States. Eventually, they found only one cross-default in U.S. debt, in a principal amount of about $500 million.

> "I asked our treasury people how that got in there," [the chairman and chief executive] said. "Nobody has been able to give me a reason." . . .

> There are other issues. [The executive] said that the company had hoped to be able to use "structured transactions" to meet earnings goals this year, but that the market for such trades had virtually closed in Britain. He explained that such trades could have moved profits from one period to another, thus improving reported results. In the current atmosphere, such things are not viewed as a positive for a company.

TXU to Write Off $4.2 Billion from Failed European Venture, WALL ST. J., Nov. 7, 2002.

Chapter 11: Housekeeping, Insurance, and Information Covenants

See generally Carolyn E.C. Paris, How to Draft for Corporate Finance, ch. 6 (PLI 2006).

Examples of housekeeping covenants:

Sample 11-A *Housekeeping Covenants—Version 1*

Payment of Obligations. The Borrower will pay and discharge, and will cause each Subsidiary to pay and discharge, at or before maturity, all their respective material obligations and liabilities (including, without limitation, tax liabilities and claims of materialmen, warehousemen and the like which if unpaid might by law give rise to a Lien), except where the same may be contested in good faith by appropriate proceedings, and will maintain, and will cause each Subsidiary to maintain, in accordance with generally accepted accounting principles, appropriate reserves for the accrual of any of the same.

Conduct of Business and Maintenance of Existence. The Borrower will continue, and will cause each Subsidiary to continue, to engage in business of the same general type as now conducted by the Borrower and its Subsidiaries, and will preserve, renew and keep in full force and effect, and will cause each Subsidiary to preserve, renew and keep in full force and effect their respective corporate existence and their respective rights, privileges and franchises necessary or desirable in the normal conduct of business; *provided* that nothing in this Section shall prohibit (i) the merger of a Subsidiary into the Borrower or the merger or consolidation of a Subsidiary of the Borrower with or into another Person if the corporation surviving such consolidation or merger is a Subsidiary of the Borrower and if, in each case, after giving effect thereto, no Default shall have occurred and be continuing or (ii) the termination of the corporate existence of any Subsidiary if the Borrower in the good faith exercise of its business judgment determines that such termination is desirable for the Borrower and is not materially disadvantageous to the Banks; *provided further*, that Holdings and the Borrower may not merge.

Compliance with Laws. The Borrower will comply, and will cause each Subsidiary to comply, in all material respects with all applicable laws, ordinances, rules, regulations, and requirements of governmental authorities (including, without limitation, Environmental Laws and ERISA and the rules and regulations thereunder) except where the necessity of compliance therewith is contested in good faith by appropriate proceedings.

Inspection of Property, Books and Records; Annual Bank Meeting.

(a)   The Borrower will keep, and will cause each Subsidiary to keep, proper books of record and account in which full, true and correct entries shall be made of all dealings and transactions in relation to its business and activities; and will permit, and will cause each Subsidiary to permit upon reasonable prior request therefor, a reasonable number of representatives of the Banks (designated by the Agent or the Required Banks) at expense of (i) if at the time no Default shall have occurred and be continuing, the Banks (as they may agree among themselves) and (ii) if at the time a Default shall have occurred and be continuing, the Borrower, to visit and inspect any of their respective properties, to examine and make abstracts from any of their respective books and records and to discuss their respective affairs, finances and accounts with their respective officers, employees and independent public accountants, all at such reasonable times during normal business hours and as often as may reasonably be desired.

(b)   Unless the Administrative Agent shall notify the Borrower that no meeting is required, within 120 days after the end of each fiscal year, the Borrower will conduct a meeting of the Banks to discuss such fiscal year's results and the financial condition of the Borrower at which shall be present the chief executive officer and the chief financial officer of the Borrower and such other officers of the Borrowers as Borrower's chief executive officer shall designate. Such meetings shall be held at a time and place convenient to the Banks and to the Borrower.

Sample 11-B *Housekeeping Covenants—Version 2*

The Borrower covenants and agrees that on and after the Effective Date and until the later to occur of (a) the Commitment Termination Date and (b) the payment in full of the Loans, the Fees and all other sums payable under the Loan Documents, the Borrower will:

Legal Existence

Except as may otherwise be permitted by [merger covenant], maintain, and cause each Subsidiary to maintain, its corporate existence in good standing in the jurisdiction of its incorporation or formation and in each other jurisdiction in which the failure so to do could reasonably be expected to have a Material Adverse effect, except that the corporate existence of Subsidiaries operating closing or discontinued operations may be terminated.

Taxes

Pay and discharge when due, and cause each Subsidiary so to do, all taxes, assessments, governmental charges, license fees and levies upon or with respect to the Borrower and such Subsidiary, and upon the income, profits and Property thereof unless, and only to the extent, that either (i)(a) such taxes, assessments, governmental charges, license fees and levies shall be contested in good faith and by appropriate proceedings diligently conducted by the Borrower or such Subsidiary, and (b) such reserve or other appropriate provision as shall be required by GAAP shall have been made therefor, or (ii) the failure to pay or discharge such taxes, assessments, governmental charges, license fees and levies could not reasonably be expected to have a Material Adverse effect.

Performance of Obligations

Pay and discharge promptly when due, and cause each Subsidiary so to do, all lawful Indebtedness, obligations and claims for labor, materials and supplies or otherwise which, if unpaid, could reasonably be expected to (a) have a Material Adverse effect, or (b) become a Lien on the Property of the Borrower or any Subsidiary, except those Liens permitted under [lien covenant], *provided* that neither the Borrower nor such Subsidiary shall be required to pay or discharge or cause to be paid or discharged any such Indebtedness, obligation or claim so long as (i) the validity thereof shall be contested in good faith and by appropriate proceedings diligently conducted by the Borrower or such Subsidiary, and (ii) such reserve or other appropriate provision as shall be required by GAAP shall have been made therefor.

Condition of Property

Except for ordinary wear and tear, at all times, maintain, protect and keep in good repair, working order and condition, all material Property necessary for the operation of its business (other than Property which is replaced with similar Property) as then being operated, and cause each Subsidiary so to do.

Observance of Legal Requirements

Observe and comply in all material respects, and cause each Subsidiary so to do, with all laws, ordinances, orders, judgments, rules, regulations, certifications, franchises, permits, licenses, directions and requirements of all Governmental Authorities, which now or at any time hereafter may be applicable to it or to such Subsidiary, a violation of which could reasonably be expected to have a Material Adverse effect.

Records

Upon reasonable notice and during normal business hours, permit representatives of the Administrative Agent and each Lender to visit the offices of the Borrower and each Subsidiary, to examine the books and records (other than tax returns and work papers related to tax returns) thereof and auditors' reports relating thereto, to discuss the affairs of the Borrower and each Subsidiary with the respective officers thereof, and to meet and discuss the affairs of the Borrower and each Subsidiary with the Borrower's auditors.

Authorizations

Maintain and cause each Subsidiary to maintain, in full force and effect, all copyrights, patents, trademarks, trade names, franchises, licenses, permits, applications, reports, and other authorizations and rights, which, if not so maintained, would individually or in the aggregate have a Material Adverse effect.

Sample 11-C *Housekeeping Covenants—Version 3*

Each Borrower covenants and agrees with each Lender that so long as this Agreement shall remain in effect or the principal of or interest on any Loan, any Fees or any other expenses or amounts payable under any Loan Document shall be unpaid, unless the Required Lenders shall otherwise consent in writing, it will, and will cause each of the Subsidiaries (except Subsidiaries not material individually or in the aggregate to the consolidated financial position or results of operations of the Borrowers, to the extent the failure of such Subsidiaries to comply with the covenants set forth in this Article V could not result in a Material Adverse Effect) to:

> Existence: Businesses and Properties. (a) Do or cause to be done all things necessary to preserve, renew and keep in full force and effect its legal existence, except as otherwise expressly permitted under [merger covenant].

> (b) Do or cause to be done all things necessary to obtain, preserve, renew, extend and keep in full force and effect the rights, licenses, permits, franchises, authorizations, patents, copyrights, trademarks and trade names material to the conduct of its business; comply in all material respects with all applicable laws, rules, regulations and orders of any Governmen-

tal Authority, whether now in effect or hereafter enacted; and at all times maintain and preserve all property material to the conduct of such business and keep such property in good repair, working order and condition and from time to time make, or cause to be made, all needful and proper repairs, renewals, additions, improvements and replacements thereto necessary in order that the business carried on in connection therewith may be properly conducted at all times.

Obligations and Taxes. Pay its Indebtedness and other obligations promptly and in accordance with their terms and pay and discharge promptly when due all taxes, assessments and governmental charges or levies imposed upon it or upon its income or profits or in respect of its property, before the same shall become delinquent or in default, as well as all lawful claims for labor, materials and supplies or otherwise which, if unpaid, might give rise to a Lien upon such properties or any part thereof; *provided, however,* that such payment and discharge shall not be required with respect to any such tax, assessment, charge, levy or claim so long as the validity or amount thereof shall be contested in good faith by appropriate proceedings and the Borrowers shall have set aside on its books adequate reserves with respect thereto to the extent required by GAAP.

Maintaining Records; Access to Properties and Inspections. Maintain all financial records in accordance with GAAP and arrange with the Administrative Agent for (a) any representatives designated by any Lender to visit and inspect the financial records and the properties of any Borrower or Subsidiary at reasonable times and as often as reasonably requested and (b) at the request of any Lender, any representatives designated by such Lender to discuss the affairs, finances and condition of any Borrower or Subsidiary with the senior officers of the Borrowers and independent accountants therefor.

Sample 11-D *Simple Insurance Covenant—Common Version*

Insurance. The Borrower shall maintain such property, liability and other insurance to such extent and against such risks as shall be customary with companies in the same or similar business or as shall be required by law, such insurance to be maintained with financially sound and reputable insurers or, to the extent customary with companies in the same or similar businesses, through self-insurance.

Sample 11-E *Simple Insurance Covenant—Unusual Variation*

Insurance. Keep, and cause each Subsidiary to keep, insurance with responsible insurance companies in such amounts and against such risks as is usually carried by the Borrower or such Subsidiary.

Sample 11-F *Insurance Covenant in a Secured Credit Agreement*

Insurance. Each of the Obligors will maintain, and will cause each of its Subsidiaries to maintain, insurance with responsible companies in such amounts and against such risks as is usually carried by owners of similar businesses and properties in the same general areas in which each such Person operates, provided that in any event each such Person shall maintain:

(1) *Property/Business Interruption Insurance*—insurance as shall be reasonable and customary, but in no event less than the greater of (A) the aggregate outstanding principal amount of the Term Loans or such lesser amount as the Majority Lenders shall have consented to in writing and (B) the amounts necessary to avoid the insured named therein from becoming a co-insurer of any loss under such policy, (x) against loss or damage covering all of the tangible real and personal property and improvements of such Person and its Subsidiaries, by reason of any Peril (as defined below), (y) covering any construction or repair or improvements, for the total value of the work performed and equipment, supplies and material furnished against any Peril and (z) against loss of operating income earned from the operation of the Plants, by reason of any Peril affecting the operation thereof, and insurance against any other insurable loss of operating income by reason of any business interruption affecting such Person and its Subsidiaries to the extent covered by standard business interruption policies in the States in which the Plants are located, which insurance shall in each case cover gross earnings by reason of the particular Peril or other insurable business interruption in amounts (subject to such deductibles which shall not exceed $5 million in the case of any policy for any such insurance described in the foregoing clause (x) or (y) or, in the case of any policy for any such insurance described in the foregoing clause (z), thirty days).

(2) *Automobile Liability Insurance for Bodily Injury and Property Damage*— carry or cause to be carried insurance in respect of all vehicles (whether owned, hired or rented by such Person or any of its Subsidiaries) at any time located at the Plants in such amounts (and subject to such deductibles) as are then customary for vehicles

used in connection with property similar in use to the Plants and as otherwise may be required by applicable law.

(3)   *Comprehensive General Liability Insurance*—insurance against (i) claims for bodily injury, death or property damage occurring on, in or about the Plants and adjoining streets and sidewalks, (ii) claims for bodily injury, death or property damage resulting from the use of products sold by such Person or any of its Subsidiaries in such amounts as are then customary for property similar in use, and for operations and businesses similar, to the Plants located in the States in which the Plants are located, but in any event in an amount per occurrence of at least $10 million and $10 million annually in the aggregate and with a deductible (or self-insured amount) not in excess of $1 million.

(4)   *Workers' Compensation Insurance*—insurance (including Employers' Liability Insurance) to the extent required by applicable law and with a deductible not in excess of $1 million.

(5)   *Marine Liability Insurance*—insurance against claims for bodily injury, death or property damage occurring on, in or about waterways, in such amounts as are then customary for operations and property similar to the Plants located in the States in which the Plants are located but in any event in an amount per occurrence of at least $2 million and with a deductible (or self-insured amount) not in excess of $1 million.

(6)   *Other Insurance*—such other insurance, in each case as generally carried by owners of similar properties in the States in which the Plants are located, in such amounts and against such risks as are then customary for property similar in use to such Plants.

Such insurance shall be written by financially responsible companies selected by such Person, having an A.M. Best rating of "A–" or better at the time of such insurance is written and renewed and in a financial size category of XI or larger, or by other companies acceptable to the Majority Lenders, and (other than third party liability and workers' compensation) shall name the Administrative Agent as loss payee and as additional insured as its interests may appear. Each policy referred to in this Section shall include effective waivers by the insurer of all claims for insurance premiums against the Administrative Agent or any Lender, provide that all insurance proceeds (other than proceeds of business interruption insurance) in excess of $1 million per claim which would otherwise be payable to such Person or any Subsidiary of such Person under any of the policies described in this Section shall be adjusted with and payable to the Administrative Agent (for deposit in the Collateral Account maintained pursuant to the Security Documents and application in accordance with [prepayment provisions], provide that it will not be cancelled or reduced except after not less than thirty days' written notice to the Administrative Agent and provide that the interests of the Administrative Agent and the Lenders shall not be invalidated by any act or negligence of any Person having an interest in the Plants nor by occupancy or use of the Plants for purposes more hazardous than permitted by such policy nor by any foreclosure or other proceedings relating to the Plants. The Borrower will advise the Administrative Agent promptly of any policy cancellation, reduction or amendment.

On the Closing Date the Borrower will deliver to the Administrative Agent certificates of insurance satisfactory to the Administrative Agent evidencing the existence of all insurance required to be maintained hereunder and showing the termination or expiry date of such insurance. Thereafter, not later than five Business Days prior to the termination or expiry date of any such insurance the Borrower shall confirm to the Administrative Agent that such insurance will be renewed or replaced and, prior to the termination or expiry date of such insurance, shall deliver to the Administrative Agent certificates of insurance evidencing that such insurance has been renewed or replaced, subject only to the payment of premiums as they become due. None of the Obligors will obtain or carry separate insurance concurrent in form or contributing in the event of loss with that required by this Section unless the Administrative Agent is named insured therein, with loss payable as provided herein. The Borrower will immediately notify the Administrative Agent whenever any such separate insurance is obtained and shall deliver to the Administrative Agent the certificates evidencing the same.

If, in the opinion of the Borrower, any of the insurance which the Obligors are required to maintain pursuant to this Section is not available on commercially reasonable terms, the Borrower shall so notify the Administrative Agent and the Lenders and, with the consent of the Majority Lenders, may elect not to purchase such insurance; *provided* that if the Borrower shall not have received notice of disapproval from the Majority Lenders within twenty days of receipt by the Lenders of such notice from the Borrower, the Lenders shall be deemed to have consented, for the purposes of this Section, to the election not to purchase such insurance.

For purposes hereof, the term "Peril" shall mean, collectively, (i) fire, lightning, flood, windstorm, hail, explosion, riot and civil commotion, vandalism and malicious mischief, damage from aircraft, vehicles and smoke and (ii) all other perils covered by the "all-risk" endorsement then in use in the States in which the Plants are located.

Sample 11-G *Information Covenant—Version 1*

Financial Statements, Reports, etc.

Furnish to the Administrative Agent and each Lender:

(a)   within 120 days after the end of each fiscal year, a consolidated balance sheet and related consolidated statements of income and retained earnings and of cash flows of the Borrower showing the financial condition of the Borrower and its consolidated subsidiaries as of the close of such fiscal year and the results of the operations of the Borrower and its consolidated subsidiaries during such year, all audited by Ernst & Young LLP or other independent public accountants of recognized national standing acceptable to the Required Lenders and accompanied by an opinion of such accountants (which shall not be qualified in any material respect) to the effect that such consolidated financial statements present fairly the financial condition and results of operations of the Borrower on a consolidated basis, in accordance with GAAP;

(b)   within sixty days after the end of each of the first three fiscal quarters of each fiscal year, a consolidated balance sheet and related consolidated statements of income and retained earnings and of cash flows of the Borrower showing the financial condition of the Borrower and its consolidated subsidiaries as of the close of such fiscal quarter and the results of the operations of the Borrower and its consolidated subsidiaries during such fiscal quarter and the then elapsed portion of the fiscal year, all certified by one of its Financial Officers to the effect that such consolidated financial statements present fairly the financial condition and results of operations of the Borrower on a consolidated basis, in accordance with GAAP consistently applied, subject to normal year-end audit adjustments;

(c)   concurrently with any delivery of financial statements under (a) above, (i) a certificate of the accounting firm opining on such statements (which certificate may be limited to accounting matters and disclaim responsibility for legal interpretations) stating whether or not anything has come to the attention of such firm in the normal course of its audit to indicate that an Event of Default or Default has occurred and, if an Event of Default or Default has come to the attention of such firm, a certificate of a Financial Officer specifying the nature and extent thereof and any corrective action taken or proposed to be taken with respect thereto and (ii) a statement of a Financial Officer setting forth computations in reasonable detail satisfactory to the Administrative Agent (and accompanied by any

supporting information which shall have been reasonably requested by the Administrative Agent or the Required Lenders) demonstrating compliance with the [financial covenants];

(d)   concurrently with any delivery of financial statements under (b)
above, a certificate of the Financial Officer (i) certifying that no
Event of Default or Default has occurred or, if an Event of Default
or Default has occurred, specifying the nature and extent thereof
and any corrective action taken or proposed to be taken with respect thereto and (ii) setting forth computations in reasonable detail satisfactory to the Administrative Agent (and accompanied by
any supporting information which shall have been reasonably requested by the Administrative Agent or the Required Lenders)
demonstrating compliance with the [financial covenants];

(e)   promptly after the same become publicly available, copies of all periodic and other reports, proxy statements and other materials filed
by the Borrower or Subsidiary with the Securities and Exchange
Commission, or any Governmental Authority succeeding to any of
or all the functions of said Commission, or with any national securities exchange, or distributed to its public shareholders, as the case
may be (other than registration statements relating to employee
benefit plans or to the registration of securities for selling security
holders or pre-effective amendments, that shall not be declared effective, to registration statements);

(f)   promptly after obtaining knowledge thereof, notice of any Event of
Default or Default, specifying the nature and extent thereof and the
corrective action (if any) proposed to be taken with respect thereto;
and

(g)   promptly, from time to time, such other information regarding the
operations, business affairs and financial condition of the Borrower
and the Subsidiaries, or compliance with the terms of any Loan
Document (including a certificate with respect thereto), as the Administrative Agent or any Lender may reasonably request.

Sample 11-H *Information Covenant—Version 2*

<u>Financial Information, Reports, Notices, etc.</u> The Borrower will furnish,
or will cause to be furnished, to each Lender and the Agent copies of the following financial statements, reports, notices and information:

(a)   no later than the filing of each 10-K of, but in no event later than
120 days after the end of each Fiscal Year, copies of the audited annual financial statements for such Fiscal Year for the Borrower and

its Subsidiaries, in each case including therein consolidated balance sheets for each of the Borrower and its Subsidiaries as of the end of such Fiscal Year and consolidated statements of income, cash flow and changes in shareholders' equity of the Borrower and its Subsidiaries for such Fiscal Year, in each case, reported on (without any Impermissible Qualification) as to fairness of presentation, generally accepted accounting principles and consistency by independent public accountants of nationally recognized standing, together with a certificate from such accountants stating whether, in making the examination necessary for such report, such accountants have become aware of any Default that has occurred and is continuing;

(b)   no later than 120 days after the end of each Fiscal Year, annual consolidating balance sheets as of the end of such Fiscal Year and consolidating statements of income and cash flow for such Fiscal Year of the Borrower and its Subsidiaries, certified by the chief financial Authorized Officer of the Borrower, as to fairness of presentation, generally accepted accounting principles and consistency;

(c)   promptly and in any event prior to the thirtieth day of each Fiscal Year, a certified copy of the annual budget of the Borrower on a consolidated basis for such Fiscal Year, in form and scope consistent with the annual budget of the Borrower for the 1998 Fiscal Year furnished to the Agent prior to the Effective Date;

(d)   promptly and in any event within sixty days after the end of each of the first three Fiscal Quarters of each Fiscal Year, quarterly unaudited consolidated balance sheets as of the end of such Fiscal Quarter for each of the Borrower and its Subsidiaries, and quarterly unaudited consolidated statements of income, cash flow and changes in shareholders' equity of each of the Borrower and its Subsidiaries for such Fiscal Quarter and for the period commencing at the end of the previous Fiscal Year and ending with the end of such Fiscal Quarter, in each case, certified (subject to normal year-end adjustments) as to fairness of presentation, generally accepted accounting principles and consistency by the chief financial Authorized Officer of the Borrower;

(e)   within ten Business Days of the delivery of the financial statements required by clauses (a) and (d) of this Section, a Compliance Certificate, executed by the chief financial Authorized Officer of the Borrower, (i) showing (in reasonable detail and with appropriate calculations and computations in all respects reasonably satisfactory to the Agent) compliance with the [financial covenants] and (ii) giving notice of the other items referred to in the Compliance Certificate;

(f)   promptly after the sending or filing thereof, copies of all reports which the Borrower sends to any class of its security holders generally, and all reports and registration statements (other than the exhibits thereto and any registration statements on Form S-8 or its equivalent) which the Borrower or any of its Subsidiaries files with the Securities and Exchange Commission (or any foreign equivalent) or any national securities exchange, including, without limitation, Form 10-Ks and 10-Qs;

(g)   as soon as possible and in any event within five Business Days after any officer of the Borrower obtains knowledge of the occurrence of any Default, a statement of the chief financial Authorized Officer of the Borrower setting forth details of such Default and the action which the Borrower has taken and proposes to take with respect thereto;

(h)   as soon as possible and in any event within five Business Days after the commencement of any litigation, action, proceeding or labor controversy as to which there is a material possibility of an adverse determination and which if adversely determined could result in a Material Adverse Effect, notice thereof describing in reasonable detail such litigation, action, proceeding or labor controversy;

(i)   immediately upon becoming aware of the institution of any steps by the Borrower or any other Person to terminate any Pension Plan, or the failure to make a required contribution to any Pension Plan if such failure is sufficient to give rise to a Lien under section 302(f) of ERISA, or the taking of any action with respect to a Pension Plan which could result in the requirement that the Borrower furnish a bond or other security to the PBGC or such Pension Plan, or the occurrence of any event with respect to any Pension Plan which could result in the incurrence by the Borrower of any material liability, fine or penalty, or any material increase in the contingent liability of the Borrower with respect to any post-retirement Welfare Plan benefit, notice thereof and copies of all documentation relating thereto; and

(j)   such other information respecting the condition or operations, financial or otherwise, of the Borrower or any Subsidiary as any Lender through the Agent may from time to time reasonably request.

Sample 11-I *Information Covenant—Version 3*

At all times from and after the earlier of (i) the date of the commencement of an Exchange Offer or the effectiveness of the Shelf Registration Statement (the "Registration") and (ii) the date that is six months after the Closing Date, in either case, whether or not the Company and the Obligors are then required to file reports with the Commission, the Company and the Obligors shall file with the Commission all such reports and other information as they would be required to file with the Commission by Sections 13(a) or 15(d) under the Securities Exchange Act of 1934 if they were subject thereto. The Company and the Obligors shall supply the Trustee and each Holder or shall supply to the Trustee for forwarding to each such Holder, without cost to such Holder, copies of such reports and other information. In addition, at all times prior to the earlier of the date of the Registration and the date that is six months after the Closing Date, the Company and the Obligors shall, at their cost, deliver to each Holder of the Notes quarterly and annual reports substantially equivalent to those which would be required by the Exchange Act. In addition, at all times prior to the Registration, upon the request of any Holder or any prospective purchaser of the Notes designated by a Holder, the Company and the Obligors shall supply to such Holder or such prospective purchaser the information required under Rule 144A under the Securities Act.

Chapter 12: Debt and Liens (Negative Pledges)

See generally:

Carolyn E.C. Paris, How to Draft for Corporate Finance, ch. 7 (PLI 2006).

Examples of debt and lien covenants:

Sample 12-A *Priority Debt Covenant Package*

"*Attributable Debt*" means, when used in connection with a sale and lease-back transaction, on any date as of which the amount thereof is to be determined, the product of (a) the net proceeds from such sale and lease-back transaction multiplied by (b) a fraction, the numerator of which is the number of full years of the term of the lease relating to the property involved in such sale and lease-back transaction (without regard to any option to renew or extend such term) remaining on the date of the making of such computation and the denominator of which is the number of full years of the term of such lease measured from the first day of such term.

"*Consolidated Net Tangible Assets*" means the excess over the current liabilities of the Issuer of all of its assets as determined by the Issuer and set forth in a consolidated balance sheet prepared in accordance with generally accepted accounting principles as of a date within ninety days of the date of such determination, after deducting goodwill, trademarks, patents, other like intangibles and the minority interest of others.

"*Exempted Debt*" means the sum, without duplication, of the following items outstanding as of the date Exempted Debt is being determined: (i) indebtedness of the Issuer and its Restricted Subsidiaries incurred after the date of this Indenture and secured by liens created or assumed or permitted to exist pursuant to [subsection (b) of the negative pledge], (ii) Attributable Debt of the Issuer and its Restricted Subsidiaries in respect of all sale and lease-back transactions with regard to any Principal Property entered into pursuant to [subsection (b) of the sale lease-back covenant] and (iii) Funded Debt of Restricted Subsidiaries created, assumed or guaranteed or permitted to exist pursuant to [subsection (b) of the debt covenant].

"*Funded Debt*" means all indebtedness for money borrowed, including purchase money indebtedness, having a maturity of more than one year from the date of its creation or having a maturity of less than one year but by its terms being renewable or extendible, at the option of the obligor in respect thereof, beyond one year from its creation.

"*Principal Property*" means land, land improvements, buildings and associated factory and laboratory equipment owned or leased pursuant to a capital lease and used by the Issuer or a Restricted Subsidiary primarily for processing, producing, packaging or storing its products, raw materials, inventories or other materials and supplies and located within the United States of America and having an acquisition cost plus capitalized improvements in excess of 5% of Consolidated Net Tangible Assets as of the date of such determination, but shall not include any such property financed through the issuance of tax exempt governmental obligations, or any such property that has been determined by Board Resolution of the Issuer not to be of material importance to the respective businesses conducted by the Issuer or such Restricted Subsidiary, effective as of the date such resolution is adopted.

"*Restricted Subsidiary*" means any Subsidiary organized and existing under the laws of the United States of America and the principal business of which is carried on within the United States of America which owns or is a lessee pursuant to a capital lease of any Principal Property and in which the investment of the Issuer and all its Subsidiaries exceeds 10% of Consolidated Net Tangible Assets as of the date of such determination other than:

(i)　　each Subsidiary the major part of whose business consists of finance, banking, credit, leasing, insurance, financial services or other similar operations, or any combination thereof; and

(ii)　　each Subsidiary formed or acquired after the date hereof for the purpose of acquiring the business or assets of another Person and which does not acquire all or any substantial part of the business or assets of the Issuer or any Restricted Subsidiary;

provided, however, that the Board of Directors of the Issuer may by Board Resolution declare any such Subsidiary to be a Restricted Subsidiary, effective as of the date such resolution is adopted.

Negative Pledge.

(a)　　The Issuer will not, and will not permit any Restricted Subsidiary to, mortgage or pledge as security for any indebtedness any shares of stock, indebtedness or other obligations of a Restricted Subsidiary or any Principal Property of the Issuer or a Restricted Subsidiary, whether such shares of stock, indebtedness or other obligations of a Restricted Subsidiary or Principal Property is owned at the date of this Indenture or hereafter acquired, unless the Issuer secures or causes such Restricted Subsidiary to secure the outstanding Securities equally and ratably with all indebtedness secured by such mortgage or pledge, so long as such indebtedness shall be so secured; *provided,* however, that this covenant shall not apply in the case of: (i) the creation of any mortgage, pledge or other lien on any shares of stock, indebtedness or other obligations of a Restricted Subsidiary or any Principal Property hereafter acquired (including acquisitions by way or merger or consolidation) by the Issuer or a Restricted Subsidiary contemporaneously with such acquisition, or within 120 days thereafter, to secure or provide for the payment or financing of any part of the purchase price thereof, or the assumption of any mortgage, pledge or other lien upon any shares of stock, indebtedness or other obligations of a Restricted Subsidiary or any Principal Property hereafter acquired existing at the time of such acquisition, or the acquisition of any shares of stock, indebtedness or other obligations of a Restricted Subsidiary or any Principal Property subject to any mortgage, pledge or other lien without the assumption thereof, *provided* that every such mortgage, pledge or lien referred to in this clause (i) shall attach only to the shares of stock, indebtedness or other obligations of a Restricted Subsidiary or any Principal Property so acquired and fixed improvements thereon; (ii) any mortgage, pledge or other lien on any shares of stock, indebtedness or other obligations of a Restricted Subsidiary or any Principal Property existing at the date of this Indenture; (iii) any mortgage, pledge or other lien on any shares of stock, indebtedness or other obligations of a Restricted Subsidiary or any Principal Property in favor of the Issuer or any Restricted Subsidiary; (iv) any mortgage, pledge or other lien on Principal Property being constructed or improved securing loans to finance such construction or improvements; (v) any mortgage, pledge or other lien on shares of stock, indebtedness or other obligations of a Restricted Subsidiary or any Principal Property incurred in connection with the issuance by a state or political subdivision thereof of any securities the interest on which is exempt from Federal income taxes by virtue of Section 103 of the United States Internal Revenue Code of 1986, as amended, or any other laws and regulations in effect at the time of such issuance; and (vi) any renewal of or substitution for any mortgage, pledge or other lien permitted by any of the preceding clauses (i) through (v), *provided,* in the case of a mortgage, pledge or other lien permitted under clause (i), (ii) or (iv), the debt secured is not increased nor the lien extended to any additional assets.

(b)   Notwithstanding the provisions of subsection (a) of this Section, the Issuer or any Restricted Subsidiary may create or assume liens in addition to those permitted by subsection (a) of this Section, and renew, extend or replace such liens, *provided* that at the time of such creation, assumption, renewal, extension or replacement, and after giving effect thereto, Exempted Debt does not exceed 10% of Consolidated Net Tangible Assets.

Certain Sale and Leaseback Transactions.

(a)   The Issuer will not, and will not permit any Restricted Subsidiary to, sell or transfer, directly or indirectly, except to the Issuer or a Restricted Subsidiary, any Principal Property as an entirety, or any substantial portion thereof, with the intention of taking back a lease of such property, except a lease for a period of three years or less at the end of which it is intended that the use of such property by the lessee will be discontinued; *provided* that, notwithstanding the foregoing, the Issuer or any Restricted Subsidiary may sell any such Principal Property and lease it back for a longer period (i) if the Issuer or such Restricted Subsidiary would be entitled, pursuant to the provisions of [subsection (a) of negative pledge], to create a mortgage on the property to be leased securing Funded Debt in an amount equal to the Attributable Debt with respect to such sale and lease-back transaction without equally and ratably securing the outstanding Securities or (ii) if (A) the Issuer promptly informs the Trustee of such transaction, (B) the net proceeds of such transaction are at least equal to the fair value (as determined by Board Resolution of the Issuer) of such property and (C) the Issuer causes an amount equal to the net proceeds of the sale to be applied to the retirement, within 120 days after receipt of such proceeds, of Funded Debt incurred or assumed by the Issuer or a Restricted Subsidiary (including the Securities); *provided* further that, in lieu of applying all of or any part of such net proceeds to such retirement, the Issuer may, within seventy-five days after such sale, deliver or cause to be delivered to the applicable trustee for cancellation either debentures or notes evidencing Funded Debt of the Issuer (which may include the Outstanding Securities) or of a Restricted Subsidiary previously authenticated and delivered by the applicable trustee, and not theretofore tendered for sinking fund purposes or called for a sinking fund or otherwise applied as a credit against an obligation to redeem or retire such notes or debentures, and an Officers' Certificate stating that the Issuer elects to deliver or cause to be delivered such debentures or notes in lieu of retiring Funded Debt as hereinabove provided. If the Issuer shall so deliver debentures or notes to the applicable trustee and the Issuer shall duly deliver such Officers' Certificate, the amount of cash which the Issuer shall be required to apply to the retirement of Funded Debt under this subsection (a) shall be reduced by an amount equal to the aggregate of the then applicable optional redemption prices (not including any optional sinking fund redemption prices) of such debentures or notes, or, if there are no such redemption prices, the principal amount of such debentures or notes; *provided*, that in the case of debentures or notes which provide for an amount less than the principal amount thereof to be due and payable upon a declaration of the maturity thereof, such amount of cash shall be reduced by the amount of principal of such debentures or notes that would be due and payable as of the date of such application upon a declaration of acceleration of the maturity thereof pursuant to the terms of the indenture pursuant to which such debentures or notes were issued.

(b)   Notwithstanding the provisions of subsection (a) of this Section, the Issuer or any Restricted Subsidiary may enter into sale and leaseback transactions in addition to those permitted by subsection (a) of this Section and without any obligation to retire any outstanding Securities or other Funded Debt, *provided* that at the time of entering into such sale and lease-back transactions and after giving effect thereto, Exempted Debt does not exceed 10% of Consolidated Net Tangible Assets.

Funded Debt of Restricted Subsidiaries.

(a)   The Issuer will not permit any Restricted Subsidiary

  (A)   To create, assume or permit to exist any Funded Debt other than (i) Funded Debt secured by a mortgage, pledge or lien which is permitted to such Restricted Subsidiary under the provisions of [subsection (a) of negative pledge], (ii) Funded Debt owed to the Issuer or any Restricted Subsidiary, (iii) Funded Debt of a corporation existing at the time it becomes a Restricted Subsidiary, (iv) Funded Debt existing on the date of this Indenture, or (v) Funded Debt created in connection with, or with a view to, compliance by such Restricted Subsidiary with the requirements of any program adopted by any federal, state or local governmental authority and applicable to such Restricted Subsidiary and providing financial or tax benefits to such Restricted Subsidiary which are not available directly to the Issuer; or

  (B)   To guarantee, directly or indirectly through any arrangement which is substantially the equivalent of a guarantee, any Funded Debt except for (i) guarantees existing on the date of this Indenture, (ii) guarantees which, on the date of this Indenture, a Restricted Subsidiary is obligated to give, and (iii) guarantees of Funded Debt secured by a mortgage, pledge or lien which is permitted to such Restricted Subsidiary under the provisions of [subsection (a) of negative pledge].

(b)   Notwithstanding the provisions of subsection (a) of this Section, any Restricted Subsidiary may create, assume or guarantee Funded Debt in addition to that permitted by subsection (a) of this Section, and renew, extend or replace such Funded Debt, *provided* that at the time of such creation, assumption, guarantee, renewal, extension or replacement, and after giving effect thereto, Exempted Debt does not exceed 10% of Consolidated Net Tangible Assets.

Sample 12-B *Negative Pledge—Indenture (Investment Grade)*

"Principal Manufacturing Property" means any manufacturing property located within the United States of America (other than its territories or possessions) and owned by the Company or any Subsidiary, except for any manufacturing property that, in the opinion of the Board of Directors, is not of material importance to the business conducted by the Company and its Subsidiaries, taken as a whole.

Limitation Upon Mortgages and Liens. The Company will not at any time directly or indirectly create or assume and will not cause or permit a Subsidiary directly or indirectly to create or assume, otherwise than in favor of the Company or a Wholly-Owned Subsidiary, any mortgage, pledge or other lien or encumbrance upon any Principal Manufacturing Property or any interest it may have therein or upon any stock or indebtedness of any Subsidiary, whether now owned or hereafter acquired, without making effective provision (and the Company covenants that in such case it will make or cause to be made effective provision) whereby the Outstanding Debt Securities and any other indebtedness of the Company then entitled thereto shall be secured by such mortgage, pledge, lien or encumbrance equally and ratably with any and all other obligations and indebtedness thereby secured, so long as any such other obligations and indebtedness shall be so secured; *provided, however,* that the foregoing covenant shall not be applicable to the following:

(a) (i) any mortgage, pledge or other lien or encumbrance on any property, hereafter acquired or constructed by the Company or a Subsidiary, or on which property so constructed is located, and created prior to, contemporaneously with or within 180 days after, such acquisition or construction or the commencement of commercial operation of such property to secure or provide for the payment of any part of the purchase or construction price of such property, or (ii) the acquisition by the Company or a Subsidiary of such property subject to any mortgage, pledge, or other lien or encumbrance upon such property existing at the time of acquisition thereof, whether or not assumed by the Company or such Subsidiary, or (iii) any mortgage, pledge, or other lien or encumbrance existing on the property, shares of stock or indebtedness of a corporation at the time such corporation shall become a Subsidiary, or (iv) any conditional sales agreement or other title retention agreement with respect to any property hereafter acquired or constructed; *provided* that the lien of any such mortgage, pledge or other lien does not spread to property owned prior to such acquisition or construction or to other property thereafter acquired or constructed other than additions to such acquired or constructed property and other than property on which property so acquired or constructed is located;

(b) any mortgage, pledge or other lien or encumbrance created for the sole purpose of extending, renewing or refunding any mortgage, pledge, lien or encumbrance permitted by subsection (a) of the Section; *provided, however,* that the principal amount of indebtedness secured therein shall not exceed the principal amount of indebtedness so secured at the time of such extension, renewal or refunding and that such extension, renewal or refunding mortgage, pledge, lien or encumbrance shall be limited to all or any part of the same property that secured the mortgage, pledge or other lien or encumbrance extended, renewed or refunded;

(c) Liens for taxes or assessments or governmental charges or levies not then due and delinquent or the validity of which is being contested in good faith, and against which an adequate reserve has been established; pledges or deposits to secure public or statutory obligations or to secure permits in connection with bids or contracts; materialmen's, mechanics', carrier's, workmen's, repairmen's or other like liens, or deposits to obtain the release of such liens; deposits to secure surety, stay, appeal or customs bonds; liens created by or resulting from any litigation or legal proceeding which is currently being contested in good faith by appropriate proceedings; leases and liens, right of reverter and other possessory rights of the lessor thereunder; zoning restrictions, easements, rights-of-way or other restrictions on the use of real property or minor irregularities in the title thereto; and any other liens and encumbrances similar to those described in this subsection, the existence of which does not, in the opinion of the Company, materially impair the use by the Company or a Subsidiary of the affected property in the operation of the business of the Company or a Subsidiary, or the value of such property for the purposes of such business;

(d) any contracts for production, research or development, providing for advance, partial or progress payments on such contracts and for a lien, paramount to all other liens, upon money advanced or paid pursuant to such contracts, or upon any material or supplies in connection with the performance of such contracts to secure such payments;

(e) any mortgage, pledge or other lien or encumbrance created after the date of this Indenture on any property leased to or purchased by the Company or a Subsidiary after that date and securing, directly or indirectly, obligations issued by a State, a territory or a possession of the United States, or any political subdivision of any of the foregoing, or the District of Columbia, to finance the cost of acquisition or cost of construction of such property, provided that the interest paid on such obligations is entitled to be excluded from gross income of the recipient pursuant to Section 103(a)(1) of the

Code (or any successor to such provision) as in effect at the time of the issuance of such obligations;

(f)   any pledge of notes, chattel mortgages, leases, accounts receivable, trade acceptances and other paper arising in the ordinary course of business, out of installment or conditional sales to or by, or other transactions involving title retention with, distributors, dealers or other customers, of merchandise, equipment or services; and

(g)   any mortgage, pledge or other lien or encumbrance not otherwise permitted under this Section, *provided*, the aggregate amount of indebtedness secured by all such mortgages, pledges, liens or encumbrances, together with the aggregate sale price of property involved in sale and leaseback transactions not otherwise permitted except under [basket under sale and leaseback covenant] does not exceed the greater of $20 million or 5% of Consolidated Shareholders' Equity.

Sample 12-C *Negative Pledge—Indenture (High-Yield)*

Limitation on Liens. The Company will not, and will not permit any Restricted Subsidiary to, directly or indirectly, create, incur, assume or suffer to exist any Lien of any kind (other than Permitted Liens) on or with respect to any of its property or assets, including any shares of stock or indebtedness of any Restricted Subsidiary, whether owned at the date of the Indenture or thereafter acquired, or any income, profits or proceeds therefrom, or assign or otherwise convey any right to receive income thereon, unless (x) in the case of any Lien securing Subordinated Indebtedness, the Notes are secured by a Lien on such property, assets or proceeds that is senior in priority to such Lien and (y) in the case of any other Lien, the Notes are equally and ratably secured with the obligation or liability secured by such Lien.

"Permitted Liens" means the following types of Liens:

(a)   Liens existing as of the Original Issue Date;

(b)   Liens on property or assets of the Company or any Restricted Subsidiary securing Indebtedness and all other obligations under any revolving line of credit referred to in clause (a) of the definition of "Permitted Indebtedness" or under Interest Rate Agreements or Currency Agreements which constitute Permitted Indebtedness or Permitted Subsidiary Indebtedness;

(c)   Liens on any property or assets of a Restricted Subsidiary granted in favor of the Company or any wholly owned Restricted Subsidiary;

(d)   Liens on any property or assets of the Company or any Restricted Subsidiary securing the Notes or the Guarantees;

(e)   any interest or title of a lessor under any Capitalized Lease Obligation or Sale and Leaseback Transaction so long as the amount of such Capitalized Lease Obligation or the Attributable Value of such Sale and Leaseback Transaction secured by such Lien does not exceed the amount permitted in the covenant entitled "Limitation on Indebtedness" or the covenant entitled "Limitation on Sale and Leaseback Transactions," as the case may be;

(f)   statutory Liens of landlords and carriers, warehousemen, mechanics, suppliers, materialmen, repairmen or other similar Liens arising in the ordinary course of business of the Company or any Restricted Subsidiary and with respect to amounts not yet delinquent or being contested in good faith by appropriate proceedings, if a reserve or other appropriate provision, if any, as shall be required in conformity with GAAP shall have been made therefor;

(g)   Liens for taxes, assessments, government charges or claims that are being contested in good faith by appropriate proceedings promptly instituted and diligently conducted and if a reserve or other appropriate provision, if any, as shall be required in conformity with GAAP shall have been made therefor;

(h)   easements, rights-of-way, restrictions and other similar charges or encumbrances not interfering in any material respect with the business of the Company or any Restricted Subsidiary incurred in the ordinary course of business;

(i)   Liens arising out of judgments or orders that have been adequately bonded or with respect to which a stay of execution has been obtained pending an appeal or proceeding for review;

(j)   Liens securing Acquired Indebtedness created prior to (and not in connection with or in contemplation of) the incurrence of such Indebtedness by the Company or any Restricted Subsidiary, *provided* that such Lien does not extend to any property or assets of the Company or any Restricted Subsidiary other than the assets acquired in connection with the incurrence of such Acquired Indebtedness;

(k)   Liens incurred or deposits made in the ordinary course of business in connection with workers' compensation, unemployment insurance and other types of social security;

(l)   Liens securing reimbursement obligations of the Company or any Restricted Subsidiary with respect to letters of credit that encumber documents and other property relating to such letters of credit and the products and proceeds thereof;

(m)   Liens incurred or deposits made to secure the performance of tenders, bids, leases, statutory or regulatory obligations, surety and appeal bonds, contracts (other than for Indebtedness), performance and return-of-money bonds and other obligations of a similar nature incurred in the ordinary course of business (exclusive of obligations for the payment of borrowed money);

(n)   Liens in favor of customs and revenue authorities arising as a matter of law to secure payment of customs duties in connection with the importation of goods;

(o)   Liens arising solely by virtue of any statutory provision relating to banker's liens, rights of set-off or similar rights and remedies as to deposit accounts or other funds maintained with a creditor depository institution, *provided, however,* that (x) such deposit account is not a dedicated cash collateral account and is not subject to restrictions against access by the Company or any of its Restricted Subsidiaries and (y) such deposit account is not intended by Holdings or any of its Subsidiaries to provide collateral to the depository institution; and

(p)   any extension, renewal or replacement, in whole or in part, of any Lien described in the foregoing clauses (a) through (o); *provided* that any such extension, renewal or replacement shall be no more restrictive in any material respect than the Lien so extended, renewed or replaced and shall not extend to any additional property or assets.

Sample 12-D *Negative Pledge—Indenture (Subordinated)*

Limitation on Liens

(a)   The Company will not, and will not permit any Subsidiary to, directly or indirectly, create, incur or affirm any Lien of any kind securing any Pari Passu Indebtedness or Subordinated Indebtedness (including any assumption, guarantee or other liability with respect thereto by any Subsidiary) upon any property or assets (including any intercompany notes) of the Company or any Subsidiary owned on the date of this Indenture or acquired after the date of the Note Indenture, or any income or profits therefrom, unless the Securities are directly secured equally and ratably with (or, in the case of Subordinated Indebtedness, prior or senior thereto, with the same relative priority as the Securities shall have with respect to such Subordinated Indebtedness) the obligation or liability secured by such Lien, and except for any Lien securing Acquired Indebtedness created prior to (and not created in connection with, or in contemplation of) the incurrence of such Pari Passu Indebtedness or Subordinated Indebtedness by the Company or any Subsidiary which Indebtedness is permitted under the provisions of [debt covenant] *provided* that any such Lien extends only to the assets that were subject to such Lien securing such Acquired Indebtedness prior to the related acquisition by the Company or its Subsidiaries.

(b)   The Company will not permit any Subsidiary, directly or indirectly, to secure the payment of any Senior Indebtedness of the Company or pledge any intercompany notes representing obligations of any Subsidiary to secure the payment of any Senior Indebtedness, unless in each case such Subsidiary simultaneously executes and delivers a supplemental indenture to this Indenture providing for a guarantee of payment of the Securities by such Subsidiary, which guarantee shall be on the same terms as the guarantee of such Senior Indebtedness (if a guarantee of such Senior Indebtedness is granted by any such Subsidiary) except that the guarantee of the Securities need not be secured and shall be subordinated to the claims against such Subsidiary in respect of Senior Indebtedness to the same extent as the Securities are subordinated to Senior Indebtedness of the Company under this Indenture.

Sample 12-E *Negative Pledge—Credit Agreement Version 1*

"Indebtedness" of any person means, without duplication, (a) all obligations of such person for borrowed money or with respect to deposits or advances of any kind, (b) all obligations of such person evidenced by bonds, debentures, notes or similar instruments, (c) all obligations of such person under conditional sale or other title retention agreements relating to property or assets purchased by such person, (d) all obligations of such person issued or assumed as the deferred purchase price of property or services, (e) all Indebtedness of others secured by (or for which the holder of such Indebtedness has an existing right, contingent or otherwise, to be secured by) any Lien on property owned or acquired by such person, whether or not the obligations secured thereby have been assumed, (f) all Guarantees by such person of Indebtedness of others, (g) all Capitalized Lease Obligations of such person, (h) all obligations of such person in respect of interest rate swaps or other interest rate protection or interest rate hedging arrangements, (i) all obligations of such person as an account party in respect of letters of credit and bankers' acceptances and (j) all obligations of such person to pay a specified purchase price for goods or services whether or not delivered or accepted (e.g., take-or-pay and similar obligations); *provided, however,* that Indebtedness shall not include trade payables or trade receivables (including, without limitation, customer deposits and advances in respect of purchases of inventory) and accrued expenses, in each case, arising in the ordinary course of business. The Indebtedness of any person shall include, without limitation, the Indebtedness of any partnership in which such person is a general partner.

"Lien" means any lien, security interest or other charge or encumbrance of any kind, or any other type of preferential arrangement that has the practical effect of creating a security interest or similar charge or an encumbrance, including, without limitation, the lien or retained security title of a conditional vendor.

"Permitted Liens" means such of the following as to which no enforcement, collection, execution, levy or foreclosure proceeding shall have been commenced:

(a) Liens for taxes, assessments and governmental charges or levies to the extent not required to be paid under [payment of taxes covenant];

(b) Liens imposed by law, such as materialmen's, mechanics', carriers', workmen's and repairmen's Liens and other similar Liens arising in the ordinary course of business securing obligations that are not overdue for a period of more than thirty days or are being contested in good faith and by proper proceedings and as to which adequate reserves are being maintained;

(c) pledges or deposits to secure obligations under workers' compensation laws or similar legislation or to secure public or statutory obligations that are not overdue for a period of more than thirty days or are being contested in good faith by proper proceedings and for which adequate reserves are being maintained;

(d) undertakings to secure the performance of bids, tenders, contracts or leases or to secure surety, stay or appeal or other similar types of deposits, liens or pledges (to the extent such undertakings do not secure obligations for the payment of borrowed money or the deferred purchase of property or services);

(e) judgment Liens to the extent such Liens are being contested in good faith and by proper proceedings and as to which adequate reserves are being maintained or for which an adequate bond has been obtained; *provided* that such Liens do not, in the aggregate, secure judgments in excess of $25 million; and

(f)   easements, rights of way and other encumbrances on title to real property that do not render title to the property encumbered thereby unmarketable or materially adversely affect the use of such property for its present or intended purposes.

<u>Negative Covenant</u>. So long as any Advance shall remain unpaid, any Letter of Credit shall be outstanding or any Lender shall have any Commitment hereunder, the Borrower will not, without the written consent of the Required Lenders:

(a)   <u>Liens, Etc</u>. Create, incur, assume or suffer to exist, or permit any of its Subsidiaries to create, incur, assume or suffer to exist, any Lien on or with respect to any of its properties of any character (including, without limitation, accounts and intercompany obligations) whether now owned or hereafter acquired, or sign or file, or permit any of its Subsidiaries to sign or file, under the Uniform Commercial Code of any jurisdiction, a financing statement that names the Borrower or any of its Subsidiaries as debtor, or sign, or permit any of their respective Subsidiaries to sign, any security agreement authorizing any secured party thereunder to file such financing statement, or assign, or permit any of their respective Subsidiaries to assign, any accounts or other right to receive income; *excluding, however,* from the operation of the foregoing restrictions the following:

     (1)   Permitted Liens;

     (2)   the Liens described in Schedule L, and the extension, renewal or replacement of such Liens upon or in the same properties subject thereto in connection with the extension, renewal or replacement (without increase of the principal amount) of the Indebtedness secured thereby;

     (3)   Liens created by leases permitted by [lease covenant];

     (4)   purchase money Liens upon or in one or more items of personal property or Real Property acquired or held by the Borrower or any of its Subsidiaries in the ordinary course of business to secure Indebtedness incurred solely for the purpose of financing the acquisition, construction or improvement of any such property to be subject to such Liens, or Liens existing on any such property at the time of acquisi-

tion, or extensions, renewals or replacements of any of the foregoing for the same or a lesser amount; *provided, however,* that no such Lien shall extend to or cover any property other than the property being acquired, constructed or improved, and no such extension, renewal or replacement shall extend to or cover any property not theretofore subject to the Lien or Liens being extended, renewed or replaced; and *provided further* that the aggregate principal amount of the Indebtedness at any one time outstanding secured by Liens permitted by this clause (4) shall not exceed $50 million; and

(5) iens not otherwise permitted by this Section that secure Indebtedness in an aggregate principal amount at any time outstanding not to exceed $10 million.

Sample 12-F *Negative Pledge—Credit Agreement Version 2*

Negative Covenants. So long as any Loan shall remain unpaid or any Bank shall have any Commitment hereunder, the Borrower will not, without the written consent of the Majority Banks:

(a) *Liens, Etc.* Create or suffer to exist, or permit any of its subsidiaries to create or suffer to exist, any lien, security interest or other charge or encumbrance, or any other type of preferential arrangement, upon or with respect to any of its properties, whether now owned or hereafter acquired, or assign, or permit any of its subsidiaries to assign, any right to receive income, in each case to secure or provide for the payment of any Debt of any Person, other than (i) purchase money liens or purchase money security interests upon or in any property acquired or held by the Borrower or any subsidiary in the ordinary course of business to secure the purchase price of such property or to secure indebtedness incurred solely for the purpose of financing the acquisition of such property, or (ii) liens or security interests existing on such property at the time of its acquisition (other than any such lien or security interest created in contemplation of such acquisition), *provided* that the aggregate principal amount of the indebtedness secured by the liens or security interests referred to in clauses (i) and (ii) above shall not exceed $10 million at any time outstanding.

Sample 12-G *Negative Pledge—Credit Agreement Version 3*

"*Lien*" means any lien, security interest or other charge or encumbrance of any kind, or any other type of preferential arrangement, including, without limitation, the lien or retained security title of a conditional vendor and any easement, right of way or other encumbrance on title to real property.

Limitation on Liens. The Company will not, nor will it permit any of its Subsidiaries to, create, incur, assume or suffer to exist, any Lien upon any of its property, assets or revenues, whether now owned or hereafter acquired, except:

(a)   Liens imposed by any governmental authority for taxes, assessments or charges not yet due or which are being contested in good faith and by appropriate proceedings if adequate reserves with respect thereto are maintained on the books of the Company or any of its Subsidiaries, as the case may be, in accordance with GAAP;

(b)   carriers', warehousemen's, mechanics', materialmen's, repairmen's or other like liens arising in the ordinary course of business which are not overdue for a period of more than thirty days or which are being contested in good faith and by appropriate proceedings;

(c)   pledges or deposits under worker's compensation, unemployment insurance and other social security legislation;

(d)   deposits to secure the performance of bids, trade contracts (other than for borrowed money), leases, statutory obligations, surety and appeal bonds, performance bonds and other obligations of a like nature incurred in the ordinary course of business;

(e)   easements, rights-of-way, restrictions and other similar encumbrances incurred in the ordinary course of business and encumbrances consisting of zoning restrictions, easements, licenses, restrictions on the use of property or minor imperfections in title thereto which, in the aggregate, are not material in amount, and which do not in any case materially detract from the value of the property subject thereto or interfere with the ordinary conduct of the business of the Company or any of its Subsidiaries;

(f)   Liens on assets of corporations which become Subsidiaries of the Company after the date of this Agreement, provided that such Liens are in existence at the time the respective corporations become Subsidiaries of the Company and were not created in anticipation thereof;

(g)   Liens upon real and/or tangible personal property acquired after the date hereof (by purchase, construction or otherwise) by the

Company or any of its Subsidiaries, each of which Liens either (A) existed on such property before the time of its acquisition and was not created in anticipation thereof, or (B) was created solely for the purpose of securing Indebtedness representing, or incurred to finance, refinance or refund, the cost (including the cost of construction) of the respective property; provided that no such Lien shall extend to or cover any property of the Company or such Subsidiary other than the respective property so acquired and improvements thereon; and provided, further that the principal amount of Indebtedness secured by any such Lien shall at no time exceed 100% of the fair market value (as determined in good faith by a senior financial officer of the Company) of the respective property at the time it was acquired (by purchase, construction or otherwise);

(h)   additional Liens upon real and/or personal property created after the date hereof, provided that the aggregate Indebtedness secured thereby and incurred on and after the date hereof shall not exceed $500,000 in the aggregate at any one time outstanding; and

(i)   any extension, renewal or replacement of the foregoing, provided, however, that the Liens permitted hereunder shall not be spread to cover any additional Indebtedness or property (other than a substitution of like property).

Sample 12-H *Negative Pledge—Credit Agreement Version 4*

"*Lien*" shall mean, with respect to any asset, any mortgage, lien, pledge, charge, security interest or encumbrance of any kind in respect of such asset. For the purposes of this Agreement, a Person shall be deemed to own subject to a Lien any asset which it has acquired or holds subject to the interest of a vendor or lessor under any conditional sale agreement, capital lease or other title retention agreement relating to such asset.

Negative Pledge. The Borrower will not, and will not permit any of its Restricted Subsidiaries to, create, assume or suffer to exist any Lien securing Debt on any asset now owned or hereafter acquired by it, except:

(a)   any Lien existing on any asset of any corporation at the time such corporation becomes a Restricted Subsidiary and not created in contemplation of such event;

(b)   any Lien on any asset securing Debt incurred or assumed for the purpose of financing all or any part of the cost of acquiring such asset, *provided* that such Lien attaches to such asset concurrently with or within ninety days after the acquisition thereof;

(c)   any Lien on any improvements constructed on any property of the Borrower or any such Restricted Subsidiary and any theretofore unimproved real property on which such improvements are located securing Debt incurred for the purpose of financing all or any part of the cost of constructing such improvements, *provided* that such Lien attaches to such improvements within ninety days after the later of (1) completion of construction of such improvements and (2) commencement of full operation of such improvements;

(d)   any Lien existing on any asset prior to the acquisition thereof by the Borrower or a Restricted Subsidiary and not created in contemplation of such acquisition;

(e)   any Lien arising out of the refinancing, extension, renewal or refunding of any Debt secured by any Lien permitted by any of the foregoing clauses of this Section, *provided* that such Debt is not increased and is not secured by any additional assets;

(f)   Liens created in connection with the sale or pledge of Receivables; and

(g)   Liens not otherwise permitted by the foregoing clauses of this Section securing Debt in an aggregate principal amount at any time outstanding not to exceed $100 million.

Sample 12-I *Debt Covenant—Leverage Ratio*

"*Debt*" means (i) indebtedness for borrowed money, (ii) obligations evidenced by bonds, debentures, notes or other similar instruments, (iii) obligations to pay the deferred purchase price of property or services, (iv) obligations as lessee under leases which shall have been or should be, in accordance with generally accepted accounting principles, recorded as capital leases, and (v) obligations under direct or indirect guaranties in respect of, and obligations (contingent or otherwise) to purchase or otherwise acquire, or otherwise to assure a creditor against loss in respect of, indebtedness or obligations of others of the kinds referred to in clauses (i) through (iv) above.

Debt. The Borrower will not create or suffer to exist, or permit any of its subsidiaries to create or suffer to exist, any Debt if, immediately after giving effect to such Debt and the receipt and application of any proceeds thereof, the ratio of the aggregate amount of Debt of the Borrower and its subsidiaries, on a consolidated basis, to the aggregate amount of total tangible assets of the Borrower and its subsidiaries, on a consolidated basis, would be greater than .50 to 1.00.

Sample 12-J   *Debt Covenant—Credit Agreement Version 1*

"*Guarantee*" shall mean a guarantee, an endorsement, a contingent agreement to purchase or to furnish funds for the payment or maintenance of, or otherwise to be or become contingently liable under or with respect to, the Indebtedness, other obligations, net worth, working capital or earnings of any Person, or a guarantee of the payment of dividends or other distributions upon the stock of any corporation, or an agreement to purchase, sell or lease (as lessee or lessor) property, products, materials, supplies or services primarily for the purpose of enabling a debtor to make payment of his, her or its obligations or an agreement to assure a creditor against loss, and including without limitation, causing a bank to open a letter of credit for the benefit of another Person, but excluding endorsements for collection or deposit in the ordinary course of business. The terms "*Guarantee*" and "*Guaranteed*" used as a verb shall have a correlative meaning.

"*Indebtedness*" shall mean, as to any Person: (a) indebtedness created, issued or incurred by such Person for borrowed money (whether by loan or the issuance and sale of debt securities); (b) obligations of such Person to pay the deferred purchase or acquisition price of property or services, other than trade accounts payable (other than for borrowed money) arising, and accrued expenses incurred, in the ordinary course of business; (c) indebtedness of others secured by a Lien on the property of such Person, whether or not the respective indebtedness so secured has been assumed by such Person; (d) obligations of such Person in respect of letters of credit or similar instruments issued or accepted by banks and other financial institutions for the account of such Person; (e) Capital Lease Obligations of such Person; (f) indebtedness of others Guaranteed by such Person; and (g) obligations of such Person in respect of Interest Rate Protection Agreements.

"*Interest Rate Protection Agreement*" shall mean an interest rate swap, cap or collar agreement or similar arrangement between any Person and a financial institution providing for the transfer or mitigation of interest risks either generally or under specific contingencies. For purposes hereof, the "*exposure*" at any time of any Person under an Interest Rate Protection Agreement to which such Person is a party shall be determined at such time in accordance with the standard methods of calculating such exposure under similar arrangements as prescribed from time to time by the Agent, taking into account the respective termination provisions set forth therein.

"*Subordinated Indebtedness*" shall mean, Indebtedness for which the Company is directly and primarily liable, in respect of which none of its Subsidiaries is contingently or otherwise obligated, and which is subordinated to the obligations of the Company to pay principal of and interest on the Loans and the Notes hereunder on terms, and which contains other terms (including interest, amortization and financial covenants), in form and substance satisfactory to the Majority Banks.

Indebtedness. The Company will not, and will not permit any of its Subsidiaries to, create, incur or suffer to exist any Indebtedness except:

(a)   Indebtedness to the Banks hereunder;

(b)   Indebtedness outstanding on the date hereof and listed in Schedule I hereto;

(c)   Indebtedness under Interest Rate Protection Agreements so long as the aggregate exposure under all Interest Rate Protection Agreements calculated at the time any Interest Rate Protection Agreement is entered into does not exceed $20 million;

(d)   Subordinated Indebtedness;

(e)   Indebtedness of Subsidiaries of the Company to the Company or to other Subsidiaries of the Company;

(f)   Indebtedness of the Company and its Subsidiaries secured by Liens permitted under [lien covenant] up to but not exceeding $5 million at any one time outstanding; and

(g)   additional Indebtedness of the Company up to but not exceeding $5 million at any one time outstanding.

Sample 12-K *Debt Covenant—Credit Agreement Version 2*

"Guarantee" of or by any person shall mean any obligation, contingent or otherwise, of such person guaranteeing or having the economic effect of guaranteeing any Indebtedness of any other person (the "primary obligor") in any manner, whether directly or indirectly, and including any obligation of such person, direct or indirect, (a) to purchase or pay (or advance or supply funds for the purchase or payment of) such Indebtedness or to purchase (or to advance or supply funds for the purchase of) any security for the payment of such Indebtedness, (b) to purchase property, securities or services for the purpose of assuring the owner of such Indebtedness of the payment of such Indebtedness or (c) to maintain working capital, equity capital or other financial statement condition or liquidity of the primary obligor so as to enable the primary obligor to pay such Indebtedness; *provided, however,* that the term Guarantee shall not include endorsements for collection or deposit, in either case in the ordinary course of business.

"Indebtedness" of any person shall mean, without duplication, (a) all obligations of such person for borrowed money or with respect to deposits or advances of any kind (other than deposits or advance payments on contracts entered into in the ordinary course of business), (b) all obligations of such

person evidenced by bonds, debentures, notes or similar instruments, (c) all obligations of such person under conditional sale or other title retention arrangements relating to property or assets purchased by such person (but in no event including operating leases), (d) all obligations of such person issued or assumed as the deferred purchase price of property or services (other than trade accounts payable and deferred compensation to officers and employees in the ordinary course of business), (e) all Indebtedness of others secured by (or for which the holder of such Indebtedness has an existing right, contingent or otherwise, to be secured by) any Lien on property owned or acquired by such person, whether or not the obligations secured thereby have been assumed, (f) all Guarantees by such person of Indebtedness of others, (g) all Capital Lease Obligations of such person, (h) all obligations of such person in respect of interest rate protection agreements, foreign currency exchange agreements or other interest or exchange rate hedging arrangements (the amount of any such obligation to be the amount that would be payable upon the acceleration, termination or liquidation thereof) and (i) all obligations, contingent or otherwise, of such person as an account party in respect of letters of credit and bankers' acceptances. The Indebtedness of any person (i) shall include the Indebtedness of any partnership in which such person is a general partner but (ii) shall not include the Indebtedness of such person to any of its subsidiaries or of any such subsidiary to such person or any other such subsidiary.

Negative Covenants. The Borrower covenants and agrees with each Lender that, so long as this Agreement shall remain in effect or the principal of or interest on any Loan, any Fees or any other expenses or amounts payable under any Loan Document shall be unpaid, unless the Required Lenders shall otherwise consent in writing, it will not, and will not cause or permit any of the Subsidiaries (or, to the extent the covenants set forth below are expressly so limited, any of the Restricted Subsidiaries) to:

Indebtedness. (a) Incur, create, assume or permit to exist any Indebtedness, except:

    (i)   Indebtedness existing of the date hereof and set forth in Schedule I or reflected on the most recent balance sheet of the Borrower referred to in [financial statement representation] (*provided* that no additional Subsidiary shall become liable for any such Indebtedness);

    (ii)   Indebtedness the proceeds of which are used to refinance any Indebtedness permitted under clause (i) above so long as (A) the obligor or obligors in respect of such refinancing Indebtedness are the same as those in respect of the Indebtedness being refinanced, (B) the principal amount of such refinancing Indebtedness does not exceed that of the Indebtedness being refinanced and (C) in the case of any Indebtedness being refinanced which is subordinated in whole or in part to the obligations of the Borrower hereunder, such refinancing Indebtedness shall be subordinated to such obligations to at least the same extent as the Indebtedness being refinanced, shall mature or be required to be prepaid, redeemed or repurchased no earlier than the Revolving Credit Maturity Date and shall be on terms no less favorable to the Lenders than the Indebtedness being refinanced, and the Borrower shall have notified the Administrative Agent of such refinancing and furnished to the Administrative Agent a copy of each agreement or instrument governing the refinancing Indebtedness;

(iii) Indebtedness represented by the Loans made under this Agreement;

(iv) Indebtedness of the Borrower and its Subsidiaries not permitted by the foregoing clauses of this Section so long as the aggregate amount of such Indebtedness does not exceed $100 million; and

(v) any Indebtedness created or deemed to be created in connection with any Receivables Facility; provided; however, that the holders of such Indebtedness have recourse only to the accounts receivable and related assets transferred pursuant to such Receivables Facility.

(b) Pay or prepay any principal of, or redeem, defease or acquire, any Indebtedness, or amend the terms of the Subordinated Indebtedness in a manner adverse to the rights or interests of the Lenders; *provided* that the Subordinated Indebtedness may be refinanced in accordance with clause (ii) of paragraph (a) of this Section.

Sample 12-L *Debt Covenant—High-Yield Indenture*

The Company will not, and will not permit any of its Subsidiaries to, create, issue, incur, assume, guarantee or otherwise in any manner become directly or indirectly liable for the payment of or otherwise incur (collectively, "incur"), any Indebtedness (including any Acquired Indebtedness but excluding Permitted Indebtedness) unless the Company's Consolidated Fixed Charge Coverage Ratio for the four full fiscal quarters immediately preceding the incurrence of such Indebtedness, taken as one period (and after giving pro forma effect to (i) the incurrence of such Indebtedness and (if applicable) the application of the net proceeds therefrom, including to refinance other Indebtedness, as if such Indebtedness was incurred, and the application of such proceeds occurred, on the first day of such applicable period; (ii) the incurrence, repayment or retirement of any other Indebtedness by the Company and its Subsidiaries since the first day of such applicable period as if such Indebtedness was incurred, repaid or retired at the beginning of such applicable period (except that, in making such computation, the amount of Indebtedness under any revolving credit facility shall be computed based upon the average daily balance of such Indebtedness during such applicable period); (iii) in the case of Acquired Indebtedness or any acquisition occurring at the time of the incurrence of such Indebtedness, the related acquisition, assuming such acquisition had been consummated on the first day of such applicable period; and (iv) any acquisition or disposition by the Company and its Subsidiaries of any company or any business or any assets out of the ordinary course of business, whether by merger, stock purchase or asset purchase or sale, or any related repayment of Indebtedness, in each case since the first day of such applicable period, assuming such acquisition or disposition had been consummated on the first day of such applicable period) is at least equal to or greater than 2.15:1.0x.

"Permitted Indebtedness" means any of the following:

(a) Indebtedness under any revolving line of credit in an aggregate principal amount not to exceed at any time outstanding the excess of (x) US$100 million (or, to the extent non-US dollar denominated, the US Dollar Equivalent of such amount) over (y) the US Dollar Equivalent of the amount of financing provided for in the documentation in respect of any Permitted Receivables Financing;

(b) Indebtedness pursuant to the Notes;

(c) Indebtedness outstanding on the date of the Indenture;

(d) Indebtedness owing to any wholly owned Restricted Subsidiary; *provided* that any Indebtedness of the Company owing to any such Restricted Subsidiary is subordinated in right of payment from and after such time as the Notes shall become due and payable (whether at Stated Maturity, acceleration or otherwise) to the payment and performance of the Company's obligations under the Notes; *provided further* that any disposition, pledge or transfer of any such Indebtedness to a Person (other than a disposition, pledge or transfer to the Company or another wholly owned Restricted Subsidiary) shall be deemed to be an incurrence of such Indebtedness not permitted by this clause (d);

(e) Indebtedness of the Company under Interest Rate Agreements relating to Indebtedness of the Company otherwise permitted under the Indenture that are entered into for the purpose of protecting against fluctuations in interest rates in respect of such Indebtedness and not for speculative purposes;

(f)   Indebtedness of the Company under Currency Agreements, provided that (x) such Currency Agreements relate to Indebtedness otherwise permitted under the Indenture or the purchase price of goods purchased or sold by the Company in the ordinary course of its business and (y) such Currency Agreements do not increase the Indebtedness or other obligations of the Company outstanding other than as a result of fluctuations in foreign currency exchange rates or by reason of fees, indemnities and compensation payable thereunder;

(g)   Capitalized Lease Obligations, the aggregate amount of which (including any refinancings thereof) does not exceed US$150 million (or, to the extent non-US dollar denominated, the US Dollar Equivalent of such amount) at any one time outstanding;

(h)   Indebtedness in respect of performance, surety or appeal bonds provided in the ordinary course of business;

(i)   the incurrence of Indebtedness which serves to refund, refinance or replace (each such incurrence, for purposes of this clause, a "refinancing") any Indebtedness as permitted under the first paragraph above (other than Permitted Indebtedness) and clauses (b) and (c) above, so long as (i) any such new Indebtedness shall be in a principal amount that does not exceed the principal amount (or, if such Indebtedness being refinanced provides for an amount less than the principal amount thereof to be due and payable upon a declaration of acceleration thereof, such lesser amount as of the date of determination) so refinanced, plus the amount of any premium required to be paid in connection with such refinancing pursuant to the original terms of the Indebtedness being refinanced or, if the original terms of such Indebtedness do not so provide, the amount of any premium reasonably determined by the Company as necessary to accomplish such refinancing, plus, in either case, the amount of reasonable expenses incurred by the Company in connection with such refinancing, (ii) in the case of any refinancing of Pari Passu Indebtedness or Subordinated Indebtedness, such new Indebtedness is (A) in the case of any refinancing of the Notes or Pari Passu Indebtedness, expressly made pari passu with or subordinate in right of payment to the Notes and (B) in the case of any refinancing of Subordinated Indebtedness, made subordinate to the Notes at least to the same extent as the Subordinated Indebtedness being refinanced, (iii) such new Indebtedness has an Average Life longer than the Average Life of the Indebtedness being refinanced and a final Stated Maturity later than the final Stated Maturity of the Indebtedness being refinanced and (iv) if the Indebtedness being refinanced is Indebtedness of the Company, the new Indebtedness cannot be incurred by a Restricted Subsidiary;

(j)   to the extent considered Indebtedness, contractual obligations arising under any Permitted Receivables Financing; and

(k)   Indebtedness of the Company in an aggregate principal amount not in excess of US$50 million (or, to the extent non-US dollar denominated, the US Dollar Equivalent of such amount) at any one time outstanding.

Sample 12-M   *Debt Covenant—Credit Agreement Version 3*

Indebtedness. None of the Obligors will, or will permit any of its Subsidiaries to, create, incur or suffer to exist after the Closing Date any Indebtedness except: (i) Indebtedness to the Lenders hereunder, (ii) the Equity Investor Group Notes, (iii) Subordinated Indebtedness and (iv) other Indebtedness in an aggregate amount at any time outstanding not to exceed $8 million.

Chapter 13:   General Business Covenants

See generally:
CAROLYN E.C. PARIS, HOW TO DRAFT FOR CORPORATE FINANCE ch. 8 (PLI 2006).

Regarding change of control and related issues, see generally:
CAROLYN E.C. PARIS, HOW TO DRAFT FOR CORPORATE FINANCE § 9:1.2 (PLI 2006).

Regarding "event risk" for bondholders:
As we've noted, holders of investment grade bonds with no "event risk" protection can find themselves in a pretty unenviable position when the formerly investment grade issuer is suddenly levered up in the course of an acquisition or recapitalization.
Debt-Driven Deals Shake Up Holders of Highly Rated Bonds, WALL ST. J., Feb. 8, 2007:

> Holders of highly rated bonds in companies like casino operator Harrah's Entertainment Inc. or energy firm Kinder Morgan Inc. have

seen their investments dropped in value overnight after private-equity shops launched bids for their companies.

[The article cites price drops for HCA of about 8% and for Kinder Morgan of about 9% at date of the announcement of acquisitions of these companies. In the case of Equity Office Properties bonds,] bondholders had some leverage against the company. They were protected by provisions in the debt, known as covenants, that limited the amount of new debt that EOP could take on in a buyout. . . . AIG Global Investment Group . . . banded together with other investors against the offer. By Jan. 11, EOP and Blackstone agreed to boost the offer to long-term bondholders by about 20%, paying nearly $950 million for the $725 million in outstanding bonds. . . .

In total, bondholders will be paid about $9 billion for their $8.4 billion in bonds. . . .

In many other cases, high-grade bondholders don't have these protections, making them vulnerable, even targets. . . . [B]ecause the bonds are high-grade and pay relatively low interest rates, they are appealing to buyout shops looking for companies that can bear more debt. . . .

Even with the [change of control] provisions, some bond investors are finding themselves vulnerable. This week, some bondholders in junk-rated Lear Corp. found themselves on the losing end of a buyout offer by Carl Icahn even though their bonds contained change-of-control provisions.

Lear had issued $900 million in bonds last November with terms that ensured the bonds would be paid off in full if ownership of the company changed—but not if certain "permitted holders" took control of it. These holders were defined elsewhere in the bond agreement as Mr. Icahn, his affiliates and funds controlled by him. As a result, prices of the newly issued bonds slumped on news of the buyout.

Examples of general business covenants:

Sample 13-A *Merger Provisions—Indenture (Investment-Grade)*

Merger. Nothing contained in this Indenture or in any of the Securities shall prevent any consolidation or merger of the Issuer into any other corporation or corporations (whether or not affiliated with the Issuer), or successive consolidations or mergers to which the Issuer or its respective successor or successors shall be a party or parties, or shall prevent any sale, lease or conveyance of the property of the Issuer as an entirety or substantially as an entirety; *provided*, that upon any such consolidation, merger, sale, or lease or conveyance to which the Issuer is a party and in which the Issuer is not the surviving corporation, the due and punctual performance and observance of all of the covenants and conditions of this Indenture to be performed or observed by the Issuer and the due and punctual payment of the principal of and interest on all of the Securities, according to their tenor, shall be expressly assumed by supplemental indenture satisfactory in form to the Trustee, executed and delivered to the Trustee, by the corporation formed by such consolidation, or into which the Issuer shall have been merged, or which shall have acquired such property.

Successor Corporation Substituted. In case of any such consolidation, merger, sale or conveyance, and following such an assumption by the successor corporation, such successor corporation shall succeed to and be substituted for the Issuer, with the same effect as if it had been named herein. Such successor corporation may cause to be signed, and may issue either in its own name or in the name of the Issuer prior to such succession any or all of the Securities issuable hereunder which theretofore shall not have been signed by the Issuer and delivered to the Trustee; and, upon the order of such successor corporation instead of the Issuer and subject to all the terms, conditions and limitations in this Indenture prescribed, the Trustee shall authenticate and shall deliver any Securities which previously shall have been signed and delivered by the officers of the Issuer to the Trustee for authentication, and any Securities which such successor corporation thereafter shall cause to be signed and delivered to the Trustee for that purpose. All of the Securities so issued shall in all respects have the same legal rank and benefit under this Indenture as the Securities theretofore or thereafter issued in accordance with the terms of this Indenture as though all of such Securities had been issued at the date of the execution hereof.

In case of any such consolidation, merger, sale, lease or conveyance such changes in phraseology and form (but not in substance) may be made in the Securities thereafter to be issued as may be appropriate.

In the event of any such sale or conveyance (other than a conveyance by way of lease) the Issuer or any successor corporation which shall theretofore have become such in the manner described in this Article shall be discharged from all obligations and covenants under this Indenture and the Securities and may be liquidated and dissolved.

Sample 13-B *Merger and Asset Sale Covenant— Credit Agreement Version 1*

Consolidations, Mergers and Sales of Assets. The Borrower will not (i) consolidate or merge with or into any other Person (other than a Subsidiary of the Borrower) or (ii) sell, lease or otherwise transfer, directly or indirectly, all or any substantial part of the assets of the Borrower and its Subsidiaries, taken as a whole, to any other Person.

Sample 13-C *Merger and Asset Sale Covenant—Credit Agreement Version 2*

The Borrower will not, and will not permit any of its Subsidiaries to, merge or consolidate with or into any Person, or sell all or substantially all of its assets to any Person, *except*:

(a) A merger of Borrower into a wholly-owned Subsidiary of Borrower that has nominal assets and liabilities, the primary purpose of which is to effect the reincorporation of Borrower in another state;

(b) Mergers or consolidations of a Subsidiary of Borrower into Borrower (with Borrower as the surviving corporation) or into any other wholly-owned Subsidiary of Borrower;

(c) Liquidations of any Subsidiary of Borrower into Borrower or into a wholly-owned Subsidiary of Borrower; or

(d) A merger of Borrower with another Person if (i) Borrower is the corporation surviving such merger, (ii) immediately after giving effect to such merger, no Default shall have occurred and be continuing, and (iii) immediately after giving effect to such merger, there shall have occurred no material diminution in Consolidated Tangible Net Worth, nor any material deterioration in the ratio of Senior Indebtedness to Adjusted Consolidated Tangible Net Worth, in each case from that existing immediately prior to the merger.

Sample 13-D *Merger and Asset Sale Covenant—Credit Agreement Version 3*

Consolidation, Merger or Disposition of Assets. The Company will not, and will not permit any of its Subsidiaries to become a party to any merger or consolidation other than mergers or consolidations of any Subsidiary of the Company into the Company (so long as the Company is the surviving corporation) or of any Subsidiary of the Company into any other Subsidiary of the Company, or otherwise take any action to effect the dissolution or liquidation of any such Person (other than Subsidiaries of the Company that are not Material Subsidiaries). The Company will not and will not permit any of its Subsidiaries to sell, lease or otherwise dispose of any of its assets except for (a) assets routinely sold in the ordinary course of business for fair and reasonable value in a manner consistent with past practice, both as to type of property sold and aggregate amount sold, (b) accounts receivable sold on a nonrecourse basis and otherwise in a manner that does not result in the incurrence of any Indebtedness and (c) other assets to the extent that the aggregate book value (at the time of disposition thereof) of all assets theretofore disposed of by the Company and its Subsidiaries subsequent to the Closing Date under this clause (c) plus the aggregate book value of all assets then proposed to be disposed of pursuant to this clause (c) does not exceed 10% of Consolidated Tangible Net Worth as of the end of the then most recently completed fiscal year.

Sample 13-E *Fundamental Changes Covenant*

Mergers, Consolidations, Sales of Assets and Acquisitions. Neither the Borrower nor any of its subsidiaries may merge into or consolidate with any other person, or permit any other person to merge into or consolidate with it, or sell, transfer, lease or otherwise dispose of any asset (whether now owned or hereafter acquired), or purchase, lease or otherwise acquire (in one transaction or a series of transactions) all or any substantial part of the assets of any other person, except that the Borrower and its subsidiaries may (a) consummate the Merger, (b) sell inventory in the ordinary course of business, (c) dispose of Cash Equivalents in the ordinary course of business, (d) sell for cash assets not useful in the operation of the business of the Borrower or one of its subsidiaries provided that any such sale is for a price not less than fair market value, (e) in each fiscal year, sell for cash assets whose fair market value in the aggregate does not exceed $1 million provided that any such sale is for a price not less than fair market value, (f) in the case of the Borrower, acquire any subsidiary to the extent permitted by [investment covenant], (g) acquire assets (other than capital stock) representing all or any substantial part of the assets of any other person to the extent permitted by [capital expenditures covenant], (h) in the case of any subsidiary of the Borrower, merge into the Borrower in a transaction in which the Borrower is the surviving corporation and (i) in the case of any subsidiary of the Borrower, merge into or consolidate with any other subsidiary of the Borrower. To the extent the Required Lenders (or such greater number of Lenders as may be required) waive the provisions of this Section with respect to the sale of any Collateral, or any Collateral is sold as permitted by this Section, such Collateral shall be sold free and clear of the Liens created by the Security Documents, and the Collateral Agent shall promptly take such actions at the expense of the Borrower as it reasonably deems appropriate in connection therewith or as the Borrower may reasonably request.

Sample 13-F *Fundamental Changes and Asset Sales Covenants*

Limitations on Fundamental Changes. The Borrower will not, and will not permit any of its Subsidiaries to, enter into any transaction of acquisition or merger or consolidation or amalgamation, or liquidate, wind up or dissolve itself (or suffer any liquidation or dissolution), or convey, sell, lease, assign, transfer or otherwise dispose of, all or substantially all of its property, business or assets, or make any material change in the present method of conducting business.

Limitation on Sale of Assets. The Borrower will not, and will not permit any of its Subsidiaries to, convey, sell, lease, assign, transfer or otherwise dispose of, any of its property, business or assets (including, without limitation, receivables and leasehold interests) whether now owned or hereafter acquired except:

(a)   obsolete or worn out property disposed of in the ordinary course of business;

(b)   the sale or other disposition of any property (other than inventory or Cash Equivalents) for cash, *provided* that if the Net Proceeds realized from any sales or other dispositions in any fiscal year are greater than $1 million, such Net Proceeds shall be applied to the prepayment of the Loans (or to provide cover for Letter of Credit Liabilities) as further provided in [mandatory prepayment provision]; and

(c)   the sale of inventory in the ordinary course of business and the sale of Cash Equivalents from time to time.

Sample 13-G *Merger and Asset Sale Covenant—Credit Agreement Version 4*

Consolidations, Mergers and Sales of Assets. (a) The Borrower will not (i) consolidate or merge with or into any other Person or (ii) sell, lease or otherwise transfer all or any substantial part of its assets to any other Person; *provided* that (x) the Borrower may merge with another Person if (1) the Borrower is the corporation surviving such merger and (2) immediately after giving effect to such merger, no Default shall have occurred and be continuing and (y) the Borrower may transfer assets as described in subsections (c) and (d) below. The Borrower will not permit any Significant Subsidiary to (i) consolidate or merge with or into, (ii) transfer assets constituting a substantial part of the assets of the Borrower and its Subsidiaries, taken as a whole, to, or (iii) issue any shares of its capital stock to, any Person other than the Borrower or a Wholly-Owned Consolidated Subsidiary; *provided* that (x) a Significant Subsidiary may merge with or into or issue shares to another Person if (A) the percentage of each class of the surviving corporation's capital stock owned directly or indirectly by the Borrower is not less than the percentage of such Significant Subsidiary's capital stock previously so owned and (B) immediately after giving effect to such merger or issuance, no Default shall have occurred and be continuing and (y) a Significant Subsidiary may transfer assets as described in subsections (c) and (d).

(b) Neither the Borrower nor any Subsidiary shall, directly or indirectly, sell or otherwise dispose of the whole of, or any integral part of, any of its operating businesses now owned or hereafter built, acquired or formed or commenced by the Borrower or any Subsidiary; *provided* the foregoing shall not prohibit (1) any merger of the Borrower specifically permitted under subsection (a) above, (2) any consolidation or merger by any Subsidiary with or into, or transfer of assets of a Subsidiary to, the Borrower or a Wholly-Owned Consolidated Subsidiary, (3) any merger of a Subsidiary into another Person if (A) the percentage of each class of the surviving corporation's capital stock owned directly or indirectly by the Borrower is not less than the percentage of such Subsidiary's capital stock previously so owned and (B) immediately after giving effect to such merger, no Default shall have occurred and be continuing, or (4) any transfer of assets by the Borrower or a Subsidiary described in subsections (c) and (d) below.

(c) The Borrower shall not, and shall not permit any Subsidiary to, sell, pledge, assign or otherwise dispose of any Accounts (as defined in the Security Agreement) other than pursuant to the Security Agreement; *provided* that the Borrower and its Subsidiaries may sell or assign Accounts receivable from payors located in jurisdictions outside the United States; *provided further* that the aggregate outstanding amount of all such Accounts sold shall not at any time exceed $15 million.

(d) Notwithstanding the foregoing provisions of subsections (a) and (b), the Borrower or its Subsidiaries may make Asset Dispositions having a fair market value not in excess of $5 million in aggregate for all such Asset Dispositions occurring after the date hereof, *provided* that each such Asset Disposition is approved by the board of directors of the Borrower and is on an arm's-length fair market value basis.

"Asset Disposition" means any sale, lease, transfer or other disposition of assets (each referred to for the purposes of this definition as a "disposition") by the Borrower or any of its Subsidiaries other than (1) a disposition by a Subsidiary or the Borrower of the type described in clauses (1) through (3) of subsection (b) or (2) a disposition of assets in the ordinary course of business, including, without limitation, (i) dispositions of inventory in the ordinary course of business, (ii) dispositions of surplus or obsolete equipment in the ordinary course of business, (iii) dispositions of Temporary Cash Investments or cash and (iv) sales of Accounts (as defined in the Security Agreement) permitted by subsection (c).

Sample 13-H *Asset Sales Covenant and Merger Provisions— Indenture (High-Yield)*

Limitation on Subsidiary Mergers; Sales of Assets and Subsidiary Stock. (a) The Company will not dispose of the Capital Stock of any of its Subsidiaries or any other property or assets of the Company and will not permit any of its Subsidiaries to merge or consolidate with any Person or dispose of any Capital Stock of any of its Subsidiaries or any other property or assets, except for the following transactions, (i) the merger or consolidation of any Subsidiary of the Company with or into, or the disposition of any assets or Capital Stock of any Subsidiary of the Company to, the Company or any Wholly-Owned Subsidiary of the Company; *provided* that if the Subsidiary of the Company merging into, or disposing of any assets or Capital Stock of any other Subsidiary of the Company to, the Company or any Wholly-Owned Subsidiary of the Company is a Guarantor, such Wholly-Owned Subsidiary is or becomes a Guarantor in connection therewith; *provided* that the Company may dispose of its property and assets to Subsidiaries that are not Foreign Subsidiaries, (ii) the disposition by the Company or any of its Subsidiaries of any of its property or assets in the ordinary course of business, and (iii) except as provided in clause (i) above, the merger or consolidation of any Subsidiary of the Company with or into any Person or the disposition by the Company or any Subsidiary of the Company of the Capital Stock of any Subsidiary of the Company (whether by primary or secondary sale) or any property or assets of the Company or any Subsidiary of the Company outside of the ordinary course of business, so long as within six months following such merger, consolidation or disposition (or, in the case of installment notes or other deferred payment arrangements, within six months of the receipt of cash proceeds therefrom), the Company or such Subsidiary utilizes the Net Cash Proceeds from the transaction for purposes of repaying (and, to the extent of revolving commitments, permanently reducing) Senior Indebtedness; *provided* that the Company shall not be required to apply the Net Cash Proceeds in accordance with clause (iii) above except to the extent that the aggregate Net Cash Proceeds from all Asset Sales which are not so applied in accordance with this proviso exceed $25 million in any fiscal year; *provided, further*, that (x) to the extent that any or all of the Net Cash Proceeds of any Foreign Asset Sale are prohibited or delayed by applicable local law from being repatriated to the United States, the portion of such Net Cash Proceeds so affected will not be required to be applied to repay Senior Indebtedness at the time provided above but may be retained by the applicable Subsidiary so long, but only so long, as the applicable local law will not permit repatriation to the United States; and (y) to the extent that the Company has determined in good faith that repatriation of any or all of the Net Cash Proceeds of any Foreign Asset Sale would have a material adverse tax cost consequence, the Net Cash Proceeds so affected may be retained by the applicable Subsidiary for so long as such material adverse tax cost event would continue. In the event that the Net Cash Proceeds required to be applied to repay Senior Indebtedness are not so fully utilized in accordance with the immediately preceding sentence within six months following such merger, consolidation or disposition (or in the case of installment notes or other deferred payment arrangements, within six months of receipt of the proceeds therefrom), the Company shall make an offer to purchase outstanding Securities and other Indebtedness ranking pari passu with the Securities (the "Offer Securities") (a "Net Proceeds Offer"), and shall purchase from holders of Offer Securities accepting such offer (in accordance with the procedures set forth in paragraph (b), on a pro rata basis, Offer Securities in an aggregate principal amount equal to the Net Cash Proceeds remaining after any such required application at a purchase price equal to 100% of the principal amount of the Offer Securities, plus, in each case, accrued interest to the date fixed for payment therefor (which date shall not be later than thirty Business Days after the date of mailing of the notice of the Net Proceeds Offer) (the "Net Proceeds Payment Date"); *provided, further*, that the Company may defer the Net Proceeds Offer until the aggregate Net Cash Proceeds to be so applied equals or exceeds $10 million. Notwithstanding anything to the contrary contained herein, the Company shall not dispose of property or assets comprising all or substantially all of the properties or assets of the Company unless such disposition is made in compliance with the provisions of Article X and any disposition made in accordance with Article X shall not be subject to the provisions of this Section.

(b)   At least fifteen Business Days prior to the Company's mailing of a notice of a Net Proceeds Offer, the Company shall notify the Trustee of the Company's obligation to make such Net Proceeds Offer. Notice of a Net Proceeds Offer shall be mailed by the Company not less than twenty Business Days nor more than thirty Business Days before the Net Proceeds Payment Date to the Holders of the Offer Securities at their last registered addresses with a copy to the Trustee and the Paying Agent. The Net Proceeds Offer shall remain open from the time of mailing until the Net Proceeds Payment Date. The notice shall contain all instructions and materials necessary to enable such Holders to tender Securities pursuant to the Net Proceeds Offer. The notice, which shall govern the terms of the Net Proceeds Offer, shall state:

(1) that the Net Proceeds Offer is being made pursuant to this Section and that Offer Securities will be accepted for payment on a pro rata basis (rounded to the nearest $1,000), if necessary;

(2) the purchase price and the Net Proceeds Payment Date;

(3) that any Offer Security not tendered or accepted for payment will continue to accrue interest or accrete value (as applicable);

(4) that any Offer Security accepted for payment pursuant to the Net Proceeds Offer shall cease to accrue interest or accrete value (as applicable) after the Net Proceeds Payment Date;

(5) that each Holder of a Security which is an Offer Security electing to have such Offer Security purchased pursuant to a Net Proceeds Offer will be required to surrender the Offer Security, with the form entitled "Option of Holder to Elect Purchase" on the reverse of the Offer Security completed, to the Trustee at the address specified in the notice prior to the close of business on the Business Day prior to the Net Proceeds Payment Date;

(6) that Holders will be entitled to withdraw their election if the Trustee receives, not later than the close of business on the fifth Business Day next preceding the Net Proceeds Payment Date, a telegram, telex, facsimile transmission or letter setting forth the name of the Holder, the principal amount of Offer Securities the Holder delivered for purchase and a statement that such Holder is withdrawing his election to have such Offer Securities purchased; and

(7) that Holders whose Offer Securities are purchased only in part will be issued new Securities of the same series equal in principal amount to the unpurchased portion of the Offer Securities surrendered.

On the Net Proceeds Payment Date, the Company shall (i) accept for payment on a pro rata basis (if necessary) Offer Securities or portions thereof tendered pursuant to the Net Proceeds Offer, (ii) deposit with the Paying Agent money sufficient to pay the purchase price of all Securities or portions thereof so accepted and (iii) deliver or cause to be delivered to the Trustee all Securities so accepted together with an Officers' Certificate stating the Securities or portions thereof accepted for payment by the Company. The Paying Agent shall promptly mail or deliver to Holders of Securities so accepted, payment in an amount equal to the purchase price, and the Trustee shall promptly authenticate and mail or deliver to such Holders a new Security equal in principal amount to any unpurchased portion of the Security surrendered. For purposes of any proration pursuant to this paragraph, all series of Offer Securities shall be treated as one series with no distinction among series of Offer Securities. Any Securities not so accepted shall be promptly mailed or delivered by the Company to the Holder thereof. The Company will publicly announce the results of the Net Proceeds Offer on or as soon as practicable after the Net Proceeds Payment Date. For purposes of this Section, the Trustee shall act as the Paying Agent.

"Net Cash Proceeds" means, with respect to any Asset Sale, the proceeds thereof in the form of cash or Cash Equivalents including payments in respect of deferred payment obligations when received in the form of, or stock or other assets when disposed for, cash or Cash Equivalents (except to the extent that such obligations are financed or sold with recourse to the Company or any Restricted Subsidiary), net of (i) brokerage commissions and other fees and expenses (including fees and expenses of legal counsel and investment banks) related to such Asset Sale, (ii) provisions for all taxes payable as a result of such Asset Sale, (iii) payments made to retire Indebtedness where payment of such Indebtedness is secured by the assets or properties the subject of such Asset Sale, (iv) amounts required to be paid to any Person (other than the Company or any Restricted Subsidiary) owning a beneficial interest in the assets subject to the Asset Sale and (v) appropriate amounts to be provided by the Company or any Restricted Subsidiary, as the case may be, as a reserve, whether or not required by GAAP, against any liabilities associated with such Asset Sale and retained by the Company or any Restricted Subsidiary, as the case may be, after such Asset Sale, including, without limitation, pension and other post-employment benefit liabilities, liabilities related to environmental matters and liabilities under any indemnification obligations associated with such Asset Sale, all as reflected in an Officers' Certificate delivered to the Trustee.

"Asset Sale" means any sale, issuance, conveyance, transfer, lease or other disposition (including, without limitation, by way of merger, consolidation or sale and leaseback transaction) (collectively, a "transfer"), directly or indirectly, in one or a series of related transactions, of (a) any Capital Stock of any Restricted Subsidiary; (b) all or substantially all of the properties and assets of any division or line of business of the Company or its Restricted Subsidiaries; or (c) any other properties or assets of the Company or any Restricted Subsidiary, other than in the ordinary course of business. For the purpose of this definition, the term "Asset Sale" shall not include any transfer of properties or assets (i) that is governed by the provisions of Article X, (ii) between or among the Company and any wholly owned Restricted Subsidiaries in accordance with the terms of the Indenture, (iii) having a Fair Market Value of not more than US$500,000 (or, to the extent non-US dollar denominated, the US Dollar Equivalent of such amount) in any given fiscal year, (iv) by the Company or any Restricted Subsidiary of damaged, worn out or other obsolete property or assets in the ordinary course of business, (v) that is permitted to be made, and is made, under paragraph (a) of the [restricted payments covenant] or (vi) that is permitted to be made, and is made, pursuant to the definition of "Permitted Investments."

Successor Corporation

When the Company May Merge, etc. The Company shall not consolidate with or merge with or into or sell, assign, transfer or lease all or substantially all of its properties and assets as an entirety to any Person (other than a Subsidiary), or permit any Person (other than a Subsidiary) to merge with or into the Company unless:

(1)   the Company shall be the continuing Person, or the Person (if other than the Company) formed by such consolidation or into which the Company is merged or to which the properties and assets of the Company substantially as an entirety are transferred (the "surviving entity") shall be a corporation organized and existing under the laws of the United States or any State thereof or the District of Columbia and shall expressly assume, by an indenture supplemental hereto, executed and delivered to the Trustee, in form satisfactory to the Trustee, all the obligations of the Company under the Securities and this Indenture, and this Indenture remains in full force and effect;

(2)   immediately before and immediately after giving effect to such transaction, no Event of Default and no Default shall have occurred and be continuing and the Company (or the surviving entity if the Company is not the continuing obligor hereunder), giving effect to such transaction, could incur $1 of additional Indebtedness under the [coverage test] of [the debt incurrence test];

(3)   immediately after giving effect to such transaction on a pro forma basis, the Adjusted Consolidated Net Worth of the Company (or

the surviving entity if the Company is not continuing) is at least equal to the Adjusted Consolidated Net Worth of the Company immediately before such transaction; and

(4)   immediately after giving effect to such transaction on a pro forma basis, the Consolidated Fixed Charge Ratio of the Company (or of the surviving entity if the Company is not continuing) is at least 4 to 1, or if the Consolidated Fixed Charge Ratio of the Company prior to such transaction is within the range set forth in Column A below, then the Consolidated Fixed Charge Ratio of the Company or the surviving entity, as the case may be, giving effect to such transaction shall be at least equal to the percentage set forth in Column B below of such prior Consolidated Fixed Charge Ratio of the Company.

A	B
equal to or greater than 2 to 1, but less than 2.5 to 1	90%
equal to or greater than 2.5 to 1, but less than 3 to 1	80%
equal to or greater than 3 to 1, but less than 3.5 to 1	70%
equal to or greater than 3.5 to 1, but less than 4 to 1	60%

In connection with any consolidation, merger, transfer or lease contemplated by this Section, the Company shall deliver, or cause to be delivered, to the Trustee, in form and substance reasonably satisfactory to the Trustee, an Officers' Certificate and an Opinion of Counsel, each stating that such consolidation, merger, transfer or lease and the supplemental indenture in respect thereto comply with this Article and that all conditions precedent herein provided for relating to such transaction have been complied with.

Upon any consolidation or merger or any transfer of all or substantially all of the assets of the Company in accordance with this Section, the successor corporation formed by such consolidation or into which the Company is merged or to which such transfer is made, shall succeed to, and be substituted for, and may exercise every right and power of, the Company under this Indenture with the same effect as if such successor corporation had been named as the Company herein.

Sample 13-1 *Mandatory Prepayment Provision— Credit Agreement*

(b) *Mandatory Prepayments and Cover.*

  (1) *Borrowing Base.* The Borrower shall from time to time prepay the Working Capital Loans (or provide cover for Letter of Credit Liabilities as provided below) in such amounts as shall be necessary so that at all times the aggregate outstanding amount of the Working Capital Obligations shall be less than or equal to the Borrowing Base.

  (2) *Issuance of Shares and Indebtedness.* The Borrower shall prepay the Loans (or provide cover for Letter of Credit Liabilities as provided below) in the amount of and on the date of each receipt by the Borrower or any Subsidiary thereof of Net Proceeds from (x) issuance subsequent to the Closing Date of its shares (upon the exercise of options or otherwise) or (y) incurrence of any Funded Indebtedness not otherwise permitted under [debt covenant] to which the Majority Lenders have consented.

  (3) *Excess Cash Flow.* In the event that, for any fiscal year of the Borrower (commencing with the fiscal year ending on December 31, 1998), (x) Adjusted Cash Flow exceeds (y) to the extent paid in cash during such year, the sum (calculated without duplication) of (i) Scheduled Amortization, (ii) Interest Expense and (iii) Capital Expenditures, then the Borrower shall, on the first Quarterly Date following the end of such fiscal year, prepay the Loans (or provide cover for Letter of Credit Liabilities as provided below) in an amount equal to the remainder of 50% of such excess *minus* optional prepayments during such fiscal year pursuant to [optional prepayment provisions].

  (4) *Asset Dispositions.* The Borrower shall prepay the Loans (or provide cover for Letter of Credit Liabilities as provided below) in the amount of and on the date of each receipt by such Person or any of its Subsidiaries of (x) the Net Proceeds of any sale or other disposition of property pursuant to subsection (b) of [asset sale covenant], if and as required by such subsection (b).

Any payment by the Borrower pursuant to paragraph (2), (3) or (4) above shall be applied, *first,* to the Term Loans and *second,* to the Working Capital Loans or Letter of Credit Liabilities in accordance with this paragraph. If upon the occurrence of any event requiring a prepayment of Loans pursuant to paragraphs (2) through (4) above, a Lender waives the requirement that a portion of such prepayment be applied to its Tranche B Term Loans, any amounts that would otherwise have been so applied shall be applied in accordance with the other provisions of the preceding sentence. In the event that any Person shall be required pursuant to paragraphs (1) through (4) above to prepay any Working Capital Loans or provide cover for any Letter of Credit Liabilities, such Person shall, until the relevant Working Capital Loans have been paid in full, first prepay the principal of such Loans and then, following such payment in full, provide cover for the relevant Letter of Credit Liabilities. Cover for Letter of Credit Liabilities shall be effected by paying to the Administrative Agent immediately available funds, to be held by the Administrative Agent in the Collateral Account maintained pursuant to the Security Documents, in an amount equal to the required prepayment, which amount shall be retained by the Administrative Agent in such Collateral Account until such time as the Letters of Credit shall have been terminated and all of the Letter of Credit Liabilities paid in full; *provided* that if the Working Capital Commitments shall have been terminated, all other amounts payable hereunder shall have been paid in full and no Default shall have occurred and be continuing, the Administrative Agent shall from time to time upon the request of the Borrower return to the Borrower such portion of such amount as the Administrative Agent in its sole discretion determines is no longer needed to provide cover for Letter of Credit Liabilities and related fees and expenses payable under this Agreement.

Sample 13-J   *Covenant Restricting Dividends and Other Payments on Stock (Borrower and Subsidiaries)— Version 1*

"Restricted Payment" shall mean dividends (in cash, property or obligations) on, or other payments or distributions on account of, or the setting apart of money for a sinking or other analogous fund for the purchase, redemption, retirement or other acquisition of, any shares of the Borrower or any Subsidiary, or the exchange or conversion of any shares of the Borrower or any Subsidiary for or into any obligations of or shares, Subordinated Indebtedness or any other property, other than dividends payable solely in, or exchanges or conversions for or into, shares of the same class of the Borrower.

Restricted Payments. Neither the Borrower nor any Subsidiary will make any Restricted Payment *except*:

(a) Restricted Payments by a Subsidiary of Borrower to Borrower or to a wholly-owned Subsidiary of Borrower;

(b) Restricted Payments consisting of the stated cash dividends on the Preferred Stock;

(c) the Restricted Payment consisting of the Special Dividend;

(d) a Restricted Payment consisting of exchange of the Preferred Stock for the Exchange Subordinated Notes; and

(e) Restricted Payments (*other than* the Restricted Payments referred to in clauses (a) through (d) of this Section) if, giving effect thereto, the aggregate of all such Restricted Payments (*other than* the Restricted Payments referred to in clauses (a) through (d) of this Section) subsequent to the Closing Date would not exceed an amount equal to the sum of (i) $10 million plus (ii) an amount equal to 50% of Consolidated Net Income for the fiscal period commencing on January 1, 1998, through the last day of the Fiscal Quarter then most recently ended, computed on a cumulative basis for the said entire period (but in no event shall the amount calculated for purposes of this clause be less than zero), plus (iii) an amount equal to the sum of (A) the aggregate net cash proceeds received by Borrower from the issuance and sale of its capital stock subsequent to the Closing Date and (B) the aggregate amount by which shareholders' equity of Borrower and its Consolidated Subsidiaries shall have been increased upon the conversion after the Closing Date of any convertible debenture, note, bond or other similar security to common or preferred stock of Borrower.

Sample 13-K *Covenant Restricting Dividends and Other Payments on Stock (Borrower and Subsidiaries)— Version 2*

Distributions. The Company will not permit (x) any of its wholly owned Subsidiaries, directly or indirectly, to make or declare any Distribution other than Distributions to the Company or (y) any of its Subsidiaries that are not wholly owned, directly or indirectly, to make or declare any Distribution other than Distributions in which the Company receives its pro rata share thereof.

The Company will not make or declare any Distribution, *provided* that the Company may, from and after January 1, 1998, declare and pay cash dividends if:

(a) the aggregate amount of such cash dividends declared or paid shall not exceed the sum of (i) $10 million plus (ii) 50% of the Consolidated Net Income of the Company for each fiscal quarter of the Company beginning on or after January 1, 1998, in which the Company had a positive Consolidated Net Income minus (iii) 100% the amount of the Company's consolidated net loss for each fiscal quarter of the Company beginning on or after January 1, 1998, in which the Company had a consolidated net loss plus (iv) 100% of the proceeds of each issuance of the Company's capital stock occurring after the Closing Date, and

(b) no Default or Event of Default shall have occurred and be continuing at the time such cash dividend is to be declared or paid, and no Default or Event of Default shall result from the payment of such cash dividend.

Sample 13-L *Covenant Restricting Dividends and Other Payments on Stock (Borrower Only)*

Dividends and Distributions. The Borrower shall not declare or pay, directly or indirectly, any dividend or make any other distribution (by reduction of capital or otherwise), whether in cash, property, securities or a combination thereof, with respect to any shares of its capital stock or directly or indirectly redeem, purchase, retire or otherwise acquire for value any shares of any class of its capital stock or set aside any amount for any such purpose; *provided, however,* that the foregoing restriction shall not prohibit the Borrower from repurchasing its common stock or stock options from holders thereof that are employees of the Borrower (or the estates or successors of deceased employees) as a result of the death, disability, retirement or termination of employment of any employee in an aggregate amount for all employees not to exceed $100,000.

Sample 13-M *Covenant Restricting Optional Payments on Subordinated Indebtedness—Version 1*

Subordinated Indebtedness. Neither the Guarantor nor the Company will, and the Company will not permit any of its Subsidiaries to, effect or give any notice of optional redemption or optional prepayment or offer to repurchase, or, directly or indirectly, exchange any securities or other obligations for or make any payment of principal of or interest on, or in redemption, retirement or repurchase of, or otherwise acquire for value, any Subordinated Indebtedness, except for:

(a)   in the case of the Company, regularly scheduled payments required by the terms of the Subordinated Indebtedness and not prohibited by the subordination provisions of the Subordinated Indebtedness;

(b)   in the case of the Guarantor, any redemption, retirement or repurchase of any Subordinated Indebtedness in exchange for the issuance by the Guarantor of its common stock, *provided* that any Subordinated Indebtedness acquired by the Guarantor shall be contributed by the Guarantor to the Company; and

(c)   in the case of the Company, any redemption, retirement or repurchase of any Subordinated Indebtedness, *provided* that the source of funds therefor shall have been solely from cash proceeds from the issuance by the Guarantor of its common stock contributed to the equity capital of the Company or the issuance by the Company of additional Subordinated Indebtedness.

Sample 13-N *Covenant Restricting Optional Payments on Subordinated Indebtedness—Version 2*

As long as any Loan remains unpaid, or any other Obligation remains unpaid, or any portion of the Commitment remains outstanding, Borrower shall not, and shall not permit any of its Subsidiaries to, unless the Agent (with the approval of the Majority Banks) otherwise consents in writing:

Payment or Prepayment of Subordinated Obligations. Make an optional or unscheduled payment or prepayment of any principal (including an optional or unscheduled sinking fund payment), interest or any other amount with respect to any Subordinated Obligation or make an optional purchase or redemption of any Subordinated Obligation or make any optional payment with respect to any Subordinated Obligation in violation of the subordination provisions in the instruments governing such Subordinated Obligation; *provided* that the Borrower may prepay and refinance Subordinated Obligations of Borrower if through the issuance of new Subordinated Obligations (a) no principal or sinking fund payments are due under the new Subordinated Obligations prior to the Maturity Date, (b) the subordination provisions, including interest blockage, standstill and related provisions, under the new Subordinated Obligations are at least as favorable to the Banks as those set forth in the Subordinated Obligations being refinanced or have been approved in writing by the Majority Banks, (c) the restrictive covenants and events of default in the new Subordinated Obligations (*except* such covenants or events of default as may be approved in writing by the Majority Banks) are no more onerous to the Borrower than those contained in the Subordinated Obligations being refinanced, and (d) the incurrence of such new Subordinated Obligations is permitted under [debt covenant].

Sample 13-O *Restricted Payments Covenant— Indenture (High-Yield)*

Limitation on Restricted Payments. (a) The Company will not, and will not permit any Restricted Subsidiary to, directly or indirectly, take any of the following action:

(i)   declare or pay any dividend on, or make any distribution to holders of, any shares of the Capital Stock of the Company (other than dividends or distributions payable solely in shares of its qualified Capital Stock or in options, warrants or other rights to acquire such shares of Qualified Capital Stock);

(ii)   purchase, redeem or otherwise acquire or retire for value, directly or indirectly, any shares of Capital Stock of the Company or any options, warrants or other rights to acquire such shares of Capital Stock;

(iii)   make any principal payment on, or repurchase, redeem, defease or otherwise acquire or retire for value, prior to any scheduled principal payment, sinking fund payment or final maturity, any Subordinated Indebtedness;

(iv)   make any Investment (other than any Permitted Investment) in any Person (including, without limitations, any Unrestricted Subsidiary); or

(v)   (x) declare or pay any dividend or distribution on any Capital Stock of any Restricted Subsidiary (other than to the Company or any wholly owned Restricted Subsidiary or to minority holders of Capital Stock of a Restricted Subsidiary on a pro rata basis) or (y) purchase, redeem or otherwise acquire or retire for value any Capital Stock of any Restricted Subsidiary other than (a) Capital Stock of a wholly owned Restricted Subsidiary or (b) from all holders of Capital Stock of a Restricted Subsidiary on a pro rata basis (such payments or other actions described in (but not excluded from) clauses (i) through (v) are collectively referred to as "Restricted Payments"), unless at the time of, and immediately after giving effect to, the proposed Restricted Payment (the amount of any such Restricted Payment, if other than cash, as determined by the Board of Directors of the Company, whose determination shall be conclusive and evidenced by a Board Resolution), (1) no Default or Event of Default shall have occurred and be continuing, (2) the Company could incur at least US$1 of additional Indebtedness (other than Permitted Indebtedness) pursuant to the "Limitation on Indebtedness" covenant and (3) the aggregate amount of all Restricted Payments declared or made after the Original Issue Date shall not exceed the sum of:

(A) 50% of the Consolidated Net Income of the Company accrued on a cumulative basis during the period (taken as one accounting period) beginning on the first day of the Company's first fiscal quarter after the date of the Indenture and ending on the last day of the Company's last fiscal quarter ending prior to the date of such proposed Restricted Payment (or, if such aggregate cumulative Consolidated Net Income shall be a loss, minus 100% of such loss), plus

(B) the aggregate net cash proceeds received after the Original Issue Date by the Company as capital contributions or from the issuance or sale (other than to a Restricted Subsidiary) of shares of Qualified Capital Stock of the Company (including upon the exercise of options, warrants or rights) or warrants, options or rights to purchase shares of Qualified Capital Stock of the Company, *plus*

(C) the aggregate net cash proceeds received after the Original Issue Date by the Company from the issuance or sale (other than to a Restricted Subsidiary) of debt securities or Redeemable Capital Stock that have been converted into or exchanged for Qualified Capital Stock of the Company, to the extent such securities were originally sold for cash, together with the aggregate net cash proceeds received by the Company at the time of such conversion or exchange, *plus*

(D) to the extent not otherwise included in the Consolidated Net Income of the Company, an amount equal to the sum of (i) the net reduction in Investments in any Person (other than reductions in Permitted Investments) resulting from the payment in cash of interest on Indebtedness, dividends, repayments of loans or advances, or other transfers of assets, in each case to the Company or any Restricted Subsidiary after the Original Issue Date from such person and (ii) the portion (proportionate to the Company's equity interest in such Subsidiary) of the Fair Market Value of the net assets of any Unrestricted Subsidiary at the time such Unrestricted Subsidiary is designated a Restricted Subsidiary; *provided, however,* that in the case of (i) or (ii) above the foregoing sum shall not exceed the amount of Investments previously made (and treated as a Restricted Payment) by the Company or any Restricted Subsidiary in such Person or Unrestricted Subsidiary, *plus*

    (E)   US$25 million.

(b)   Notwithstanding paragraph (a) above, the Company and any Restricted Subsidiary may take the following actions so long as (with respect to clauses (ii), (iii), (iv) and (v) below) no Default or Event of Default shall have occurred and be continuing:

    (i)   the payment of any dividend within sixty days after the date of declaration thereof, if at such date of declaration the payment of such dividend would have complied with the provisions of paragraph (a) above and such payment will be deemed to have been paid on such date of declaration for purposes of the calculation required by paragraph (a) above;

    (ii)   the purchase, redemption or other acquisition or retirement for value of any shares of Capital Stock of the Company in exchange for, or out of the net cash proceeds of a substantially concurrent issuance and sale (other than to a Restricted Subsidiary) of, shares of Qualified Capital Stock of the Company;

    (iii)   the purchase, redemption, defeasance or other acquisition or retirement for value of any Subordinated Indebtedness in exchange for, or out of the net cash proceeds of a substantially concurrent issuance and sale (other than to a Restricted Subsidiary) of, shares of Qualified Capital Stock of the Company;

    (iv)   the purchase, redemption, defeasance or other acquisition or retirement for value of Subordinated Indebtedness in exchange for, or out of the net cash proceeds of a substantially concurrent incurrence (other than to a Restricted Subsidiary) of, new Subordinated Indebtedness so long as (A) the principal amount of such new Subordinated Indebtedness does not exceed the principal amount (or, if such Subordinated Indebtedness being refinanced provides for an amount less than the principal amount thereof to be due and payable upon a declaration of acceleration thereof, such lesser amount as of the date of determination) of the Subordinated Indebtedness being so purchased, redeemed, defeased, acquired or retired, plus the amount of any premium required to be paid in connection with such refinancing pursuant to the original terms of the Subordinated Indebtedness being refinanced or, if the original terms of such Subordinated Indebtedness do not so provide, the amount of any premium reasonably determined by the Company as necessary to accomplish such refinancing, plus, in either case, the amount of reasonable expenses of the Company incurred in connection with such refinancing, (B) such new Subordinated Indebtedness is subordinated to the Notes to the same extent as such Subordinated Indebtedness so purchased, redeemed, defeased, acquired or retired and (C) such new Subordinated Indebtedness has an Average Life longer than the Average Life of the Notes and a final Stated Maturity of principal later than the final Stated Maturity of principal of the Notes; and

(v)   to the extent otherwise deemed Restricted Payments, loans, advances, dividends or distributions to Holdings for the purpose, and in an aggregate amount not to exceed (x) US$1 million per annum, to pay (A) the then currently due operating and administrative expense of Holdings incurred in the ordinary course of business that are for the benefit of, or are attributable to, Holdings' investment in Holdings, and (B) the then currently due taxes payable by Holdings solely on account of the Company and its Subsidiaries or on account of the income of Holdings related to its investment in the Company and its Subsidiaries and (y) the management fees permitted to be paid to the [sponsor] pursuant to the [transactions with affiliates covenant].

The actions described in clauses (i), (ii), (iii) and (v)(x) of this paragraph (b) shall be Restricted Payments that shall be permitted to be taken in accordance with this paragraph (b) but shall reduce the amount that would otherwise be available for Restricted Payments under clause (3) of paragraph (a) above and the actions described in clauses (iv) and (v)(y) of this paragraph (b) shall be Restricted Payments that shall be permitted to be taken in accordance with this paragraph (b) and shall not reduce the amount that would otherwise be available for Restricted Payments under clause (3) of paragraph (a).

(c)   in computing Consolidated Adjusted Net Income of the Company under paragraph (a) above, (1) the Company shall use audited financial statements for the portions of the relevant period for which audited financial statements are available on the date of determination and unaudited financial statements and other current financial data based on the books and records of the Company for the remaining portion of such period and (2) the Company shall be permitted to rely in good faith on the financial statements and other financial data derived from the books and records of the Company that are available on the date of determination. If the Company makes a Restricted Payment which, at the time of the making of such Restricted Payment would in the good faith determination of the Company be permitted under the requirements of the Indenture, such Restricted Payment shall be deemed to have been made in compliance with the Indenture notwithstanding any subsequent adjustments made in good faith to the Company's financial statements affecting Consolidated Adjusted Net Income of the Company for any period.

"*Permitted Investments*" means (i) Investments in marketable, direct obligations issued or guaranteed by the United States of America, or any governmental entity or agency or political subdivision thereof (provided that the full faith and credit of the United States of America is pledged in support thereof), maturing within one year of the date of purchase; (ii) Investments in commercial paper issued by corporations or financial institutions maturing within 180 days from the date of the original issue thereof, and rated "P-1" or better by Moody's Investors Service or "A-1" or better by Standard & Poor's Corporation or an equivalent rating or better by any other nationally recognized securities rating agency; (iii) Investments in time deposits and certificates of deposit issued or acceptances accepted by or guaranteed by any bank or trust company organized under the laws of the United States of America or any state thereof or the District of Columbia or incorporated in a foreign jurisdiction and having a branch office in the United States (each, an "Approved Bank"), in each case having capital, surplus and undivided profits totaling more than $500 million, maturing within one year of the date of purchase; (iv) Investments representing Capital Stock or obligations issued to the Company or any of its Restricted Subsidiaries in the course of the good faith settlement of claims against any other Person or by means of a composition or readjustment of debt or a reorganization of any debtor of the Company or any of its Restricted Subsidiaries; (v) deposits, including interest-bearing deposits, maintained in the ordinary course of business in banks; (vi) repurchase obligations of an Approved Bank for government obligations with a term of not more than seven days; (vii) investments in money market mutual funds having assets in excess of $2.5 billion all of whose assets are comprised of government obligations; (viii) any acquisition of the capital stock of any Person; *provided, however,* that after giving effect to any such acquisition such Person shall become a Restricted Subsidiary of the Company; (ix) trade receivables and prepaid expenses, in each case arising in the ordinary course of business; *provided, however,* that such receivables and prepaid expenses would be recorded as assets of such Person in accordance with GAAP; (x) endorsements for collection or deposit in the ordinary course of business by such Person of bank drafts and similar negotiable instruments of such other Person received as payment for ordinary course of business trade receivables; (xi) any interest swap or hedging obligation with an unaffiliated Person otherwise permitted by the Indenture; (xii) Investments received as consideration for an Asset Disposition in compliance with the [asset sale covenant]; (xiii) Investments in Restricted Subsidiaries or by virtue of which a person becomes a Restricted Subsidiary; (xiv) loans and advances to employees made in the ordinary course of business; and (xv) Investments the sole consideration for which consists of Capital Stock of the Company.

Sample 13-P *Investments Covenant—Version 1*

Investments, Loans and Advances. Neither the Borrower nor any Subsidiary shall purchase, hold or acquire any Investment in, any other person, except:

(a) cash and Cash Equivalents;

(b) receivables created or acquired in the ordinary course of business and payable or dischargeable in accordance with customary trade terms;

(c) loans and advances to employees made in the ordinary course of business in an aggregate principal amount not exceeding $500,000 at any time outstanding;

(d) Rate Protection Agreements permitted by [debt covenant];

(e) in the case of the Borrower, investments in any wholly-owned subsidiary of the Borrower owning the assets of the Borrower's business and no other significant assets, provided that at the time the Borrower contributes such assets to such subsidiary, (i) such subsidiary delivers to the Agent, in consideration of such contribution, (A) a guarantee of the Obligations and (B) mortgages, security agreements and other instruments and documents, and evidence of all filings and recordings, necessary or advisable in the judgment of the Agent to create first priority perfected Liens on all its property and assets as security for the Obligations, all satisfactory in form and substance to the Agent and (ii) the Borrower pledges the capital stock of such subsidiary to the Collateral Agent pursuant to a pledge agreement satisfactory in form and substance to the Agent;

(f)   investments in any wholly owned subsidiary acquired from one or more third parties in a transaction permitted under [capital expenditure covenant]; provided that at the time of such acquisition (i) such subsidiary delivers to the Agent (A) a guarantee of the Obligations and (B) mortgages, security agreements and other instruments and documents, and evidence of all filings and recordings, necessary or advisable in the judgment of the Agent to create first priority perfected Liens on all its property and assets as security for the Obligations, all satisfactory in form and substance to the Agent, and (ii) the capital stock of such subsidiary is pledged pursuant to a pledge agreement satisfactory in form and substance to the Agent; provided further that the subsidiaries in which the Borrower or a subsidiary of the Borrower is permitted to invest under this clause (f) shall not hold or account for more than 10% of the assets (based on book value), or more than 10% of the revenues for any period of four consecutive fiscal quarters, of the Borrower and its subsidiaries taken as a whole;

(g)   investments received from any supplier or customer (i) in connection with a bankruptcy or other insolvency proceeding relating to such supplier or customer or (ii) in settlement or compromise of a dispute; and

(h)   other Investments in an aggregate amount not exceeding $500,000.

"Investment", as applied to any person (the "Investor"), means any direct or indirect purchase or other acquisition by the Investor of, or a beneficial interest in, stock or other Securities of any other person or capital contribution by the Investor to any other person, including all indebtedness and accounts receivable owing to the Investor from that other person or Contingent Obligations of the Investor in respect of obligations of that other person. The amount of any Investment shall be the original cost of such Investment plus the cost of all additions thereto, without any adjustments for increases or decreases in value, or write-ups, write-downs, or write-offs with respect to such Investment, but less any return of capital, provided that the amount of any Investment in the form of a Contingent Obligation shall be, until it is funded, the amount which can reasonably be expected to be funded in respect thereof.

Sample 13-Q *Investments Covenant—Version 2*

Investments. The Borrower will not purchase or acquire any Investment in any Person, or permit any Subsidiary to do so, except (i) obligations issued or guaranteed by the United States of America with a remaining maturity not exceeding 180 days, (ii) commercial paper with maturities of not more than 180 days and a published rating of not less than A-1 and P-1 (or the equivalent rating), (iii) certificates of deposit and bankers' acceptances having maturities of not more than 180 days of any Bank or other commercial bank if (a) such bank has a combined capital and surplus of at least $100 million and (b) its debt obligations, or those of a holding company of which it is a Subsidiary, are rated not less than A (or the equivalent rating) by a nationally recognized investment rating agency, (iv) repurchase agreements with any Bank for periods not in excess of 180 days fully collateralized by securities constituting direct obligations of the United States of America, (v) notes and other instruments which are exempt from Federal income taxation with a remaining maturity not exceeding 180 days, provided that such notes and other instruments are rated in the highest safety category (MIG-1 or equivalent) by Moody's Investors Service, Inc., (vi) stock or interests in, or loans or advances to, the Company or any of its Subsidiaries, provided that no such loans or advances to a Subsidiary shall remain outstanding after any sale, exchange or disposition of such Subsidiary, (vii) loans or advances to any Person (other than to the Company or any Subsidiary of the Company) not exceeding in the aggregate for the Company and its Subsidiaries $5 million principal amount at any one time outstanding, (viii) stock or other equity interests and notes or other debt obligations received as consideration in sales permitted by [asset sales covenant], and (ix) any other obligations or stock not exceeding in the aggregate $5 million in cost, net of return of capital.

Sample 13-R *Investments Covenant—Version 3*

Advances, Investments, and Loans. The Company will not, and will not permit any of its Subsidiaries to, directly or indirectly, lend money or credit or make advances to any Person, or purchase or acquire any stock, obligations or securities of, or any other interest in, or make any capital contribution to, any other Person, or purchase or own a futures contract or otherwise become liable for the purchase or sale of currency or other commodities at a future date in the nature of a futures contract or hold any cash or Cash Equivalents ("Investments"), except that the following shall be permitted:

(i)   the Company may acquire and hold accounts receivables owing to it, if created or acquired in the ordinary course of business and payable or dischargeable in accordance with customary terms;

(ii)   the Company may acquire and hold cash and Cash Equivalents, *provided* that to the extent that the aggregate amount of cash and Cash Equivalents held by the Company shall exceed $5 million at any time, then all such excess amounts shall be applied to repay Working Capital Loans;

(iii)   the Company may make or maintain advances to employees of the Company in the ordinary course of business not exceeding in aggregate principal amount $250,000 at any one time outstanding;

(iv)   the Company may enter into Interest Rate Protection Agreements;

(v)   the Company may enter into forward purchase contracts to meet its normal raw material supply requirements in the ordinary course of business or futures contracts entered into for delivery in the ordinary course of business; and

(vi)   the Company may make loans or advances to, or investments in, Subsidiaries so long as the fair market value of the assets loaned, advanced to, or invested in, all such Subsidiaries, together with the fair market value of all assets transferred to, all such Subsidiaries does not exceed $2,500,000 at any time and provided further that all such loans and advances shall be evidenced by a promissory note pledged to the Agent for the benefit of the Banks pursuant to the Pledge Agreement and all such investments shall be evidenced by capital stock of the Subsidiary and shall be pledged to the Agent for the benefit of the Banks pursuant to the Pledge Agreement.

Notwithstanding the foregoing, in no event will the Company or any of its Subsidiaries be permitted to make any Investment in any Affiliate.

Sample 13-S *Line of Business Covenant—Version 1*

Business. The Borrower will not engage, or permit any of its Subsidiaries to engage, in any business other than the ownership and operation of cable television systems and related business.

Sample 13-T *Line of Business Covenant—Version 2*

Business. The Company will not engage (directly or indirectly) in any business other than the business in which it is engaged on the Initial Borrowing Date and any other reasonably related businesses.

Sample 13-U *Line of Business Covenant—Version 3*

Business. The Borrower and its Subsidiaries will not engage to any material extent at any time in any business or business activity other than oil and gas refining and marketing activities and activities reasonably related or incidental thereto.

Sample 13-V *Line of Business Covenant—Version 4*

Change in Business. The Borrower and its Subsidiaries will not engage in any business other than the businesses as now conducted by the Borrower.

Sample 13-W *Line of Business Covenant—Version 5*

Lines of Business. The Company will not and will not permit any of its Subsidiaries to engage in any line of business not substantially similar to the businesses such Persons were conducting on the date hereof.

Sample 13-X *Line of Business Covenant—Version 6*

Conduct of Business. From and after the Closing Date, Company will not permit Target or any of its Subsidiaries and, from and after the Effective Time, the Surviving Corporation will not and will not permit any of its Subsidiaries to engage in any business other than (i) the business engaged in by Target and its Subsidiaries on the date hereof as described in the Tender Offer Materials and the 2014 10-K and similar or related businesses, (ii) such other businesses as are engaged in by Target and its Subsidiaries on the date hereof which are not material to Target and its Subsidiaries, and (iii) such other lines of business as may be consented to by Requisite Lenders (such consent may not be unreasonably withheld). Company will not prior to the Effective Time engage in any type of business activity other than the ownership of the Target Shares, the issuance of the Notes and the Securities or other activities to facilitate the Tender Offer or Merger.

Sample 13-Y　　*Line of Business Covenant—Version 7*

Limitation on Lines of Business.

The Company shall, and shall cause each Restricted Subsidiary of the Company to, directly or indirectly engage primarily in a Related Business.

"Related Business" means any business in which the Company and its Subsidiaries are engaged, directly or indirectly, that consists primarily of, or is related to, operating, acquiring, developing and constructing any telecommunications services and related businesses.

Sample 13-Z　　*Capital Expenditure Covenant—Version 1*

Limitation on Consolidated Capital Expenditures

Company will not, and will not permit its Subsidiaries to, incur Consolidated Capital Expenditures in any fiscal year of Company and its Subsidiaries indicated below in excess of the corresponding amount (the "Maximum Amount") set forth below opposite such fiscal year; *provided, that,* the Maximum Amount for each fiscal year shall be increased by an amount equal to 100% of the unused amount of Capital Expenditures in respect of the prior fiscal year permitted under this subsection ("Carryover Amount") (except that in no event may the increase in the Maximum Amount in any year attributable to the Carryover Amount from a prior year or years exceed $4 million):

Fiscal Year	Maximum Consolidated Capital Expenditures
2015	$21 million
2016	$20 million
2017	$11 million
2018	$14 million
2019	$13 million
2020	$15 million

provided, however, that Foreign Subsidiaries of Company may not incur Capital Expenditures in excess of more than $6 million in any fiscal year of Company; and *provided further,* that Capital Expenditures shall exclude (i) expenditures of insurance proceeds received upon destruction of property to the extent such proceeds are used to effect restoration, replacement or repair of such property and (ii) expenditures of up to $10 million to build or purchase facilities or invest in assets located outside the United States of America, its territories and possessions to the extent such expenditures are made with the proceeds of sales of assets by Foreign Subsidiaries.

"Capital Expenditures" means, with respect to any Person for any period, the sum (without duplication) of (A) the aggregate amount of all expenditures of such Person and its Subsidiaries for fixed or capital assets made during such period which, in accordance with GAAP, would be classified as capital expenditures and (B) to the extent not covered in the preceding subclause (A), the aggregate amount of all expenditures of such Person and its Subsidiaries made during such period to acquire, by purchase or otherwise, all or substantially all of the assets (or any part of the assets constituting all or substantially all of a business or line of business) of any other Person, whether such acquisition is direct or indirect, including through the acquisition of the business of, or capital stock, equity interests or other evidence of beneficial ownership of, such other Person.

Sample 13-AA *Capital Expenditure Covenant—Version 2*

Capital Expenditures. (a) The Borrower and its Subsidiaries will not make or permit Capital Expenditures (other than Capital Expenditures made with respect to lost, damaged, destroyed or condemned assets to the extent funded with the proceeds of any insurance or condemnation award received in connection with such loss, damage, destruction or condemnation) during any period identified below in excess of the sum of (i) the amount set forth below opposite such period (as such amount may be increased pursuant to paragraph (b)) (the "scheduled amount") and (ii) an amount equal to the remainder (if positive) of (A) the scheduled amount for the immediately preceding period (as such amount may have been increased pursuant to paragraph (b) of this Section) minus (B) the actual amount of Capital Expenditures made by the Borrower during such immediately preceding period and applied against the scheduled amount pursuant to the next sentence. For purposes of this Section, Capital Expenditures made in any period will first be applied against the scheduled amount for such period.

Period	Amount
From the Closing Date, to and including June 30, 2015	$13 million
From July 1, 2015, to and including June 30, 2016	$15 million
From July 1, 2016, to and including June 30, 2017	$17 million
From July 1, 2017, to and including June 30, 2018	$19 million
From July 1, 2018, to and including the Maturity Date	$21 million

(b)   The amount set forth opposite each period shall be increased by an amount equal to the lesser of (i) 50% of the amount by which EDITDA for the fiscal year ending during such period exceeds $17 million and (ii) $5 million.

"Capital Expenditures" shall mean, as to any Person, expenditures in respect of fixed or capital assets by such Person or any of its Subsidiaries, including the capital portion of lease payments made in respect of Capital Lease Obligations, but excluding expenditures for the restoration or replacement of fixed assets to the extent financed by the proceeds of insurance.

Sample 13-BB   *Capital Expenditure Covenant—Version 3*

Capital Expenditures. The Borrower shall not make payments for Capital Expenditures in excess of (i) $10 million from the Closing Date through the end of the Borrower's fiscal year 1998; (ii) $20 million for the Borrower's fiscal year 1999; and (iii) $30 million for the Borrower's fiscal year 2000; *provided, however,* that Capital Expenditures directly funded with cash proceeds of (A) capital contributions to the Borrower, (B) Indebtedness incurred pursuant to [purchase money liens, including capital leases of new property] or (C) the proceeds of asset sales that are reinvested in the business of the Borrower or its Subsidiaries pursuant to [asset sale covenant], in each case shall not be included in determining the maximum annual amount of Capital Expenditures permitted by this Section. To the extent that all or any portion of the permitted amount is not used in any fiscal year, it may be carried forward to the immediately following fiscal year and used for Capital Expenditures during such immediately following fiscal year. The Borrower shall not make any Capital Expenditures that are not directly related to the businesses conducted on the Closing Date by the Borrower.

Sample 13-CC   *Capital Expenditure Covenant—Version 4*

Capital Expenditures. (a) The Company will not, and will not permit any of its Subsidiaries to, make any Capital Expenditures, except that the Company may make Capital Expenditures in aggregate amounts (i) during the period commencing on the Initial Borrowing Date and ending the last day of the 1998 fiscal year, not in excess of $500,000 in the aggregate and (ii) during the fiscal years set forth below, not in excess of the respective amounts set forth opposite such fiscal year below:

Fiscal Year	Amount per Year
2015	$1 million
2016	$1 million
2017 and thereafter	$1 million

To the extent that the amount of Capital Expenditures made by the Company and its Subsidiaries during any fiscal year of the Company ended after the Initial Borrowing Date (including the period from the Initial Borrowing Date to and including the last day of the fiscal year ended in December 1998) is less than the amount applicable to the respective fiscal year (including the period from the Initial Borrowing Date to the fiscal year ended in December 1998) as described above, such unutilized amount may be carried forward and utilized to make Capital Expenditures in excess of the amount permitted above in any subsequent fiscal year. In addition, the amount of Capital Expenditures permitted during any fiscal year set forth above may be increased by an amount equal to (x) 25% of the amount of Excess Cash Flow generated during the period commencing on the Initial Borrowing Date and ending on the last day of the fiscal year of the Company ended immediately preceding the date on which the amount of permitted Capital Expenditures is being determined less (y) the aggregate amount of Capital Expenditures previously made in excess of the otherwise applicable permitted amount as set forth above (without giving effect to this sentence).

Sample 13-DD *Limitation on Acquisitions—Version 1*

<u>Investments and Acquisitions</u>. Neither the Borrower nor any Subsidiary will make any Acquisition, or enter into an agreement to make any Acquisition, or make or suffer to exist any Investment, *other than*:

(a) Investments consisting of Cash or Cash Equivalents;

(b) Advances to employees of Borrower or its Subsidiaries for travel, housing expenses, stock option plans, or otherwise in connection with their employment or the business of Borrower or any of its Subsidiaries;

(c) Investments of Borrower in any of its wholly-owned Subsidiaries and Investments of any Subsidiary of Borrower in Borrower or any of Borrower's wholly-owned Subsidiaries;

(d) Acquisitions of or Investments in Persons engaged in (i) the grocery retail business in those areas in which Borrower or any of its Subsidiaries now conducts such business, (ii) the grocery retail business in Wisconsin, and (iii) the convenience store business in Wisconsin, Illinois, Iowa and Missouri, *provided* that the aggregate cost of such Acquisitions and Investments made after the Closing Date pursuant to this clause (iii) does not exceed $10 million;

(e) Investments in existence on the Closing Date disclosed on Schedule V; and

(f) Acquisitions of or Investments in Persons engaged primarily in businesses other than those permitted by subsection (d); *provided* that the aggregate cost of all such Acquisitions and Investments made after the Closing Date does not exceed $5 million.

"Investment" means, with respect to any Person, any investment by that Person, whether by means of purchase or other acquisition of capital stock or other Securities of any other Person or by means of loan, advance, capital contribution, guarantee, or other debt or equity participation or interest in any other Person, *including* any partnership or joint venture interest in any other Person; *provided* that an Investment of a Person shall not include any trade or account receivable arising in the ordinary course of the business of such Person. The amount of any Investment shall be the amount actually invested, without adjustment for subsequent increases or decreases in the market value of such Investment.

"Acquisition" means any transaction, or any series of related transactions, consummated after the Closing Date, by which Borrower and/or any of its Subsidiaries directly or indirectly (a) acquires any ongoing business or all or substantially all of the assets of any firm, corporation or division thereof, whether through purchase of assets, merger or otherwise, (b) acquires con-trol of securities of a corporation representing 50% or more of the ordinary voting power for the election of directors or (c) acquires control of a 50% or more ownership interest in any partnership, joint venture or other business entity.

Sample 13-EE   *Limitation on Acquisitions—Version 2*

<u>Consolidation, Merger, Purchase or Sale of Assets, etc.</u> The Company will not, and will not permit any of its Subsidiaries to, wind up, liquidate or dis-solve its affairs or enter into any transaction of merger or consolidation, or convey, sell, lease or otherwise dispose of (or agree to do any of the foregoing at any future time) all or any part of its property or assets, or enter into any partnerships, joint ventures or sale-leaseback transactions, or purchase or otherwise acquire (in one or a series of related transactions) any part of the property or assets (other than purchases or other acquisitions of inventory, materials and equipment in the ordinary course of business) of any Person, except that:

(i)   Capital Expenditures by the Company shall be permitted to the ex-tent not in violation of [capital expenditure covenant];

(ii)   the Company may, in the ordinary course of business, sell, lease or otherwise dispose of any assets which, in the reasonable judgment of the Company, have become uneconomic, obsolete or worn out so long as the aggregate amount of Net Sale Proceeds from all such sales in any one fiscal year does not exceed $7,500,000;

(iii)   the Company may lease (as lessee) real or personal property to the extent permitted by [lease covenant] (so long as such lease does not create Capitalized Lease Obligations);

(iv)   the Company may make sales or other dispositions of inventory and Cash Equivalents in the ordinary course of business and the Company may otherwise dispose of inventory by providing sam-ples to potential customers, vendors and other parties in amounts and at times and otherwise in the ordinary course of business and consistent with past practice;

(v)   Investments may be made to the extent permitted by [investments covenant];

(vi)   sales of receivables as described in, and in accordance with the pro-visions of, [receivables financing covenant] shall be permitted; and

(vii) the Company may transfer assets to newly created or established Subsidiaries in accordance with [provision permitting subsidiaries].

In the event the Required Banks waive the provisions of this Section with respect to the sale of any Collateral, or any Collateral is sold as permitted by this Section, such Collateral shall be sold free and clear of the Liens created by the Security Documents, and the Agent and Collateral Agent shall be authorized to take any actions deemed appropriate in order to effect the foregoing.

Sample 13-FF   *Limitation on Acquisitions—Version 3*

Restriction on Fundamental Changes

Subject to [merger covenant], Company and its Subsidiaries will not enter into any transaction of merger or consolidate, or liquidate, wind-up or dissolve itself (or suffer any liquidation or dissolution), or convey, sell, lease, transfer or otherwise dispose of, in one transaction or a series of transactions, all or any part of its business, property or fixed assets, whether now owned or hereafter acquired, or acquire by purchase or otherwise all or substantially all the business, property or fixed assets of, or stock or other evidence of beneficial ownership of, any Person, except:

(i) the Loan Parties may enter into transactions contemplated by the Merger Agreement;

(ii) any Subsidiary of Company may be merged or consolidated with or into Company or any wholly-owned subsidiary of Company (other than a Foreign Subsidiary), or be liquidated, wound up or dissolved, or all or substantially all of its business, property or assets may be conveyed, sold, leased, transferred or otherwise disposed of, in one transaction or a series of transactions, to Company or any wholly-owned subsidiary of Company (other than a Foreign Subsidiary); *provided* that (x) any Foreign Subsidiary of Company (other than a Foreign Subsidiary that is a Material Subsidiary) may be merged or consolidated with or into any other Foreign Subsidiary, or be liquidated, wound up or dissolved, or (y) all or substantially all of the business, property or assets of any Foreign Subsidiary (other than a Foreign Subsidiary that is a Material Subsidiary) may be conveyed, sold, leased, or transferred or otherwise disposed of, in one transaction or a series of transactions to another Foreign Subsidiary (other than to a Foreign Subsidiary that is also a Material Subsidiary) or (z) any of the foregoing transactions may occur between two Foreign Subsidiaries that are Material Subsidiaries; *provided further* that, in the case of such a merger or consolidation of a Subsidiary and Company, Company shall be the continuing or surviving corporation, or, in the case of a merger or consolidation of a Subsidiary and a wholly-owned subsidiary, the wholly-owned subsidiary shall be the continuing or surviving corporation, or, in the case of a merger or consolidation of two wholly-owned subsidiaries, either of such Subsidiaries shall be the surviving or continuing corporation; *provided further* that, in the case of such a merger or consolidation or disposition of a majority of the stock of a Guarantor Subsidiary or of substantially all of the business, property or assets of a Guarantor Subsidiary, (a) the continuing, surviving or transferee corporation shall expressly assume the obligations of such Guarantor Subsidiary under the relevant Guarantor Subsidiary Guarantee and (b) in the case of a merger or consolidation, the net worth of the continuing or surviving corporation (calculated without giving effect to any increase in the amount of intercompany Indebtedness for which the continuing or surviving corporation is liable as compared to the amount of intercompany Indebtedness for which such Guarantor Subsidiary was liable immediately prior to such merger or consolidation) shall not be less than the net worth of such Guarantor Subsidiary immediately prior to such merger or consolidation; and *provided further* that, subject to the terms of the applicable Collateral Document, in the case of such a merger or consolidation or disposition of a majority of the stock of a Subsidiary or of all or substantially all of the business, property or assets of such a Subsidiary of Company the stock of which is pledged to secure the Obligations, the stock of the continuing, surviving or transferee corporation shall, at the time of consummation of such merger, consolidation or transfer, be pledged to secure the Obligations;

(iii) Company or any of its Subsidiaries may convey, sell, transfer or otherwise dispose of any Margin Stock, whether now owned or hereafter acquired; *provided* that such disposition is for fair value and, the proceeds are held in Cash or Cash Equivalents;

(iv) Company and its Subsidiaries may sell or dispose of in the ordinary course of business (a) property which is obsolete or no longer useful in any of its businesses or is of de minimis value, and, in the case of any property the value of which is in excess of $50 million, all as determined in good faith by the Board of Directors of Company or such Subsidiary, as the case may be, (b) Cash and Cash

Equivalents and (c) other Investments described in [certain subsections of the investments covenant], *provided* that any such sale or other disposition is made for at least the fair value of such assets;

(v) so long as no Event of Default has occurred and is continuing or shall be caused thereby, Company and its Subsidiaries may sell or otherwise dispose of any of their respective assets outside the ordinary course of business; *provided* that (a) any such sale or other disposition is made for at least the fair market value of such assets, and (b) any sale or other disposition of more than $500 million in fair market value of stock or other assets in any one transaction or a related series of transactions shall be subject to the prior written consent of Requisite Lenders unless such sale or other disposition is of Margin Stock;

(vi) Company and its Subsidiaries may sell, resell or otherwise dispose of real or personal property held for sale or resale in the ordinary course of business; and

(vii) Company and its Subsidiaries may make Investments otherwise permitted pursuant to [investments covenant] and Capital Expenditures permitted pursuant to [capital expenditure covenant].

Sample 13-GG *Limitation on Acquisitions—Version 4*

Purchase of Assets. Subject to [capital expenditure covenant], neither the Company nor any of its Subsidiaries shall acquire any assets (including and Investment in any Person) other than in the ordinary course of business.

Sample 13-HH *Covenant Limiting Contingent Obligations*

"Contingent Obligation," as applied to any Person, means any direct or indirect liability, contingent or otherwise, of that Person (i) with respect to any indebtedness, lease, dividend, letter of credit or other obligation of another if the primary purpose or intent thereof by the Person incurring the Contingent Obligation is to provide assurance to the obligee of such obligation of another that such obligation of another will be paid or discharged, or that any agreements relating thereto will be complied with, or that the holders of such obligation will be protected (in whole or in part) against loss in respect thereof, (ii) under any letter of credit issued for the account of that Person or for which that Person is otherwise liable for reimbursement thereof, or (iii) under Currency Agreements or Interest Rate Agreements. Contingent Obligations shall include, without limitation, (a) the direct or indirect guarantee, endorsement (otherwise than for collection or deposit in the ordinary course of business), co-making, discounting with recourse or sale with recourse by such Person of the obligation of another, and (b) any liability of such Person for the obligations of another through any agreement (contingent or otherwise) (x) to purchase, repurchase or otherwise acquire such obligation or any security therefor, or to provide funds for the payment or discharge of such obligation (whether in the form of loans, advances, stock purchases, capital contributions or otherwise), (y) to maintain the solvency or any balance sheet item, level of income or financial condition of another, or (z) to make take-or-pay or similar payments if required regardless of nonperformance by any other party or parties to an agreement, if in the case of any such agreement the primary purpose or intent thereof is as described in the preceding sentence. The amount of any Contingent Obligation shall be equal to, in the case of a Contingent Obligation described in clause (i) above, the amount of the obligation so guaranteed or otherwise supported, in the case of a Contingent Obligation described in clause (ii) above, the amount available to be drawn under the relevant letter of credit and in the case of a Contingent Obligation described in clause (iii) above, the relevant Termination Value.

Contingent Obligations

Company will not, and will not permit any of its Subsidiaries to, directly or indirectly, create or become or be liable with respect to any Contingent Obligation except:

(i)   Guarantees resulting from endorsement of negotiable instruments for collection in the ordinary course of business;

(ii)   obligations under the Guarantor Subsidiary Guarantees;

(iii)   Guarantees of Interest Rate Agreements and Currency Agreements that are permitted by (iv) and (v);

(iv)   (A) Interest Rate Agreements and Currency Agreements entered into by Company and any Lender and (B) Interest Rate Agreements entered into by Company with a bank or other financial institutions;

(v)   Currency Agreements entered into by Company or any Subsidiary and any financial institution in the ordinary course of business or in connection with Asset Sales;

(vi)   contingent reimbursement obligations not exceeding $5 million in the aggregate outstanding at one time under letters of credit (including any such letters of credit in existence as of the date hereof) other than Letters of Credit under this Agreement;

(vii)   Contingent Obligations in existence on the date hereof described in Schedule X and extensions and renewals thereof so long as the amount of any such Contingent Obligations so extended or renewed is not increased thereby;

(viii) Contingent Obligations in respect of any obligation (other than any obligation with respect to Indebtedness) of (x) Company or one of its Domestic Subsidiaries and (y) Foreign Subsidiaries and Foreign Joint Ventures to the extent such Contingent Obligation is permitted under the [investments covenant];

(ix)   Contingent Obligations in respect of performance bonds and similar obligations relating to the sale of Company's or Subsidiaries' products incurred in the ordinary course of business (exclusive of obligations for payment of borrowed money) not to exceed $5 million at any time;

(x)   Contingent Obligations in respect of surety and appeal bonds and similar obligations incurred in the ordinary course of business (exclusive of obligations for payment of borrowed money) not to exceed $5 million at any time;

(xi)   Contingent Obligations in respect of Indebtedness of (x) Company or a Domestic Subsidiary and (y) Foreign Subsidiaries and Foreign Joint Ventures to the extent such Contingent Obligation is permitted under [investments and indebtedness covenants]; and

(xii)   in addition to the Contingent Obligations permitted by clauses (i)-(xi), Company and its Subsidiaries may become and remain liable with respect to other Contingent Obligations; *provided* that the maximum aggregate liability of Company and its Subsidiaries in respect of all such other Contingent Obligations shall at no time exceed $10 million.

Sample 13-II   *Covenant Limiting Contingent Obligations and Guarantees of Subsidiaries*

"*Contingent Guaranty Obligation*" means, as to any Person, any (a) direct or indirect guarantee of Indebtedness of, or other obligation performable by, any other Person (*other than* a performance obligation undertaken in the ordinary and usual course of business), *including* any endorsement (*other than* for collection or deposit in the ordinary course of business), co-making or sale with recourse of the obligations of any other Person or (b) assurance given to an obligee with respect to the performance of an obligation (*other than* a performance obligation undertaken in the ordinary and usual course of business) by, or the financial condition of, any other Person, whether direct, indirect or contingent, *including* any purchase or repurchase agreement covering such obligation or any collateral security therefor, any agreement to provide funds (by means of loans, capital contributions or otherwise) to such other Person, any agreement to support the solvency or level of any balance sheet item of such other Person, or any "keep-well," "take-or-pay," "throughput" or other arrangement of whatever nature having the effect of assuring or holding harmless any obligee against loss with respect to any obligation of such other Person. The amount of any Contingent Guaranty Obligation shall be deemed to be an amount equal to the stated or determinable amount of the related primary obligation (unless the Contingent Guaranty Obligation is limited by its terms to a lesser amount, in which case to the extent of such amount) or, if not stated or determinable, the maximum reasonably anticipated liability in respect thereof as determined by such Person in good faith.

Subsidiary Indebtedness and Contingent Guaranty Obligations. Company shall not permit any Domestic Subsidiary to create, incur, assume or suffer to exist any Indebtedness, or any Contingent Guaranty Obligation *except*:

(a)   the Subsidiary Guaranty;

(b)   Indebtedness of a Financial Subsidiary;

(c)   Nonrecourse Indebtedness;

(d)   Indebtedness owed to Borrower or to a wholly-owned Subsidiary of Borrower;

(e)   Contingent Guaranty Obligations of Indebtedness owed to Borrower or to a wholly-owned Subsidiary of Borrower; and

(f)   Indebtedness the aggregate principal outstanding amount of which does not exceed $5 million at any time.

Sample 13-JJ   *Covenant Limiting Guarantees*

No Guarantees. Neither the Borrower nor any Subsidiary shall assume, guarantee, endorse, or otherwise become liable upon the obligations of any other Person, including, without limitation, any Subsidiary or Affiliate of the Borrower, except (i) by the endorsement of negotiable instruments for deposit or collection or similar transactions in the ordinary course of business, (ii) by the giving of indemnities in connection with the sale of Inventory or other asset dispositions permitted hereunder and (iii) in connection with the incurrence of Permitted Indebtedness.

Sample 13-KK   *Sale-Leaseback Covenant—Credit Agreement Version 1*

Sale and Lease-Back Transactions. Neither the Company nor any Subsidiary will enter into any arrangement, directly or indirectly, with any person whereby it shall sell or transfer any property, real or personal, used in its business, whether now owned or hereafter acquired, and thereafter rent or lease such property or other property which it intends to use for substantially the same purpose or purposes as the property being sold or transferred, other than any such arrangements the total sales proceeds in respect of which do not exceed $500,000 in the aggregate.

Sample 13-LL   *Sale-Leaseback Covenant—Credit Agreement Version 2*

Sale-Leasebacks. The Company will not and will not permit any of its Subsidiaries to enter into any sale-leaseback transaction as seller-lessee without the prior written consent of the Majority Holders unless the Indebtedness and Liens incurred or created in connection therewith would be permitted to be incurred or created under [debt covenant] and [lien covenant].

Sample 13-MM *Sale-Leaseback Covenant— Indenture (High-Yield)*

Limitation on Sale and Leaseback Transaction. The Company will not, and will not permit any Restricted Subsidiary to, directly or indirectly, enter into any Sale and Leaseback Transaction with respect to any property or assets (whether now owned or hereafter acquired), unless (i) the sale or transfer of such property or assets to be leased is treated as an Asset Sale and the Company complies with the [asset sale covenant], (ii) the Company or such Restricted Subsidiary would be permitted to incur Indebtedness under the [debt covenant] in the amount of the Attributable Value incurred in respect of such Sale and Leaseback Transaction and (iii) the Company or such Restricted Subsidiary would be permitted to grant a Lien under the [negative pledge] to secure the amount of the Attributable Value in respect of such Sale and Leaseback Transaction.

"*Sale and Leaseback Transaction*" means any transaction or series of related transactions pursuant to which the Company or a Restricted Subsidiary sells or transfers any property or asset in connection with the leasing, or the resale against installment payments, of such property or asset to the seller or transferor.

Sample 13-NN *Lease Covenant—Version 1*

Lease Payments. Neither the Company nor any of its Subsidiaries will incur or assume (whether pursuant to a Guarantee or otherwise) any liability for rental payments under a lease with a lease term (as defined in Financial Accounting Standards Board Statement No. 13, as in effect on the date hereof) of one year or more if, after giving effect thereto, the aggregate amount of minimum lease payments that the Company and its Consolidated Subsidiaries have so incurred or assumed will exceed, on a consolidated basis, $100,000 for any calendar year under all such leases (excluding Capital Leases).

Sample 13-OO *Lease Covenant—Version 2*

Restriction on Leases

Company will not, and will not permit any of its Subsidiaries to, become liable in any way, whether directly or by assignment or as a guarantor or other surety, for the obligations of the lessee under any lease (other than intercompany leases between Company and its Subsidiaries (other than Foreign Subsidiary)), whether an Operating Lease or a Capital Lease, unless, immediately after giving effect to the incurrence of liability with respect to such lease, the Consolidated Rental Payments at the time in effect during the then current fiscal year of Company shall not exceed the applicable amount set forth below:

Fiscal Year	Amount
2015	$3 million
2016	$4 million
2017	$5 million

Sample 13-PP *Prohibition on Sale of Receivables*

Sale or Discount of Receivables

Company will not, and will not permit any of its Subsidiaries directly or indirectly to, sell with or without recourse, or discount or otherwise sell for less than the face value thereof, notes or accounts receivable except notes issued in favor of Company or any of its Subsidiaries in connection with an Asset Sale so long as Company or such Subsidiary, as the case may be, receives fair value for such notes, as determined in good faith by the Board of Directors of Company, and such notes are sold without recourse.

Sample 13-QQ *Receivables Financing Covenant Provisions for an Indenture (High-Yield)*

Limitation of Indebtedness. The Indenture will provide that Issuer will not, and will not permit any of its Restricted Subsidiaries to, directly or indirectly, Incur any Indebtedness (including Acquired Indebtedness), except: . . . (ii) Indebtedness of the Issuer and its Restricted Subsidiaries Incurred under the Credit Agreement in an amount not to exceed $50.0 million; . . . (viii) Indebtedness pursuant to a Permitted Receivables Financing; *provided, however,* that indebtedness incurred under such Permitted Receivables Financing and Indebtedness Incurred pursuant to clause (ii) above shall not exceed $50.0 million in the aggregate at any time outstanding.

Limitation on Restricted Payments. The Indenture will provide that Issuer will not, and will not permit any of its Restricted Subsidiaries to, directly or indirectly, (i) declare or pay any dividend, or make any distribution of any kind or character (whether in cash, property or securities), in respect of any class of the Capital Stock of Issuer or any of its Restricted Subsidiaries or to the holders thereof, excluding any (x) dividend or distribution payable solely in shares of Capital Stock of Issuer (other than Disqualified Stock) or in options, warrants or other rights to acquire Capital Stock of Issuer (other than Disqualified Stock), or (y) in the case of any Restricted Subsidiary of Issuer, dividends or distributions payable to Issuer or a Restricted Subsidiary of Issuer, (ii) purchase, redeem, or otherwise acquire or retire for value shares of Capital Stock of Issuer or any of its Restricted Subsidiaries, any options, warrants or rights to purchase or acquire shares of Capital Stock of Issuer or any of its Restricted Subsidiaries or any securities convertible or exchangeable into shares of Capital Stock of Issuer or any of its Restricted Subsidiaries, excluding any such shares of Capital Stock, options, warrants, rights or securities which are owned by Issuer or a Restricted Subsidiary of Issuer, (iii) make any Investment (other than a Permitted Investment) in, or payment on a guarantee of any obligation of, any Person, other than Issuer or a direct or indirect Wholly-Owned Restricted Subsidiary of Issuer, or (iv) redeem, defease, repurchase, retire or otherwise acquire or retire for value, prior to any scheduled maturity, repayment or sinking fund payment, Subordinated Indebtedness (each of the transactions described in clauses (i) through (iv) (other than any exception to any such clause) being a "Restricted Payment") other than [provision setting forth limitations on Restricted Payments].

"Permitted Investments" means . . . (xv) Investments required in connection with any Permitted Receivables Financing to the extent that such Investments are customary in respect of transactions of such nature.

Limitation Concerning Distributions and Transfers by Restricted Subsidiaries. The Indenture will provide that Issuer will not, and will not permit any of its Restricted Subsidiaries to, directly or indirectly, create or otherwise cause or suffer to exist any consensual encumbrance or restriction on the ability of any Restricted Subsidiary of Issuer to (i) pay, directly or indirectly, dividends or make any other distributions in respect of its Capital Stock or pay any Indebtedness or other obligations owed to Issuer or any Restricted Subsidiary of Issuer, (ii) make loans or advances to Issuer or any Restricted Subsidiary of Issuer or (iii) transfer any of its property or assets to Issuer or any Restricted Subsidiary of Issuer, except for such encumbrances or restrictions existing under or by reason of: . . . (j) any agreement relating to a Permitted Receivables Financing.

Limitation on Liens. The Indenture will provide that Issuer will not, and will not permit any of its Restricted Subsidiaries to, incur any lien on or with respect to any property or assets of Issuer or such Restricted Subsidiary owned on the Issue Date or thereafter acquired or on the income or profits thereof, which Lien secures Indebtedness, without making, or causing any such Restricted Subsidiary to make, effective provisions for securing the Notes and all other amounts due under the Indenture (and, if Issuer shall so determine, any other Indebtedness of Issuer or such Restricted Subsidiary, including Subordinated Indebtedness; *provided, however,* that Liens securing the Notes and any Indebtedness pari passu with the Notes are senior to such Liens securing such Subordinated Indebtedness) equally and ratably with such Indebtedness or, in the event such Indebtedness is subordinate in right of payment to the Notes or the Subsidiary Guarantee prior to such Indebtedness, as to such property or assets for so long as such Indebtedness shall be so secured.

The foregoing restrictions shall not apply to . . . (x) Liens incurred in connection with a Permitted Receivables Financing.

Limitation on Certain Asset Dispositions. The Indenture will provide that Issuer will not, and will not permit any of its Restricted Subsidiaries to, directly or indirectly, make one or more Asset Dispositions unless [provisions applicable to Asset Dispositions].

"Asset Disposition" means any sale, transfer or other disposition (including, without limitation, by merger, consolidation or sale-and-leaseback transaction) of (i) shares of Capital Stock of a Subsidiary of Issuer (other than directors' qualifying shares) or (ii) property or assets of Issuer or any Subsidiary of Issuer; *provided, however,* that an Asset Disposition shall not include . . . (l) any permitted Receivables Financing.

Limitation on Transactions with Affiliates and Related Persons. The Indenture will provide that Issuer will not, and will not permit any of its Restricted Subsidiaries to, enter into directly or indirectly any transaction with any of their respective Affiliates or Related Persons (other than Issuer or a Restricted Subsidiary of Issuer), including, without limitation, the purchase, sale, lease or exchange of property, the rendering of any service, or the making of any guarantee, loan, advance or Investment, either directly or indirectly, involving aggregate consideration in excess of $1 million unless a majority of the disinterested directors of the Board of Directors of Issuer determines, in its good faith judgment evidenced by a resolution of such Board of Directors filed with the Trustee, that the terms of such transaction are at least as favorable as the terms that could be obtained by Issuer or such Restricted Subsidiary, as the case may be, in a comparable transaction made on an arms-length basis between unaffiliated parties. The provisions of this covenant shall not apply to . . . (iv) transactions in connection with a Permitted Receivables Financing.

"Permitted Receivables Financing" means a transaction or series of transactions (including amendments, supplements, extensions, renewals, replacements, refinancings or modifications thereof) pursuant to which (a) a Securitization Subsidiary purchases Receivables and Related Assets from Issuer or any Restricted Subsidiary and finances such Receivables and Related purchase Receivables and Related Assets through the issuance of indebtedness or equity interests or through the sale of the Receivables and Related Assets or a fractional undivided interest in the Receivables and Related Assets or (b) the Company or a Restricted Subsidiary finances Receivables and Related Assets through the sale of the Receivables and Related Assets or fractional undivided interests therein; *provided* that (i) the Board of Directors shall have determined in good faith that such Permitted Receivables Financing is economically fair and reasonable to Issuer and the Securitization Subsidiary, (ii) all sales of Receivables and Related Assets to the Securitization Subsidiary are made at fair market value (as determined in good faith by the Board of Directors), (iii) the financing terms, covenants, termination events and other provisions thereof shall be market terms (as determined in good faith by the Board of Directors), (iv) no portion of the Indebtedness of a Securitization Subsidiary is guaranteed by or is recourse to Issuer or any Restricted Subsidiary (other than recourse for customary representations, warranties, covenants and indemnities, none of which shall relate to the collectibility of the Receivables and Related Assets) and (v) neither Issuer nor any Subsidiary has any obligation to maintain or preserve the Securitization Subsidiary's financial condition.

"Receivables and Related Assets" means accounts receivable and instruments, chattel paper, obligations, general intangibles and other similar assets, in each case, relating to such receivables, including interests in merchandise or goods, the sale or lease of which gave rise to such receivable, related contractual rights, guarantees, insurance proceeds, collections, other related assets and proceeds of all of the foregoing.

"*Securitization Subsidiary*" means a Wholly Owned Subsidiary of Issuer, which is established for the limited purpose of acquiring and financing Receivables and Related Assets and engaging in activities ancillary thereto.

"*Subsidiary*" of any Person means (i) a corporation more than 50% of the outstanding Voting Stock of which is owned, directly or indirectly, by such Person or by one or more other Subsidiaries of such Person or by such Person and one or more other Subsidiaries thereof or (ii) any other Person (other than a corporation) in which such Person, or one or more other Subsidiaries of such Person or such Person and one or more other Subsidiaries thereof, directly or indirectly, has at least a majority ownership and voting power relating to the policies, management and affairs thereof.

"*Subsidiary Guarantee*" means the guarantee of the Notes by each Subsidiary Guarantor under the Indenture.

"*Subsidiary Guarantor*" means each Restricted Subsidiary of Issuer existing as of the Issue Date, or formed or acquired after the Issue Date, (other than a Securitization Subsidiary).

Sample 13-RR   *Transactions with Affiliates Covenant— Credit Agreement Version 1*

Transactions with Affiliates. Neither the Borrower nor any Subsidiary shall enter into any transaction of any kind with any Affiliate of the Borrower other than (a) the borrowing of Subordinated Indebtedness, or (b) a transaction between or among Borrower and its wholly-owned Subsidiaries, or (c) a transaction that has been approved by a resolution adopted by the board of directors of Borrower with the favorable vote of a majority of the directors who have no financial or other interest in the transaction or by the vote of a majority of the outstanding shares of capital stock of Borrower, or (d) an arm's-length transaction entered into on terms and under conditions not less favorable to Borrower or any of its Subsidiaries than could be obtained from a Person that is not an Affiliate of Borrower.

"*Affiliate*" of the Borrower means any other Person directly or indirectly controlling, controlled by, or under direct or indirect common control with the Borrower (other than the Subsidiaries of the Borrower). For purposes of this definition, "control" (including, with correlative meanings, the terms "controlling," "controlled by" and "under common control with"), as applied to any Person, means the possession, directly or indirectly, of the power to direct or cause the direction of the management and policies of such Person, whether through the ownership of voting securities, by contract or otherwise.

Sample 13-SS   *Transactions with Affiliates Covenant— Credit Agreement Version 2*

Transactions with Affiliates. The Borrower will not, and will not permit any subsidiary to, sell or transfer any property or assets to, or purchase or acquire any property or assets from, or otherwise engage in any other transactions with, any of its Affiliates (other than the Borrower or any subsidiary of the Borrower), except that the Borrower or any of its subsidiaries may engage in any of the foregoing transactions in the ordinary course of business at prices and on terms and conditions not less favorable to the Borrower or such subsidiary than could be obtained on an arm's-length basis from unrelated third parties; *provided, however,* that the foregoing restriction shall not prohibit (a) the payment of customary fees to members of the Board of Directors of the Borrower, (b) any transaction between the Borrower or any of its subsidiaries and any employee of the Borrower or such subsidiary that is approved by the Board of Directors of the Borrower or such subsidiary, provided that such transaction is not otherwise prohibited by this Agreement, (c) the payment of fees to [sponsor] or its Affiliates from time to time for financial consulting and underwriting services, such fees not to exceed the then usual and customary fees of [sponsor] or its Affiliates for similar services, (d) transactions expressly permitted by [restricted payments covenant] and (e) transactions expressly contemplated by the Merger Agreement.

"Affiliate" means, as applied to any Person, any other Person directly or indirectly controlling, controlled by, or under direct or indirect common control with, such Person. For purposes of this definition, "control" (including, with correlative meanings, the terms "controlling," "controlled by" and "under common control with"), as applied to any Person, means the possession, directly or indirectly, of the power to direct or cause the direction of the management and policies of such Person, whether through the ownership of voting securities, by contract or otherwise; having the power to vote 5% or more of a Person's voting securities shall be deemed to constitute "control" of such Person.

Sample 13-TT   *Transactions with Affiliates Covenant— Indenture (High-Yield)*

Limitation on Transactions with Shareholders and Affiliates

The Company will not, and will not permit any Restricted Subsidiary to, directly or indirectly, enter into, renew or extend any transaction (including, without limitation, the purchase, sale, lease or exchange of property or assets, or the rendering of any service) with any Person known to the Company to be the holder (or any Affiliate of such holder) of 10% or more of any class of Capital Stock of the Company or with any Affiliate of the Company or any Restricted Subsidiary (each, a "Related Party Transaction"), except upon fair and reasonable terms no less favorable to the Company or such restricted Subsidiary than could be obtained, at the time of such transaction or at the time of the execution of the agreement providing therefor, in a comparable arm's-length transaction with a Person that is not such a holder or an Affiliate.

Without limiting the foregoing, (i) any Related Party Transaction or series of Related Party Transactions with an aggregate value in excess of $5.0 million must be approved by a majority of the Board of Directors of the Company who are disinterested in the subject matter of the transaction pursuant to a Board Resolution, and (ii) with respect to any Related Party Transaction or series of Related Party Transactions with an aggregate value in excess of $15.0 million, the Company must obtain a favorable written opinion from a nationally recognized investment banking firm as to the fairness from a financial point of view of such transaction to the Company or such Restricted Subsidiary, as the case may be.

The foregoing limitation does not limit, and shall not apply to: (i) the payment of reasonable and customary regular fees to directors of the Company who are not employees of the Company; (ii) any Restricted Payments not prohibited by the "Limitation on Restricted Payments" covenant; (iii) any loans or advances by the Company to employees of the Company or a Restricted Subsidiary in the ordinary course of business and in furtherance of the Company's business, in an aggregate amount not to exceed $25.0 million at any one time outstanding; (iv) any grant of stock options or other rights to employees or directors of the Company or any of its Subsidiaries pursuant to benefit plans or agreement adopted or authorized by the Company's nonemployee Directors; and (v) any transaction between the Company and any Wholly Owned Restricted Subsidiary or between any Wholly Owned Restricted Subsidiaries.

"*Affiliate*" means, as applied to any Person, any other Person directly or indirectly controlling, controlled by, or under direct or indirect common control with, such Person. For purposes of this definition, "control" (including, with correlative meanings, the terms "controlling," "controlled by" and "under common control with"), as applied to any Person, means the possession, directly or indirectly, of the power to direct or cause the direction of the management and policies of such Person, whether through the ownership of voting securities, by contract or otherwise.

Sample 13-UU *Capital Structures and Other Agreements—Version 1*

Limitation on Optional Payments and Modification of Debt Instruments. Neither the Borrower nor any Subsidiary will (a) make any optional payment or prepayment on or redemption of any Indebtedness (other than Indebtedness pursuant to this Agreement), or (b) amend, modify or change, or consent or agree to any amendment, modification or change to any of the terms of any such Indebtedness (other than any such amendment, modification or change which would extend the maturity or reduce the amount of any payment of principal thereof or which would reduce the rate or extend the date for payment of interest thereon) *provided* that the Company may redeem the Subordinated Notes with the proceeds of the issuance of other Subordinated Debt.

Rights under Other Agreements. Neither the Borrower nor any Subsidiary will waive or otherwise relinquish any of its rights or causes of action under or arising out of the Purchase Agreement or amend in any material respect the Purchase Agreement without the prior written consent of the Required Banks.

Sample 13-VV *Capital Structures and Other Agreements—Version 2*

Modifications of Other Documents. The Company will not, at any time following the Closing Date, amend, waive, or otherwise modify, or request or consent to any amendment, waiver, or other modification of, any provision of:

(a)   the Senior Subordinated Debenture Indenture; or

(b)   the Other Credit Agreement, any promissory note issued thereunder or the Parent Guaranty (as defined therein), or any document or instrument pertaining thereto, if the effect of such amendment or modification would be to commence payment or repayment of the Indebtedness outstanding thereunder prior to the first scheduled principal payment date therefor (as in effect on the Closing Date) or shorten the time or schedule of repayment of such Indebtedness, or change in a manner adverse to the Company or any of its Subsidiaries the rate, computation, amount, or time of payment of, interest, prepayment premiums, penalties, charges, fees or other amounts payable under any of such documents. In addition, the Company will not effect or permit any change in or amendment to the Other Credit Agreement, such notes or such guaranty, or any document or instrument pertaining thereto, which would change, amend, or otherwise affect the defaults, events of default, any mandatory prepayment provisions, financial covenants or other affirmative or negative covenants in any such document if the effect of any such amendment or modification is to subject the Company or any of its Subsidiaries to any more onerous or restrictive provisions or to impose any additional covenants on the Company or any of its Subsidiaries. Notwithstanding the foregoing, the Other Credit Agreement may be amended to conform the covenants in the Other Credit Agreement to any amendments of the covenants contained in this Agreement.

Sample 13-WW   *Capital Structures and Other Agreements— Version 3*

No Payment of Subordinated Debt; Amendments or Waivers. Without the prior written consent of the Required Lenders, neither the Company nor any of its Subsidiaries will (i) consent to the transfer of the Holdings Note, (ii) pay, repay, prepay, redeem, purchase, acquire or make any other payment in respect of the Holdings Note, except (1) as specifically provided in the Holdings Note or (2) with the proceeds of a refinancing approved in writing by the Required Lenders or (3) with the proceeds from any sale of common stock or other equity securities to officers or employees of the Company or Holdings to the extent that such proceeds are not required to be applied to prepay the Term Loans pursuant hereto or (iii) agree to any material amendment or waiver of any material contract constituting a part of the Collateral if such amendment or waiver could reasonably be expected to be adverse to the Agent or any Lender or their rights under any Financing Document.

Capital Stock. Neither the Company nor Holdings will amend or otherwise change any provision of any class of its capital stock.

Sample 13-XX   *Fiscal Year*

Fiscal Year. The Company shall not change its fiscal year from a fiscal year ending December 31.

Sample 13-YY   *Control of Cash*

No Additional Bank Accounts. Neither the Borrower nor any Subsidiary will open, maintain or otherwise have any checking, savings or other accounts at any bank or other financial institution, or any other account where money is or may be deposited or maintained with any Person, other than the accounts set forth on Schedule I hereto or as otherwise agreed to in writing by the Agent.

No Excess Cash. Neither the Borrower nor any Subsidiary will maintain, in the aggregate in all of the checking accounts of the Borrower, total cash balances in excess of $1 million at any time.

Sample 13-ZZ   *No Negative Pledges*

No Additional Negative Pledges. Neither the Borrower nor any Subsidiary will create or otherwise suffer to exist or become effective, or permit any of the Subsidiaries to create or otherwise cause or suffer to exist or become effective, directly or indirectly, (i) any prohibition or restriction (including any agreement to provide equal and ratable security to any other Person) on the creation or existence of any Lien upon the assets of the Borrower or the Subsidiaries granted to or for the benefit of the Agent and the Lenders (other than in connection with purchase money liens and capitalized leases granted by the Borrower pursuant to [lien covenant], in which case such prohibition or restriction shall apply only to the individual asset subject to such purchase money lien or capitalized lease, as the case may be) or (ii) any Contractual Obligation which may restrict or inhibit the Agent's rights or ability to sell or otherwise dispose of the Collateral.

Examples of change of control provisions:

Sample 13-AAA   *Change of Control—Version 1*

"Change of Control" means:

(i)   any "person" or "group" (as such terms are used for purposes of Sections 13(d) and 14(d) of the Exchange Act, whether or not applicable, except that for purposes of this clause (i) such person or group shall be deemed to have "beneficial ownership" of all shares that such person or group has the right to acquire, whether such right is exercisable immediately or only after the passage of time) is or becomes the "beneficial owner" (as such term is used in Rule 13d-3 promulgated pursuant to the Exchange Act), directly or indirectly, of more than 35% of the aggregate voting power of the Voting Stock of the Company; or

(ii)   individuals who on the Issue Date constituted the Board of Directors of the Company (together with any new directors whose election by such Board or whose nomination for election by the stockholders of the Company was approved by a majority of the directors then still in office who were either directors on the Issue Date or whose election or nomination for election was previously so approved) cease for any reason to constitute a majority of the Board of Directors of the Company then in office.

Sample 13-BBB   *Change of Control—Version 2*

"Change of Control" means the occurrence of any of the following events: (i) any "person" or "group" (as such terms are used in Sections 13(d) and 14(d) of the Exchange Act) is or becomes the "beneficial owner" (as defined in Rules 13d-3 and 13d-5 under the Exchange Act, except that a Person shall be deemed to have beneficial ownership of all shares that such Person has the right to acquire, whether such right is exercisable immediately or only after the passage of time), directly or indirectly, of more than 50% of the total outstanding Voting Stock of the Company or Holdings, as the case may be; (ii) during any period of two consecutive years, individuals who at the beginning of such period constituted the Board of Directors of the Company or Holdings, as the case may be (together with any new directors whose election to such Board of Directors or whose nomination for election by the stockholders of the Company or Holdings, as the case may be, was approved by a vote of 66 2/3% of the directors then still in office who were either directors at the beginning of such period or whose election or nomination for election was previously so approved), cease for any reason to constitute a majority of such board of directors then in office; (iii) the Company or Holdings, as the case may be, consolidates with or merges with or into any Person or conveys, transfers or leases all or substantially all of its assets to any Person, or any corporation consolidates with or merges into or with the Company or Holdings, as the case may be, in any such event pursuant to a transaction in which the outstanding Voting Stock of the Company or Holdings, as the case may be, is changed into or exchanged for cash, securities or other property, other than any such transaction where the outstanding Voting Stock of the Company or Holdings, as the case may be, is not changed or exchanged at all (except to the extent necessary to reflect a change in the jurisdiction of incorporation of the Company or Holdings, as the case may be) or where (A) the outstanding Voting Stock of the Company or Holdings, as the case may be, is changed into or exchanged for (x) Voting Stock of the surviving corporation which is not Redeemable Capital Stock or (y) cash, securities, and other property (other than Capital Stock of the surviving corporation) in an amount which could be paid by the Company as a Restricted Payment in accordance with [restricted payments covenant] (and such amount shall be treated as a Restricted Payment subject to the provisions described under [restricted payments covenant]), and (B) no "person" or "group" owns immediately after such transaction, directly or indirectly, more than 50% of the total outstanding Voting Stock of the surviving corporation; or (iv) the Company or Holdings, as the case may be, is liquidated or dissolved or

adopts a plan of liquidation or dissolution other than in a transaction which complies with the provisions described under [merger covenant].

Sample 13-CCC   *Change of Control—Version 3*

"*Change of Control*" means the occurrence of any of the following events: (i) any "person" or "group" (as such terms are used in Sections 13(d) and 14(d) of the Exchange Act) is or becomes the "beneficial owner" (as defined in Rules 13d-3 and 13d-5 under the Exchange Act, except that a Person shall be deemed to have beneficial ownership of all shares that such Person has the right to acquire, whether such right is exercisable immediately or only after the passage of time), directly or indirectly, of more than 50% of the total outstanding Voting Stock of Holdings; (ii) during any period of two consecutive years, individuals who at the beginning of such period constituted the Board of Directors of Holdings (together with any new directors whose election to such Board of Directors or whose nomination for election by the stockholders of Holdings, as the case may be, was approved by a vote of 66 2/3% of the directors then still in office who were either directors at the beginning of such period or whose election or nomination for election was previously so approved), cease for any reason to constitute a majority of such board of directors then in office; (iii) Holdings consolidates with or merges with or into any Person or conveys, transfers, or leases all or substantially all of its assets to any Person, or any corporation consolidates with or merges into or with Holdings, as the case may be, in any such event pursuant to a transaction in which the outstanding Voting Stock of Holdings is changed into or exchanged for cash, securities or other property, other than any such transaction where the outstanding Voting Stock of Holdings, is not changed or exchanged at all (except to the extent necessary to reflect a change in the jurisdiction of incorporation of Holdings) or where (A) the outstanding Voting Stock of Holdings is changed into or exchanged for (x) Voting Stock of the surviving corporation which is not Redeemable Capital Stock or (y) cash, securities and other property (other than Capital Stock of the surviving corporation) in an amount which could be paid by the Company as a Restricted Payment in accordance with [restricted payments covenant] (and such amount shall be treated as a Restricted Payment subject to the provisions described under [restricted payments covenant] and (B) no "person" or "group" owns immediately after such transaction, directly or indirectly, more than 50% of the total outstanding Voting Stock of the surviving corporation; (iv) the Company or Holdings, as the case may be, is liquidated or dissolved or adopts a plan of liquidation or dissolution other than in a transaction which complies with the provisions described under [merger covenant]; or (v) except by virtue of a permitted merger of the Company and Holdings, Holdings ceases to own 100% of the Capital Stock of the Company.

Sample 13-DDD *Change of Control—Version 4*

A "Change of Control" will be deemed to have occurred in the event that (whether or not otherwise permitted by the Indenture), after the Issue Date (a) any Person or any Persons acting together that would constitute a group (for purposes of Section 13(d) of the Exchange Act, or any successor provision thereto) (a "Group"), together with any Affiliates or Related Persons thereof, other than Permitted Holders, shall "beneficially own" (as defined in Rule 13d-3 under the Exchange Act, or any successor provision thereto) at least 40% of the voting power of the outstanding Voting Stock of the Issuer; (b) any sale, lease, or other transfer (in one transaction or a series of related transactions) is made by the Issuer or any of its Restricted Subsidiaries of all or substantially all of the consolidated assets of the Issuer and its Restricted Subsidiaries to any Person; (c) the Issuer consolidates with or merges with or into another Person or any Person consolidates with, or merges with or into the Issuer, in any such event pursuant to a transaction in which immediately after the consummation thereof Persons owning a majority of the Voting Stock of the Issuer immediately prior to such consummation shall cease to own a majority of the Voting Stock of the Issuer or the surviving entity if other than the Issuer, (d) Continuing Directors cease to constitute at least a majority of the Board of Directors of the Issuer; or (e) the stockholders of the Issuer approve any plan or proposal for the liquidation or dissolution of the Issuer.

"*Affiliate*" of any specified Person means any other Person directly or indirectly controlling or controlled by or under direct or indirect common control with any specified Person. For purposes of this definition, "control" when used with respect to any Person means the power to direct the management and policies of such Person, directly or indirectly, whether through the ownership of voting securities, by contract or otherwise; and the terms "controlling" and "controlled" have meanings correlative to the foregoing.

"*Continuing Director*" means a director who either was a member of the Board of Directors of the Issuer on the Issue Date or who became a director of the Issuer subsequent to the Issue Date and (i) whose election, or nomination for election by the Issuer's stockholders, was duly approved by a majority of the Continuing Directors then on the Board of Directors of the Issuer either by a specific vote or by approval of the proxy statement issued by the Issuer on behalf of the entire Board of Directors of the Issuer in which such individual is named as nominee for director or (ii) whose election was duly approved by the Principals at a meeting of stockholders of the Issuer called for such purpose.

"*Management Investors*" means full-time members of management of the Issuer who acquire stock of the Issuer on or after the Issue Date and any of their Permitted Transferees.

"*Permitted Holder*" means any of (i) the Principals and their Related Persons and Affiliates and (ii) the Management Investors.

"*Permitted Transferee*" means, with respect to any Management Investor (i) any spouse or lineal descendant (including by adoption and stepchildren) of such Management Investor and (ii) any trust, corporation or partnership, the beneficiaries, stockholders or partners of which consist entirely of one or more Management Investors or individuals described in clause (i) above.

"*Principals*" means Equity Fund, L.L.C. and any Person controlled by Equity Fund, L.L.C., any Related Person of Equity Fund, L.L.C. and certain other Persons related to Equity Fund, L.L.C.

"*Related Person*" of any Person means any other Person directly or indirectly owning (a) 5% or more of the outstanding Common Stock of such Person (or, in the case of a Person that is not a corporation, 5% or more of the equity interest in such Person), or (b) 5% or more of the combined voting power of the Voting Stock of such Person.

Sample 13-EEE   *Change of Control—Version 5*

Offer to Repurchase Upon a Change of Control Repurchase Event— Excerpt from Prospectus

If a Change of Control Repurchase Event occurs, unless we have exercised our right to redeem the Notes as described above, we will make an offer to each holder of Notes to repurchase all or any part (in multiples of $1,000 principal amount) of that holder's Notes at a repurchase price in cash equal to 101% of the aggregate principal amount of Notes repurchased plus any accrued and unpaid interest on the Notes repurchased to the date of purchase. Within 30 days following any Change of Control Repurchase Event or, at our option, prior to any Change of Control, but after the public announcement of the Change of Control, we will mail a notice to each holder describing the transaction or transactions that constitute or may constitute the Change of Control Repurchase Event and offering to repurchase Notes on the payment date specified in the notice, which date will be no earlier than 30 days and no later than 60 days from the date such notice is mailed. The notice shall, if mailed prior to the date of consummation of the Change of Control, state that the offer to purchase is conditioned on the Change of Control Repurchase Event occurring on or prior to the payment date specified in the notice. We will comply with the requirements of Rule 14e-1 under the Securities Exchange Act of 1934 (the "Exchange Act") and any other securities laws and regulations thereunder to the extent those laws and regulations are applicable in connection with the repurchase of the Notes as a result of a Change of Control Repurchase Event. To the extent that the provisions of any securities laws or regulations conflict with the Change of Control Repurchase Event provisions of the Notes, we will comply with the applicable securities laws and regulations and will not be deemed to have breached our obligations under the Change of Control Repurchase Event provisions of the Notes by virtue of such conflict.

On the Change of Control Repurchase Event payment date, we will, to the extent lawful:

(1) accept for payment all Notes or portions of Notes properly tendered pursuant to our offer;

(2) deposit with the paying agent an amount equal to the aggregate purchase price in respect of all Notes or portions of Notes properly tendered; and

(3) deliver or cause to be delivered to the trustee the Notes properly accepted, together with an officers' certificate stating the aggregate principal amount of Notes being purchased by us.

The paying agent will promptly mail to each holder of Notes properly tendered the purchase price for the Notes, and the trustee will promptly authenticate and mail (or cause to be transferred by book-entry) to each holder a new note equal in principal amount to any unpurchased portion of any Notes surrendered; *provided* that each new note will be in a principal amount of $1,000 or an integral multiple of $1,000.

We will not be required to make an offer to repurchase the Notes upon a Change of Control Repurchase Event if a third party makes an offer in the manner, at the times and otherwise in compliance with the requirements for an offer made by us and such third party purchases all Notes properly tendered and not withdrawn under its offer.

The definition of Change of Control includes a phrase relating to the direct or indirect sale, lease, transfer, conveyance or other disposition of "all or substantially all" of our properties or assets and those of our Subsidiaries taken as a whole. Although there is a limited body of case law interpreting the phrase "substantially all", there is no precise established definition of the phrase under applicable law. Accordingly, the ability of a holder of Notes to require us to repurchase our Notes as a result of a sale, lease, transfer, conveyance or other disposition of less than all of our assets and the assets of our Subsidiaries taken as a whole to another person or group may be uncertain.

For purposes of the Notes:

"Below Investment Grade Rating Event" means the Notes are rated below Investment Grade by both Rating Agencies on any date from the date of the public notice of an arrangement that could result in a Change of Control until the end of the 60-day period following public notice of the occurrence of a Change of Control (which period shall be extended so long as the rating of the Notes is under publicly announced consideration for possible downgrade by either of the Rating Agencies).

"Change of Control" means the occurrence of any of the following:

(1)   the direct or indirect sale, transfer, conveyance or other disposition (other than by way of merger or consolidation), in one or a series of related transactions, of all or substantially all of our properties or assets and those of our Subsidiaries, taken as a whole, to any "person" (as that term is used in Section 13(d)(3) of the Exchange Act), other than us or a Subsidiary Guarantor that is one of our wholly owned Subsidiaries;

(2)   the adoption of a plan relating to our liquidation or dissolution;

(3)   the consummation of any transaction (including, without limitation, any merger or consolidation) the result of which is that any "person" (as that term is used in Section 13(d)(3) of the Exchange Act), other than us or a Subsidiary Guarantor that is one of our wholly owned Subsidiaries, becomes the beneficial owner, directly or indirectly, of more than 50% of our Voting Stock, measured by voting power rather than number of shares; or

(4)   the first day on which a majority of the members of our Board of Directors are not Continuing Directors.

Notwithstanding the foregoing, a transaction effected to create a holding company for us will not be deemed to involve a Change of Control if (1) pursuant to such transaction we become a wholly owned Subsidiary of such holding company and (2) the holders of the Voting Stock of such holding company immediately following such transaction are the same as the holders of our Voting Stock immediately prior to such transaction.

"Change of Control Repurchase Event" means the occurrence of a Change of Control and a Below Investment Grade Rating Event.

"Continuing Directors" means, as of any date of determination, any member of our Board of Directors who:

(1)   was a member of such Board of Directors on the first date that any of the Notes were issued; or

(2)   was nominated for election or elected to our Board of Directors with the approval of a majority of the Continuing Directors who were members of our Board at the time of such nomination or election.

"Investment Grade" means a rating of Baa3 or better by Moody's (or its equivalent under any successor rating categories of Moody's) and BBB- or better by S&P (or its equivalent under any successor rating categories of S&P) (or, in each case, if such Rating Agency ceases to rate the Notes for reasons outside of our control, the equivalent investment grade credit rating from any Rating Agency selected by us as a replacement Rating Agency).

"Moody's" means Moody's Investors Service Inc.

"Rating Agency" means:

(1)   each of Moody's and S&P; and

(2)   if either of Moody's or S&P ceases to rate the Notes or fails to make a rating of the Notes publicly available for reasons outside of our control, a "nationally recognized statistical rating organization" within the meaning of Rule 15c3-1(c)(2)(vi)(F) under the Exchange Act selected by us as a replacement agency for Moody's or S&P, or both, as the case may be.

"S&P" means Standard & Poor's Ratings Services, a division of McGraw-Hill, Inc.

"Voting Stock" as applied to stock of any person, means shares, interests, participations or other equivalents in the equity interest (however designated) in such person having ordinary voting power for the election of a majority of the directors (or the equivalent) of such person, other than shares, interests, participations or other equivalents having such power only by reason of the occurrence of a contingency.

Sample 13-FFF   *Limitations on Activities*

Limitations on Activities by Holdings. Holdings shall not, directly or indirectly, (i) enter into or permit to exist any transaction or agreement (including any agreement for incurrence or assumption of Debt, any purchase, sale, lease or exchange of any property or the rendering of any service), between itself and any other Person, other than this Agreement, the Holdings Pledge Agreement, the Registration Rights Agreement and the Common Stockholders Agreement (the "Holdings Documents"), (ii) engage in any business or conduct any activity (including the making of any Investment or payment) or hold any assets, other than holding the common stock of the Company, the performance of the Holdings Documents in accordance with the terms thereof and performance of ministerial activities and payment of taxes and administrative fees necessary for compliance with the next succeeding sentence, or (iii) consolidate or merge with or into any other Person.

Chapter 14:   Financial Covenants

See generally:

Carolyn E.C. Paris, How to Draft for Corporate Finance, ch. 10 (PLI 2006).

EBITDA ratios:

The temptations of private equity, The Deal, Nov. 21, 2006:

In a review of a leveraged acquisition of Michaels Stores, this article cites an EBITDA ratio (EBITDA to interest expense) of only 1.3 times. The same article reports Debt to EBITDA and EBITDA to Interest plus Capital Expenditures for then recent and pending acquisitions and recapitalizations: Toys 'R' Us, July 2005: 8.2 and 1.1; LifeCare Holdings, August 2005: 6.2 and 0.9; Perkins & Marie Callender's Inc., September 2005: 5.3 and 1.1; Neiman Marcus Inc., October 2005: 5.9 and 1.3; Burlington Coat Factory Warehouse Corp., April 2006: 6.5 and 1.1; HCA: 6.8 and 1; Petco: 5.6 and 1; Burger King: 4.1 and 1.6; Intelsat: 6.1 and 1.2. While the leveraged buyouts of the 1980s were done with very little equity, say 10%, equity in recent leveraged buyouts has been 20–30% of the purchase price. However, the article notes that Debt to EBITDA ratios have been going up from an average of 4.3 in 2000 to 5.8 in the third quarter of 2006; Tony James of Blackstone cites (perhaps rhetorically) banks offering staple finance packages at 7.5 times EBITDA. From the same article:

> If there is one metric that effectively reflects credit risk, it is the coverage ratio after capital expenses. This is calculated by dividing a company's EBITDA in one period by the company's interest expenses plus capital expenditures of the same period. The lower the ratio, the tougher it is for the company to pay down debt. An interest coverage ratio of below 1 means that the company is not generating enough free cash flow to pay interest expenses and to make necessary investments in operations.

Regarding the acquisition of Petco, with a coverage ratio of about 1:

> . . . the San Diego pet store change has a large undrawn revolver, roughly $1.2 billion, and no maintenance financial covenants. That means it isn't required to maintain certain leverage ratios and coverage ratios on a quarterly basis and has no limits on capex. Petco has historically generated profits by opening new stores. Moreover, maintenance capex, to refurbish stores and such, is very low. Also, as with many deals, Petco's

debt payment is back-ended, rather than amortized, other than the typical [and token] 1% per year. Absent covenants, the company has time to fix any issues or ride through a cycle. If there's a hiccup, capex can be cut near zero, and the company would have enough liquidity and time to grow EBITDA.

The Petco story is interesting because it explains the interplay between the company's covenant structure, and thus the availability of funds, and further the "liquidity cushion" that the condition-light revolver provides for the deal as a whole.

Examples of financial covenants:

Sample 14-A *Cash Flow Charge Coverage*

Cash Flow Charge Coverage. As of the last day of each fiscal quarter of the Borrower ended during each of the periods set forth below, the ratio of aggregated Consolidated Adjusted Cash Flow to aggregate Consolidated Cash Flow Charges, in each case for the four consecutive fiscal quarters ending on such day, shall not be less than the ratio set forth below opposite such fiscal period:

Period	Ratio
From November 1, 2014 through November 30, 2015	1.2:1
From December 1, 2015 through November 30, 2016	1.3:1
From December 1, 2016 through November 30, 2017	1.3:1
From December 1, 2017 through November 30, 2018	1.3:1
From December 1, 2018 and thereafter	1.3:1

"*Consolidated Adjusted Cash Flow*" means for any period (a) the sum of (i) Consolidated Net Income for such period *plus* (ii) to the extent deducted in determining Consolidated Net Income for such period, the aggregate amount of depreciation, amortization, deferred income taxes and other similar noncash charges for such period *plus* (iii) consolidated cash rental expense incurred or accrued by the Borrower and its Consolidated Subsidiaries during such period *plus* (iv) to the extent reflected in Consolidated Net Income for such period, any loss (or minus any gain) in respect of sales of assets outside the ordinary course of business, in each case net of tax effect, *plus* (v) Consolidated Interest Charges for such period, *minus* (b) to the extent reflected in Consolidated Net Income for such period, all equity in earnings of Equity Affiliates in excess of cash dividends received by the Borrower and its Consolidated Subsidiaries from Equity Affiliates.

"*Consolidated Cash Flow Charges*" means for any period, without duplication, the sum of (i) consolidated cash rental expense incurred or accrued by the Borrower and its Consolidated Subsidiaries during such period, (ii) Consolidated Interest Charges for such period, and (iii) the consolidated gross amount of additions to property, plant and equipment of the Borrower and its Consolidated Subsidiaries during such period.

Sample 14-B　　*EBITDA to Interest*

Interest Coverage Ratio. The Interest Coverage Ratio will, at the end of each fiscal quarter of the Company ending (x) on or prior to December 31, 1998, be greater than 3.0 to 1, (y) after December 31, 1998, but on or prior to December 31, 1999, be greater than 3.5 to 1, and (z) after December 31, 1999, be greater than 4.0 to 1.

"*Consolidated Cash Flow*" means, for any period, (i) Consolidated Net Income for such period excluding therefrom (x) the net positive amount (if any) of all extraordinary items during such period, (y) the net positive amount of all gains and losses on dispositions and acquisitions of assets (other than any disposition and acquisition of inventory in the ordinary course and any extraordinary items) during such period, *provided* that if such amount determined pursuant to this clause (y) for any fiscal quarter of the Company is less than $1 million, then the amount determined pursuant to this clause (y) for such fiscal quarter shall be deemed to be zero, and (z) any equity in earnings of unconsolidated Affiliates plus (ii) the sum of (A) the aggregate amount of all cash distributions during such period by unconsolidated Affiliates to the Company and its Consolidated Subsidiaries and (B) consolidated depreciation and amortization expense of the Company and its Consolidated Subsidiaries for such period.

"*Consolidated Net Income*" means, for any period, the consolidated net income of the Company and its Consolidated Subsidiaries for such period.

"*Interest Coverage Ratio*" means, at the end of any fiscal quarter, the ratio of (i) Consolidated Cash Flow for the period of four consecutive fiscal quarters then ended plus consolidated tax expense and net interest expense for the Company and its Consolidated Subsidiaries, to the extent deducted in determining Consolidated Cash Flow for such period to (ii) consolidated net interest expense for the Company and its Consolidated Subsidiaries for such period.

Sample 14-C   *EBITDA to Cash Interest*

Interest Coverage Ratio. The Company will not permit the ratio of (i) EBITDA to (ii) Consolidated Cash Interest Expense (A) for the period from April 1, 2015 through (x) the last day of the fiscal quarter ended on June 30, 2015 (taken as one accounting period), to be less than 2.0:1, (y) the last day of the fiscal quarter ended on September 30, 2015 (taken as one accounting period), to be less than 1.5:1, and (z) the last day of the fiscal quarter ended on December 31, 2015 (taken as one accounting period), to be less than 1.4:1, and (B) for any period of four consecutive fiscal quarters (taken as one accounting period) ended on each fiscal quarter set forth below to be less than the ratio set forth opposite such quarter:

Fiscal Quarter Ended	Ratio
March 31, 2016	1.5:1
June 30, 2016	1.5:1
September 30, 2016	1.5:1
December 31, 2016	1.5:1
March 31, 2017	1.65:1
June 30, 2017	1.65:1
September 30, 2017	1.65:1
December 31, 2017	1.65:1
March 31, 2018	1.9:1
June 30, 2018	1.9:1
September 30, 2018	1.9:1
December 31, 2018	1.9:1
March 31, 2019	2.1:1
June 30, 2019	2.1:1
September 30, 2019	2.1:1
December 31, 2019	2.1:1
March 31, 2020	2.4:1

June 30, 2020	2.4:1
September 30, 2020	2.4:1
December 31, 2020	2.4:1
March 31, 2021	3.0:1
June 30, 2021	3.0:1
September 30, 2021	3.0:1
December 31, 2021	3.0:1

"*Consolidated Cash Interest Expense*" for any period shall mean Consolidated Interest Expense for such period less the sum of (i) amortization of debt discount and debt issuance costs, and (ii) amortization of noncash discount and noncash costs of any Swap Agreements of the Company and its Subsidiaries on a consolidated basis for such period.

"*EBIT*" shall mean, for any period, the consolidated net income of the Company and its Subsidiaries, before interest expense and provision for income taxes, and without giving effect to any extraordinary gains and gains from sales of assets (other than sales of inventory in the ordinary course of business; *provided* that the gains resulting from aggregate gross proceeds of all sales of up to $1 million of assets in the ordinary course of business (other than any such sale of assets the value of which individually exceeds $500,000) in the fiscal year in which such period occurs shall be considered gains from sales of assets for the purposes of the foregoing calculation only to the extent such gains exceed losses relating to such sales; and *provided* further that any losses (not exceeding $2 million in the aggregate) relating to the divestiture on or before January 31, 2000, of certain assets of the Printemps business shall not be considered losses when calculating net income for the purposes of the foregoing calculation), for such period.

"*EBITDA*" for any period shall mean EBIT, adjusted by (i) adding thereto the amount of (a) all amortization of goodwill and other intangibles and, in respect of any period occurring in 1998, fees relating to the transactions contemplated hereby paid during such period not exceeding $35 million in the aggregate for all such periods, (b) depreciation, (c) all noncash contributions or accruals to or with respect to deferred profit sharing plans and (d) all noncash contributions and accruals to and/or with respect to deferred compensation plans, in each case to the extent deducted in arriving at EBIT for such period, and (ii) subtracting therefrom the amount of all noncash gains that were added in arriving at EBIT for such period other than such gains arising from sales of inventory in the ordinary course of business.

Sample 14-D   *Cash Flow to Debt Service*

Total Debt Coverage Ratio. The Company shall not permit the ratio on any Testing Date of (i) Consolidated Free Cash Flow for the Testing Period then ended to (ii) Total Debt Service for the Testing Period then ended (or, prior to the completion of one Testing Period after the Closing Date, for such shorter period beginning on the Closing Date and ending on such Testing Date), to be less than the ratio set forth below opposite the period in which such Testing Date occurs:

Period			Ratio
From		through	
08/31/2015	–	11/30/2015	1.20:1
12/01/2015	–	02/28/2016	1.20:1
03/01/2016	–	05/31/2016	1.25:1
06/01/2016	–	07/31/2016	1.25:1
08/01/2016	–	07/31/2017	1.35:1
08/01/2017	–	07/31/2018	1.40:1
08/01/2018	–	08/31/2019	1.45:1

"*Consolidated Free Cash Flow*" means, for any period, the consolidated net income of the Company and its Consolidated Subsidiaries for such period before interest expense and provision for income taxes and without giving effect to any extraordinary gains or extraordinary losses, plus the following amounts:

(a)   all amortization of goodwill and other intangibles (including, without limitation, amortization of any inventory write-up) to the extent deducted in arriving at consolidated net income for such period;

(b)   depreciation to the extent deducted in arriving at consolidated net income for such period; and

(c)   the excess, if any, of (i) any decrease, if any, in Net Working Investment during such period over (ii) the absolute amount of any net reduction, if any, during such period in the outstanding principle amount of Working Capital Loans; and minus the following amounts:

(d)   all cash payments of income taxes by the Company and its Consolidated Subsidiaries during such period;

(e)   Consolidated Capital Expenditures for such period; and

(f)   the excess, if any, of (i) any increase in Net Working Investment during such period over (ii) the sum of (A) the absolute amount of any net increase, if any, during such period in the outstanding principal amount of Working Capital Loans and (B) the excess on the last day of such period of (1) the aggregate amount of the Working Capital Commitments over (2) the outstanding principal amount of Working Capital Loans.

"*Consolidated Capital Expenditures*" means, for any period, the aggregate amount of expenditures by the Company and its Consolidated Subsidiaries for plant, property, and equipment during such period (including any such expenditure by way of acquisition of a Person, to the extent reflected as plant, property, and equipment), but excluding any such expenditures made in connection with the replacement or restoration of assets to the extent financed by condemnation awards or proceeds of insurance received with respect to the loss or taking of or damage to the asset or assets being replaced or restored.

"*Net Working Investment*" means at any date consolidated current assets (excluding cash and cash equivalents) minus consolidated current liabilities (excluding Debt).

"*Testing Date*" means (a) the last day of each Fiscal Quarter if the term "Testing Period" means a period of four consecutive Fiscal Quarters or (b) the last day of each month if the term "Testing Period" means a period of twelve consecutive months.

"*Testing Period*" means a period of four consecutive Fiscal Quarters; *provided* that if the Required Lenders shall have given the Company at least fifteen days' prior written notice to such effect, "Testing Period" shall mean a period of twelve consecutive months.

"*Total Debt Service*" means, for any period, the sum of (i) the aggregate interest charges incurred (other than in respect of the Subordinated Note) by the Company and its Consolidated Subsidiaries for such period, whether expensed or capitalized, including, without limitation, the portion of any obligation under Capital Leases allocable to interest expense in accordance with GAAP and the portion of any debt discount (but not expenses of issuance) that shall be amortized in such period and (ii) the aggregate amount scheduled to be paid during such period of mandatory principal payments pursuant to [scheduled prepayment provisions] (as such scheduled payments may be reduced from time to time pursuant to [scheduled prepayment provisions]) and all other scheduled principal payments on all other Debt of the Company and its Consolidated Subsidiaries (other than the Subordinated Note) including the portion of any payments under Capital Leases that is allocable to principal.

Sample 14-E   *Cash Flow to Interest*

Consolidated Cash Flow Coverage. The Company shall not permit the ratio on the last day of any fiscal quarter of the Company of (i) Adjusted Consolidated Cash Flow to (ii) Consolidated Interest Expense, in each case for the four consecutive fiscal quarters then ended considered as a single accounting period (or, prior to the first anniversary of the Closing, for such shorter period beginning on the date of Closing and ending on such date), to be less than the ratio set forth below opposite such fiscal quarter:

Fiscal Quarter Ended	Ratio
September 30, 2015	3.00:1.0
December 31, 2015	2.85:1.0
March 31, 2016	2.55:1.0
June 30, 2016	2.50:1.0
September 30, 2016	2.25:1.0
December 31, 2016	2.50:1.0
March 31, 2017	2.25:1.0
June 30, 2017	2.00:1.0
September 30, 2017	1.75:1.0
December 31, 2017 and thereafter	1.50:1.0

"Adjusted Consolidated Cash Flow" means, for any period, the sum (without duplication) of (i) Consolidated Net Income (including income or loss attributable to equity in Equity Affiliates) for such period *plus* (ii) Consolidated Interest Expense and depreciation, amortization and other similar noncash charges (to the extent deducted in determining Consolidated Net Income) for such period *plus* (iii) any increase (or minus any decrease) in net deferred tax liabilities of the Company and its Consolidated Subsidiaries

(adjusted to exclude any increase or decrease arising in connection with Asset Sales) with respect to such period *minus* (iv) any income (or plus any loss) attributable to equity in all Equity Affiliates during such period *plus* (v) cash distributions from Equity Affiliates received during such period.

"*Consolidated Interest Expense*" means, for any period, the sum of the amounts deducted for consolidated interest expense in determining Consolidated Net Income for such period.

Sample 14-F   *Cash Flow to Fixed Charges*

Coverage Ratios. The Borrower will not permit the ratio of (i) Consolidated Cash Flow Available for Fixed Charges to (ii) Consolidated Fixed Charges for any Test Period to be less than 1.10 to 1.00, or the ratio of (i) Consolidated EBITDA to (ii) Consolidated Cash Interest Expense for any Test Period to be less than 2.25 to 1.00.

"*Consolidated Capital Expenditures*" shall mean, for any period, the aggregate of all expenditures (whether paid in cash or accrued as liabilities and including in all events all amounts expended or capitalized under Capital Leases, but excluding any amount representing capitalized interest) by the Borrower and its Subsidiaries during that period that, in conformity with GAAP, are or are required to be included in the property, plant, or equipment reflected in the consolidated balance sheet of the Borrower and its Subsidiaries, but excluding expenditures made in connection with the replacement, substitution, or restoration of assets (i) to the extent financed from insurance proceeds paid on account of the loss of or damage to the assets being replaced or restored, or (ii) with awards of compensation arising from the taking by eminent domain or condemnation of the assets being replaced, *provided* that Consolidated Capital Expenditures shall in any event include the purchase price paid in connection with the acquisition of any Person (including through the purchase of all of the capital stock or other ownership interests of such Person or through merger or consolidation) to the extent allocable to property, plant, and equipment.

"*Consolidated Cash Capital Expenditures*" shall mean, for any period, Consolidated Capital Expenditures, but excluding, however, the amount thereof not actually paid by the end of such period, but including the unpaid amount thereof at the beginning of such period to the extent paid during such period.

"*Consolidated Cash Flow Available for Fixed Charges*" shall mean, for any period, the sum of the amounts for such period of (i) Consolidated EBIT, (ii) Consolidated Operating Rental Payments and (iii) noncash items (including depreciation) reducing Consolidated EBIT for such period (including LIFO inventory adjustments).

"*Consolidated Cash Interest Expense*" shall mean, for any period, (i) Consolidated Interest Expense, but excluding, however, interest expense not payable in cash, amortization of discount and deferred financing costs, *plus* (ii) cash dividends paid on the Series A Preferred Stock during such period.

"*Consolidated EBIT*" shall mean, for any period, (A) the sum of the amounts for such period of (i) Consolidated Net Income, (ii) provisions for taxes based on income, (iii) Consolidated Interest Expense, (iv) dividends accrued on the Series A Preferred Stock, (v) amortization or write-off of deferred financing costs to the extent deducted in determining Consolidated Net Income and (vi) losses on sales of assets (excluding sales in the ordinary course of business) and other extraordinary losses, *less* (B) the amount for such period of (i) interest income and (ii) gains on sales of assets (excluding sales in the ordinary course of business) and other extraordinary gains, all as determined on a consolidated basis in accordance with GAAP.

"*Consolidated EBITDA*" shall mean, for any period, the sum of the amounts for such period of (i) Consolidated EBIT, (ii) depreciation expense, and (iii) amortization expense, all as determined on a consolidated basis in accordance with GAAP.

"*Consolidated Fixed Charges*" shall mean, for any period, the sum, without duplication, of the amounts for such period of (i) Consolidated Cash Interest Expense, (ii) Consolidated Rental Payments, (iii) provisions for taxes based on income other than (w) the noncash portion of current tax provisions, (x) changes in deferred taxes, (y) taxes on gains resulting from sales of assets (other than sales in the ordinary course of business) and (z) taxes on gains on extraordinary items, (iv) Consolidated Cash Capital Expenditures and (v) scheduled payments on the Term Loans and on the Schedule A Debt, all as determined on a consolidated basis for the Borrower and its Subsidiaries in accordance with GAAP.

"*Consolidated Interest Expense*" shall mean, for any period, total interest expense (including that attributable to Capital Leases in accordance with GAAP) of the Borrower and its Subsidiaries on a consolidated basis with respect to all outstanding Indebtedness of the Borrower and its Subsidiaries, including, without limitation, all commissions, discounts, and other fees and charges owed with respect to letters of credit and bankers' acceptance financing and net costs under Interest Rate Agreements, but excluding, however, any amortization of deferred financing costs, all as determined in accordance with GAAP.

"*Consolidated Net Income*" shall mean, for any period, the net income (or loss) of the Borrower and its Subsidiaries on a consolidated basis for such period taken as a single accounting period determined in conformity with GAAP (determined in any event by deducting any dividends accruing during such period on the Series A Preferred Stock), *provided* that there shall be excluded (i) the income (or loss) of any Person (other than Subsidiaries of the Borrower) in which any other Person (other than the Borrower or any of its Subsidiaries) has a joint interest, except to the extent of the amount of dividends or other distributions actually paid to the Borrower or any of its Subsidiaries by such Person during such period, (ii) the income (or loss) of any Person accrued prior to the date it becomes a Subsidiary of the Borrower or is merged into or consolidated with the Borrower or any of its Subsidiaries, or that Person's assets are acquired by the Borrower or any of its Subsidiaries, and (iii) the income of any Subsidiary of the Borrower to the extent that the declaration or payment of dividends or similar distributions by that Subsidiary of that income is not at the time permitted by operation of the terms of its charter or any agreement, instrument, judgment, decree, order, statute, rule, or governmental regulation applicable to that Subsidiary.

"*Consolidated Operating Rental Payments*" shall mean, for any period, all Consolidated Rental Payments attributable to Operating Leases.

"*Consolidated Rental Payments*" shall mean, for any period, the aggregate amount of all fixed and percentage rents (but excluding the interest component of all rentals under Capital Leases) paid under all leases (whether Capital Leases or Operating Leases) of the Borrower and its Subsidiaries as lessee, all as determined on a consolidated basis in accordance with GAAP.

Sample 14-G   *Cash Flow to Debt*

Ratio of Consolidated Cash Flow to Consolidated Debt. For any fiscal quarter listed below, the ratio of Consolidated Cash Flow for the period of four consecutive fiscal quarters ending with such fiscal quarter (or, in the case of (x) September 30, 1998, such fiscal quarter, times 4, (y) December 31, 1998, the two consecutive fiscal quarters ending with such quarter, times 2, and (z) March 31, 1999, the three consecutive fiscal quarters ending with such quarter, times $4/3$), to Consolidated Debt as at the end of such fiscal quarter will not be less than the ratio set forth below with respect to such fiscal quarter:

Year	March 31	June 30	September 30	December 31
2015	–	–	.09	.05
2016	.04	.05	.06	.07
2017	.07	.09	.09	.10
2018	.10	.10	.10	.20
2019	.20	.20	.20	.20

2020	.20	.20	.20	.20
2021	.20	.20	.20	.20
2022	.20	.20	.20	.20

"*Consolidated Cash Flow*" means with respect to Borrower and its Consolidated Subsidiaries for any fiscal period, without duplication, (i) the sum of (A) payments received during such period in respect of accounts receivable, (B) interest income during such period, to the extent received in cash, and (C) net proceeds received during such period from the sale of accounts receivable, *minus* (ii) the sum of (D) the cost of goods sold during such period, (E) operating expenses during such period, (F) cash dividends paid on the Preferred Stock during such period, (G) taxes paid during such period, (H) interest accrued during such period on Debt, (I) extraordinary losses incurred during such period and (J) Consolidated Net Capital Expenditures during such period.

Sample 14-H   *Debt to EBITDA*

Leverage. At no time during the Fiscal Years set forth below shall the ratio of (i) Consolidated Total Debt at such time to (ii) EBITDA for the four fiscal quarters of the Company then most recently ended (considered as a single accounting period) exceed the ratio set forth below opposite such Fiscal Year:

Fiscal Year Ending December 31	Ratio
2015	3.50:1.0
2016	3.25:1.0
2017	2.75:1.0
2018	2.00:1.0
2019	1.50:1.0
2020	1.50:1.0
2021 and thereafter	1.50:1.0

"EBITDA" means, for any period, the consolidated net income of the Company and its Consolidated Subsidiaries for such period *plus* any amount deducted (or, in the case of extraordinary gains, minus any amount added) in the computation thereof for (i) charges against income for all federal, state and local income and franchise taxes, (ii) the consolidated interest expense of the Company and its Consolidated Subsidiaries, (iii) any extraordinary gains or losses, (iv) amortization of goodwill and other intangibles, (including, without limitation, amortization of any inventory write-up) and (v) depreciation.

"Consolidated Total Debt" means at any date the Debt of the Company and its Subsidiaries, determined on a consolidated basis of such date.

Sample 14-1   *Minimum EBITDA*

Minimum EBITDA. The Company will not permit EBITDA for the period (a) from April 1, 1998, through (x) the last day of the fiscal quarter ended on June 30, 1998 (taken as one accounting period), to be less than $10 million, (y) the last day of the fiscal quarter ended on September 30, 1998, to be less than $17 million, and (z) the last day of fiscal quarter ended on December 31, 1998, to be less than $30 million, and (b) for any period of four consecutive fiscal quarters (taken as one accounting period) ended on the last day of any fiscal quarter set forth below to be less than the amount set forth opposite such fiscal quarter:

Fiscal Quarter Ending	Amount
March 31, 2015	$38,000,000
June 30, 2015	$38,000,000
September 30, 2015	$38,000,000
December 31, 2015	$38,000,000
March 31, 2016	$42,000,000
June 30, 2016	$42,000,000
September 30, 2016	$42,000,000
December 31, 2016	$42,000,000
March 31, 2017	$46,000,000
June 30, 2017	$46,000,000

September 30, 2017	$46,000,000
December 31, 2017	$46,000,000
March 31, 2018	$50,000,000
June 30, 2018	$50,000,000
September 30, 2018	$50,000,000
December 31, 2018	$50,000,000
March 31, 2019	$55,000,000
June 30, 2019	$55,000,000
September 30, 2019	$55,000,000
December 31, 2019	$55,000,000
March 31, 2020	$60,000,000
June 30, 2020	$60,000,000

Sample 14-J   *Cumulative EBITDA*

Cumulative Consolidated EBITDA. As at each date listed below, the Borrower will not permit Cumulative Consolidated EBITDA to be less than the amount set forth below opposite such date:

Date of Determination	Cumulative Consolidated EBITDA Amount
November 30, 2015	$ 5,000,000
December 31, 2015	$10,000,000
January 31, 2016	$15,000,000
February 28, 2016	$25,000,000
March 31, 2016	$35,000,000
April 30, 2016	$45,000,000
May 31, 2016	$50,000,000
June 30, 2016	$57,000,000

July 31, 2016	$65,000,000
August 31, 2016	$75,000,000
September 30, 2016	$80,000,000

Sample 14-K   *Minimum Net Worth*

Minimum Net Worth. Consolidated stockholders' equity of the Borrower and its Consolidated Subsidiaries will at no time be less than $250 million.

Sample 14-L   *Consolidated Tangible Net Worth—Version 1*

Minimum Consolidated Tangible Net Worth. Consolidated Tangible Net Worth will at no time be less than $400 million.

"*Consolidated Tangible Net Worth*" shall mean at any date the consolidated stockholders' equity (other than any redeemable or other similar preferred stock) of the Company and its Consolidated Subsidiaries less their consolidated Intangible Assets, all determined as of such date. For purposes of this definition, "Intangible Assets" means the amount (to the extent reflected in determining such consolidated stockholders' equity) of (i) all write-ups (other than write-ups resulting from foreign currency translations and write-ups of assets of a going concern business made within twelve months after the acquisition of such business) subsequent to December 31, 1997, in the book value of any asset owned by the Company or a Consolidated Subsidiary, (ii) all Investments in unconsolidated Subsidiaries, (iii) all equity investments in Persons which are not Subsidiaries, and (iv) all unamortized debt discount and expense, unamortized deferred charges, goodwill, patents, trademarks, service marks, trade names, copyrights, organization or developmental expenses, and other intangible assets.

Sample 14-M   *Consolidated Tangible Net Worth—Version 2*

Maintenance of Consolidated Tangible Net Worth. Consolidated Tangible Net Worth will not, at any time during any period set forth below, be less than the applicable amount set forth below opposite such period:

Period		
From and including the last day of Fiscal Year	**To but not including the last day of Fiscal Year**	**Amount**
The Effective Date	2015	$100,000,000
2015	2016	$130,000,000
2016	2017	$175,000,000
2017	2018	$200,000,000
2018	2019	$300,000,000
2019	2020	$420,000,000
2020	2021	$530,000,000
2021	2022 and thereafter	$600,000,000

"Consolidated Tangible Net Worth" means at any date the consolidated stockholders' equity of the Borrower and its Consolidated Subsidiaries less their consolidated Intangible Assets, all determined as of such date. For purposes of this definition, "Intangible Assets" shall be determined in accordance with generally accepted accounting principles and includes, without limitation, goodwill, patents, trademarks, service marks, trade names, copyrights, organization or developmental expenses, and other intangible assets.

Sample 14-N   *Consolidated Tangible Net Worth—Version 3*

Minimum Consolidated Tangible Net Worth. Consolidated Tangible Net worth will at no time be less than the sum of (i) $500,000,000 and (ii) 50% of the consolidated net income of the Company and its Consolidated Subsidiaries for each fiscal year of the Company ending after December 31, 1997. For purposes of this Section, if, for any such fiscal year consolidated net income of the Company and its Consolidated Subsidiaries shall be less than zero, the amount calculated pursuant to clause (ii) above for such fiscal year shall be zero.

"Consolidated Tangible Net Worth" shall mean at any date the consolidated stockholders' equity (other than any redeemable or other similar preferred stock) of the Company and its Consolidated Subsidiaries less their consolidated Intangible Assets, all determined as of such date. For purposes of this definition, "Intangible Assets" means the amount (to the extent reflected in determining such consolidated stockholders' equity) of (i) all write-ups (other than write-ups resulting from foreign currency translations and write-ups of assets of a going concern business made within twelve months after the acquisition of such business) subsequent to December 31, 1997, in the book value of any asset owned by the Company or a Consolidated Subsidiary, (ii) all Investments in unconsolidated Subsidiaries, (iii) all equity investments in Persons which are not Subsidiaries carried other than at market value on the consolidated balance sheets of the Company and its Consolidated Subsidiaries, and (iv) all unamortized debt discount and expense, unamortized deferred charges, goodwill, patents, trademarks, service marks, trade names, copyrights, organization or developmental expenses and other intangible items (including, without limitation, any asset identified in the consolidated balance sheets of the Company and its Consolidated Subsidiaries to the extent such asset consists of or includes the present value of future profits or any other similar item).

Sample 14-O   *Consolidated Tangible Net Worth—Version 4*

Minimum Consolidated Tangible Net Worth. Consolidated Tangible Net Worth will at no time be less than Minimum Adjusted Net Worth. "Minimum Adjusted Net Worth" means, at any date, the amount of $500 million adjusted from time to time as follows:

(i)   if and whenever the consolidated stockholders' equity of the Borrower and its Consolidated Subsidiaries is increased after the date hereof as a result of the issuance or sale of capital stock of the Borrower (or options, rights or warrants to acquire such stock), Minimum Adjusted Net Worth shall be increased by an amount equal to such increase in consolidated stockholders' equity; and

(ii)   at the end of each of the Borrower's fiscal quarters ending after the date hereof, Minimum Adjusted Net Worth shall be increased from time to time above its previous level (but not decreased) by the amount (if any) necessary so that cumulative increases pursuant to this clause (ii) equal 50% of the consolidated net income of the Borrower and its Consolidated Subsidiaries for the period (treated as one accounting period) beginning on January 1, 1998 and ending at the end of such fiscal quarter.

Sample 14-P   *Leverage Ratio—Version 1*

Debt. Consolidated Debt will at no time exceed 150% of Consolidated Tangible Net Worth, and total Debt of all Consolidated Subsidiaries (excluding Debt of a Consolidated Subsidiary to the Borrower or to a Wholly-

Owned Consolidated Subsidiary) will at no time exceed 20% of Consolidated Tangible Net Worth. For purposes of this Section any preferred stock of a Consolidated Subsidiary held by a Person other than the Borrower or a Wholly-Owned Consolidated Subsidiary shall be included, at the higher of its voluntary or involuntary liquidation value, in "Consolidated Debt" and in the "Debt" of such Consolidated Subsidiary.

Sample 14-Q   *Leverage Ratio—Version 2*

Leverage Ratio. At all times during each period set forth below, the ratio of (i) Consolidated Senior Debt of the Parent and its Subsidiaries to (ii) Consolidated Tangible Net Worth plus Subordinated Debt of the Company shall not exceed the ratio set forth below opposite such period:

Period		
From and including the last day of Fiscal Year	To but not including the last day of Fiscal Year	Ratio
The Effective Date	2015	4.0:1
2015	2016	3.5:1
2016	2017	2.5:1
2017	2018	1.5:1

Sample 14-R   *Cumulative EBITDA*

Cumulative Consolidated EBITDA. As at each date listed below, the Borrower will not permit Cumulative Consolidated EBITDA to be less than the amount set forth below opposite such date:

Date of Determination	Cumulative Consolidated EBITDA Amount
November 30, 2015	$5,000,000
December 31, 2015	$10,000,000
January 31, 2016	$15,000,000
February 28, 2016	$25,000,000
March 31, 2016	$35,000,000

April 30, 2016	$45,000,000
May 31, 2016	$50,000,000
June 30, 2016	$57,000,000
July 31, 2016	$65,000,000
August 31, 2016	$75,000,000
September 30, 2016	$80,000,000

Sample 14-S   *Working Capital*

Working Capital. Consolidated Current Assets will at no time be less than 1.25% of Consolidated Current Liabilities, and Consolidated Working Capital will at no time be less than $10 million.

"*Consolidated Current Assets*" means at any date the consolidated current assets of the Borrower and its Consolidated Subsidiaries determined as of such date.

"*Consolidated Current Liabilities*" means at any date (i) the consolidated current liabilities of the Borrower and its Consolidated Subsidiaries plus (ii) the current liabilities of any Person (other than the Borrower or a Consolidated Subsidiary) which are Guaranteed by the Borrower or a Consolidated Subsidiary, all determined as of such date.

"*Consolidated Working Capital*" means at any date the amount by which Consolidated Current Assets exceeds Consolidated Current Liabilities as of such date.

Sample 14-T   *Current Ratio*

Current Ratio. The Company will not permit the ratio of (i) consolidated current assets of the Company and its Subsidiaries to (ii) consolidated current liabilities of the Company and its Subsidiaries at any time to be less than 1.25 to 1. For purposes of this Section 9.08, the terms "*consolidated current assets*" and "*consolidated current liabilities*" shall have the respective meanings assigned to them by GAAP, provided that there shall be excluded from consolidated current assets all cash and cash equivalents and all prepaid expenses and that there shall be excluded from consolidated current liabilities the currently maturing portion of all long-term Indebtedness of the Company and its Subsidiaries and accrued interest expense.

Sample 14-U   *Quick Ratio*

Quick Ratio. The ratio of cash, cash equivalents and receivables to current liabilities shall at no time be less than 1.10 to 1.

Sample 14-V   *Excess Cash Flow—Version 1*

Mandatory Incremental Prepayments. (i) There shall become due and payable, and the Company shall prepay, on the ninetieth day following the last day of each fiscal year of the Company beginning with the fiscal year ending December 31, 2015, an aggregate principal amount of the Notes equal to 80% of Excess Cash Flow for such fiscal year (or, in the case of the payment for the first such period, for the period beginning on the Closing Date and ending on the last day of such fiscal year).

"*Consolidated Cash Flow*" means, for any period, (i) the consolidated net income of the Company and its Consolidated Subsidiaries for such period before interest expense and provision for income taxes and without giving effect to any extraordinary gains or extraordinary losses, plus the amount of (x) all amortization of goodwill and other intangibles, (y) depreciation and (z) all accruals for retiree health costs to the extent deducted in arriving at consolidated net income for such period, *minus* (ii) the sum of (x) all current accrued income taxes of the Company and its Consolidated Subsidiaries during such period and (y) Consolidated Capital Expenditures for such period.

"*Excess Cash Flow*" means, for any period, an amount equal to (i) Consolidated Cash Flow for such period plus (or minus) any net cash extraordinary gains (or net cash extraordinary losses) for such period of the Company and its Consolidated Subsidiaries *minus* (ii) the sum for such period of (x) Total Debt Service plus (y) all optional payments of the Notes during such period.

Sample 14-W   *Excess Cash Flow—Version 2*

On the date that is ninety days after the last day of each fiscal year of the Borrower, 75% of Excess Cash Flow for the fiscal year then last ended shall be applied: (x) first, to the prepayment of the outstanding principal amount of Term Loans and (y) second, to the extent remaining after the application required by preceding clause (x), to the prepayment of the outstanding principal amount of Revolving Loans.

"*Excess Cash Flow*" shall mean, for each annual period ending December 31, an amount, if positive, equal to (a) the net increase or net decrease (which decrease shall be stated as a negative number for the purposes of the remainder of this definition) for such period, if any, in "cash and cash equivalents" as set forth on a Consolidated Statement of Cash Flows of the Borrower and its Subsidiaries *plus* (b) the decrease, if any, or *less* the increase, if any, from the beginning of the period to the end of such period in the aggregate outstanding principal amount of Revolving Loans except that any such decrease will not be added to the extent that (i) such decrease permanently reduced the Total Revolving Loan Commitment or (ii) such decrease is attributable to a repayment of Revolving Loans during such period which may not be reborrowed for any purpose *less* the sum of (c) Net Cash Proceeds of Asset Sales occurring during such period not required as of the end of such period to be applied to the Loans pursuant to [asset sale proceeds paydown provision] and being held for reinvestment in the business, (d) the excess of Maximum Capex Amount for such period over Consolidated Capital Expenditures for such period to the extent such amount is permitted to be expended in the next period or periods (which amounts shall not exceed $50 million for each period), (e) any increase in "cash and cash equivalents" which is held outside of the United States to the extent that (i) repatriation of such amount is prohibited or delayed by applicable local law or (ii) the Borrower has determined in good faith that repatriation of such amount would have a material adverse tax consequence, (f) amounts received from casualty insurance proceeds and condemnation and eminent domain awards during such period and not yet applied as at the end of such period to restore or replace the assets damaged, destroyed or taken and (g) cash proceeds from the sale of receivables *plus* the sum of (h) the sum of all amounts deducted in determining Excess Cash Flow (w) in respect of the prior period pursuant to clause (c) of this definition and not reinvested, (x) in respect of prior periods pursuant to clause (e) of this definition, to the extent repatriated during such current period and (z) in respect of the prior period pursuant to clause (f) of this definition, to the extent not expended during such current period and *less* (i) the amount, if any, of Term Loans repaid during such period pursuant to [optional prepayment provisions].

Sample 14-X   *Excess Cash Flow—Version 3*

"*Excess Cash Flow*" means, for any period the excess (if any) of:

> the sum of (i) Available Cash Flow for such fiscal period and (ii) any decrease in Consolidated Net Working Investment between the beginning and the end of such period;

over

the sum of (i) Consolidated Capital Expenditures for such period, (ii) any increase in Consolidated Net Working Investment between the beginning and the end of such period, (iii) cash dividends paid on preferred stock during such period, (iv) mandatory reductions of long-term Debt of the Borrower and its Consolidated Subsidiaries during such period (adjusted to eliminate the effect of prepayments on account of Excess Cash Flow for a prior period) and (v) repayments during such period of the revolving credit loans and short-term Debt of the Borrower and its Consolidated Subsidiaries that were not made with the proceeds of other Debt.

"*Available Cash Flow*" means, for any fiscal period, the sum of (i) Consolidated Net Income for such period *plus* (ii) to the extent deducted in determining Consolidated Net Income for such period, depreciation, amortization and other similar noncash charges *plus* (iii) any increase (or minus any decrease) during such period in deferred tax liabilities of the Borrower and its Consolidated Subsidiaries, taken as a whole.

Sample 14-Y   *Excess Cash Flow—Version 4*

"*Excess Cash Flow*" means, for any period, the excess, if any, of (a) EBITDA of the Borrower and its Subsidiaries for such period over (b) the sum of (i) cash tax expense of the Borrower and its Subsidiaries for such period, (ii) cash interest expense paid by the Borrower and its Subsidiaries for such period, (iii) the aggregate amount of (a) all mandatory payments of the principal amount of the Term Advances made during such period, and (b) all scheduled payments of the principal amount of any other funded debt or other indebtedness for borrowed money (including Capitalized Leases) of the Borrower and its Subsidiaries (determined in accordance with GAAP but excluding any Revolving Advances and L/C Advances) required to be made during such period, (iv) the aggregate amount equal to the amount of all Capital Expenditures of the Borrower and its Subsidiaries paid in cash during such period to the extent permitted by this Agreement, (v) if there was a net decrease in consolidated current accounts payable and current accrued liabilities of the Borrower and its Subsidiaries during such period, the amount of such net decrease, (vi) if there was a net increase in consolidated current receivables and current inventories of the Borrower and its Subsidiaries during such period, the amount of such net increase, and (vii) cash dividends paid by the Borrower to Holdings during such period to the extent permitted under [specified clause of restricted payments covenant].

Sample 14-Z　　*Excess Cash Flow—Version 5*

On each Business Day, the Company shall repay the Working Capital Loans in an aggregate principal amount equal to the excess, if any, of (i) the aggregate amount of Cash and Temporary Cash Investments of the Company and its Subsidiaries at such date (excluding any such amounts then in the insurance Account referred to in the Security Agreement) over (ii) the sum of (x) $5 million plus (y) the aggregate amount of expenditures of the Company and its Subsidiaries to be paid before the end of the second Business Day after such day, as estimated in good faith by the chief financial officer or the treasurer of the Company, together with accrued and unpaid interest on the amount so prepaid to but excluding the date of such prepayment.

Sample 14-AA　*Limit on Cash*

Limitation on Available Liquid Assets. The Company shall prepay Revolving Credit Loans from time to time outstanding to the extent necessary so that Available Liquid Assets do not exceed $3 million in aggregate amount at the close of business on any three consecutive Domestic Business Days on which Revolving Credit Loans are outstanding.

Sample 14-BB　*Weekly Cash Sweep*

Cash Sweep Amount. On Tuesday of each week, the Borrower shall deliver to the Agent (a) an amount (the "Cash Sweep Amount") equal to the amount, if any, by which (i) the sum of (A) Aggregate Cash On Hand at the close of business on the preceding Friday *plus* (B) the aggregate principal amount of each Borrowing and each withdrawal from the Cash Collateral Account, if any, effected since such preceding Friday *minus* (C) Anticipated Cash Needs as of such Tuesday exceeds (ii) $1 million and (b) a certificate of the Borrower's chief financial officer dated such date as to such Aggregate Cash On Hand, Borrowings and Cash Collateral Account withdrawals, Anticipated Cash Needs and Cash Sweep Amount.

"*Aggregate Cash on Hand*" means, at any time, without duplication, (a) all funds in the Collection Accounts, the General Account and the Concentration Account at such time, (b) all Temporary Cash Investments at such time and (c) all other cash on hand, but does not include (i) amounts in any bank account representing funds in respect of third-party instrument that are uncollected and undrawable at such time, (ii) up to $2 million of cash on hand or (iii) any amounts in the Cash Collateral Account at such time.

"*Anticipated Cash Needs*" means, as of any date, the aggregate amount of cash disbursements in excess of cash receipts reasonably anticipated to be required in the operations of the Borrower during the period from (but excluding) the Determination Date immediately prior to such date to (and including) the next Determination Date after such date (or, if such date is a Determination Date, to and including such date), as such anticipated cash requirements may be adjusted in light of actual cash receipts and disbursements during such period as of such date that result in a material deviation from such cash requirements as previously anticipated; and will take into account amounts required to cover checks issued by the Borrower and expected to be presented for collection during such period, but will not take into account any amounts with respect to Letters of Credit expected to be issued or drawn during such period other than the amount of any Reimbursement Obligation expected to be paid in cash during such period.

Chapter 15: Amendments, Waivers, and Control Provisions

See generally:

CAROLYN E.C. PARIS, HOW TO DRAFT FOR CORPORATE FINANCE, ch. 17 (PLI 2006).

For a discussion of collective action clauses (to mitigate the "hold-out" or "free-rider" problem) in sovereign debt offerings:

CAROLYN E.C. PARIS, HOW TO DRAFT FOR CORPORATE FINANCE § 17:5 (PLI 2006).

In June 2014, the United States Supreme Court declined to hear an appeal by Argentina of a lower court judgment requiring it to pay holdouts from earlier restructurings, a decision that has provoked much commentary. It should be interesting to follow the developments and trace the implications for sovereign debt markets and for choice of law.

Chapter 16: Risk-Based Review; Transactions Analysis

Cases that test corporate or financial transactions under debt agreement terms include the following:

"Can't do indirectly":

In re Associated Gas & Elec. Co., 61 F. Supp. 11 (S.D.N.Y. 1944), *aff'd*, 149 F.2d 996 (2d Cir. 1945).

"All or substantially all":

Sharon Steel Corp. v. Chase Manhattan Bank, N.A., 691 F.2d 1039 (2d Cir. 1982); *compare* 8 DEL. CODE § 271, *e.g.*, as relevant in Hollinger Inc. v. Hollinger Int'l, Inc., 858 A.2d 342 (Del. Ch. 2004).

Phila. Nat'l Bank v. B.S.F. Co., 199 A.2d 557 (Del. Ch. 1964), *rev'd on other grounds*, 204 A.2d 746 (Del. 1964).

Floyd Norris, *Bondholders Scream Foul as Tyco Splits*, N.Y. Times, June 29, 2007 (noting the *Sharon Steel* case; after Tyco split, the obligor on Tyco bonds estimated to represent 40% of the pre-split company, and "bondholders fear the new Tyco will be a prime candidate for a leveraged buyout, which could saddle the company with more debt and reduce the value of existing bonds.").

BCE Bondholders Eye Lawsuit Over Deal, Globe and Mail, July 11, 2007 (bond rating and value drops at prospect of buyout; timing of disclosure also at issue).

Cases on calls:

Morgan Stanley & Co. v. Archer Daniels Midland Co., 570 F. Supp. 1529 (S.D.N.Y. 1983) ("clean money" call); Mutual Sav. Life Ins. Co. v. James River Corp. of Va., 716 So. 2d 1172 (Ala. 1998) (simultaneous tender and call did not violate indenture).

Intentional default and early call cases:

In re LHD Realty Corp., 726 F.2d 327 (7th Cir. 1984); Sharon Steel Corp. v. Chase Manhattan Bank, N.A., 691 F.2d 1039 (2d Cir. 1982); *In re* Hennepin Cnty. 1986 Recycling Bond Litig., 540 N.W.2d 494 (Minn. 1995).

New York Housing Agency Settles Case Arising from Early Bond Redemption, Bond Buyer 4, Dec. 7, 1988.

Some Investors Accept Accord in Suit Against New York HDC, Bond Buyer 1, May 11, 1988.

Challenges to leveraged buyouts and restructurings:

Metro. Life Ins. Co. v. RJR Nabisco, Inc., 716 F. Supp. 1504 (S.D.N.Y. 1989); Geren v. Quantum Chem. Corp., 832 F. Supp. 728 (S.D.N.Y. 1993); Harris Trust & Sav. Bank v. E-II Holdings, Inc., 926 F.2d 636 (7th Cir. 1991) (general challenges to leveraged buyouts did not prevail).

F. John Stark, III, J. Andrew Rahl, Jr. & Lori C. Seegers, *"Marriott Risk," A New Model Covenant to Restrict Transfer of Wealth from Bondholders to Stockholders*, 1994 Colum. Bus. L. Rev. 503 (1994).

Interpretation of term loan B and high yield bond provisions

The term loan B and high yield markets have generated a few disputes and some case law in the last few years. One example was the *Realogy* case, see: http://www.jonesday.com/files/Publication/f717800c-934e-4737-8b8c-

89c5b2633736/Presentation/PublicationAttachment/794567da-f366-40dd-a99f-5c4a99597a53/Exchange%20Offer.pdf

The *Realogy* case demonstrates that the complexity of financing documents—referring to and depending on one another, full of exceptions to exceptions and amorphous or expandable concepts such as "the Credit Agreement"—can easily give rise to disputes and unintended results, particularly where non-traditional participants bring different expectations to the table and read the documents accordingly.

Chapter 17:   Best Practices

Drafting errors on the increase:

See Aaron E. Hoffman & Lawrence E. Zabinski, *Drafting Errors and More—Claims Arising From Documents*, ALAS Loss Prevention J., Fall 2003 (noting failure to make parallel changes in a companion document as the cause of a malpractice action; other costly mistakes involved errors in the drafting of mathematical formulas, or the use of the wrong mathematical formula). "[Most drafting errors] could be avoided by a careful and thorough proofreading and review of all of the documents. That would uncover inconsistencies within and between documents, and flush out stray holdover clauses (from an earlier transaction that was used as "precedent"), which have no place in the current transaction."

Small change, big impact:

An important case that turned on the interpretation of contract wording was Interactivecorp (f/k/a USA Interactive) and USANI Sub. LLK v. Vivendi Universal, et al. (Del. Ch. July 6, 2004). In this case, the judge decided to give effect to the plain words of a limited partnership agreement drafted by Vivendi's lawyers, disregarding Vivendi's claims that what appeared to be an income tax gross-up was not intended to be.

On April 6, 2007, Charter Communications, Inc. filed a complaint against Irell & Manella in Federal court (Central District of California, Southern Division) alleging significant damages were caused by the "mistaken and negligent" omission of a key clause by "an associate (the 'Associate') [sic]", and then the failure by others, partners and associates, to spot the deletion. It is further alleged that distributions did not highlight the omission through proper blacklining. In addition, the complaint alleges that the firm "further failed to exercise reasonable care in coordinating the terms of various transactional documents that it prepared." The background described in the complaint is typical as an overture to alleged error—parties were reasonably close to closing when a regulatory problem was spotted. To work around the regulatory problem, a major structural change in the deal was required, and to give effect to that quite significant changes needed to be made to multiple, complex agreements. Something as simple as incorrect blacklining and perhaps working off an incorrect draft could have been at the root of the alleged errors. The complaint is worth reading also for its description of the complex holding company structure used in the deal—again a typical feature of today's M&A transactions. The case was settled.

A missing cross-reference?

In the rather odd case *In re* Sonicblue, Inc., 2007 Bankr. LEXIS 1057 (Bankr. N.D. Cal. Mar. 26, 2007), Pillsbury Winthrop Shaw Pittman was disqualified from acting for a debtor in possession (the bankrupt company) where it had given an ordinary enforceability opinion on some bonds issued earlier by the company and the bondholders had (disingenuously in my view) advanced a claim against Pillsbury on the basis that the opinion did not accurate reflect that bankruptcy of the obligor might affect bondholder recovery (in this case because the bonds were issued with original issue discount). Failure of the law firm to disclose this claim by the bondholders and thus an alleged conflict of interest resulted in their disqualification. *See Pillsbury Ejected from Bankruptcy Case*, law.com, Mar. 27, 2007. The opinion at issue however seems merely to have included a mistake, where the bankruptcy qualification did not contain a complete cross-reference to all of the enforceability paragraphs in the opinion—an error hardly more substantive than a typo. The case is a fascinating read if you are looking to understand the dynamics of how bondholder actions and intercreditor relations play out in a troubled credit situation.

Regarding the use of standard forms, see generally:

CAROLYN E.C. PARIS, HOW TO DRAFT FOR CORPORATE FINANCE, ch. 18 (PLI 2006).

Regarding computer-based drafting, see generally:

CAROLYN E.C. PARIS, HOW TO DRAFT FOR CORPORATE FINANCE, ch. 20 (PLI 2006).

Regarding document retention:

The Enron case, and the role and fate of Arthur Andersen in particular, put the spotlight on document retention (or document destruction) policies and practices. What is noteworthy, in that case and in several high profile stories of (alleged) financial wrongdoing, is how institutions and individuals have found themselves hung, not on the merits of what they did or did not do, but, but based on what they said or wrote and what they subsequently did with the records of what they said or wrote.

Though it was not much use to Andersen by the time the decision was handed down, in 2005 the Supreme Court held that the jury instruction under which Andersen had been convicted of obstruction of justice by virtue of "corrupt persuasion" related to the destruction of files was in error, and that Andersen did not have the requisite intent. Arthur Andersen LLP v. United States, No. 04-368 (May 31, 2005). At the time of the relevant actions, it was likely that Andersen and indeed many others were operating a document retention program that focused on whether an action or investigation had in fact commenced as the cut-off for "file cleanup." The following provision from Sarbanes-Oxley (18 U.S.C. § 1519), enacted after the Enron collapse, includes the concept of "in contemplation of":

> Whoever knowingly alters, destroys, mutilates, conceals, covers up, falsifies, or makes a false entry in any record, document, or tangible object with the intent to impede, obstruct, or influence the investigation or proper administration of any matter within the jurisdiction of any department or agency of the United States or any case filed under title 11, or in relation to or contemplation of any such matter or case, shall be fined under this title, imprisoned not more than 20 years, or both.

This provision, the Enron case, and other legal developments, have put pressure on the well-known practice in legal and financial circles of "file cleanup." The state of files and records within a financial institution or law firm is hardly ever ideal from a litigation perspective, a problem that has become nearly intractable in today's ubiquitous computing environment.

In terms of retaining drafts, for example, it is the practice of some firms to maintain files of drafts of documents; historically, it has been as firmly the practice, or at least policy, of other firms to destroy such files. But what do those policies really mean in an era of electronic documents, where documents are stored within a document management system, distributed electronically and so forth? An important case interpreting a contract provision placed heavy weight on the exchange of drafts showing what appears to be electronic redlining. Interactivecorp. (f/k/a USA Interactive) and USANI Sub. LLK v. Vivendi Universal, et. al. (Del. Ch. July 6, 2004).

One thing that seems very clear is that emails must be considered as fully real and evidentiary as paper documents sent to files or out of the office—and, since they are treated as more informal and evanescent communications, much more likely to yield up embarrassments. For a time, those who pursued a ruthless strategy of file destruction (including the quick and permanent deletion of emails) could be advantaged by that fact alone. But now there are requirements for email preservation, and financial institutions must monitor email for compliance purposes. In addition, firms have sustained significant liabilities based on their inability to comply with email discovery orders.

Some important and useful work has been done to help businesses (including law firms) think through the issues surrounding document retention (*see* The Sedona Guidelines: Best Practice Guidelines for Managing Information & Records in the Electronic Age—A Project of the Sedona Conference Working Group on Best Practices for Electronic Document Retention & Production, November 2007), and there is convergence on some key points that lawyers working with documents in the electronic environment (which includes all finance lawyers, of course) should keep in mind:

1. The company's or firm's IS department will run backup cycles on electronic records for disaster recovery purposes. These cycles are typically rather short. The IS department may also use software "archiving" solutions that move records into cheaper and less accessible storage based on currency, usage, and so forth. Neither of these IS-driven "document retention" activities is a substitute for an active documents and records retention policy, which instead looks to maintain in an organized fashion those records that the company or firm needs to retain and to discard or destroy other documents and items of information.

2. All of the above is subject to override by a "litigation hold"—the need to preserve all information in the company's possession that has potential evidentiary value in a pending or threatened action or investigation. A litigation hold can reach beyond the company's IS system to any other IT environment where relevant information may reside, for example, on an employee's home PC.

3. It is nearly impossible to conclude that a given electronic record has been or can be deleted; pressing the "delete" key will result in complete deletion in only relatively rare circumstances.

4. The need to consciously manage electronic documents extends to metadata. Even the fact that a document has been viewed or printed creates a metadata record.

5. Email creates a very comprehensive correspondence file. All email exchanges with third parties should be considered of record for discovery purposes, which means that the drafting history of documents will be an open book, at least to the extent the drafts were sent out of the firm.

6. All internal electronic records that have not been destroyed in accordance with a proper documents retention policy will be subject to discovery; the appropriateness of the policy and whether it has

been implemented on a regular basis can determine whether a "negative inference" can be drawn that evidence has been wrongly destroyed.

Technical Drafting Checklist

1 Proper Connections

Have the proper connections been made to show how pieces of the contract fit together using: ❑

(a) cross-references ❑

(b) prioritizing words (*subject to, notwithstanding*) ❑

(c) linking words (*in accordance with*) ❑

Are there too many cross references and prioritizing and linking words? ❑

If so, have you gone back and reorganized or constructed definitions? ❑

Have you used cross-references in ways that are likely to confuse or mislead the reader? ❑

2 Consequential and Conforming Changes

Have you scrubbed the document at least once solely to make sure consequential and conforming changes have been made? ❑

Have you used brevity and clear organization as aids to achieving consistency? ❑

3 Language from Precedent

Do you know the provenance of the document and the purpose of each provision in it? ❑

Have you reserved some time for disengaged and careful reading of the contract word for word, including the boilerplate? In this, two heads are better than one, and it is better yet if one of the two heads can read with "fresh eyes." ❑

If the precedent seems cluttered with off-point wording, or is
simply too wordy for the matter at hand, have you junked it and
started from an outline or term sheet instead? ❑

4 Appropriate Level of Generality/Specificity

Have you read literally and imagined or even charted different
scenarios to test for unintended scope, *i.e.*, too much generality? ❑

Do the words apply when they should not? ❑

Have you imagined likely variations to test for too much
specificity? ❑

Are nonessential elements included such that a concept is too ·
limited, or limiting? ❑

5 Ambiguity and Vagueness

Have you eliminated structural or syntactic ambiguity by
reordering or using logical markers (if (p)(x) and (y)(a) or (b),
then (q))? ❑

Where there is vagueness in language, have you decided whether
it is helpful, or instead likely to be the source of misunderstanding
or conflict? ❑

If the latter, have you clarified or expressly deferred to subsequent
resolution? ❑

6 Logical Completeness and Correctness

Have you used flowcharts, outlines or diagrams as necessary to see
if your formal contract constructions lack logical completeness or
have overlapping coverage? ❑

Do you set up concepts of (a) versus (b) where (b) is short of
covering not-(a), or are there items that fall within both (a) and (b)?
Do you specify the consequences of (a), but not of not-(a)? ❑

Beyond the level of formal construction, does your contract deal
with likely scenarios, but not go on at length to address remote
hypothetical situations? Note that the expected term of the contract
is a key variable in this analysis. ❑

7 Over-Drafting

Have you made sure that you have not written more than is necessary for the purpose at hand? ❑

If something is not working right or is collecting barnacles (too many exceptions, parentheticals, "subject to's"), have you asked yourself whether it should be scrapped or reworked altogether, rather than made the subject of further elaboration? ❑

8 Too Many Words

Have you been concise? ❑

Have you eliminated unnecessary words/wording; updated archaic constructions; kept an eye out for overlapping provisions; reorganized to eliminate duplication and proliferating complexity? ❑

9 Definitions

Have you made sure that your definitions (admittedly formal and artificial) are not in fact counterintuitive? ❑

Have you made a definition whenever you find yourself repeating a lengthy formula of words, and considered making a definition when you find yourself repeating a cross-reference? ❑

Have you used definitions to encapsulate technical concepts or procedures that otherwise would slow the flow of reading comprehension? ❑

Have you made sure definitions do not contain active, substantive provisions, which are, in effect, hidden covenants? ❑

Have you made sure that you did not define obvious concepts? ❑

Have you kept a definition in the body of a contract if it is used in only that one place? ❑

Have you used defined terms that have no definition, or have you included definitions for defined terms that are not used? ❑

Once you have a defined term, have you used it everywhere it applies, but been careful about not using it when instead the ordinary language word is meant? ❑

Have you built related definitions logically, without repeating basic concepts and without adding nonintuitive qualifiers as you built? ❑

Have you made sure the definitions are not circular? ❑

Have you been careful to check for incorrect usage of "includes," which is illustrative, but is not definitive? ❑

Have you been careful that definition construction does not have unintended operational effect, and looked back at the definition each time it is used? ❑

10 Provisions in Related Documents

Have you analyzed through side-by-side reading to make sure the related agreements "tie" and "dovetail"? ❑

11 Lists

Have you used parallel construction? ❑

Have you fixed your lists when you added or deleted items? ❑

In particular: Suppose a concluding item in a list of exceptions was a basket or other clause defined by reference to all of the items above it, such as "in addition to the foregoing, Liens securing obligations of not more than $____ in aggregate". When you add to the list, are you careful to make the addition above the concluding clause, so that the new item is encompassed within "the foregoing"? ❑

12 Gender-Neutral Terms

Have you minimized the use of gender words? ❑

Appendix C

Indicative Terms for Bank Debt and Public Debt, Investment Grade Versus Non-Investment Grade

The basic terms for a particular deal will in the first instance drive off precedent and market. In fact, there is increasing standardization of terms from deal to deal and across types of deals. This is occurring for many reasons, ranging from the convergence of the traditionally separate private credit and public capital markets, to the ready availability of more market information, to the use of computer word-processing (which militates in favor of inertia, that is, precedent), to the pressure to produce documents and close deals on ever-shorter timetables.

A review of precedent is therefore extremely helpful in ascertaining the baseline for negotiations. Such a review would lead you to such "big-picture" generalities as the following:

- Covenants in investment grade debt are minimal and focus on one or two measures of creditworthiness or, in public debt, may merely preserve the public debt's priority relative to other debt, whereas non-investment grade debt agreements contain more covenants and "tighter" (that is, more restrictive) covenants.

- Covenants in private debt (where banks or insurance companies act as lenders) can be "tighter" than those in public debt instruments (where holdings can be widespread) because waivers and amendments are easier to obtain from private lenders than from a potentially large group of public debtholders.

- For the same reason, public debt tends to have "incurrence" tests (covenants that the company cannot breach except by "incurring" a debt or a lien, or otherwise taking some voluntary action), whereas financial "maintenance" covenants (where poor financial performance alone might result in a borrower's falling out of compliance) are customary in private debt.

Having a sense of the content and design of general terms and covenant packages for deals comparable to yours is a necessary prerequisite in professional representation of a business client. You need to make sure your deal is "in the ballpark," that is, that your client is not overreaching, on the one hand, or being unfairly treated, on the other hand. You and your client will save much time and preserve goodwill by graciously accepting those things that must be accepted as "market" (assuming the client can live with them). It is very wasteful to engage in, or to have to deal with, a lot of hand-waving and table-pounding over inevitabilities. Having a sense of other deals also helps you propose creative and constructive alternatives that are still "in the ballpark." An ancillary benefit to the lawyer who carefully prepares in this way is that a sophisticated client will almost always react with real appreciation to a firm grasp of market realities and possibilities. One of the things that lawyers can legitimately and honestly bring to the table as "value-added" (*cf.* hand-waving and table-pounding, above) by virtue of their day-in, day-out exposure is market expertise.

That said, it is the poorly advised client that agrees to a covenant package from some other deal just because it is "precedent" or "market." Locating the proposed covenant package within the relevant universe of market precedent is an important starting point, but not a substitute for particularized covenant analysis and negotiation. Well-advised clients spend time analyzing the scope and implications of covenants as those covenants apply to their particular businesses. It is the lawyer's job to make sure that the covenant package the client agrees to is understood by the client, is well-constructed, error-free and, insofar as practical, tailored to the client's needs and expectations. Covenants are not "just words," but have real and material ongoing impact on the client; and senior officers at a business are unlikely to be sympathetic to their line officers and well-paid lawyers when a contract negotiated at perhaps considerable expense does not reflect the business understanding or inadvertently prohibits a desired or even contemplated course of action.

The following charts are *indicative* only of terms you might find in a credit agreement versus public bond indenture, investment grade versus non-investment grade. To do your own analysis for a deal you should locate current comparables and prepare similar spreadsheets.

INDICATIVE TERMS COMPARISON
U.S. MARKET, DOLLAR-BASED FINANCINGS
(AS OF Q3 2014)

GENERAL TERMS	TYPE OF DEAL			
	Investment grade credit agreement (including commercial paper backstop)	Investment grade bonds	Leveraged credit agreement	High-yield bonds
Preliminary agreement	Commitment letter with term sheet, plus fee letter	Engagement letter, with no funding commitment; no commitment letter	Commitment letter with term sheet, plus fee letter	Engagement letter with no funding commitment—EXCEPT in deal context there may be a bridge financing which is committed with, if funded, anticipated high yield bond takeout
Nature of commitment	Commitment by lead banks, or possibly part firm and part "best efforts"	No commitment at engagement letter stage; firm underwriting commitment in underwriting agreement signed at pricing and T+3 before closing (if not registered, initial purchase agreement instead of underwriting agreement)	A firm commitment by lead banks if M&A-related or possibly "best efforts"; committed financing will often include market flex to adjust terms as necessary (within limits) for successful syndication	No commitment at engagement letter stage; firm underwriting commitment in underwriting agreement signed at pricing and T+3 before closing (if not registered, initial purchase agreement instead of underwriting agreement). Any backstop bridge loan commitment (for example, for bid) more like credit agreement commitment

GENERAL TERMS (cont'd)	Investment grade credit agreement	Investment grade bonds	Leveraged credit agreement	High-yield bonds
Indicative upfront fee structure (order of magnitude)	<1%	<1% at funding to underwriters out of spread between gross proceeds and net proceeds to issuer	1%–3% or more, if second-lien, mezzanine or other specialized issuance	2%–3% at funding to underwriters as spread between gross proceeds and net proceeds to issuer. Bridge could be similar or somewhat less split between "committed" and "funding" fees with another conversion or takeout fee when rolled or exchanged
Parties to definitive agreements	Company (could be multiple group borrowers with company guarantee; usually no subsidiary guarantees), plus possibly administrative agent, swingline lenders, letter of credit issuing banks, syndication agents, arrangers and bookrunners	Issuer, guarantors if any, and trustee (underwriter and issuer sign underwriting agreement)	Company (could be multiple group borrowers (including new ones added after closing); borrower could be acquired company upon upstream merger with acquisition company), typically with guarantors (parent holding company and subsidiaries), administrative agent, plus possibly documentation agent, swingline lenders, letter of credit issuing banks, syndication agents, arrangers and bookrunners	Issuer, guarantors, if any, and trustee (underwriter and issuer sign underwriting agreement)

GENERAL TERMS (cont'd)	Investment grade credit agreement	Investment grade bonds	Leveraged credit agreement	High-yield bonds
Definitive documentation	Credit agreement	Indenture (if public, qualified under the Trust Indenture Act of 1939; conditions precedent and representations are in the underwriting agreement)	Credit agreement, guarantees and security agreements (including mortgages, stock pledge agreements, intellectual property security agreements and any intercreditor agreements if security is shared among different creditor groups)	Indenture (if public, qualified under the Trust Indenture Act of 1939; conditions precedent and representations are in the underwriting agreement); bridge loan in leveraged acquisition is a hybrid credit agreement with high-yield bond terms
Disclosure document	Perhaps none, or possibly a "bank book"—private information book for the lending syndicate; no legal disclosure letters or accountants letters	Prospectus or similar offering memorandum; lawyers provide "10-b5" disclosure letters; accountants provide audit/comfort letters	"Bank book"—private information book (but may include public-only information) for the lending syndicate; no legal disclosure letters or accountants letters	Prospectus or similar offering memorandum; lawyers provide "10-b5" disclosure letters; accountants provide audit/comfort letters
Pricing on debt (and commitments during life of revolving credit)	LIBOR rate plus margin ranging from .1% to .75% (depending on ratings) or Base Rate (highest of Prime/Fed Funds rate + .5%) and one-month LIBOR; competitive or auction bid rates also available; facility fee (on total deal whether used or unused) ranging from, for example, .05% to .25% (typical where there is an auction feature or multiple facilities in which lenders will not participate ratably) and/or commitment fee on unused portion (ranging proportionately); letter of credit fee = margin over LIBOR with .125% p.a. fronting fee to letter of credit issuing bank; default rate on overdue amounts; may include multi-currency options	Fixed based on market conditions at time of pricing; based on comparables and spread over treasuries for the rating at the time (occasionally the indenture will cover a floating rate note issue)	Depending on credit rating, and market conditions generally, a spread over LIBOR, over Base Rate; letter of credit fee = margin over LIBOR with .125% p.a. fronting fee to letter of credit issuing bank; commitment fee of .375% to .5% on unused revolving commitments—but pricing may be subject to adjustments based on, for example, credit rating or total leverage ratio; default rate on overdue amounts; longer term tranche available at perhaps higher rates; may include multi-currency options	Fixed based on market conditions at time of pricing; based on comparables and spread over treasuries for the rating at the time

GENERAL TERMS (cont'd)	Investment grade credit agreement	Investment grade bonds	Leveraged credit agreement	High-yield bonds
Accrual	360 days (or, for Base Rate Loans, 365 days) and actual days elapsed	A year of twelve 30-day months	360 days (or, for Base Rate Loans, 365 days) and actual days elapsed	A year of twelve 30-day months
Maturity; type of facility	Usually a 364-day revolving facility or 3- or 5-year facility that occasionally includes a term loan component as well as revolving loans; may include swingline and letter of credit subfacilities, and foreign currency subfacilities; company may be able to request extension or increase of commitments on non-ratable basis	A fixed maturity; could contain sinking fund or other early mandatory redemptions	5-year revolving portion including swingline and letter of credit sub-facility; 5- to 7-year "term loan A" with scheduled amortization; 7- to 8-year "term loan B" with de minimis amortization before maturity	7 to 10 years fixed maturity dates with no sinking fund or other early mandatory redemptions

GENERAL TERMS (cont'd)	Investment grade credit agreement	Investment grade bonds	Leveraged credit agreement	High-yield bonds
Optional repayment or redemption; defeasance; satisfaction and discharge	Optional repayment in part or in full without premium at the end of any interest period	Possible early redemption at a premium; legal defeasance and covenant defeasance (making covenants inapplicable) available, in each case subject to certain conditions; notes may be discharged up to a year in advance of final maturity through deposit of funds with trustee (standard provision)	Optional repayment in part or in full at the end of any interest period; there may be soft-call (or hard-call) protection in the form of a premium for early refinancing of term tranches to preserve the margin and discourage opportunistic "repricing" refinancing	Starting at half the number of years to maturity (plus one if odd number of years to maturity), at a fixed premium (starting at 50% of coupon) that reduces each year; before that at a make-whole premium; up to 35% can be redeemed with the proceeds of an equity offering at a fixed premium equal to the interest rate so long as a minimum amount remains outstanding thereafter (for example, 65% of original issue); legal defeasance and covenant defeasance (making covenants inapplicable) available, in each case subject to certain conditions; notes may be discharged up to a year in advance of final maturity through deposit of funds with trustee (standard provision)

GENERAL TERMS (cont'd)	Investment grade credit agreement	Investment grade bonds	Leveraged credit agreement	High-yield bonds
Mandatory repayment (excluding acceleration upon default)	Excess exposure due to currency fluctuation (if multiple-currency options are available)	Might contain a Change of Control or "event risk" (change of control coupled with ratings downgrade) Offer to Purchase, but not for strongest issuers; some types of indentures may include sinking fund redemptions	For example: 50% of Excess Cash Flow less same-period optional prepayments; Net Cash Proceeds of asset sales or casualty subject to reinvestment rights; Net Cash Proceeds of Debt incurred not permitted under the agreement; excess exposure due to currency fluctuation (if multiple currency options are available)	Offer to Purchase at par plus interest must be made with proceeds of asset sales (with exceptions) to the extent not reinvested in the business or used to retire other senior debt within a negotiated period (for example, 12 or 18 months).
Yield protection; premium	Standard bank yield protection provisions: payments net of (negotiated) certain taxes; alternative pricing for illegality or inability to determine rate (historical Eurodollar provisions); increased costs provision; capital adequacy reserve costs; break-funding losses if payments made on day other than the end of an interest period.	Per optional redemption provisions; but generally not upon mandatory redemption or Offer to Purchase, or acceleration	Standard bank yield protection provisions: payments net of (negotiated) certain taxes; alternative pricing for illegality or inability to determine rate (historical Eurodollar provisions); increased costs provision; capital adequacy reserve costs; break-funding losses if payments made on day other than the end of an interest period	Per optional redemption provisions; but generally not upon mandatory redemption or Offer to Purchase (except change of control offer at 101%), or acceleration

GENERAL TERMS (cont'd)	Investment grade credit agreement	Investment grade bonds	Leveraged credit agreement	High-yield bonds
Acceleration and remedies	Majority can accelerate	Trustee or 25% of affected series can accelerate; majority may rescind acceleration upon cure; majority controls remedies (standard bondholder action provisions; notes held by issuer not counted)	Majority can accelerate	Trustee or 25% can accelerate; majority may rescind acceleration upon cure; majority controls remedies (standard bondholder action provisions; notes held by issuer not counted; notice and blockage provisions apply in subordinated debt)
Waiver and amendment	Majority can waive, except on standard money terms or voting provisions; there may be provisions that require hold-outs from votes requiring unanimity to sell at par	Waiver of defaults other than non-payment, by majority of series affected; technical amendments or amendments for the benefit of holders can be agreed to by the trustee; each holder affected for changes in money terms, amendment and waiver provisions or rank or guaranties; otherwise a majority of all series affected (notes held by issuer not counted)	Majority can waive, except on standard money terms, voting provisions or for release of all or substantially all (or sometimes "a substantial portion") of the collateral or guarantees; there may be provisions that require hold-outs from votes requiring unanimity to sell at par	Waiver of defaults other than non-payment, by majority; technical amendments or amendments for the benefit of holders can be agreed to by the trustee; each holder affected for changes in money terms, amendment and waiver provisions or rank or guaranties (notes held by issuer not counted)

GENERAL TERMS (cont'd)	Investment grade credit agreement	Investment grade bonds	Leveraged credit agreement	High-yield bonds
Security	None	None	Stock of main borrower by parent company guarantor; grant of security interest in "substantially" all assets of the borrower(s) and guarantor subsidiaries, but often with significant exceptions, including capital stock (but stock pledge of foreign subsidiaries of a U.S. company will be limited if the pledge would create a tax liability)	Senior notes may share in collateral but more typically unsecured
Guarantees	If specified subsidiaries can borrow, company guaranties those borrowings	Generally none	From parent holding company and all subsidiaries, including ones formed after closing; foreign subsidiaries of a U.S. company will typically be excluded if the guarantee would create tax liability	From, for example, Domestic Restricted Subsidiaries, subordinated for subordinated notes
Rank	Intended to be Senior Debt if there is any subordinated debt	Typically senior; specialized issues (regulatory capital, for example) may be subordinated	Senior debt—usually specifically included in the definition of Senior Debt	May be senior or subordinated
Transferability	With certain exceptions, consent of company and administrative agent (and for revolving exposure, swingline lenders and letter of credit banks) required to assign; participations may be granted without consent (limited flow-through of rights)	Normal for the market and subject to securities laws in relevant jurisdictions, depending of course on status of notes under the securities laws (144A, Reg. S, registered)	With certain exceptions, consent of company and administrative agent (and for revolving exposure, swingline lenders and letter of credit banks) required to assign; participations may be granted without consent (limited flow-through of rights)	Normal for the market and subject to securities laws in relevant jurisdictions, depending of course on status of notes under the securities laws (144A, Reg. S, registered)

GENERAL TERMS (cont'd)	Investment grade credit agreement	Investment grade bonds	Leveraged credit agreement	High-yield bonds
Entities restricted by agreement covenants	Generally, borrower and subsidiaries	Generally, issuer and Restricted Subsidiaries (sometimes limited to Significant Subsidiaries)	Generally, parent holding company, company and all subsidiaries or Restricted Subsidiaries	Generally, parent holding company if guarantor, company, and Restricted Subsidiaries
Effect of financial performance and ratings	Financial ratios and/or ratings may affect pricing directly through a pricing grid	Some investment grade indentures protect against event risk—where a change of control is accompanied with a ratings downgrade—with an Offer to Purchase requirement applicable in that event	Financial ratios and/or ratings may affect pricing directly through a pricing grid	May provide that, when (and so long as) notes are rated investment grade, covenants indicated * in the covenant summary are dropped
Change of control	May include a change of control default with change of control meaning (for a public company) that a person acquires more than a specified percentage (typically, 30%–50%) of the voting stock of the company	Merger provisions will generally permit/require successor to assume the debt, though the indenture might include "event risk" protection where a change of control is coupled with a ratings downgrade (triggering Offer to Purchase requirements)	Change of control outside the Permitted Holders (in private context) or a person acquiring more than a specified percentage (typically, 30%–50% of the voting stock of the company or parent holding company (in public context) will be a default	Change of control outside the Permitted Holders (in private context) or a person acquiring more than a specified percentage (typically, 30%–50% of the voting stock of the company or parent holding company (in public context) will trigger Offer to Purchase at 101% of principal plus interest

GENERAL TERMS *(cont'd)*	Investment grade credit agreement	Investment grade bonds	Leveraged credit agreement	High-yield bonds
Other general provisions	Normal sharing provisions; normal agent provisions; currency equivalents and business day adjustment provisions; notice; no waiver; attorney costs; indemnification; set-off adjustment; confidentiality; pledge of notes to Federal Reserve Bank permitted; set-off rights; usury savings clause; counterpart signature; integration; severability; confidentiality; tax forms; governing law; right to trial by jury waived; binding effect; judgment currency; PATRIOT Act; agent for service of process; margin rule compliance	Normal notes mechanics and trustee provisions (quite standard); Trust Indenture Act controls; notice provisions; statements required in certificates and opinions (TIA requirement); no personal liability; governing law; waiver of trial by jury; trustee excused by force majeure; successors are bound; no interpretation of other documents intended and other documents not to be used to interpret indenture; severability; counterpart signatures; table of contents and headings for convenience only; qualification of indenture under Trust Indenture Act	Normal sharing provisions; normal agent provisions; currency equivalents and business day adjustment provisions; notice; no waiver; attorney costs; indemnification; set-off adjustment; confidentiality; pledge of notes to Federal Reserve Bank permitted; set-off rights; usury savings clause; counterpart signature; integration; severability; confidentiality; tax forms; governing law; right to trial by jury waived; binding effect; judgment currency; PATRIOT Act; agent for service of process; margin rule compliance; effect of the merger of the acquisition vehicle into the acquired company, if applicable	Normal notes mechanics and trustee provisions (quite standard); consideration for consents must be offered same to all; Trust Indenture Act controls; notice provisions; statements required in certificates and opinions (TIA requirement); no personal liability; governing law; waiver of trial by jury; trustee excused by force majeure; successors are bound; no interpretation of other documents intended and other documents not to be used to interpret indenture; severability; counterpart signatures; table of contents and headings for convenience only; qualification of indenture under Trust Indenture Act

REPRESENTATIONS	Investment grade credit agreement	Investment grade bonds NB: representations contained in underwriting agreement only	Leveraged credit agreement	High-yield bonds NB: representations contained in underwriting agreement only
Corporate existence, power and compliance with laws	YES	YES	YES	YES
Duly authorized, non-contravention	YES	YES	YES	YES
Government authorizations and other consents either not required or obtained	YES	YES	YES	YES
Binding effect (enforceability)	YES	YES	YES	YES
Financial statements accurate (audited year-end and unaudited quarterly); no MAC; no material liabilities; information	Financial statements accurate (audited year-end and unaudited quarterly); no MAC since last [audited] financial statements as of commitment	Financial statements accurate (audited year-end and unaudited quarterly); representations as to prospectus; no MAC since prospectus; all information materially accurate; debt documents accurately described in the prospectus	Financial statements accurate (audited year-end, unaudited quarterly and pro forma); no MAC or material liabilities since last [audited] financial statements as of commitment; rep as to forecasts; all liabilities disclosed; all information (including any bank book) materially accurate	Financial statements accurate (audited year-end, unaudited quarterly and pro forma); representations as to prospectus; no MAC since prospectus; all information materially accurate; debt and transaction documents accurately described in prospectus; no material liabilities not in prospectus
No material litigation	Possibly	YES, except as disclosed in prospectus	YES	YES, except as disclosed in prospectus
No default under other agreements	NO	YES	YES	YES

REPRESENTATIONS (cont'd)	Investment grade credit agreement	Investment grade bonds NB: representations contained in underwriting agreement only	Leveraged credit agreement	High-yield bonds NB: representations contained in underwriting agreement only
Ownership of property	Possibly	NO	YES	YES
Insurance	NO	NO	YES	YES
Environmental issues	NO	NO	YES	YES
Labor disputes	NO	NO	Possibly	YES
Taxes	YES	NO	YES	YES
ERISA	YES	NO	YES	YES
No violation of law	YES	NO	YES	YES
Subsidiaries	NO	NO	YES	YES
Representations as no issues under margin rules and Investment Company Act	YES	Possibly	YES	YES
Intellectual property	NO	NO	YES	YES
Solvency	NO	NO	YES	YES
Senior Debt	YES, if known about and relevant	YES, if known about and relevant	YES	YES, if relevant
As to use of proceeds	YES	YES, as disclosed	YES	YES, as disclosed

REPRESENTATIONS *(cont'd)*	Investment grade credit agreement	Investment grade bonds NB: representations contained in underwriting agreement only	Leveraged credit agreement	High-yield bonds NB: representations contained in underwriting agreement only
Compliance: Sarbanes-Oxley, controls, FCPA, money laundering, OFAC	NO (may be PATRIOT Act provisions)	NO (may be PATRIOT Act provisions)	NO (may be PATRIOT Act provisions)	YES
Representations re securities law matters	NO	YES	NO	YES
No restriction on ability of subsidiaries to upstream dividends	NO	NO	Probably, through covenants	YES

CONDITIONS PRECEDENT	Investment grade credit agreement N.B.: conditions are contained in commitment letter (CL) and then in credit agreement (CA) ((FF) First funding only)	Investment grade bonds N.B.: Conditions are contained in underwriting agreement	Leveraged credit agreement N.B.: conditions are contained in commitment letter (CL) and then in credit agreement (CA) ((FF) First funding only)	High-yield bonds N.B.: Conditions are contained in underwriting agreement
Market out	NO	YES as termination event in the underwriting agreement	CL—market flex	YES as termination event in the underwriting agreement but in deal context (for example, bid) limited or no market out for bridge
Due diligence	NO	Due diligence update on date of issue, tied to representations as to disclosure; otherwise due diligence is done in connection with preparation of the prospectus	CL—may include due diligence out but not in deal context	Due diligence update on date of issue, tied to representations as to disclosure; otherwise due diligence is done in connection with preparation of the prospectus; in deal context (for example, bid) bridge will piggyback on acquiror's conditions
Clear market condition	CL—company typically undertakes that there won't be competing offerings	Company typically undertakes that there won't be competing offerings	CL—company typically undertakes that there won't be competing offerings	Company typically undertakes that there won't be competing offerings

CONDITIONS PRECEDENT *(cont'd)*	Investment grade credit agreement	Investment grade bonds	Leveraged credit agreement	High-yield bonds
MAC (including material litigation)	CL—MAC is a condition to signing definitive agreements; CA(FF) No material adverse change from information at time of commitment; may or may not be condition for subsequent fundings, depending on leverage of borrower and purpose of credit agreement (for example, rating agency may not permit it in a backstop)	YES	CL and CA—YES; N.B. acquiror in deal context (for example, bid) will not want an independent condition on initial funding and will seek to conform to purchase agreement	YES; documents for bridge may contain MAC clause but acquiror in deal context (for example, bid) will not want an independent condition and will seek to conform to purchase agreement
Documents and filings	CA(FF) YES	YES	CA(FF) YES	YES
Corporate authorization and incumbency	CA(FF) YES	YES	CA(FF) YES	YES
Opinions	CA(FF) YES	YES (will include 10b-5)	CA(FF) YES	YES, (will include 10b-5)
Solvency certificate (leveraged acquisitions and recapitalizations only)	NO	NO	CA(FF) YES	YES, or by way of representations and officer's certificate
Insurance	NO	NO	CA(FF) YES	NO
Deal effective	NO	NO	CA(FF) YES, if applicable	YES, if applicable (by way of disclosure representations if not specifically)
Fees and expenses	(FF) Fees and expenses then due paid	Paid out of proceeds	CA(FF) Fees and expenses then due paid	Paid out of proceeds

CONDITIONS PRECEDENT *(cont'd)*	Investment grade credit agreement	Investment grade bonds	Leveraged credit agreement	High-yield bonds
Other financings in place	NO	NO	CA(FF) YES, if applicable	YES, if applicable (by way of disclosure representations if not specifically)
Pay-off of debt to be refinanced	NO	NO	(FF) YES, if applicable	YES, if applicable (by way of disclosure representations if not specifically)
Information update	By way of MAC and representations	By way of MAC and bringdown of representations as to prospectus and disclosure	(FF) By way of MAC and representations; financial information and pro formas to be as expected	By way of MAC and bringdown of representations as to prospectus and disclosure
Auditors' comfort letter (re prospectus)	NO	YES	NO	YES
Notice of borrowing	Notice of borrowing	Indenture is effective at issuance T+3 after underwriting agreement is signed	Notice of borrowing	Indenture is effective at issuance T+3 after underwriting agreement is signed (bridge can be more like a credit agreement)
Representations and warranties	Representations and warranties true and correct but may be tailored so quite unlikely to be a problem (for example, MAC, material litigation reps may not have to be repeated)	YES	Representations and warranties true and correct, including no MAC and no material litigation	YES
No default	No Event of Default and no Default	May not be express	No Event of Default and no Default	May not be express

CONDITIONS PRECEDENT (cont'd)	Investment grade credit agreement	Investment grade bonds	Leveraged credit agreement	High-yield bonds
Securities laws related conditions, possible listing	NO	YES	NO	YES
No ratings downgrade and not on credit watch	NO	YES	NO	YES

COVENANTS	Investment grade credit agreement	Investment grade bonds	Leveraged credit agreement	High-yield bonds
AFFIRMATIVE				
Payment of notes and paying office	NO	Pay notes; maintenance of paying office	NO	Pay notes; maintenance of paying office
Information	Information: 10-K, 10-Q, other SEC filings, other information (may say other *public* information) as requested, possibly notices of ratings changes	NO	Information: audited annual financial statements without qualification and quarterly unaudited (as filed with SEC acceptable); annual budget and projections; other information as requested	Financial statements and other reports per SEC standards
Compliance certifications and notices	Compliance certificates; notice of default under agreement	Annual compliance certificate	Compliance certificates; SEC filings; notice of default under agreement; notices of events that could give rise to MAE; notices given or received under other debt	Compliance certificates; notice of default under indenture; notice of default under other debt
Pay obligations	NO	NO	YES	NO

COVENANTS (cont'd)	Investment grade credit agreement	Investment grade bonds	Leveraged credit agreement	High-yield bonds
Preserve existence	YES	YES	YES	YES
Maintenance of properties	YES	NO	YES	NO
Insurance	NO	NO	Maintain insurance per industry standard or to specific requirements (especially with respect to collateral)	NO
Compliance with laws	Possibly	NO	YES	NO
Books and records	NO	NO	Keep books and records in accordance with GAAP	NO
Inspection rights	NO	NO	Inspection rights granted to lenders	NO
Subsidiaries to provide guarantees	NO	NO	Guarantees from new subsidiaries. Guarantees from Domestic Restricted Subsidiaries, with agreed exceptions	Guarantees from Domestic Restricted Subsidiaries, with agreed exceptions
Environmental laws	NO	NO	Comply with environmental laws	NO
Further assurances	NO	NO	"Further assurances" and post-closing actions	YES
Unrestricted subsidiaries	NO	Designation of Subsidiaries as Unrestricted Subsidiaries	Only if the Restricted Subsidiaries construct is used	Designation of Subsidiaries as Unrestricted Subsidiaries (usually has significant tests and covenant implications)

COVENANTS (cont'd)	Investment grade credit agreement	Investment grade bonds	Leveraged credit agreement	High-yield bonds
Pay taxes	NO	NO	YES	NO
Waiver of defenses	NO	YES	NO	YES
NEGATIVE				
Negative pledge	Negative pledge, for example, secured debt and attributable debt (with respect to sale-leasebacks) cannot exceed 10% of net tangible assets	If senior debt, *may* include an "equal and ratable" negative pledge, (for example, secured debt and attributable debt (with respect to sale-leasebacks) cannot exceed 10% of net tangible assets)	Negative pledge (prohibition on liens with list of permitted exceptions)	No liens except as listed (including liens to secure senior debt) unless notes equally and ratably secured (on a senior basis if debt being secured is subordinated to notes)
Sale-leasebacks	Sale-leasebacks may be restricted along with liens	If senior debt, *may* include restriction on sale and leasebacks	Restriction on sale and leasebacks as if liens, possible treatment as if asset sales	Restriction on sale and leasebacks as if liens, possible treatment as if asset sales
Investments	NO	NO	Restriction on investments except as listed	Restricted as Restricted Payments
Debt	Possible restriction on debt through leverage ratio or other financial covenant	NO	Debt exceptions provided. Often includes debt subject to a ratio (for example, leverage)	For example, no issuance of Debt, preferred stock or Disqualified Stock, unless Fixed Charge Coverage Ratio is met, tested at time of, and giving effect to, incurrence; exceptions listed

COVENANTS *(cont'd)*	Investment grade credit agreement	Investment grade bonds	Leveraged credit agreement	High-yield bonds
Merger or sale of all or substantially all assets (but see Change of Control provisions, which may also apply)	Merger covenant: Succession by merger permitted if successor assumes and financial covenant would not be breached; no other sale of all or substantially all assets	Merger covenant: Succession by merger or sale of all or substantially all the assets permitted if successor assumes, would not create a default and, if the transaction would give rise to a Lien not permitted under the indenture, equal and ratable security is granted	Merger covenant: Succession by merger or sale of all or substantially all the assets permitted: if successor assumes; the transaction, would not create a default; and, if the transaction would give rise to a lien not permitted under the indenture, equal and ratable security is granted	Merger covenant: Succession by merger or sale of all or substantially all the assets permitted if: successor assumes; the transaction would not create a default; if the transaction would give rise to a Lien not permitted under the indenture, equal and ratable security is granted; and $1 of Debt could be incurred or transaction results in increase of Fixed Charge Coverage Ratio
Asset sales	NO	NO	Historically, limited to an agreed list of permitted transactions and a basket. Has been moving increasingly toward more flexible high-yield bond model	Asset sales (except as provided) to be for at least 75% cash and used to reduce debt, including in Excess Proceeds Offer to Purchase
Restricted payments	NO	NO	Historically, limited to an agreed list of permitted transactions and a basket. Has been moving increasingly toward more flexible high-yield bond model	Restrictions on Restricted Payments (unless no default, $1 of additional debt could be incurred, and then only out of accumulating basket for Restricted Payments)
Transactions with affiliates	NO	NO	Transactions with affiliates (meaning entities under common control) are restricted	Transactions with affiliates (meaning entities under common control) are restricted

COVENANTS (cont'd)	Investment grade credit agreement	Investment grade bonds	Leveraged credit agreement	High-yield bonds
Restrictions on restrictions at the subsidiary level	NO	NO	"Burdensome agreements" (includes restrictions on restrictions on ability of subsidiaries to upstream money to company)	Restriction on dividend and other restrictions affecting Restricted Subsidiaries
Margin rule provisions	Use of proceeds to be in compliance with margin rules	No specific provision	Use of proceeds (term loans to close deal; revolving credit for general corporate purposes; proceeds not to be used to purchase or carry margin stock (or compliance with margin rules)	No specific provision
Prepayment of junior debt	NO	NO	Restricted as a Restricted Payment	Restricted as a Restricted Payment
Subsidiaries to be wholly owned	NO	NO	NO, though covenants may discourage	NO, though covenants may discourage
Limitation on holding company	NO	NO	Holding company business limited to holding company only	NO
Capital expenditures	NO	NO	NO	NO
Anti-layering	NO	If senior subordinated, anti-layering	NO	If senior subordinated, anti-layering

COVENANTS (cont'd)	Investment grade credit agreement	Investment grade bonds	Leveraged credit agreement	High-yield bonds
FINANCIAL COVENANTS				
Balance sheet test	For example, a minimum net worth or maximum leverage ratio	NO	For example, maximum total leverage ratio at quarter-ends (total debt to 4-quarter EBITDA; reducing over the life of the facility)	NO
Coverage test	Minimum interest expense ratio	NO	For example, minimum coverage ratio for each period of 4 rolling quarters (increasing over the life of the facility)	NO, except as incurrence test for debt and other covenants

EVENTS OF DEFAULT	Investment grade credit agreement	Investment grade bonds	Leveraged credit agreement	High-yield bonds
Failure to pay	Failure to pay principal when due, or interest or fees within 5 days	Failure to pay principal or premium when due at stated maturity or on mandatory redemption, or interest within 30 days; if relevant, failure to make an Offer to Purchase when required (30 days grace)	Failure to pay principal when due, or interest or fees within 3–5 days	Failure to pay principal or premium when due at stated maturity or on mandatory redemption, or interest within 30 days; failure to make an Offer to Purchase when required (30 days grace)
Covenant default— immediate	Financial covenant default, possible negative covenant default	NO	Breach of negative covenants or financial covenants; it may be provided that financial covenant defaults can be cured with an equity injection	NO
Covenant default—after grace and/or notice	Breach of other covenants continuing 30 days after notice from agent or majority	Covenant default continuing 60 days after notice from trustee or 25% of affected series	Breach of other covenants continuing for 30 days after notice from agent or majority	Covenant default continuing 60 days after notice from trustee or 25%
Misrepresentation	Material misrepresentation	NO	Material misrepresentation	NO

EVENTS OF DEFAULT (cont'd)	Investment grade credit agreement	Investment grade bonds	Leveraged credit agreement	High-yield bonds
Cross-default	Other debt above a threshold amount is not paid when due or default occurs under other debt in excess of threshold amount that results or could result in acceleration or mandatory prepayment (not including normal due-on-sale clauses of, for example, mortgage debt)	NO	Other debt above a threshold amount is not paid when due or default occurs under other debt in excess of threshold amount that results or could result in acceleration or mandatory prepayment (not including normal due-on-sale clauses of, for example, mortgage debt)	Other debt above a threshold amount is not paid when due or accelerated (if not cured)
Bankruptcy (including failure to pay debts generally when due)	Bankruptcy etc. of company, other borrower or Significant Subsidiary	Bankruptcy etc. of company or Significant Subsidiary	Bankruptcy etc. of company, parent holding company or Restricted Subsidiary	Bankruptcy etc. of company, parent holding company or Restricted Subsidiary (or Significant Subsidiary)
Judgment default	Entry of judgment against borrower or Significant Subsidiary in excess of threshold amount (not covered by insurance) not stayed or satisfied within 30 or 60 days, or enforcement proceeding is commenced	NO	Entry of judgment against borrower or subsidiary in excess of threshold amount (not covered by insurance) not stayed or satisfied within 30 or 60 days, or enforcement proceeding is commenced	Entry of judgment against issuer or Restricted Subsidiary in excess of threshold amount (not covered by insurance) not stayed or satisfied within 60 days, or enforcement proceeding is commenced
ERISA default	NO	NO	YES	NO
Invalidity, etc.	Not unless relevant because there are guarantees	NO	Invalidity of loan documents; if there are guarantees, guarantees not valid or disavowed	If there are guarantees, guarantees not valid or disavowed

EVENTS OF DEFAULT (cont'd)	Investment grade credit agreement	Investment grade bonds	Leveraged credit agreement	High-yield bonds
Change of control	May include a change of control default with change of control meaning (for a public company) that a person acquires more than a specified percentage (typically 30%–50%) of the voting stock of the company	Possible "event risk" protection (Offer to Purchase) but unlikely to be an event of default	Change of control outside the Permitted Holders (in private context) or a person acquiring more than a specified percentage (typically 30%–50%) of the voting stock of the company or parent holding company (in public context) will be a default	*Cf.* change of control will require an Offer to Purchase but will not be cast as an event of default
Failure of security or other security-related defaults	NO	NO	YES	Possibly, if secured
Senior debt	NO	NO	Credit agreement debt failing to constitute "Senior Debt"	Only if tiering specifically applies in the deal
Other	NO	Other defaults that might be prescribed for a particular series	NO	NO

Appendix D

Newco Goes to Wall Street—
8½ Balance Sheets

So, this bit of old New York, the sepia, horsecar Manhattan, Wall Street. Bartleby and the god-blessed lawyer. They were created by Melville before the Civil War and were coeval with John Jacob Astor's old age and the prime of Cornelius Vanderbilt. And yet here they are, strange apparitions in the metonymic Wall Street district where the exertions, as described by Mark Twain, were "A year ago I didn't have a penny, and now I owe you a million dollars."

—Elizabeth Hardwick, *Bartleby in Manhattan*

Elizabeth Hardwick, *Bartleby in Manhattan, in* AMERICAN FICTIONS (Modern Library 1999) (1986).

BALANCE SHEET 1:
NEWCO
Balance sheet (amounts in thousands of dollars)

Assets		Liabilities	
Cash and cash equivalents	$250	Accounts payable	$150
Accounts receivable	500	Accrued expenses	250
Inventory	500	Note payable to bank	50
Prepaid expenses	25		
Total current assets	1,275	*Total current liabilities*	450
		Term loan payable to bank	300
Plant, property and equipment	2,000	Mortgage loan 6% due year 10	1,500
Total long-term assets	2,000	*Total long-term liabilities*	1,800
		TOTAL LIABILITIES	2,250
		Stockholders' equity	
		Common stock	1,025
		TOTAL STOCKHOLDERS' EQUITY	1,025
TOTAL ASSETS	$3,275	TOTAL LIABILITIES AND STOCKHOLDERS' EQUITY	$3,275

Newco is newly formed. It has no subsidiaries and a simple capital structure. It has borrowed $350,000 from a bank, $50,000 of which is in the form of a note due within a year. It has bought a building for $2 million, borrowing $1.5 million of the purchase price.

BALANCE SHEET 2:
NEWCO SUB 1

Balance Sheet (amounts in thousands of dollars)

Assets		Liabilities	
Cash and cash equivalents	$225	Accounts payable	$100
Accounts receivable	500	Accrued expenses	150
Inventory	500		
Prepaid expenses	25		
Total current assets	1,250	Total current liabilities	250
Plant, property and equipment	2,000	Mortgage loan 6% due year 10	1,500
Total long-term assets	2,000	*Total long-term liabilities*	1,500
		TOTAL LIABILITIES	1,750
		Stockholders' equity	
		Common stock	1,500
		TOTAL STOCKHOLDERS' EQUITY	1,500
		TOTAL LIABILITIES AND	
TOTAL ASSETS	$3,250	STOCKHOLDERS' EQUITY	$3,250

Newco has formed a subsidiary, Newco Sub 1, which holds all of Newco's operations and assets, except for $25,000 of cash.

The bank loan of $350,000 is still owed by Newco, which has contributed most of the cash to Newco Sub 1 in the form of equity.

Newco's balance sheet (not consolidated) has two assets: cash of $25,000 and stock of Newco Sub 1 at $1,500,000, for a total of $1,525,000.

Liabilities at Newco consist of $50,000 of accounts payable, $100,000 accrued expenses, a $50,000 note payable to the bank, and the $300,000 bank term loan—for total liabilities of $500,000 and stockholders' equity of $1,025,000.

The bank loans at Newco are now structurally subordinated to the debt and other liabilities of Newco Sub 1.

BALANCE SHEET 3:
NEWCO

Consolidated balance sheet (amounts in thousands of dollars)

Assets		Liabilities	
Cash and cash equivalents	$50	Accounts payable	$250
Accounts receivable	575	Accrued expenses	350
Inventory	500	Note payable to bank	50
Prepaid expenses	25		
Total current assets	1,150	*Total current liabilities*	650
Plant, property and equipment	3,000	Term loan payable to bank	1,400
Accumulated depreciation	-200	Mortgage loan 6% due year 9	1,500
Intangible assets other than goodwill	200		
Goodwill	225		
Total long-term assets	3,225	*Total long-term liabilities*	2,900
		TOTAL LIABILITIES	3,550
		Stockholders' equity	
		Common stock (paid-in capital)	1,025
		Retained earnings (deficit)	-200
		TOTAL STOCKHOLDERS' EQUITY	825
TOTAL ASSETS	$4,375	TOTAL LIABILITIES AND STOCKHOLDERS' EQUITY	$4,375

Newco's position is unchanged a year later, except for the depreciation of its plant, property and equipment, and the acquisition of another company, Newco Sub 2, for $1.5 million. The consideration consisted of $200,000 cash, the assumption of $200,000 of short-term liabilities ($100,000 accounts payable and $100,000 accrued expenses), and an additional $1.1 million borrowed from the bank. Assets acquired were $75,000 of accounts receivable, a factory worth $1 million, and patents worth $200,000. The remainder of the purchase price ($225,000) was allocated to goodwill. The stock of Newco Sub 2 was pledged to secure parent company bank loans, and the founder of Newco gave a personal guarantee. Newco did not have any income or loss from operations for this year, so retained earnings (deficit) reflects the depreciation of PP&E ($200,000).

BALANCE SHEET 4:
NEWCO

Consolidated balance sheet (amounts in thousands of dollars)

Assets		Liabilities	
Cash and cash equivalents	$50	Accounts payable	$250
Accounts receivable	575	Accrued expenses	350
Inventory	500	Note payable to bank	50
Prepaid expenses	25		
Total current assets	1,150	*Total current liabilities*	650
Plant, property and equipment	3,000	Term loan payable to bank	900
Accumulated depreciation	-500	Mortgage loan 6% due year 8	1,500
Intangible assets			
other than goodwill	50		
Goodwill	225		
Amortization of goodwill	-25		
Total long-term assets	2,750	*Total long-term liabilities*	2,400
		TOTAL LIABILITIES	3,050
		Stockholders' equity	
		Common stock	
		(paid-in capital)	1,025
		Retained earnings (deficit)	-175
		TOTAL STOCKHOLDERS' EQUITY	850
TOTAL ASSETS	$3,900	TOTAL LIABILITIES AND STOCKHOLDERS' EQUITY	$3,900

Newco sells rights to patent royalties to a third-party securitization vehicle for $500,000, uses the proceeds to reduce bank debt and records a gain of $350,000 (proceeds received over value of related intangible rights ($150,000 leaving intangible assets of $50,000)). There has also been another year of depreciation (a total of $300 of depreciation expense), and goodwill has started to amortize. Again, there is no gain or loss from operations. Income is equal to the gain of $350,000 less depreciation of $300,000 and amortization of $25,000, for net income of $25,000 (retained earnings (deficit) now ($175,000) instead of ($200,000)).

481

BALANCE SHEET 5:
NEWCO

Consolidated balance sheet (amounts in thousands of dollars)

Assets		Liabilities	
Cash and cash equivalents	$50	Accounts payable	$150
Marketable securities	300	Accrued expenses	150
Accounts receivable	200	Note payable to bank	100
Inventory	200		
Prepaid expenses	25		
Total current assets	775	*Total current liabilities*	400
Plant, property and equipment	3,500	Term loan payable to bank	475
Accumulated depreciation	-800	Mortgage loan 6% due year 7	1,500
Intangible assets other than goodwill	50		
Goodwill	225		
Amortization of goodwill	-50		
Total long-term assets	2,925	*Total long-term liabilities*	1,975
		TOTAL LIABILITIES	2,375
		Stockholders' equity	
		Common stock (paid-in capital)	1,025
		Retained earnings	300
		TOTAL STOCKHOLDERS' EQUITY	1,325
TOTAL ASSETS	$3,700	TOTAL LIABILITIES AND STOCKHOLDERS' EQUITY	$3,700

A year on, Newco has started to have net earnings, worked to reduce its inventory and receivables (carrying these is a use of cash), and pay down its debt. It has built up an investment position in marketable securities and spent $500,000 in capital expenditures, both out of operating cash flow.

BALANCE SHEET 6:
OLDCO
Consolidated balance sheet (amounts in millions of dollars)

Assets		Liabilities	
Cash and cash equivalents	$50	Accounts payable	$150
Marketable securities	600	Accrued expenses	150
Accounts receivable	200	Income tax payable	100
Inventory	200	Notes payable*	500
Prepaid expenses	25		
Total current assets	1,075	Total current liabilities	900
Plant, property and equipment (net of depreciation)	2,225	Notes due in 8 years, at 6%	1,000
Intangible assets and goodwill (net of amortization)	1,000	Liability reserves	100
Total long-term assets	3,225	Total long-term liabilities	1,100
		TOTAL LIABILITIES	2,000
		Stockholders' equity	
		Common stock (paid-in capital)	2,000
		Retained earnings	300
		TOTAL STOCKHOLDERS' EQUITY	2,300
TOTAL ASSETS	$4,300	TOTAL LIABILITIES AND STOCKHOLDERS' EQUITY	$4,300

Ten years later, NEWCO is now OLDCO. It is a public company, funding itself with commercial paper (with a backstop revolving credit facility) and some long-term public debt.

---

* Commercial paper notes may be treated as long-term debt with an appropriate back-stop.

BALANCE SHEET 7:
HOLDCO

Consolidated balance sheet (amounts in millions of dollars)

Assets		Liabilities	
Cash and cash equivalents	$50	Accounts payable	$150
Accounts receivable	200	Accrued expenses	150
Inventory	200	Income tax payable	100
Prepaid expenses	25	Short term bank debt payable	50
Total current assets	475	*Total current liabilities*	450
		Senior bank debt	2,000
Plant, property and equipment (net of depreciation)	5,000	Senior subordinated debt 8% due 7 years	2,000
Intangible assets and goodwill (net of amortization)	2,075	Subordinated debt 9% due 9 years	2,000
		Liability reserves	100
Total long-term assets	7,075	*Total long-term liabilities*	6,100
		TOTAL LIABILITIES	6,550
		Stockholders' equity	
		Common stock (paid-in capital)	1,000
		TOTAL STOCKHOLDERS' EQUITY	1,000
TOTAL ASSETS	$7,550	TOTAL LIABILITIES AND STOCKHOLDERS' EQUITY	$7,550

OLDCO has been bought by HOLDCO in a leveraged buyout. This is HOLDCO's balance sheet after the acquisition. To understand more about the transaction, see Balance Sheet 8.

BALANCE SHEET 8:
OLDCO (NOW OPCO)

Consolidated balance sheet (amounts in millions of dollars)*

Assets		Liabilities	
Cash and cash equivalents	$50	Accounts payable	$150
Accounts receivable	200	Accrued expenses	150
Inventory	200	Income tax payable	100
Prepaid expenses	25	Short term bank debt payable	50
Total current assets	475	Total current liabilities	450
		Senior bank debt	2,000
Plant, property and equipment (net of depreciation)	2,225	Senior subordinated debt 8% due 7 years	2,000
Intangible assets and goodwill (net of amortization)	1,000	Subordinated debt 9% due 9 years	2,000
		Liability reserves	100
Total long-term assets	3,225	Total long-term liabilities	6,100
		TOTAL LIABILITIES	6,550
		Stockholders' equity	
		Common stock (paid-in capital)	2,000
		Retained earnings	300
		[Effective Distribution to shareholders]	-5,150
		TOTAL STOCKHOLDERS' EQUITY	-2,850
TOTAL ASSETS	$3,700	TOTAL LIABILITIES AND STOCKHOLDERS' EQUITY	$3,700

OLDCO (now called OPCO) assumes the acquisition debt, but this balance sheet shows the results with no write-up in book value of assets. When HOLDCO and OPCO are merged, the asset write-up will occur and stockholders' equity will be revalued. To see the effect of the write-up and consolidation, see Balance Sheet 8½.

---

* All balance sheets in Appendix D (and this one in particular) are simplified and illustrative only; they are not meant to reflect GAAP.

BALANCE SHEET 8½:
OPCO AFTER MERGER OF HOLDCO DOWN INTO OPCO
Consolidated balance sheet (amounts in millions of dollars)

Assets		Liabilities	
Cash and cash equivalents	$50	Accounts payable	$150
Accounts receivable	200	Accrued expenses	150
Inventory	200	Income tax payable	100
Prepaid expenses	25	Short-term bank debt payable	50
Total current assets	475	*Total current liabilities*	450
		Senior bank debt	2,000
Plant, property and equipment		Senior subordinated debt 8%	
(net of depreciation)	5,000	due 7 years	2,000
Intangible assets and goodwill		Subordinated debt 9% due 9	
(net of amortization)	2,075	years	2,000
		Liability reserves	100
Total long-term assets	7,075	*Total long- term liabilities*	6,100
		TOTAL LIABILITIES	6,550
		Stockholders' equity	
		Common stock	
		(paid-in capital)	1,000
		TOTAL STOCKHOLDERS' EQUITY	1,000
		TOTAL LIABILITES AND	
TOTAL ASSETS	$7,550	STOCKHOLDERS' EQUITY	$7,550

OLDCO has been bought by HOLDCO in a leveraged buyout. Compare this balance sheet to Balance Sheet 7.

Appendix E

Diary of a Liquidity Crisis: Enron's Last Days

This summary of Enron's last days is based entirely on publicly available information. In particular, there is wealth of information contained in the so-called Powers Report, which is a report dated February 1, 2002, addressed to the Board of Directors of Enron, from a Special Investigation Committee headed by William Powers, Jr., the Dean of the University of Texas Law School. The other two members of the committee were Raymond S. Troubh and Herbert S. Winokur, Jr.; and Wilmer, Cutler & Pickering, acted as counsel to the committee. Because Mr. Winokur was a member of Enron's board of directors during the period that is the subject of the investigation, and because Enron's principal outside counsel, Vinson and Elkins, had close ties to the University of Texas, various portions of the Powers Report are stated to be by Powers and Troubh (that is, Winokur is recused), or by Troubh and Winokur (that is, Powers is recused).

It is important to note the context and purpose of the Powers Report. It was commissioned by the Board of Directors of Enron in the fall of 2001 to investigate several complex off-balance-sheet financings that were causing serious problems for the company, but before it was clear that Enron would be entering bankruptcy, and at a time when the extent of financial and accounting problems was thought perhaps to be more limited than it turned out to be. Further, the report itself cites a number of limitations on its scope, principally time constraints and lack of access.

Nevertheless, the Powers Report is quite useful to those trying to understand in some detail at least a few of the problems that brought Enron down. The Powers Report, taken together with other publicly available information, provides much learning about the limits of corporate finance techniques when they run far ahead of business reality.

In March 2003 the report of the examiner for the Enron bankruptcy was released. This report went into Enron financial and accounting matters in great depth for purposes of setting a framework for settlement of the Enron bankruptcy matters. The examiner, Neal Batson, concluded that deals without economic substance were responsible for the vast majority of Enron's earnings in its last years and that over half of Enron's actual debt load was not on its balance sheet. In particular, it was reported that commodities trading transactions—"pre-pays"—with offshore vehicles associated with banks made up large portions of cash flows. Other techniques noted in the report are bridge financings of illiquid assets; acquisitions driven wholly by tax considerations; hedging with counterparties affiliated with Enron; using trusts to move debt off the balance sheet; and using minority-owned companies to borrow money for the company's business needs. The report tracked proceeds of transactions and outlined a possible basis for getting money back from various parties for the benefit of the Enron estate and its creditors.

Though the tale of Enron has run its course, it is still of interest to look at the earliest stages of the crisis as it unfolded. Indeed it is quite interesting to compare the public disclosure over the relevant period with the allegations eventually made by the SEC against management. Enron is now a by-word for corporate wrongdoing, but in fact, at the outset, it took several months at least for the outside world to take in the magnitude of events and to understand that this was no ordinary liquidity crisis.

The Enron Chronology

> On October 16, 2001, Enron announced that it was taking a $544 million after-tax charge against earnings related to transactions with LJM2 Co-Investment, L.P. (LJM2), a partnership created and managed by [Chief Financial Officer Andrew] Fastow. It also announced a reduction of shareholders' equity of $1.2 billion related to transactions with that same entity.

Powers Report, at 2.

October 16, 2001, marked the beginning of Enron's public troubles. The charge against earnings and the equity writedown were the first indications known outside Enron of the unraveling of the elaborate financing structures apparently used to prop up earnings.

Events that followed can be tracked from Enron's filings with the SEC, in particular its 8-K's filed in November and its 10-Q for the 2001 third quarter, filed November 19.

In an 8-K filed on November 8, Enron reported the earnings charge and equity writedown previously noted. However, it also stated that its financial statements, starting with those for 1997, would be required to be restated. It announced the appointment of a special committee that would look into certain related party transactions; this is the committee that produced the Powers Report.

The November 8 8-K introduced the reader to the concept of a special purpose entity, or SPE:

> Enron, like many other companies, utilizes a variety of structured financings in the ordinary course of its business to access capital or hedge risk. Many of these transactions involve "special purpose entities," or "SPEs." Accounting guidelines allow for the non-consolidation of SPEs from the sponsoring company's financial statements in certain circumstances. Accordingly, certain transactions between the sponsoring company and the SPE may result in gain or loss and/or cash flow being recognized by the sponsor, commonly referred to by financial institutions as "monetizations."

The company then went on to state that a special committee would be appointed to look into a number of such transactions involving, on the one hand, Enron and, on the other, two partnerships—LJM1 and LJM2—formed by Enron's chief financial officer, Andrew Fastow.

In describing the restatements of prior periods' earnings, the report focused on several entities that had not been, but should have been, consolidated with Enron for financial accounting purposes. In brief, consolidating these previously non-consolidated entities eliminated the corresponding inter-company transactions, and thus the positive effects of the associated "monetization" transactions that had occurred between them and Enron. It also brought onto Enron's consolidated balance sheet the liabilities of these entities. In gross terms, off-balance-sheet borrowings by these affiliated entities had provided the cash for "purchases" by them of Enron assets. These "purchases" in some cases generated realized gain for Enron. Thus, so long as the entities were not consolidated, Enron's financial statements reflected cash from their borrowings as, effectively, income to Enron; what was actually a liability of the group was shown as Enron earnings. Consolidating the entities not only wiped out the earnings from the "monetizations," it put the entity's debt onto the Enron consolidated balance sheet as a liability.

> Enron will restate its financial statements from 1997 to 2000 and the first and second quarters of 2001 to: (1) reflect its conclusion that three entities did not meet certain accounting requirements and should have been consolidated, (2) reflect the adjustment to shareholders' equity described below, and (3) include prior-year proposed audit adjustments and reclassifications (which were previously determined to be immaterial in the year originally proposed). Specifically, Enron has concluded that based on current information:
>
> - The financial activities of Chewco Investments, L.P. ("Chewco"), a related party which was an investor in Joint Energy Development Investments Limited Partnership (JEDI), should have been consolidated beginning in November 1997;
>
> - The financial activities of JEDI, in which Enron was an investor and which was consolidated into Enron's financial statements during the first quarter of 2001, should have been consolidated beginning in November 1997; and
>
> - The financial activities of a wholly-owned subsidiary of LJM1, which engaged in derivative transactions with Enron to permit Enron to hedge market risks of an equity investment in Rhythms NetConnections, Inc., should have been consolidated into Enron's financial statements beginning in 1999.

The November 8 8-K provides in summary form a description of a number of transactions between Enron and various affiliated entities. These were the subject of the Powers Report.

Enron filed another 8-K on November 13. This 8-K filing covered $1 billion of financing commitment letters dated October 31, $550 million for Transwestern Pipeline Company and $450 million for Northern Natural Gas Company.

On November 14, yet another 8-K was filed, together with the merger agreement Enron had just signed with Dynegy. A key element of the agreement with Dynegy was a purchase option agreement, which provided Dynegy with an option, subject to certain conditions, to purchase Northern Natural Gas Company if the Enron-Dynegy merger did not close.

On November 19, Enron filed its quarterly report on Form 10-Q for the quarter ended September 30 but also covering subsequent events up to the time of filing. This document makes for very interesting reading from the viewpoint of the corporate finance lawyer.

On November 28, Dynegy gave notice of termination of the merger contract and also exercised its purchase option under the purchase option agreement.

On December 2, Enron filed for bankruptcy and sued Dynegy for breach of contract. Dynegy sued for declarative judgment that it was entitled to exercise its purchase option and to compel specific performance from Enron to carry through on the Northern Natural Gas transaction. The issue was settled in favor of Dynegy in early January; the settlement agreement can be found in Dynegy's 8-K filed January 8, 2002.

Contract Triggers and the Liquidity Crisis

The November 19 Enron 10-Q begins with the following statement:

> As explained in a November 8, 2001 Form 8-K filed by Enron Corp. (Enron) with the Securities and Exchange Commission (SEC), Enron will be filing restated consolidated financial statements for the fiscal years ended December 31, 1997 through 2000 and for the first and second quarters of 2001 but it has not yet done so. As a result, the previously issued financial statements for these periods and the audit reports covering the year-end financial statements for 1997 through 2000 should not be relied upon.

The report continues by noting that the SEC has commenced an investigation and reminds the reader that the special investigatory committee of the board has been appointed to look into the affiliated party transactions.

The November 19 10-Q is an interesting document from an accounting perspective, and its filing was a critical negative development in terms of the proposed merger with Dynegy. But it is also a compelling description of how a liquidity crisis unfolds and can quickly overwhelm a company.

> Following Enron's announcement of its third quarter 2001 results on October 16, 2001, there was a significant decrease in Enron's common share price and subsequent decreases in the credit ratings of Enron's long-term debt to BBB– and Baa3 (the lowest level of investment grade) with a warning that further downgrades were possible. This situation resulted in a loss of investor confidence and significantly affected Enron's ability to raise capital.

This is a blunt statement of investor and rating agency reaction to the announcement of the charge against earnings and equity restatement on October 16. Let's see what follows.

> Maintaining an investment grade credit rating is a critical element in maintaining liquidity for Enron's wholesale business which, together with the natural gas pipeline operations and the retail business, comprise Enron's core businesses discussed below. As a part of their standard contractual arrangements, Enron and its trading counterparties regularly post cash deposits or letters of credit to collateralize a portion of their trading obligations. A downgrade to below investment grade could lead to a substantial increase in the level of cash required for collateral and margin deposits with Enron's wholesale trading partners. Additionally, Enron and its subsidiaries have outstanding surety bonds and other instruments related to construction projects and other performance obligations. Under certain circumstances, the issuers of such sureties may request collateral.

This paragraph tells the informed reader that Enron was anticipating demands from counterparties and other financial contract parties to post collateral to support its financial obligations. Many financial arrangements such as swaps and credit accommodations are unsecured so long as the obligor meets certain credit criteria but might be required to be collateralized, with cash or other assets, by an obligor that falls below the specified threshold of creditworthiness—such as a minimum long-term credit rating from a rating agency. A typical credit threshold might be "investment grade," the lowest such grade being BBB– from Standard & Poors or Baa3 from Moody's. The reduction of Enron's long-term debt rating to the lowest investment grade rating together with an announcement that Enron was being put on credit watch for possible further downgrades would put Enron's financial staff on the alert to try to figure out how to respond to counterparty demands for collateral.

A little farther along, the 10-Q notes a slowdown in trading activity, particularly for longer term contracts. This means that counterparties are deciding that Enron is not a good credit risk, or at least have decided not to commit until things cleared up a bit.

A company in this situation would also expect liquidity problems from another direction: If the ratings fall has been precipitous, the company may have been financing itself with short-term borrowings in the commercial paper market, that is, with short-term corporate IOUs. A company with a commercial paper program typically has a back-up line of credit in the form of a revolving credit facility.

Let's read on:

> Liquidity Actions. Enron has implemented a financial strategy to restore investor confidence and will continue its initiatives in this regard. Enron has taken the following steps to assure its customers and investors that it can fulfill its commitments in the ordinary course of business:
>
> - Enron borrowed approximately $3.0 billion from its committed lines of credit to repay outstanding and expiring commercial paper obligations of approximately $1.9 billion and to provide immediate cash liquidity. This action to convert Enron's committed lines of credit to cash was done to eliminate any doubt as to their availability in the future.
>
> - In an effort to further enhance short-term liquidity, on November 13, 2001, Enron (through its wholly-owned subsidiary) obtained $550 million in a new secured line of credit from JP Morgan Chase Bank (Chase) and Citicorp North America, Inc. (Citicorp), secured by Enron's Transwestern Pipeline Company assets. Enron anticipates obtaining $450 million in a new secured line of credit on or about November 20, 2001 from Chase and Citicorp secured by Northern Natural Gas Company as-

sets. These proceeds will be used to further supplement short-term liquidity and to retire maturing obligations.

- On November 13, 2001, Enron received a $1.5 billion equity infusion in the form of a preferred stock investment in Northern Natural Gas Company, an Enron subsidiary (Northern), from Dynegy Inc. (Dynegy) in connection with the merger agreement signed between Enron and Dynegy discussed below.

- Enron anticipates the receipt of over $800 million in net proceeds from asset sales scheduled to close by year-end. However, the closings of these sale transactions are pending certain regulatory and other approvals that will impact whether such transactions close and the ultimate timing of the closings. Of the net proceeds, approximately $250 million, or a portion thereof, may be required to repay an obligation that may become a demand obligation due to a recent credit rating downgrade discussed below in note 9.

From your readings in this book, you will know that the reference in the first paragraph to the immediate borrowing of $3 billion under credit facilities "to eliminate any doubt as to their availability in the future" is a reference to the conditions precedent in those facilities. Financial officers were anticipating possible problems meeting those conditions precedent and borrowed while the funds were still available. Perhaps those facilities contained a minimum ratings requirement as a condition precedent. Much more likely, as they were probably commercial paper backstops intended to be available exactly in the event of ratings problems affecting the ability of the company to place commercial paper, is that they contained a material adverse change clause.

Even the $3 billion drawdown was not enough however, so the company had arranged the additional $1 billion in secured financings to be extended to subsidiaries. Presumably the proceeds of those financings would have been on-lent around the corporate group as needed.

In this same excerpt the reader is further put on notice of at least one other rating trigger: "an obligation that may become a demand obligation due to a recent credit rating downgrade. . . ." From note 9 of the Powers Report:

Enron has various financial arrangements which require Enron to maintain specified credit ratings. The November 12, 2001 downgrade in Enron's senior unsecured debt rating to BBB– by Standard & Poor's has caused a ratings event related to a $690 million note payable that, absent Enron posting collateral, will become a demand obligation on November 27, 2001.

. . . .

Enron consolidates a limited partnership (the Limited Partnership), for which the consolidated third party's ownership interest is reflected in minority interests on Enron's balance sheet in the amount of $691 million at September 30, 2001. The Limited Partnership assets include a $690 million note payable from Enron and certain merchant investments, both domestic and international. Enron anticipates the receipt of approximately $250 million from the sale of one of the Limited Partnership's investments, a local gas distribution company in Brazil, upon the closing of the sale which is pending certain regulatory and other approvals. Enron may be required to use the net proceeds upon the closing of the sale, or a portion thereof, to repay a portion of the note payable.

The November 12, 2001 downgrade in Enron's senior unsecured debt rating to BBB– by Standard & Poor's has caused a ratings event related to the Limited Partnership. This ratings event started a nine business day period during which Enron has the right, until November 26, 2001, to post an unsecured letter of credit equal to Enron's note payable, to repay the note payable with the Limited Partnership investing such proceeds in permitted investments, or to purchase the investors' interest in the Limited Partnership. To the extent that Enron does not satisfy this requirement by November 27, 2001, the investors have the right to immediately begin to liquidate the Limited Partnership assets. Additionally, as a result of the rating downgrade, the investors, subject to certain actions, are able to accelerate and assign the note payable. Consistent with the restructuring plan discussed in Note 2, Enron is currently working with the lenders to develop a mutually acceptable amendment or waiver to the transaction documents in order to avoid an early Enron payment obligation.

So here is another $690 million effectively due, based on a downgrade that still left Enron investment grade. The 10-Q says that Enron is negotiating with the lender for relief. But more bad news follows:

> In the event Enron were to lose its investment grade credit rating and Enron's stock price was below a specified price, a note trigger event would occur. This could require Enron to repay, refinance or cash collateralize additional facilities totaling $3.9 billion, which primarily consist of $2.4 billion of debt in Osprey Trust (Osprey) and $915 million of debt in Marlin Water Trust (Marlin). In the event such a trigger event occurs and Enron cannot timely issue equity in an amount sufficient to repay the notes or restructure the obligations, Enron is obligated to pay the difference in cash. For a description of the Marlin and Osprey Trusts, both of which are unconsolidated affiliates, and the related debt obligations, see note 8.

Another $3.9 billion of debt that could become due—the numbers are starting to add up to fairly alarming sums. This pattern is typical of even a less extraordinary liquidity crisis—the company discovers a number of credit arrangements with similar or inter-related conditions precedents, defaults (including cross-defaults) and collateralization triggers, all of which start to trip at the same time. Lenders or counterparties are demanding payment or collateral, but the company is unable to meet the conditions precedent to get cash. So it scrambles to find clean, unmortgaged assets to sell or pledge. The image of the boy sticking his fingers in the dike as it springs leak after leak is apropos. Enron sums up with a rather pro forma bit of protective (from a disclosure standpoint anyway) language.

> In the event that Enron fails to pay any debt obligations when due, including when such obligations may be accelerated, or is unable to refinance or obtain a waiver of or amendment to such obligations, a series of events would begin which could impact Enron's compliance with the terms of its Revolving Credit Agreements and certain other obligations, including bank debt facilities. It is not possible to predict whether any or all of the actions described above (including the sale of non-core businesses and assets and the refinancing or waiver of Enron obligations that may become immediately payable upon scheduled maturities or due to an acceleration event) will be adequate to maintain

Enron's investment grade credit rating or enable Enron to refinance or otherwise restructure its debt obligations that become due. An adverse outcome with respect to any of these matters would likely have a material adverse impact on Enron's ability to continue as a going concern.

Other financial arrangements contained provisions that would have required substantial issuance of Enron equity. These arrangements merited a similar warning:

Summarized below [in the 10-Q] is a description related to two of Enron's unconsolidated equity affiliates for which Enron has committed to issue equity to satisfy obligations of these equity affiliates. As discussed in Note 2, Enron's current common share stock price, liquidity situation and credit ratings may significantly impact Enron's ability to satisfy these obligations solely with equity issuances.

WHITEWING ASSOCIATES L.P. Whitewing is an entity formed by Enron and various investors, investing through an entity named Osprey, to acquire and own energy-related assets and other investments. Osprey is capitalized with approximately $2.4 billion in debt and $220 million in equity. The Osprey debt is supported by the assets within Whitewing, which include Enron Mandatorily Convertible Junior Preferred Stock, Series B (which is convertible into 50 million shares of Enron common stock), and a contingent obligation of Enron to issue additional shares, if needed, to retire such debt obligation. In the event that the sale of equity is not sufficient to retire such obligations, Enron is liable for the shortfall.

. . . .

ATLANTIC WATER TRUST. Atlantic Water Trust is an entity formed by Enron and unrelated institutional investors, investing through an entity named Marlin, for the purpose of acquiring and holding an interest in Azurix Corp. (Azurix). The primary asset of Azurix is Wessex Water Services Ltd. (Wessex), a regulated water utility in the UK. Atlantic Water Trust currently owns 67% of Azurix, with Enron owning the remaining 33%. Marlin was capitalized with approximately $915 million in debt and $125 million in equity. The Marlin debt is supported by the assets of Atlantic Water Trust and Enron's contingent obligation to cause the sale of Enron equity, if needed, in an amount sufficient to retire such obligations. In the event that the sale of equity is not sufficient to retire such obligations, Enron is liable for the shortfall.

DESCRIPTION OF TRIGGER EVENTS. Osprey and Marlin's debt obligations contain certain "Note Trigger Events" to protect the note holders, including (i) an Enron senior unsecured debt rating below investment grade by any of the three major credit rating agencies concurrent with an Enron stock closing price of $59.78 per share or below in the case of Osprey and $34.13 per share or below in the case of Marlin; (ii) a cross default to Enron senior obligations in excess of $50 million and $100 million for Osprey and Marlin, respectively; and (iii) the requirement that an amount sufficient to redeem the notes be deposited with a trustee 120 days prior to maturity dates of January 15, 2003 and July 15, 2003 for Osprey and Marlin, respectively. As of November 16, 2001 the Enron stock closing price was $9.00 per share.

In the event a Note Trigger Event was to occur, Enron has twenty-one days to file a registration statement for the issuance of equity to repay the notes and such registration statement has ninety days from the Note Trigger Event to become effective. Any Enron registration statement filed cannot become effective until Enron files its restated audited consolidated financial statements which is not expected until completion of the Special Committee investigation. In the event that Enron does not file its registration statement or the registration statement is not effective during the respective time requirements, Enron must pursue a private placement of equity, if permitted. If Enron cannot timely sell equity in an amount sufficient to repay the notes, Enron is obligated to pay the difference in cash.

In the event that Enron fails to pay any debt obligations when due, including when such obligations may be accelerated, or is unable to refinance or obtain a waiver of or amendment to such obligations, a series of events would begin which could impact Enron's compliance with the terms of its Revolving Credit Agreements and certain other obligations, including bank debt facilities.

The sum-up of these circumstances is seen in Enron's summary of its debt maturities, which showed over $6 billion of debt classified as short term. As against these looming maturities, Enron had about

$1 billion of cash and cash equivalents on September 30; at November 16, after it had presumably drawn down most of the credit available to it, it had $1.2 billion.

> Cash inflows during this period primarily consisted of net collections from business operations and trade settlements, the borrowing from committed lines of credit, obtaining new secured lines of credit, the equity infusion from Dynegy and receipt of collateral deposits from trading partners. Cash outflows during this period primarily consisted of operating costs of business operations and trade settlements, repaying expiring commercial paper obligations and maturing short- and long-term debt and payment of collateral deposits to trading partners.
>
> CREDIT LINES. As a result of Enron's loss of investor confidence discussed above, Enron exited the commercial paper market for its short-term liquidity needs and borrowed under its committed lines of credit (approximately $3.0 billion) to repay outstanding and expiring commercial paper obligations of approximately $1.9 billion and to provide additional cash liquidity. Of its $3.3 billion in committed credit lines, at November 16, 2001, Enron had unused commercial paper lines of credit of $103 million.

The words are not especially dramatic, but the picture drawn is stark and bleak: Whatever other troubles the company might be facing, it was in the grips of a full-scale liquidity crisis—billions of dollars were coming due under a complex set of financing arrangements, there was $1.2 billion of cash left, and only $100 million of credit was available. No doubt the company's best chance of getting past this particular crisis was the pending Dynegy merger, which might have stabilized the situation.

The Failed Merger with Dynegy

The merger agreement with Dynegy, a major rival to Enron in the energy and energy trading business, had come together quickly in the aftermath of Enron's October 16 announcement. Enron got out of it an immediate cash infusion and the hope of a bailout—of its corporate survival at least. Dynegy got a possible upside in this merger with a much larger cross-town rival and in any case the Northern Natural Gas purchase option.

Enron's November 19 10-Q contained disclosures of information that, according to Dynegy, was not previously known to Dynegy—certainly not known to Dynegy at the time the merger agreement was signed. The 10-Q described a company that was discovering large financial obligations coming due, and busy trying to find assets to pledge to borrow money which would go to pay off debts as soon as it came in. More worrisome was the picture of a company that did not have a good grasp of the financial arrangements to which it was a party or of the scope and risks and interconnectedness of its financial obligations. At the same time there were hints that its energy trading business was drying up while counterparties perhaps found other ways to do business but in any case sat on the sidelines in terms of Enron.

By November 28, Dynegy had decided that the risks in proceeding were too great. The company gave Enron formal notice that it was terminating the merger agreement and exercised the purchase option on Northern Natural Gas.

On December 2, Enron filed for bankruptcy and sued Dynegy for breach of contract.

Index

The Index refers to sections of the text. Appendix A: Notes, Resources and Sample Language, *also has additional explanatory or reference material associated with some of the entries below.*

A

Acceleration
    control provision considerations, 15:4.1
    default provisions, under, 10:8.2
Accountants
    role of, 2:4.3
Accounting
    accrual method, 4:1
    cash method, 4:1
    equity method of accounting, 4:6
    financial statements
        components of, 4:1
        interpretation of, 2:1.8
    "historical" starting points, 4:1
Accrual method of accounting
    overview, 4:1
Acquisitions
    limitations on, 13:2.6
    mergers and acquisitions (M&A). *See* Mergers and acquisitions (M&A)
Administrative services
    providers of, 2:4.1
Adverse developments
    risk-based review of, 16:3.13
Affiliates
    definition of, risk-based review of, 16:3.12
    transactions with, 13:2.10
Affirmative covenants
    overview, 10:7.1

C

D

E

F

H

I

M

N

O

P

R

Risk-based review (*cont'd*)
    term sheet, correspondence to, 16:3.2
    timing, 16:3.5
    waiver provisions, 16:3.15
Rule arbitrage
    financial engineering and, 3:3.3
Run on the bank
    overview, 2:1.3

S

Sale-leasebacks
    restrictions and exceptions for, 12:4
Scheduled maturity
    debt, on, 3:1.1
SEC. *See* Securities and Exchange Commission (SEC)
Second lien debt
    overview, 6:4.9
Secured creditors
    rights against collateral, exercise of, 6:4.9
Secured debt
    benefits of, 6:3.1
    definition of, scrutiny of, 6:3.6
Securities Act of 1933
    overview, 2:3.2
Securities and Exchange Commission (SEC)
    role of, 2:3.2
Securities Exchange Act of 1934 (Exchange Act)
    overview, 2:3.2
Securitization
    parties to and stages of, 3:3.1
Security
    risk-based review of, 16:3.7
Security documents
    review of, 6:3.6
Security interest
    collateral. *See* Collateral
    granting of, 6:3.2
    perfecting, 6:3.3
    pre-existing lenders, grant to, 6:3.9

T

U

Y